Labor Markets, Wages,
and Employment

Labor Markets, Wages, and Employment

Ingrid H. Rima

TEMPLE UNIVERSITY

W· W· Norton & Company ·New York· London

Copyright © 1981 by W. W. Norton & Company, Inc.
Published simultaneously in Canada by George J. McLeod Limited, Toronto.
Printed in the United States of America.
All Rights Reserved
First Edition

Library of Congress Cataloging in Publication Data
Rima, Ingrid H 1925–
    Labor markets, wages and employment.
    Includes index.
    1. Labor economics. 2. Labor supply. 3. Manpower policy. I. Title.
HD4901.R55 1981   331   80-21410
ISBN 0-393-95058-1

W. W. Norton & Company Inc. 500 Fifth Avenue New York N.Y. 10110
W. W. Norton & Company Ltd. 25 New Street Square London EC4 3JA

ISBN 0 393 95058 1

1 2 3 4 5 6 7 8 9 0

For three special persons,
Hertha Hahne, Philip Rima, and Rhoda Kanter

Contents

v/

PART III

Labor-Market Policy **327**

Preface

While the state of the teaching art typically lags behind research activities in a discipline, the divergence between them has become particularly wide in the field of labor economics. This gap has not been significantly narrowed by the teaching materials—textbooks, readings, and the like. Some texts concentrate on theory; others deal almost exclusively with the structure of labor in the United States; still others skirt the traditional concerns of the labor-economics course, turning instead to such newer (and important) topics as the economics of discrimination. This book attempts to cut a wider swathe through the field by bringing together the analytical, empirical, and policy approaches to the functions of labor markets.

One of the objectives of this book is to incorporate systematically the findings of empirical research into the theory of wages and labor markets. Until now the scope and the details of empirical studies have remained largely outside the classroom. There is no reason for that to continue. Empirical studies usually lend themselves to verbal reporting and thus can be made accessible to students who lack training in advanced statistics. By using nontechnical language, sections entitled "Economics in Action" demonstrate that in economics, as in other social sciences, deductive analysis requires the support of empirical research before it can be accepted as valid in principle and, more particularly, before it can be used as a basis for the formulation of policy.

A second objective of this book is to encourage examination of the macroeconomic aspects of the labor market. An important aspect of the wave of the "new" microeconomics has been to awaken awareness of the micro foundations of macroeconomics. Since these micro foundations relate especially, though not exclusively, to the functioning of labor markets, the field of labor economics provides a natural link between microeconomics and macroeconomics. Reflecting the fact that many labor economists turn to macroeconomics in pursuit of their research, Part II seeks to make clear the essentials of macroeconomic analysis that apply to the labor field.

A third concern has motivated this undertaking: to capture the essentials of the ongoing controversy about the functioning of labor markets. The work of those who espouse the view that labor markets are segmented is no longer limited to the *cognoscenti*. What remains is to put challenges to mainstream thinking into perspective. The most serious gap in our understanding relates to the demand for labor. While the limitations of the marginal-productivity principle in providing the foundation for understanding the demand side of the market have long been recognized and are traditionally emphasized, the dual labor-market theory brings the principle into new perspective with respect to the secondary market. Research into the functioning of the "internal" labor market sheds some light on the demand for labor by the primary sector. However, this aspect of labor-market research remains in the developmental stage. Thus, the most that can be hoped for at the textbook level is to put this work into a useful framework.

While this text is no longer in length than those that are most often used for teaching a one-semester course, the breadth of its objectives relative to other texts has made me particularly attentive to the problem of its effective use. Classroom experience suggests that intermediate students—those who have had a solid principles course—can complete the entire book with little difficulty.

Bearing in mind the traditional microeconomic orientation of most single-semester courses, the book has been organized to adapt readily to the needs of those who prefer to teach a traditional course. This is accomplished by assigning Part I (chapters 1–12), chapter 17 ("The Wage Share and Its Distribution"), and chapters 19 and 20, which examine policy questions relating to investment in human capital and income assurance and insurance. For those who would like to provide some insight into the macroeconomic aspects of labor-market behavior for students who are not yet at the intermediate level, the addition of chapter 13, "The Structure of Labor Markets: Their Relationship to the Macroeconomy", is recommended. Together with chapters 1–12, 17, 19, and 20, it will provide a workable sixteen-chapter outline for a course that expands the traditional microeconomic focus to include some of the macroeconomic and policy aspects of labor markets.

This undertaking owes a great deal to the encouragement of Donald Lamm of W. W. Norton, to his appreciation of the critical role of labor markets in the behavior of the macroeconomy, and to his conviction that the scope of a contemporary labor-markets text properly includes an inquiry into policy matters in addition to the micro- and macroeconomic aspects of labor markets.

I also owe a considerable intellectual debt to Robert Flanagan of Stanford University, who read the entire manuscript with great care. His expertise on all aspects of market behavior and policy has been invaluable. Edmund S. Phelps read the chapter on labor-market discrimination, and Part II, "The Macroeconomic Aspects of Labor Markets". His comments and suggestions are appreciated. Several anonymous readers with differing viewpoints provided comments that were helpful in developing what I hope will prove to be a well-balanced presentation of controversial topics. I extend my thanks to all of them for their help, and absolve them from any responsibility for the final product.

Ingrid H. Rima
Philadelphia, Pennsylvania
June 1980

Labor Markets, Wages,
and Employment

1   The Changing Scope of Labor Economics

Few areas of economics have experienced as extensive a change in scope as that which has taken place over the last decade and a half in the field of labor economics. Indeed, even its conventional designation as "labor economics" has given way to the more contemporary "human-resources economics" and "manpower economics." This is not simply a case of the proverbial "rose by any other name." It reflects a basic change in the focus of labor problems, the analytical tools developed to understand them, and the policies adopted to solve them.

Three decades ago, the chief concern of labor economists was to examine the development and role of trade unions in collective bargaining and labor disputes. Concern with weapons for waging industrial warfare and techniques for achieving industrial peace was an integral part of this focus, as was the impact of legislation and judicial decisions on union–management relations.

The interests of labor economists shifted during the prosperous 1950s and 1960s with the perception that organized labor had "come of age" and was no longer in a strategically weak position vis à vis employers. Accordingly, union–management relationships presented a less challenging investigatory problem than previously. Labor economists reached out in new directions, for in economics, as in virtually every other area of intellectual inquiry, there is a need from time to time to redefine and reexamine. For labor economists much of their research effort became directed to examining the microeconomic aspects of labor-market behavior.

The Microeconomic Aspects of Labor Markets

Microeconomics is concerned with explaining the determination of commodity and factor prices through the interaction of demand-

and-supply forces. The "price" in which the labor economist is interested is, of course, the wage rate. It is, however, simplistic to conceive of "the" wage rate. There are specific wage rates that relate to specific jobs in specific labor markets. Explaining the structure of wage rates is thus the chief microeconomic problem of labor economics.

The theory of household choice is at the center of much of the ongoing research into the supply aspects of the labor market. The dramatic change in the composition of the labor force in response to changing participation rates by men and women became an especially interesting and important area for inquiry. Since changes in the division of labor between the sexes in the marketplace implied corresponding changes in the economic functions of family members, the household was quickly identified as a key decision-making unit in determining the supply of labor. Its behavior lent itself readily to being examined in terms of traditional microeconomic supply analysis.

The *quality* of the labor supply is another recent direction of inquiry. New evidence about the relationship between earnings differentials and levels of education and training, access to labor-market information and migration to job opportunities, has focused interest on the development of labor as "human capital." This aspect of the labor-supply problem has emerged as an exciting research area. It became all the more so because it appears to offer a key for analyzing the root causes of the poverty problem and a basis for developing appropriate policies.

Behavior on the demand side of the labor market has invited less research attention than supply behavior, which lends itself readily to being examined within the conventional theory of household choice. Some insight into the demand side of labor markets has been gained from an analogous interpretation of the behavior of business firms that envisions them as profit maximizers. Other insights are being provided by research in the relatively new field of industrial organization.

Theoretical inquiry into the microeconomic aspects of labor-market behavior has been supplemented and has sometimes been given new direction, by the empirical testing of hypotheses. There are many instances in which the power of logical reasoning about economic behavior and the phenomena of the market place are unreliable guides for understanding what actually happens. Consider, for example, the following proposition: the response to an increase in the rate of wages that can be earned is that workers adjust the time they supply to the market in order to maximize their real income. Does this imply that they will supply *more* labor to the market? Conceivably, the answer is yes. If individuals not in the labor market at the previously prevailing wage rate are now attracted by the higher rate, the supply of effort to the market will increase. If individuals who are already employed respond to the increase in wages by working additional hours, the effect of higher wages is, similarly, to increase the supply of effort. In both cases the supply of labor is a positive function of the wage rate.

However, a different response is also possible. If it is recognized that a higher wage rate makes it possible to earn more income by working the same number of hours, it is reasonable to expect that some persons will value their leisure time too highly to work additional hours. It is even possible that some individuals will value their leisure time so highly they respond to an increased wage rate, which enables them to earn the same income in fewer hours, by supplying *less* labor to the market. The supply of effort is then a *negative* function of the wage rate. This is entirely consistent with the premise of individual maximizing behavior, for real income reflects the consumption of goods, services, and leisure time. It is apparent from this example that logic alone cannot identify whether, or under what conditions, the supply of effort to the labor market is a positive or a negative function of the wage rate.

Fortunately, the economist sometimes has access to actual data that he can test by using various statistical techniques. These may help him identify whether (1) there is, in fact, a relationship such as has been hypothesized between two variables; (2) the relationship between two variables is so weak that it can be attributed to chance; or (3) the behavior of the dependent variable reflects one or more independent variables, each of which exerts a different degree of influence.

Those who study economics at the intermediate level are often familiar with the basic tools of statistical analysis and will encounter no difficulty in understanding how the results of hypothesis testing can add dimension to theoretical inquiry. But there is no need for the uninitiated to be intimidated by the intricacies of statistical research. Although the *methods* of statistical analysis can become very complex, the conclusions that they yield can often be explained without involvement in technique. Theoretical analysis will therefore be supplemented by examples of "Economic Theory in Action" in each of the chapters of this book. These examples will emphasize the conclusions that statistical research has made possible, and that are readily understandable without inquiry into statistical methods.[1]

Part I, The Microeconomic Aspects of Labor Markets, which follows, is chiefly concerned with presenting the body of theory, together with the empirical work structured on it, that mainstream economists have developed to explain the labor-market phenomena underlying the wage structure. Most of the economics profession is persuaded that

---

[1] Two recommended sources are John E. Freund and Frank J. Welling, *Elementary Business Statistics* (Englewood Cliffs, New Jersey: Prentice-Hall, 1964); and William Mendenhall and James E. Reinsmith, *Statistics for Management and Economics* (North Scituate, Massachusetts: Duxbury Press, 1978).

labor-market behavior is most effectively examined with the analytical techniques and behavioral assumptions of a tradition of inquiry known as "neoclassicism." However, the neoclassical paradigm does not dominate without challenge. Orthodox theory has always had its critics and the present is not excepted. In the field of labor economics the challenge posed by those who dissent from neoclassicism has become increasingly difficult to ignore—even at the textbook level. It is well worth the time of any serious student of labor-market behavior to examine the issues they raise and the evidence they present. These criticisms are most meaningful when examined in the light of the orthodox theory they propose to refute. Examination of the heterodox challenge is, therefore, undertaken at the end of Part I.

The Macroeconomic Aspects of Labor Markets

While much of the research "action" is microeconomic in nature, labor economics does not consist only of the application of micro-analytical tools to study the behavior of labor markets. The macro-economic aspects of labor markets have become increasingly important as concern about the the level of employment and inflation has mounted. There is particular interest in the wage-price nexus and the relationship between the price level and unemployment. This is also an area of considerable controversy. The functional distribution of income and the historical constancy of the wage share is also a topic of inquiry. Part II of this book is thus concerned with the macroeconomic aspects of labor markets. Three chapters explore the functioning of labor markets and the level of employment, inflation, and unemployment, and the problem of distribution and the wage share.

Labor Market-Policy

The subject matter of labor economics has made concern with policy questions inevitable for the labor economist. The problem of achieving acceptably high levels of employment while holding down inflationary pressure is a major policy concern that the labor economist shares with those who are more specifically concerned with macro-economics. The emergence of human-capital theory has stimulated other policy interests that have been reinforced by a national commitment, dating from the passage of the Manpower Development and Training Act (MDTA) in 1962, to develop human resources. This act provided government assistance for training workers who became technologically displaced or who were structurally unemployed as a result of industrial relocation. Amendments to this act were intended to facilitate participation in the world of work as an alternative to welfare for disadvantaged workers. Labor economists in and out of government have played and continue to play an important role in shaping and critically evaluating education and training programs and their financing.

The policy commitment of labor economists is also apparent in their concern with various measures to provide income while maintaining work incentives for those who are unemployed. The problems of particular groups, among them the teenage worker, the welfare recipient, and persons who experience discrimination, have also invited policy recommendations. Public-policy issues are thus the focus of Part III. Building on the conceptual and theoretical framework of Parts I and II, Chapter 18 addresses itself to the quest for employment security in an inflation-prone economy and examines policy measures to achieve this objective. Chapter 19 examines the various aspects of "human resources" policy, and the concluding chapter, 20, is concerned with the role of programs providing for income insurance and assurance.

PART I

The Microeconomic Aspects
of Labor Markets

2 The Economic Aspects of Labor Supply

The chief problem of microeconomic analysis is to explain the demand-and-supply forces that underlie the determination of the commodity and factor prices and quantities that emerge in different kinds of markets. Like all prices, the wage rates that become established in different occupations, industries, and regions and for different persons reflect the interaction of the demand-and-supply forces operating in the particular labor market in which they prevail. The concern of this chapter is to examine the supply side of labor-market behavior in a theoretical context. The inquiry will be completed in Chapter 3, which will also examine some leading empirical studies that seek to test the theoretical relationships developed this chapter.

The Population Base

The key factor determining the supply of labor in the United States is the number of persons of labor-force age, i.e., age sixteen and over, and the proportion of that age group participating in the labor force. About one-third of the population growth of the United States is due to immigration, and legal immigrants make up about one-eighth of the yearly growth of the labor force.[1] The study of population behavior is chiefly the concern of demographers; however, changes in the number of persons of labor-force age are of interest to students of labor-market behavior because they are reflected in the supply of labor.

What proportion of the population is currently of labor-force age and how are these numbers expected to increase in the years ahead?

[1] Harold Wool, "Future Labor Supply in Low Level Occupations," *Monthly Labor Review* (March 1976): 22–31.

TABLE 2-1   *Annual Projections of the Popluation of the United States by Age and Sex (for Selected Years 1975-2037)*
(For Selected Years 1975-2037)

Intermediate Fertility-Level Assumptions—Female
(Thousands of People)

	1975	1980	1985	1990	2020
Age Groups					
16–19	8,188	8,288	7,092	7,873	12,094
20–24	9,514	10,360	10,329	9,013	14,200
25–34	15,668	18,360	20,195	21,007	27,162
35–44	11,499	12,938	15,827	18,486	24,994
45–54	12,278	11,566	11,350	12,762	19,246
55–64	10,609	11,369	11,536	10,890	19,516
65 and over	12,574	13,858	15,133	16,454	23,410
Total	111,059	118,710	127,825	195,669	
Median Age	29.1	29.5	30.0	30.6	31.1

Intermediate Fertility-Level Assumptions—Male

	1975	1980	1985	1990	2020
16–19	8,423	8,603	7,350	8,172	12,571
20–24	9,691	10,550	10,604	9,244	14,641
25–34	15,652	18,419	20,278	21,184	27,672
35–44	11,108	12,585	15,567	18,277	25,123
45–54	11,392	10,786	10,628	12,055	18,732
55–64	9,303	9,811	9,923	9,428	17,677
65 and over	8,930	9,634	10,341	11,113	16,793
Total	106,449	113,702	121,999	130,494	190,460
Median Age	26.8	27.3	27.7	28.2	28.9

Table 2-1 shows the age and sex distribution of the population in 1975 and the Bureau of the Census annual projections based on the assumption that fertility levels will be "intermediate" between the replacement level of 2.1 and the 2.4 fertility rate of the recent past.[2] According to the expectations of the bureau, total population and the number of persons of labor-force age are expected to become larger. The female population is consistently expected to be larger than the male population, and its median age will be somewhat higher. Figure 2-1 reflects the changes in the age structure of the population that are expected as the infant population of the "baby-boom" years of World War II and the 1950s grow to maturity. The dramatic increases in the number of teenagers and young adults was the most remarkable

[2] The fertility rate is the ratio of the number of births to the number of women aged 15–45, the childbearing years. The population-replacement rate is taken as 2.1 rather than 2.0 to offset the effect of infant mortality.

demographic and labor-force fact of the decade of the 1970s. Teenagers who were either working or looking for work increased from 5.2 million in 1960 to 9 million in 1978. Their numbers are expected to decrease to about 8 million in 1980, and about 7 million by 1990.

The twenty- to twenty-four-year-old age group has also experienced considerable growth since 1960 and, as is evident in Table 2-1, is expected to continue to increase through 1980 before experiencing a slowdown in growth that is expected to reduce the absolute size of this age group by 1990. Simultaneously the size of the "mature" population, i.e., persons in age groups twenty-five through thirty-four and thirty-five through forty-four will experience large absolute increases through 1990. This demographic fact is of great significance so far as the labor market is concerned. It means, quite simply, that the necessity for the labor force to absorb large numbers of inexperienced young people will decline in the mid 1980s. Meanwhile, the number of still relatively young mature

FIGURE 2-1   *Age Group as a Percentage of Total U.S. Work Force, 1960–90*

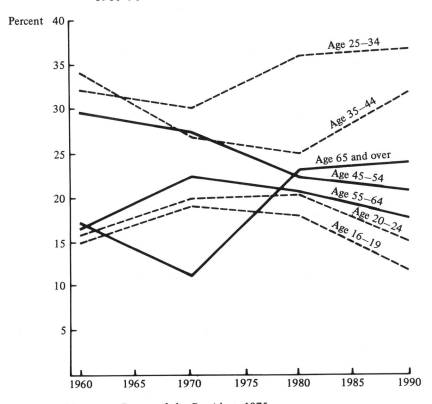

SOURCE: *Manpower Report of the President*, 1975.

adults who will already have acquired labor-market experience and training will constitute a larger proportion of the population by the middle of the next decade.

The projected rate of growth for the black population is higher than that of the white population. This projection reflects the lower age structure and the higher fertility rates of the black population. Figure 2-2 displays the projected relative increase in the teenage population for the period 1975–1990.

FIGURE 2-2   *Relative Increase of Black and All Teenagers, 1975–1990*

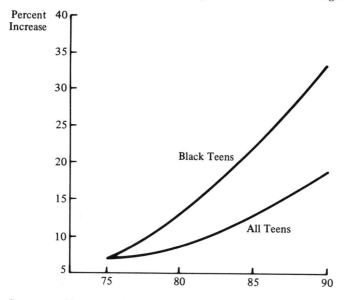

SOURCE: *Manpower Report of the President*, 1975, p. 309.

The black population is projected to reach 26.4 million by 1980, which represents an increase of 7.8 percent from its 1975 level. The number of black teenagers (age sixteen and older) is expected to increase 12 percent by 1980 and 32 percent by 1990. The comparable figures for the total population aged sixteen and over are 7.8 and 18.1 percent. In the aggregate, the black population is expected to amount to 11.6 percent of the total population aged 18 and older by 1990.

The number of persons of Latin American origin (Mexican-Americans, Puerto Ricans, and Cubans) constitutes a very small part of the total population. However, their high birth rates and the number of illegal immigrants are causing their numbers to increase at a rate that is causing some degree of concern. This is particularly true because they tend to be economically disadvantaged.

Labor-Force-Participation Rates

Although we are quite capable of predicting with considerable accuracy what proportion of the population will be of labor-force age at some future date, predictions about the *size* and especially, the *composition* of the labor force are certain to be considerably less reliable. The main difficulty lies in predicting the percentage of the noninstitutional population by age and sex group that will choose to participate. The labor-force-participation rate is the percentage of individuals aged sixteen and over who choose to be in the labor force, i.e., it is the percent of the population in that age group that is either employed or actively seeking employment.

The proportion of persons in the civilian labor force has ranged between 58.3 and 63.2 percent on an annual basis from 1947 to 1978. These data show that the relative number of persons working or seeking work has remained remarkably stable in spite of the phenomenal increases in productivity that have taken place over the same period. Can we explain why higher income levels have not and are not expected to become associated with reduced labor-force participation? The inquiry that follows into the choice which households make between work and nonmarket activity will shed some light on this question.

The Theory of the Household as It Relates to the Supply of Labor

The Choice between Work and Nonmarket Activity

The Greeks had a word for it: *Oikonomikos*, the management of the household. Modern economists have only recently focused their attention on the central role of the household in decision making. The choice made among alternative combinations of work and nonmarket activity by members of a family in order to maximize their well-being is an important aspect of household behavior because it becomes reflected in the rate of labor-force participation and the number of hours supplied to the market.

Labor-force participation is typically a family rather than an individual decision. All individuals who are older than sixteen and who are not in military service or institutionalized have a choice among various combinations of work and nonmarket activity, including the option of remaining outside the labor force at every relevant market wage. The decision that is made is determined by four broad classes of variables, which are summarized in Table 2-2. These are (1) household "tastes"; (2) the expected market-earnings rates of family members; (3) the value of the time devoted to nonmarket activities; and (4) the household's "budget time" constraint.

How do family members respond to an opportunity to work at a given wage rate? The signs in the brackets next to each category in Table 2-2 indicate the expected association between each variable that might affect his decision and the total number of hours that will be allocated to market activity by household members. For example, it is expected that a larger number of persons in a household (item A-1) will be associated with both more participation and a larger number of hours being devoted to labor-force participation. Higher anticipated expenditures (A-4) would be expected to exert a similar effect, as would a higher level of education (B-2). On the other hand, larger numbers of children (C-1), especially if they are young, larger numbers of female family members (D-1), and persons attending school (E-1) are variables that are expected to reduce labor-force participation and the number of hours devoted to market activity. Income from sources other than labor-force participation (such as rent, interest, dividends, pensions, unemployment or disability insurance, or welfare payments) is expected to exert a negative effect and reduce the number of hours allocated to market activity.

TABLE 2-2 *Outline of Variables to Be Used in Analyzing Total Hours to Be Devoted by a Household to Labor-Force Participation*

(Signs in brackets indicate expected association between each variable and total hours devoted by the household to labor force participation.)

I. *Tastes*
  A. Tastes for money income [+]
    1. Number of persons in the household [+]
    2. Differential between "permanent income" and current income: negative transitory income caused, e.g., by unemployment of a regular worker [+]
    3. Amount of fixed obligations such as interest payments, debt obligations, property taxes, etc. [+]
    4. Anticipated expenditures on such items as education, as approximated by number of children nearing college age [+]
  B. Tastes for market work per se [+]
    1. Health: poor [−]
    2. Education [+]
    3. Color and sex combined: Negro male [−], Negro female [+]
    4. Marital status and sex combined: married male [+], married female [−]
  C. Tastes for "home" goods [−]
    1. Number of young children [−]
    2. Size of house [−]
  D. Tastes for unpaid work in the home [−]
    1. Sex: Females [−]
  E. Tastes for additional schooling [−]
    1. School enrollment status: enrolled [−]
  F. Tastes for leisure [−]
    1. Location of residence: good climate [−]
  G. Family rules and decision-making processes [?]

II. *Expected Market Earnings Rates: Substitution Effects* [+]

A. General job prospects [+]
  1. Average market wage rates [+]
  2. Cost of getting to jobs in local labor market as affected by such factors as availability, convenience, and cost of public transportation [−]
  3. Unemployment rate in local labor market [−]
B. "Group" job prospects [+]
  1. Demand for the particular market skills possessed by family members as affected by the industrial and occupational mix of the area [+]
  2. Supply of persons in the area with skills and job preferences similar to those of family members [−]
C. Personal job prospects [+]
  1. Age [+ up to some age level and then −]
  2. Sex: males [+]
  3. Health: poor [−]
  4. Education [+]
  5. Experience [+]
  6. Color [generally −]
  7. Proximity of residence to job opportunities [+]

III. *Expected Non Market Earnings Rates: Substitution Effects* [−]

A. Productivity of family members in "home" tasks [−]
  1. Sex: females [−]
B. Costs of having non family members perform essential home tasks [−]
  1. Wages of domestic servants [−]
  2. Prices per unit of output of home appliances such as dishwashers [−]
C. Expected rate of return on the education of family members [−]
  1. Average rate of return on education [−]
  2. Expected rates of return for particular family members, as affected by age, sex, color, aptitude [−]

IV. *Family Resources* [−]

A. Potential labor supply [−]
  1. Number of potential earners in the household [−]
B. Expected market earnings rates: income effects [−]
  1.
  2. } Same as II, with signs reversed.
  ...
C. Expected non market earnings rates: income effects [−]
  1.
  2. } Same as III.
  ...
D. "Other (non labor) Income" and wealth of the household [−]
  1. Assets [−]
  2. Earnings on assets [−]
  3. Gifts, inheritances, and windfalls [−]
  4. Pensions and welfare payments [−]

SOURCE: W. Bowen and T. A. Finegan, *The Economics of Labor-Force Participation* (Princeton: Princeton University Press, 1969), pp. 20–21. Reprinted with permission of Princeton University Press.

The variables listed in Table 2-2 are relevant in different degrees for each family in shaping its decision about the allocation of time between market and nonmarket activity by its members. The persons in each family choose the combination of market and nonmarket activity considered "best" or, in the language of the economist, "utility maximizing."[3]

While labor-market decisions are typically family rather than individual decisions, analysis is best undertaken in terms of the behavior of individual members. A convenient way of examining the decision-making process is to recognize that there are various equally satisfactory combinations of work and nonmarket activity for every individual. An economist would say he is "indifferent" among them. Combinations of income and nonmarket activity ("leisure" for short) that are equivalent in the satisfaction or utility they represent can be identified by a curve such as I_1 in Figure 2-3. The wage rate is represented on the vertical axis and the time available to be divided between work and leisure (say, 168 hours per week) is shown on the horizontal axis. As a hypothetical individual moves rightward along I_1, he is substituting leisure (which includes schooling, job search, and unpaid work) for market activity and money income. Conversely, as he moves leftward he is substituting work (and income) for leisure. Each point on an indifference curve represent

FIGURE 2-3   *The Optimum Work-Leisure Allocation of Time*

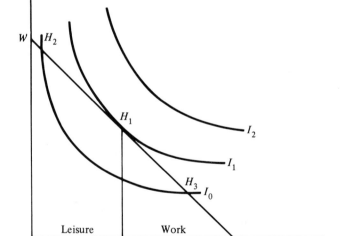

[3]The modern economic theory of the household has built in an important way on Gary Becker's "A Theory of the Allocation of Time," *Economic Journal* 75 (September 1965): 493–517.

the "marginal rate of substitution" between work and leisure, i.e., the rate at which market and nonmarket activity can be substituted for each other while leaving the individual equally well off in terms of utility. An indifference curve may, thus, also be referred to as a "utility function." Its slope reflects the "reservation wage" the individual requires in order to give up leisure and the utility it offers in preference for work and the utility of money income.

There are work-leisure combinations lying upward and to the right of I_1 that are "preferred" because they represent more money for equivalent amounts of work. Analogously, less preferred combinations than I_1 lie to the left of that curve. Every individual, whether he constitutes an independent household or is a member of a family whose choices are interdependent with his own, will seek out a combination that is "optimal" in the sense of being the best he can achieve, given his preferences and his budget-time constraint.

Figure 2-3 identifies WH as the budget-time constraint to which an individual family member might be subject. The length of the horizontal axis from O, the origin, to H represents the total time to be allocated to all activities, and OW represents the wage income that could be earned if all time were spent in market activity. Each point on the line WH thus reflects the income associated with various combinations of work and leisure at wage rate W. Reading rightward along the budget-time constraint toward H identifies less market activity and lower levels of income; reading leftward and up toward W identifies higher incomes and the allocation of more hours to work.

The relationship between the individual's indifference curves and his budget-time constraint determines the optimum allocation of time at a particular wage rate. Thus, in Figure 2-3 we identify H_1 the point at which the budget-time constraint is *tangent* to I_1, the highest attainable curve. It represents the optimum division of time between work and leisure, given the household's preferences and wage rate W. Moving from H_1 to the horizontal axis, and reading *rightward*, HA identifies the number of hours spent at work. The remaining time OA is allocated to nonmarket activity.

If the entire time OH were allocated to nonmarket activity, zero hours would be worked. This possibility is illustrated in Figure 2-4. If an individual's indifference curves are steeper than the time-budget constraint to which he is adjusting himself, there is no point of tangency between them within the area bounded by the two axes and the line passing through H, which represents zero hours of work.[4] The fact that

---

[4] Economists call such a situation a "corner solution." Whereas individuals resolve the typical choice problem by taking some positive amount of both X and Y (e.g., work and leisure) regardless of their relative prices, this need not be the case. An alternative, say Y, is *not* chosen by an individual if the marginal rate of substitution of X for Y is less than the ratio of their prices.

FIGURE 2-4   *The Case of Zero Hours of Work*

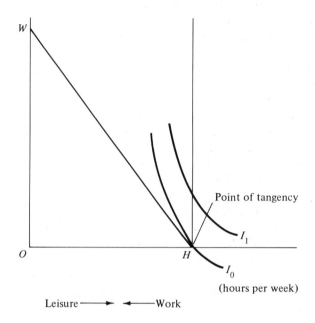

an individual works zero hours is not necessarily to be construed as a decision not to be a labor-force participant. Labor-force participation takes place if an individual is either working or searching for work. Thus, the absence of a point of tangency between an indifference curve and the time-budget constraint (i.e., a corner solution) may mean that an individual is not working but is a labor-force participant engaged in search for employment.

What would happen to our hypothetical worker's allocation of time if his wage rate is raised (or lowered)? The discussion that follows and its accompanying diagrams show that changes in wages have both substitution and income effects. If the wage rate is increased, the substitution effect operates to *increase* labor-force participation and the number of hours worked, while the income effect operates to *decrease* market activity at a higher wage rate.[5] It can be determined only empirically which of the two tendencies predominates. But it is useful to proceed by examining each effect in isolation as a first step.

If the wage rate becomes W_1, the budget-time line rotates upward but continues to terminate at H, since there is obviously no change in the

[5]Thus, the income and substitution effects of a wage change act in opposite directions. This contrasts with the situation in the theory of consumption where for a "normal" superior good the substitution effect and the income effect of price change are *reinforcing*.

FIGURE 2-5 *The Substitution Effect in Response to Wage Increases*

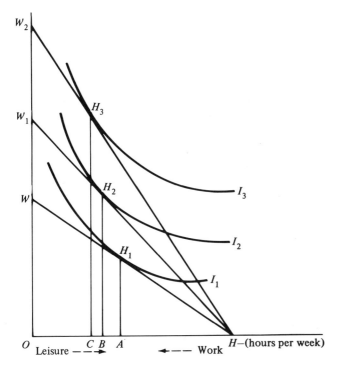

number of hours available per week. Thus, there is a *new* budget line, W_1H, as in Figure 2-5. The optimum work-nonwork choice (i.e., the point of tangency between budget-time constraint and the highest attainable indifference curve) is now H_2. At the higher wage rate, *HB* hours are worked as leisure is "traded off" for more money income. At the still higher wage of W_2, there might be a further substitution of income for leisure. Thus, at a wage of W_2 the budget-time constraint is tangent to the highest attainable indifference curve at H_3 and the optimal number of working hours is *HC*.

The increase in the number of hours of work from *HA* to *HB* or *HC* is the result of the "substitution effect." The substitution effect is present if an individual takes less of a good as its price increases. In the context of the allocation of time, an increase in the wage rate means that the "price" of nonmarket activity is rising in terms of income lost by not working; i.e., work is substituted for leisure.

It does not follow, however, that a worker will necessarily continue to substitute income for nonmarket activity. Figure 2-6 illustrates the possibility that a wage increase from W_2 to W_3 will make nonmarket

FIGURE 2-6 *The Income Effect in Response to Wage Increases*

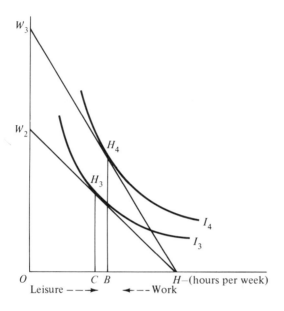

activity preferable to additional income.[6] Tangency at H_4 is indicative of an "income effect." That is, as income increases, people buy more of goods they regard as "superior" and fewer of those regarded as "inferior." If an individual regards nonmarket activity as a superior good, he will want more of it as his wage rate increases to (say) W_3. *HB*, which is the optimum work-nonwork combination when the wage rate is W_3, represents less work and more leisure than *HC*.

Separating Income and Substitution Effects

The income effect and the substitution effect are equally possible and simultaneously operative. If an increase in the wage rate induces workers to offer a larger number of hours to the market (or participate instead of remaining outside the labor force), the substitution effect is present. If, on the other hand, workers respond to a higher wage rate by working fewer hours and enjoying more leisure instead, they are responding to the income effect of the wage change.

It is possible for both the income effect and the substitution effect of a wage increase to be negative, i.e., both may have the effect of

[6]However, a worker will typically be willing to work overtime at a *premium* rate of pay even if his response to higher straight-time wages is to work fewer hours. See T. Aldrich Finnegan, "Comment: The Backward Sloping Supply Curve," *Industrial and Labor Relations Review* 15 (January 1962). This point is explored below.

decreasing the number of hours worked. This need not be the case, but if it is reasonable to assume that leisure is a "normal" good, it follows that an increase in wages will be accompanied by a reduction in hours, i.e., leisure is substituted for work. However, the theory of consumer choice does not provide a basis for deciding that the income effect of a wage increase outweighs the substitution effect. A wage increase may induce workers to offer more hours of labor, so that a substitution effect is present to a degree that offsets a negative-income effect. A larger number of hours will then be worked at a higher wage rate, as is the case in Figure 2-5.

The relative importance of the income effect and the substitution effect becomes a matter of particular concern when income other than wages provides workers (or potential workers) with an alternative to gainful employment. The term "other" income was devised by the Bureau of the Census to denote all money income received from sources other than wages, salaries, or self-employment. It thus includes rental income, dividend and alimony payments, pensions, and welfare payments. Disability payments and unemployment compensation which are related to previous work are also part of "other" income. Other things being equal, and assuming that leisure is a normal good, labor-force participation is expected to be inversely related to the availability of other income. Whether and to what extent this is the case is an empirical problem that will be examined in the next chapter.

Overtime and Moonlighting

Overtime at a Premium Wage

A large variety of interesting labor-market responses lend themselves to being examined within the framework of the theory of household choice. "Overtime" work and moonlighting activities are two that will be examined in this chapter.

It is not uncommon for employers to have labor requirements that, at least on occasion, exceed the standard work week of its regular work force. Their needs can be satisfied either by offering overtime rates of pay to regular employees or by hiring additional part-time workers, some of whom will be "moonlighting" in addition to their regular primary jobs. The theory of household choice lends itself to examining the circumstances under which overtime or moonlighting will be activities economically attractive to individuals.

The availability of "overtime"—premium pay for extra hours of work—has the effect of increasing the incentive to work. As premium pay reaches a higher reservation wage, the substitution effect comes into operation. Overtime pay causes the wage line to become steeper, which leads to the substitution of income for leisure. The marginal rate of substitution of income (work) for leisure is increased until it is equal to the slope of the new wage line. Figure 2-7 illustrates why a typical worker with a given work schedule that is paid at a standard wage rate will always choose to work overtime hours at premium pay. It reproduces our earlier Figure 2-3, making such changes as are required to illustrate the case in which a worker responds to the opportunity to earn a premium wage by working more hours than the standard work week. At the standard wage rate of OW, we again identify H_1 as the point at which the budget-time constraint is tangent to I_1, the highest attainable indifference curve. HA hours of work is the optimum division of the worker's time between work and leisure, given the household's preferences and the wage rate W. For convenience, we assume that HA hours is also the standard work week.

An offer of a premium wage of W_p for working more than HA

FIGURE 2-7 *Overtime at a Premium Wage*

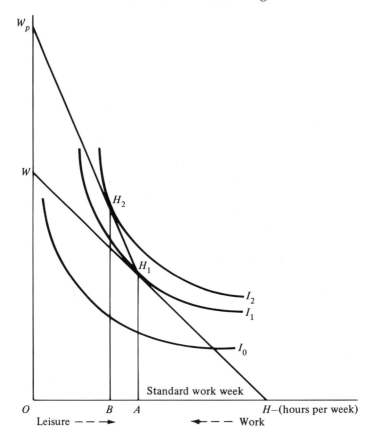

hours confronts the worker with the opportunity set $W_p H_1 H$, which is tangent to the higher indifference curve I_2 at H_2. Thus he maximizes his income-leisure position by working the standard work week of HA hours at the straight-time wage of W and additional overtime hours equal to $HB-HA$ at the premium rate W_p. A worker is likely to be willing to work overtime at a premium rate of pay even if his response to a higher straight-time wage is to work fewer hours.[7]

Moonlighting

If the work schedule that an employer offers is not compatible with a worker's preferred allocation of time at the current wage rate, he will be willing to work additional hours either at his primary job or, if this is not possible, at a second job. In Figure 2-8 the worker prefers to work HC hours at a wage rate of W. Thus, if the standard schedule is only HA hours, he will consider himself *underemployed* at the going wage rate. The vertical line $H_s A$, drawn upward from point A on the horizontal axis to designate the standard schedule, intercepts the lower indifference curve I_0. Thus, the opportunity to work more than HA hours even at a wage rate below W would enable him to improve his position. In Figure 2-8, he would be willing to work an additional number of hours equal to $HB-HA$ at a wage rate of W_0, which is below the straight-time rate of W. Any wage rate above Wm, which would place him on indifference curve I_0 as he adjusts to the time-budget constraint $W_m SH$, would induce him to offer some number of hours beyond the standard work week HA.

If additional hours of work are not available to a worker in his primary job, "moonlighting" or working at a second job may provide an alternative. It is not, however, an alternative that is likely to be attractive at a wage below the usual straight-time wage. Ignoring the cost of getting a second job, a worker will be willing to "moonlight" as long as it pays a wage above the marginal rate of substitution of income for leisure. What this rate will be depends on the adequacy of the income earned on his primary job, the opportunity for overtime on his primary job, and the flexibility of his primary-job schedule. It is unlikely that a secondary job

[7]See T. Aldrich Finnegan, "Comment: The Backward Sloping Supply Curve," *Industrial and Labor Relations Review* 15 (January 1962).

Overtime premiums and increases in the straight-line wage both have the effect of changing the slope of the wage line. However, the steepness of the wage line is increased more by the availability of overtime pay than it is by an increase in the straight-time wage rate. It is for this reason that work incentive is increased when overtime work becomes available at a premium wage, but it is reduced if the straight-time wage rate is raised so that the worker can earn the same income as he was able to earn with the addition of overtime. In short, the typical worker will become dissatisfied with his work schedule if customary overtime is eliminated, i.e., he will feel "overemployed" if the work schedule is not changed along with a shift from wage plus overtime to an equivalent higher straight-time rate.

FIGURE 2-8   *The "Moonlighting" Alternative*

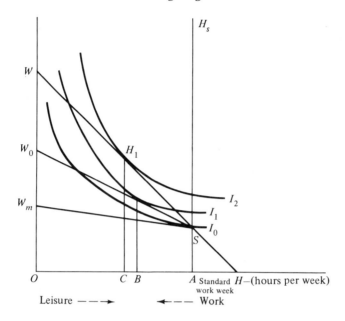

Leisure — — →   ← — — Work

will be accepted a wage much below that earned on the primary job because of the additional cost and effort that are likely to be involved.[8]

ECONOMICS IN ACTION 2:1

Evidence on Multiple-Job Holding

Most data sources, such as the decennial Census, do not disaggregate yearly earnings between primary and secondary jobs. It is thus not possible to estimate the extent of multiple-job holding from them. However, the Survey Research Center of the University of Michigan has developed an Income Dynamics Panel (IDP), which provides detailed information on family composition and earnings in addition to the wage rate and hours worked by the family head on primary and secondary jobs.

The IDP contains a representative cross-section of the United States and a supplemental sample of low-income families. The size of the representative-cross-section sample was 2,574 cases, and the supplemental sample provided 1,891 cases relating to experiences between 1968

[8] It follows that the same set of indifference curves as were used to depict work-leisure choices on a worker's primary job could be used to represent these choices with respect to secondary jobs. See Martin Bronfenbrenner and Jan Mossin, "The Shorter Work Week and the Labor Supply," *Southern Economic Journal* 33 (January 1967).

and 1970. A study that divided the sample of male heads of household between those who did some moonlighting in 1969 and those who did not established that 15 percent of those surveyed had second jobs.[9] This is a greater percentage than would be expected in the general population, because the supplemental sample contained only low-income families. The study also established that the supply of moonlighting labor increases with the moonlighting wage. An increase in the moonlighting wage increases the labor supplied to secondary jobs by inducing those already working to offer more hours and by inducing previous moonlighters to enter the secondary market. Analogously, the supply of moonlighting labor will decrease if earnings from the primary job rise.

Table 2-A summarizes the relevant characteristics of the households surveyed. It shows, in particular, that family size is positively related to moonlighting hours, while age shows a negative relationship to moonlighting hours. The latter is consistent with the hypothesis that families

TABLE 2-A *Selected Characteristics of Households from the Income Dynamics Panel[a]*

	Moonlighters		Nonmoonlighters	
Head of Household				
Age, years	37.2	(11.4)	41.6	(12.2)
Percent nonwhite	25.6		33.5	
Percent living in western United States	16.8		14.3	
Percent living in urban areas	45.3		46.0	
Percent high-school graduates	64.2		50.2	
Primary hourly-wage rate	$3.60	($1.83)	$3.80	($2.57)
Weekly hours on primary job	40.9	(9.4)	43.6	(10.4)
Secondary hourly-wage rate	$3.40	($1.27)	0.0	
Weekly hours on secondary job	8.1	(9.1)	0.0	
Family				
Family size	4.4	(2.3)	4.2	(2.2)
Annual nonmoonlighting income	$9,852	($5,109)	$10,893	($7,355)
Annual asset income	$ 361	($1,198)	$ 516	($2,256)
Annual transfer payments	$ 236	($702)	$ 263	($905)
Annual labor income less moonlighting income	$9,254	($4,828)	$10,113	($6,666)
Annual cost of housing	$1,235	($664)	$ 1,146	($740)
Sample Size	318		1,801	

[a] Numbers in parentheses are standard deviations
SOURCE: R. Shisko and B. Rostker, "The Economics of Multiple Job Holding." *American Economic Review* 66 (June 1976): p. 302. Reprinted with permission.

[9] R. Shisko and B. Rostker, "The Economics of Multiple Job Holding," *American Economic Review* 66 (June 1976): 298–309.

have life-cycle consumption plans, which they seek to fulfill by additional hours of work if necessary.

Constructing a Labor-Supply Curve

The time allocated to work (*HA, HB, HC* from Figures 2-3, 2-5, 2-6) can be translated into a labor-supply curve *SS* as in Figure 2-9. A labor-supply curve relates the number of hours that a hypothetical worker might offer to the market at the alternative wage rates to which he might be responding. These wage rates are represented on the vertical axis, and hours of effort are represented on the horizontal axis. Thus, *SS* represents the time that a hypothetical worker might allocate to market activity at various wage rates (*W*'s). (The time that is allocated to nonmarket activity is not relevant in this connection and is not represented in Figure 2-9).

The wage rates represented in Figure 2-9 are expressed in real terms rather than in money terms. Real wages reflect the purchasing power of money wages. If workers are assumed to respond to real wages, it implies that they perceive changes in the general price level and factor them into their decisions. To assume that workers respond to money wages implies that they are subject to "money illusion," which simply means that they attach special importance to the money-wage rate. Thus, they regard themselves as better off if money wages are higher and worse off when money wages are lower, quite apart from increases or decreases

FIGURE 2-9 *The Individual's Labor-Supply Curve*

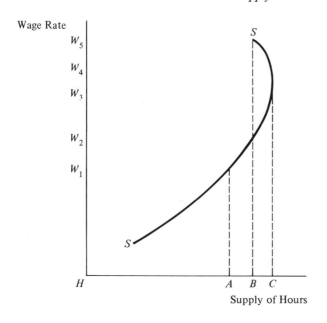

in the price level and, therefore, in the purchasing power of their money wages.

We are not concerned at this juncture with the macroeconomic problem of price-level changes. The question of whether workers respond to real wages or money wages is thus not of immediate importance. If the price level remains unchanged, or if all prices are changing proportionately, it makes no difference whether workers are envisioned as responding to money or real wages, because these are changing in the same direction. A worker who can secure a higher money wage is also improving his relative or real wage, if the price level remains constant. Conversely, a decline in his money wage is also a decline in his real wage if the price level is constant. We can thus construct a labor-supply curve such as that in Figure 2-9, which represents workers as responding to real wages, while bearing in mind that when we are later confronted with changes in the price level, it will be necessary to further examine worker responses to wage changes.[10]

The implication of a positive response in terms of hours offered to the market at a higher wage rate is that the substitution effect has predominated over the income effect. Market activity and the income that is associated with it is "preferred" to nonmarket activity. This may reflect either greater labor-force participation or more hours of work, or some combination of both possibilities.

Conversely, if the income effect swamps the substitution effect, higher wages no longer call forth more labor. In terms of the graph in Figure 2-9, the supply of labor at W_5 is no greater than it was at the lower wage W_2. This implies that the income effect dominates the substitution effect; this is represented graphically by the "backward bend" of the supply curve: i.e., as wages increase beyond some point, some workers prefer nonmarket activity to more income.

The market-supply curve of labor represents the summation of individual-supply curves. Like the individual-supply curve, it slopes upward to the right and, depending on the relative force of the income and substitution effects, it may become inelastic or even exhibit a backward bend. Each point on the curve is the product of the labor-force-participation rate of each population subgroup and the number of hours worked. The chapter that follows investigates the labor-force-participation rates of different subgroups and trends in the number of hours devoted to labor-market activity.

Concluding Remarks

This chapter has utilized the theory of choice for the purpose of examining the supply of labor to the market given the "tastes" of the

---

[10] This macroeconomic problem is addressed in Chapters 13–15.

households involved. The presumption is that the labor-market activity of household members exhibits essentially the same rational, maximizing behavior that is believed to characterize all market and market-related behavior. The presumption is that the normal response to opportunities for higher earnings is that more persons will participate in the labor force and/or that they will increase the number of hours worked.

Conversely, the presumption is that if *nonlabor* income is available, fewer individuals will participate in market activity and that those who do participate will work fewer hours. Whether or not this is the case, and whether the response differs among groups (e.g., male vs. female, prime-age as compared with older and younger persons, married vs. unmarried, white vs. nonwhite) can only be established empirically. Similarly, the question as to whether there is a difference in the supply of effort over the business cycle or in response to such nonlabor income as welfare payments and negative-income taxes is an empirical matter. These topics, and the empirical evidence that has been identified in relation to them, are the principal concerns of the chapter that follows.

Appendix A

Types of Data and Their Sources

Much of the data on which economists rely is collected by governmental agencies, among them the United States Department of Labor, the Department of Health, Education, and Welfare, and the Bureau of the Census. The annual Employment and Training Report of the President,[11] formerly the Manpower Report of the President, is the most comprehensive compilation of data collected by the United States Department of Labor and the Department of Health, Education, and Welfare. The information they collect is also published separately at regular intervals. The *Statistical Abstract of the United States* and *Historical Statistics of the United States* are comprehensive sources of historical data. Nongovernment research organizations, among them the National Bureau of Economic Research and the Brookings Institution, are also important sources of data.

Household Surveys

The United States Census Bureau conducts *Current Population Surveys* monthly among a small sample of households to supplement the

---

[11] On November 12, 1975, the Secretary of Labor changed the agency description of the Manpower Administration to the Employment and Training Administration. Program, activities, and responsibilities were not affected by the change.

very comprehensive decennial population census of the United States. Surveys by the Department of Labor ask each household to provide answers about the employment status of individual household members. They are asked whether they were 1) attending school, 2) working, 3) with a job but not at work, 4) looking for work, 5) retired, or 6) unable to work during the week prior to the survey. Questions asked of household members also provide information about numbers of persons in the family, sources and amounts of nonlabor income, level of education, earnings, hours of work, and other information useful for studying labor-market behavior.

The answers given to the questions about employment status are used to estimate employment and unemployment. According to its official definition, the labor force includes all persons who are at least sixteen years old who are working or looking for work during the survey week. The labor-force-participation rate, which is the percentage of the population in the labor force, is calculated on the basis of population and labor-force data. The estimate of unemployment, which enumerates persons who are sixteen years and older who are not working but who indicate by their responses that they are seeking employment, is also made on the basis of answers to questions asked during household surveys. Answers are then adjusted according to a statistical formula to approximate the number of persons that would have been enumerated had it been possible to interview individually everyone in the population.

Surveys of Business Firms

The *Employment and Earnings Surveys* of the Department of Labor elicits information about wage rates, wage supplements of various kinds, and social-security contributions from questionnaires sent to business firms. Information about quits and layoffs, recruitment, and training programs is also gotten this way. Additional information is gathered by the Census Bureau and published in the *Census of Manufacturers.*

Summary of Selected Data Sources

United States Department of Labor

Employment and Training Report of the President. Annual beginning 1976 (*Manpower Report of the President* to 1975).

Chartbook on Prices, Wages, and Productivity. Monthly. Current changes in prices, wages, costs, profits, and productivity in the U.S. economy.

Employment and Earnings. Monthly. Household data on labor force, employment, unemployment, job-search methods. Establishment data on employment hours, earnings, labor-turnover and job-vacancy rates, output per manhour, unit labor costs, insured unemployment.

Employment and Wages. Published quarterly.

The Employment Situation. Published monthly (free).

Labor Turnover in Manufacturing. Published monthly (free).

Occupational Outlook. Published quarterly.

Consumer Price Index. Published monthly (free).

Current Wage Developments. A monthly report on employee compensation including changes resulting from bargaining settlements.

Wage Trends for Occupational Groups in Metropolitan Areas. Published quarterly.

Special Labor-Force Reports: Data from monthly Census *Current Population Surveys*; reprints from issues of *Monthly Labor Review*.

Census Bureau

Statistical Abstract of United States. Published yearly.

Historical Statistics of the United States. Colonial times to 1970, 2 vols.

Current Population Reports. Published monthly, quarterly, annually.

P-20 Series: *Population Characteristics.*

P-25 Series: *Population Estimates and Projections.*

P-60 Series: *Consumer Income.*

Suggestions for Further Reading

G. S. Becker. "A Theory of the Allocation of Time." *Economic Journal* (September 1965), reprinted in John F. Burton, Jr., Lee K. Benham, William M. Vaughn, and Robert J. Flanagan, *Readings in Labor Market Analysis.* New York: Holt, Rinehart and Winston, 1971.

Martin Bronfenbrenner and Jan Mossin. "The Shorter Work Week and the Labor Supply." *Southern Economic Journal* 33 (January 1967).

C. E. Ferguson and Maurice S. Charles. *Economic Analysis*, rev. ed. Homewood, Ill.: R. O. Irwin, 1974, Chapters 2–3.

Richard Perlman. *Labor Theory.* New York: John Wiley and Sons, 1969, pp. 298–309.

R. Shisko and B. Rostker. "The Economics of Multiple Job Holding." *American Economic Review* (June 1976): 298–308.

3 *Labor-Force Participation and Hours of Work*

The Labor Force and Its Structure

The source of our information about labor-force participation is the decennial census, which is supplemented, on a monthly basis, by the survey which the Bureau of the Census conducts from a sample of households that are selected to represent different geographical sections of the country. The civilian labor force includes individuals who are sixteen or older who are employed or "actively seeking" work. The information given in table 3-1, Labor-Force-Participation Rates for Selected Years, 1947–1978, shows that labor-force-participation rates have been remarkably steady on an annual basis.

The seemingly simple definition of the "labor force" presents numerous difficulties, many of which are associated with the interview technique of securing information. Typically, the interviewer talks to "the lady of the house," who supplies information about the employment status of household members. The possibilities of misunderstanding and faulty reporting are myriad. This difficulty is compounded by the fact that millions of workers have relatively loose ties to the labor force. Housewives and students, in particular, often work for a short interval, sometimes part-time, and are subsequently separated from the labor force for a considerable period. Sometimes an individual says he is willing to work but is regarded by potential employers as being incapable; still others are not actively seeking employment because they think they cannot get a job. These are typical of the kinds of problems that produce a considerable range of error in the reports published on the size of the labor force.

TABLE   3-1   *Labor-Force-Participation Rates for Selected Years, 1947–1978*

Sex and age	Labor-force-participation rates annual averages *(percent of population in labor force)*			
	1947	1960	1970	1978
BOTH SEXES				
16 years and over	58.0	59.2	60.4	63.2
MALE				
16 years and over	86.8	82.4	79.2	78.4
16 − 19 years	52.5	58.6	57.5	63.5
20 − 24 years	80.5	88.9	85.1	87.1
25 − 34 years	84.9	96.4	95.0	95.5
35 − 44 years	95.8	96.4	95.7	95.8
45 − 54 years	98.0	94.3	92.9	91.3
55 − 64 years	95.5	85.2	81.5	73.5
55 − 59 years	89.6	89.9	88.0	82.9
60 − 64 years		79.5	73.6	62.0
65 years and over	47.8	32.2	25.8	20.5
65 − 69 years	*	45.8	40.7	30.1
70 years and over	*	23.5	16.9	14.2
FEMALE				
16 years and over	31.8	37.1	42.8	50.1
16 − 19 years	29.5	39.1	43.7	54.0
20 − 24 years	52.3	46.1	57.5	68.5
25 − 34 years	44.9	35.8	44.8	62.2
35 − 44 years	32.0	43.1	50.9	61.6
45 − 54 years	36.3	49.3	54.0	57.1
55 − 64 years	32.7	36.7	42.5	41.4
55 − 59 years	24.3	41.7	48.4	48.6
60 − 64 years		31.0	35.6	33.1
65 years and over	8.1	10.5	9.2	8.4
65 − 69 years	*	17.0	16.4	14.9
70 years and over	*	5.4	5.0	4.8

*Not available.

SOURCE: Department of Labor Statistics and *Employment and Training Report of the President,* 1979, Table A-4, p. 240.

Participation by Sex and Age

As was already noted in Chapter 2, in making its labor-force decisions, each person will consider, either explicitly or implicitly, the "earnings" rate per hour that he is likely to be able to get from market activity.[1] Expected market earnings are dependent on the demand-supply situation prevailing in the local labor market as well as on general economic conditions in the labor market as a whole. These operate to produce different results for different household members, depending on their sex, age, education, experience, race, health, and personal and family characteristics.

While labor-force-participation rates exhibit an overall steadiness, there have been substantial changes in the labor-force behavior of different subgroups, as is evident in Table 3-1. The proportion of males between the ages of twenty-five and fifty-four years who are labor-force participants has been between 95 percent and 98 percent throughout the period from 1947 to the present. Men who are twenty-five to fifty-four years of age are the prime age group with respect to labor-force activity in the United States and industrial economies generally. This population group comprises more than 40 percent of the labor force and typically receives more than 60 percent of the total earnings of the experienced labor force.

It is also relevant to note that the labor-force participation of men aged twenty-five to fifty-four who are divorced, separated, widowed, or never married ranged between 79.1 percent and 84.3 percent, which is considerably lower than that of married men living with their wives. This differential appears not to reflect any single cause but rather appears to be the combined result of multiple influences that probably also contributed to their single status.[2]

The participation of males between fourteen and nineteen has declined in consequence of increased school attendance. A further change in the makeup of the labor force is evident in the labor-force-participation rates of men sixty-five and over. Some 48 percent of men over sixty-five were in the labor force in 1947 as compared with 26 percent in 1970.

The large-scale participation of women in the labor force has been another major change that has taken place during the past two decades. Only 31.8 percent of the women aged sixteen and over were in the labor force in 1947. The female labor force participation rate in 1978 had reached 50 percent. This figure reflects the continuing increase in female labor-force participation that is taking place. It suggests that there have been major changes in the division of labor between the sexes in the market place and, by inference, in the home environment as well.

---

[1] The nonmonetary aspects of earnings are discussed below, p. 121.

[2] W. G. Bowen and T. A. Finnegan, *The Economics of Labor Force Participation* (Princeton: Princeton University Press, 1969), p. 45, Table 3-2.

The age distribution of women's participation is bimodal. As shown in Figure 3-1, the age pattern of work among women reflects two periods of peak participation. The first is in the young-adult period, when women leave school and are in the early years of their married lives. The second reflects their return to the labor force as their child-rearing responsibilities diminish. Participation by this group has increased considerably and is almost as high as that of younger women, who have historically had the highest participation rates. But it is the participation rate of the twenty to twenty-four-year-old woman that has been rising most rapidly since 1960. This age group had a participation rate of 68.3 percent in 1978, which exceeded that of women in the higher-age groups. The growth in participation rates among women has been so rapid that the proportion aged twenty-five to thirty-four who are in the work force today is as high as that of the most active age groups of 1950. Women with school-aged children are as likely to work at the present time as was the unmarried young woman of the 1950s.

Marital status and labor-force participation are closely related for single women, but the relationship is more complex than it is for prime-age males. Never married women register higher participation

Figure 3-1   *Women's Work-Life Patterns, 1950–1990 (Projected)*

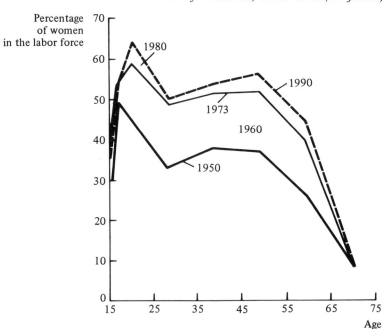

Source: U.S. Department of Labor.

rates than those who are separated or divorced; the rates of those who are widowed or who have husbands who are absent are lower. The inference is that the "taste" for work among never married women is somewhat stronger than among members of other marital groups. Conceivably, strong career interests are relevant in explaining why some women do not marry. Compared with other single women, the never married woman's higher rate of labor-force participation is related to her lesser family obligations, her greater work experience, and her higher earnings opportunities. Widows, on the other hand, have a lower-than-average tendency to participate, which appears to be related to larger asset holdings.

When such important variables as other income, schooling, and age are taken into account, participation rates are virtually the same for white and nonwhite single women. However, when these other influences are omitted from statistical-prediction equations, the finding is that white single women register labor-force-participation rates that are about seven percentage points higher than those for nonwhite women.[3]

The Labor-Force Participation of Married Women

The labor-force-participation rates of married women have invited closer scrutiny than those of other population groups. The increase in their labor-force-participation rates reflects family decisions about the distribution of leisure, market work, and homework among its members. This is consistent with changes in the opportunity cost of time devoted to nonmarket activity over a person's lifetime. The marginal cost of leisure tends to be relatively low for persons under eighteen or over sixty-five years of age, because their opportunities for gainful employment in the market are limited. Other things being equal, an increase in the market wage of a particular family member increases the cost of consumption of leisure and production of home services by that member, which tends to encourage an increased supply of effort to the market.

The reasons for the remarkable rise in the labor-force participation of married women are not readily apparent. The rise in "other family income" suggests that more wives (and other family members) could have afforded nonmarket activity. On the other hand, the rising relative cost of domestic service, which made it more expensive to hire household help, conceivably constrained labor-force participation by some women. However, the factors increasing the labor-force-participation rates of married women dominated.

The chief factors that encouraged their participation are (1) the rise in real hourly earnings; (2) the development of labor-saving appliances

---

[3] W. Bowen and T. A. Finnegan, *op. cit.*, p. 251.

and products; (3) the increase in employment opportunities associated with the shift of population from rural to urban areas; (4) the expansion of employment opportunities in clerical, service (excluding domestic service), and professional occupations, which are large employers of women; (5) the shift of the "industry mix" to the service sector (including government); (6) the decline in the length of the work week and the increase in the relative number of part-time jobs; (7) the increased number of day-care centers; (8) the decline in the proportion of married women aged fourteen to fifty-four with children less than six years of age; and (9) the growth in the average educational attainments of married women, which contributed to their "taste" for work.

To what extent is the increased participation of women a response to higher earning opportunities and how much reflects the influence of other factors? Other things being equal, the presumption is that the higher the level of prevailing wages, the greater the inclination of the worker to substitute an increment of time for labor-market activity rather than for nonmarket activity. Is this presumption as valid with respect to female labor-force participation as it is with respect to men? This is a question that economic theory alone cannot answer. Thus we examine a study by T. Aldrich Finnegan to determine whether there is a positive association between the labor-force-participation rate of married women (with husbands present) and their average annual earnings, when the other explanatory factors have been held constant.[4]

ECONOMIC THEORY IN ACTION 3:1

Labor-Force Participation of Married Women

The magnitude that Finnegan sought to explain (i.e., his dependent variable) was the labor-force participation of the 1/1000 sample of the 1960 census of population.[5] To do this he employed five labor-market measures and six control variables intended to reflect differences in individual and family characteristics among Standard Metropolitan Statistical Areas (SMSA).

The labor-market measures Finnegan identified as independent variables that are likely to affect the labor-force participation of married

---

[4]F. Aldrich Finnegan, "Participation of Married Women in the Labor Force," in C. B. Lloyd, ed., *Sex, Discrimination and the Division of Labor* (New York: Columbia University Press, 1975), pp. 27–54.

[5]In 1960, there were 100 Standard Metropolitan Statistical Areas with total populations of 250 or more in the United States. A Standard Metropolitan Statistical Area consists of one or more continuous countries with at least one fairly large city and its surrounding suburbs. It is regarded as being the best empirical approximation of a "local labor market."

women are (1) the earnings of women (measured in terms of the median annual income of women who worked fifty to fifty-two weeks); (2) the wages of domestic servants; (3) the female industry mix; (4) the supply of women (i.e. the percentage of total civilian population in the SMSA fourteen years old or older who are female); (5) the overall unemployment rate.

The influence of these variables was examined while holding constant six "control" variables. These were the mean income of husbands, the mean income from nonemployment sources, the median years of school completed by women over twenty-four, the percentage of wives who were nonwhite, the percentage with children under six, and a measure of net migration of women among SMSA's between 1955 and 1960.

The study brought to light a large number of statistically significant relationships with the expected signs. Specifically, it was found that a 1 percent difference in earnings is associated with a .44 percent difference in the participation rate. This compares with a similar study designed to predict intercity differences in the participation rates of men aged twenty-five through sixty-four, which showed that a 1 percent difference in earnings was associated with only a .06 percent difference in the participation rate for men. These findings are consistent with the expectation that married women are quite sensitive to differences in earnings, given the possibilities for substituting work in the market for work at home.[6]

As expected, there is a difference in participation behavior in response to earnings opportunities between wives with and without children under six years. Women without children are more responsive to changes in wages than those with children. Teenage wives do not exhibit a positive response to wage changes while wives in the twenty to twenty-four-year age group exhibit only a weak positive response. This suggests that job availability plays an important role in determining the participation to earnings sensitivites of married women. An industry mix that provides many jobs for women increases the percentage of married women in the labor force. The impact of this labor-market variable is greatest on the labor-force participation of very young wives who have relatively little work experience and who lack information about employment opportunities.

A high female population ratio and high wages for domestic workers was found to be a factor that discouraged labor-force participation by

---

[6] It is worth noting that this differs from an earlier finding that higher earnings by males in a city are associated with *lower* labor-force participation rate of women. See Erika Schoenberg and Paul H. Douglas, "Studies in the Supply Curve of Labor," *Journal of Political Economy* 45 (1937): 45–70.

married women. A high overall unemployment rate also was found to discourage participation. The unemployment rate has an impact on the labor-force participation of all groups and will be considered in more detail below.

Racial Differences in Labor-Force Participation

Table 3-2, Racial Labor-Force Participation Rates by Age and Sex (1974 and 1978), shows considerable difference in participation rates between whites and blacks at various ages. In the aggregate, a larger pro-

TABLE 3-2 *Racial Labor-Force-Participation Rates by Age and Sex, 1974 and 1978*

	1974 Males		1978 Males		1974 Females		1978 Females	
AGE GROUP	White	Black (and other)	White	Black (and other)	White	Black (and other)	White	Black (and other)
16 years and over	79.4	73.3	79.1	72.1	45.6	49.1	49.5	53.5
16–17	53.3	34.6	55.6	33.2	40.4	24.2	48.9	27.7
18–19	73.6	62.4	76.8	59.5	58.1	44.6	64.6	48.6
20–24	86.5	82.1	85.1	78.0	63.0	58.2	69.3	62.8
25–34	96.3	92.3	96.1	90.9	52.4	60.8	61.0	68.7
35–44	96.7	90.9	96.4	91.0	54.7	61.5	60.7	67.1
45–54	93.0	84.7	92.2	84.5	54.6	56.9	56.7	59.8
55–64	78.1	70.2	73.9	69.1	40.7	43.5	41.2	43.6
65 and over	22.5	21.7	20.4	21.3	8.2	10.0	8.1	10.7

SOURCE: *Employment and Training Report of the President*, 1979, Table A-4, p. 242.

portion of black women than white women are labor-force participants at all ages. The relatively low rates of labor-force participation among black men is probably a factor contributing to the higher participation rates of black women.[7] Discrimination in housing, which has shifted consumption among blacks toward market goods and away from goods produced in the home, also appears to have contributed to the higher female labor-force participation of black women. This stems partly from limited opportunities for home ownership that cause other commodities to become status symbols and partly from overcrowding that dictates different consumption patterns among blacks from those among whites.

---

[7] Glen C. Cain, *Married Women in the Labor Force: An Economic Analysis* (Chicago: University of Chicago Press, 1966), pp. 77–83.

The Effect of Other Income on Labor-Force Participation

The Effect of an "Offset" or Tax Rate on Participation

Assuming that leisure is a normal good, the expectation is that the availability of "other income" will tend to discourage labor-force participation and/or reduce the number of hours worked. This expectation is at the root of the generally negative attitude of the public toward the provision of income without work, except under circumstances of extraordinary need.

Programs such as *Aid for Families with Dependent Children* (AFDC) and *Aid for Families with Dependent Children Which Are Intact but Have An Unemployed Father* (AFDC-UF) typically provide payments that decline at some "offset rate" as labor-market earnings increase. One way of identifying the effect of this type of other income on labor-market decisions is to examine the way in which work incentives are altered by such an "offset" or tax rate. The offset or tax rate is the rate at which the transfer payment is reduced as the family's earned income increases. The expectation is that the availability of nonlabor income will have both a negative-income and a negative-substitution effect. These effects lend themselves to graphic representation, as in Figure 3-2. Here a hypothetical worker is assumed to have labor-leisure choice as represented by indifference curve I_0. If the wage rate he can earn is $2.50

FIGURE 3-2 *The Effect of Income Maintenance on Hours of Work*

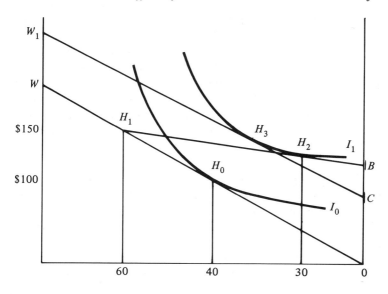

an hour, his optimal time allocation is H_0. Let us say this represents forty working hours, for which he receives a wage of $2.50 per hour or $100 per week.

Assume that this income is sufficiently low for him to qualify for a transfer like AFDC-UF. If it guarantees him $75 per week as long as he has no earned income and "taxes" earned income at (say) 50 percent, his "break-even" time allocation is represented by H_1. He works sixty hours a week and receives $150 in earned income that is taxed at a 50 percent rate. This equals $75 net, which is equivalent to the guarantee he could receive without working. If he works more than H_1 hours, he receives no payments. The opportunity set that thus confronts him is WH_1B rather than $W0$. He chooses H_2, which is the "best" combination of net wages and payments in the sense that it enables him to reach the higher indifference curve I_1. His earned income and hours of work have both decreased, but his total income has increased.

The horizontal distance from H_0 to H_2 measures the reduction in hours that results from income maintenance. As Chapter 2 noted, this reduction can be divided into an income effect and a substitution effect. Since an income-maintenance program, in effect, operates like a negative income tax, the expectation is that both the income effect and the substitution effect will be negative, i.e., the expectation is that some household members will withdraw from the labor force. This is particularly the case for those who have highly valued uses of their labor time, such as wives and young people who might wish to devote full time to housekeeping or schooling.

Figure 3-2 is drawn to reflect the likely negative-income and substitution effects of an income-maintenance program. The convex shape of the indifference curves and the "flatter" shape of WH_1B as compared with $W0$ dictates that H_2 will lie to the right of H_0. As already noted, the horizontal distance from H_0 to H_2 measures the reduction in hours resulting from income maintenance. In order to identify graphically the portion of the reduction in hours attributable to the income effect and the substitution effect, line W_1C is drawn parallel to $W0$. W_1C represents the wage increase a worker would need to achieve the same indifference curve as was possible with the original wage rate and the guaranteed income. This new budget constraint is tangent to I_1 at H_3.

Figure 3-2 is drawn on the assumption that both the income effect and the substitution effect of an income-maintenance program will be negative, although whether this assumption is valid is an empirical question that will be examined later. The horizontal distance from H_0 to H_3 reflects the income effect of the income-maintenance program; it represents the reduction in working hours (from 40 to 35 hours) that is associated with an increase in wages to W_1. The remaining reduction in hours from H_0 to H_2 is attributable to the substitution effect. The income guarantee (at the assumed tax rate) and the original wage enabled the worker to achieve the same level of satisfaction with thirty hours of work as could have been achieved with thirty-five hours of work at a higher wage rate. The level of satisfaction is the same at H_3 as at H_2, but nonwork activity is being substituted for part of the market activity represented by H_3. If the positive-substitution effect of a wage increase is large, it may outweigh the negative-income effect so that, on balance, the number of hours worked at a higher wage may be the same or larger than those worked at a lower wage.

A guarantee of $75 per week without an offsetting tax rate would enable the worker to reach an indifference curve that is to the right of I_1 by working even fewer hours than are represented by H_3. However, it is essential to recognize, once again, that this is a case in which economic theory can enlighten us only about the possibilities. Empirical research is essential for establishing how particular groups do, in fact, behave.

The Bowen-Finnegan Findings

Bowen and Finnegan identified a tendency for labor-force-participation rates to decline as the amount of "other income" rises in the range below $3,000. Their studies of the behavior of prime-age males for 1960 established this pattern for the entire group and also for single males and Negro males considered separately.[8] They interpret this finding as a basis for the inference that access to small amounts of other income permits some prime-age males who are likely to experience labor-market difficulties to stay out of the market altogether.

This evidence is not, however, as clear-cut as the preceeding generalization implies. Nonparticipation (for other reasons) is as likely to "cause" persons to become eligible for welfare payments as the payment of welfare is to "cause" nonparticipation. Thus Bowen and Finnegan point out that the association that they found between lower participation rates among prime-age males and other income "cannot be interpreted as a pure measure of the effect of other income on labor-force decisions."[9]

The Graduated Work-Incentive Experiment initiated by the Office of Economic Opportunity in 1967 provided an opportunity for the "purer measure" that Bowen and Finnegan found it impossible to obtain at the time of their study. A carefully controlled study examined the effects of eight different "negative income tax" or benefit formulas on labor-force participation. These experimental plans included a range of

[8] William Bowen and T. Aldrich Finnegan, *op. cit.*, p. 67.
[9] Bowen and Finnegan, *op. cit.*, p. 70.

basic benefits between 50 and 125 percent of the poverty line and implicit tax rates (i.e., reductions in benefits related to earnings), which ranged between 30 and 70 percent. Their impact on some 1,350 randomly selected low-income families in five New Jersey and Pennsylvania cities was examined through interviews that were conducted every three months during the three-year experiment.

Special Considerations Relative to a Negative Income Tax

The economic principles examined in Chapter 2 are the basis for the expectation that a negative income tax (i.e., a guaranteed-payment plan coupled with an offset-tax rate) will have both a negative-income effect and a negative-substitution effect. There are, however, special considerations that suggest that the analogy between a transfer income and a wage increase is less than perfect. The general expectation that guarantee plans for income without work will cause substantial reductions in the labor supply requires revision in the light of dynamic considerations that are not taken into account by the usual static analysis.

The first of these is that the market wage confronting a worker is not necessarily fixed, as is assumed in static analysis. A worker may be able to raise his wage by reducing his hours of labor-force participation in order to get training that is likely to raise future wages. To the extent that this is the case, the reduction in the supply of labor that follows from a negative income tax may be larger than is implied by the simple static theory.

Another possibility is that instead of substituting nonmarket activity for work, because a guarantee is available, workers might substitute more agreeable but lower-paying work for more disagreeable, higher-paying, work. Such behavior reflects a sacrifice of what is termed "compensating differentials"; it causes earnings to fall more than hours of work do. Earnings may similarly fall more than hours of work if workers reduce the amount of overtime work they accept or if they shift from full-time to part-time work at lower straight-time rates.

Another possible impact of a negative income tax is on job search.[10] Any payment that a worker receives when he is not working lowers the cost of job search and raises the expected wage of the job offer eventually accepted. The length of time over which a negative income tax is available is also relevant. A payment that is available on only a temporary basis is likely to have a different effect from payments that

---

[10] Job-search activity as an alternative use of time is examined in Chapter 5. Examination of the effect of the Graduated Work-Incentive Experiment on job-search activity is postponed to Chapter 19 below.

are available over a longer period. It is also likely to have a different impact on different household members. The expectation is that male heads of household will work shorter hours and engage in longer periods of search between jobs, but it is not expected that any substantial portion of them will withdraw from the labor force in consequence of payments. For wives, teenagers, and older workers, a negative income tax is expected to reduce the rate of labor-force participation. Higher tax-offset rates are, however, expected to reduce labor supply, even among male heads. All of these considerations suggest that the usual static analysis of labor-force participation may be simplistic, and that the actual response to a negative income tax may be quite different than expected.

The Graduated Work-Incentive Experiment

It is virtually impossible to identify any nonlabor income received by the working poor that is not work conditioned in existing data bases such as the census or the Survey of Economic Opportunity. Thus, the evidence brought to light about the labor-supply behavior of the 693 husband-wife families who participated in the Graduated Work-Incentive Experiment is invaluable. The findings that are the result of analysis undertaken by the Institute for Research on Poverty of the University of Wisconsin and Mathematica, Inc., are reported as *Economics in Action* 3:2.[11]

ECONOMICS IN ACTION 3:2

The Graduated Work-Incentive Experiment

The Graduated Work-Incentive Experiment provided cash payments to the included families according to eight different payment plans. The payments made under the experiment reflect the guarantee level of the plan that applies to particular families, its tax rate, the family's pre-enrollment earned income, and its size.

Table 3-A summarizes information about basic benefits for a family of four in relation to the poverty line for eight plans. The implicit tax rate is also shown. It was inferred that the responses to the experiment are most meaningful during its second year.[12] The premise is that participants would learn how to report their earnings during the first year, while the third year would reflect the expected termination of the program.

[11]"Summary Report: The New Jersey Graduated Work Incentive Experiment," Department of Health Education and Welfare December, 1973.

[12]Albert Rees, "An Overview of the Labor-Supply Results," *Journal of Human Resources* 2 (1974): 170.

TABLE 3-A *Basic Benefits and Implicit Tax Rates by Plan*

Plan	Basic Benefit (Percent of poverty line)	Basic Benefit for a Family of Four (Dollars in 1968)	Implicit Tax Rate (Percent)
I	50	$1650	30
II	50	1650	50
III	75	2475	30
IV	75	2475	50
V	75	2475	70
VI	100	3300	50
VII	100	3300	70
VIII	125	4125	50
Control Group	0	0	0

SOURCE: U.S. Department of Health, Education, and Welfare, *Summary Report: The New Jersey Graduated Work Incentive Experiment,* Office of Economic Opportunity (December 1973, p. 11).

The labor-force behavior of three broad groups of participants, married men, married women, and the family as a whole, were examined. The differences in the work behavior of those who received benefits and those who were in the control groups were so small for male household heads and continuous husband-wife families that a discernable pattern became apparent only after considerable analysis. The estimates of differentials in labor-force participation, employment, hours, and earnings for husbands in white, black, and Spanish-speaking families are summarized in Table 3-B.

The labor-supply responses to the experiment are interpreted as casting doubt on the arguments made in the nonexperimental literature that income-maintenance programs that provide benefits to intact families will have large negative effects on the labor supply.[13] Among white families, those who were in the control groups (i.e., not receiving benefits) recorded only slightly higher rates of labor-force participation that those who received benefits; they also exhibited an employment rate that was only 2.6 percentage points higher than that of the group receiving benefits. A small difference is also evidenced in hours worked per week. However, husbands receiving benefits experienced slightly *higher* earnings per week, although their labor-force-participation rate and hours worked per week were somewhat lower than those of the control group.

[13] For a discussion of the effect of income maintenance on the frequency of job change, see *Economic Theory in Action* 20-2, pp. 515–516.

TABLE 3-B *Husband Totals: Estimates of Differentials in Labor-Force Participation, Employment, Hours, and Earnings for Quarters 3–10[a]*

	Labor-Force-Participation Rate	Employment Rate	Hours Worked per Week	Earnings per Week
White				
Control-group mean	94.3	87.8	34.8	100.4
Absolute differential	− .3	−2.3	−1.9	.1
Treatment-group mean	94.0	85.5	32.9	100.5
Percent differential	− .3	−2.6	−5.6	.1
Black				
Control-group mean	95.6	85.6	31.9	93.4
Absolute differential	0	.8	.7	8.7
Treatment-group mean	95.6	86.4	32.6	102.1
Percent differential	0	.9	2.3	9.3
Spanish-speaking				
Control-group mean	95.2	89.5	34.3	92.2
Absolute differential	1.6	−2.4	−.2	5.9
Treatment-group mean	96.8	87.1	34.1	98.1
Percent differential	1.6	−2.7	−.7	6.4

[a] The data for these tables consist of 693 husband-wife families who reported for at least 8 of the 13 quarters when interviews were obtained. The reported differentials in each measure of labor supply are the experimental treatment-group mean minus the control-group mean, as measured in a regression equation in which the following variables were controlled: age of husband, education of husband, number of adults, number of children, sites, and pre-experiment labor-supply variables of the husband. These means and the associated control-treatment differentials may therefore be interpreted as applicable to control and treatment groups with identical composition in terms of these variables. Percent differentials are computed using the mean of the control as base.

Official government labor-force concepts, used in the experiment, define someone as being in the labor force if he is employed or unemployed. Someone is unemployed if he is actively seeking employment, waiting recall from layoff, or waiting to report to a new wage or salary job.

SOURCE: U.S. Department of Health, Education, and Welfare, *Summary Report: The New Jersey Graduated Work Incentive Experiment,* Office of Economic Opportunity (December 1973), p. 22.

Failure to identify that benefit payments had *any* significant effect on the labor-force-participation rate of black husbands was an unexpected finding. In spite of the fact that black husband-wife families received larger average payments than similar white and Spanish-speaking families, the estimated supply response for blacks is *positive.* No explanation is offered for this finding. The Spanish-speaking group is numerically larger than the group of black husband-and-wife families, for whom negative-supply effects were identified.

The labor-force-participation rates of wives in the experimental group was only 16 percent, which is less than half of the 1971 labor-force-participation rate among all married women in the U.S. population. This low rate is attributed partly to the fact that families with small children are overrepresented in the experiment. The measured work disincentive is particularly evident in the behavior of white wives. The effect of benefits on the labor-supply variables of black wives is close to zero and sometimes positive. The effect of payments on married Spanish-speaking women was sometimes negative and sometimes positive, but never statistically significant.

Unemployment and Labor-Force Participation

"Discouraged Worker" and "Added Worker" Effects

The number of unemployed persons is estimated by *inference* from the answers given to household-survey questions by unemployed persons. A person who responds that he is not working but is looking for work is counted as part of the labor force. The assumption is that his search activity will eventually provide suitable work. "Suitable work" implies a job that is geographically accessible, requiring skills comparable to those used for previous employment with comparable pay, job status, and other characteristics he considers important. The importance of these job characteristics to job seekers suggests the relevance of asking how the unemployment count is affected if an unemployed person has not yet become informed that he is, in fact, unlikely to find a job he will accept, either because it doesn't exist or because he is no longer considered qualified. If he had "perfect information," he might well stop his search activities, in which case he would be enumerated as "not in the labor force." Thus, the labor-force statistic on a given date will necessarily include some persons who subsequently leave as "discouraged workers." To be counted as unemployed, one must first be included in the labor force. This requires that a person who is not working be actively seeking employment. It follows that persons who are not looking for work because they are quite certain there are no jobs, i.e. they are "discouraged," are not counted as unemployed.

The magnitude and the importance of the discouraged-worker effect is a matter of considerable controversy. Table 3-3, which presents data taken from the 1979 *Employment and Training Report of the President* puts the problem of the "discouraged worker" in perspective. It indicates that besides those who cite home responsibilities, old age, poor health,

TABLE 3-3 *Persons Not in the Labor Force by Reason of Nonparticipation (1978)*

Reason for nonparticipation	Thousands	Percent
Total not in labor force	58,521	100%
In school	7,517	12.8
Poor health, disability	5,252	9.0
Home responsibilities	30,775	52.6
Retirement, old age	9,366	16.0
Think they cannot get a job	845	1.5
All other reasons	4,766	8.1
Want job now	5,328	9.1

SOURCE: *Employment and Training Report of the President,* 1979, Table A-13, p. 255.

and school attendance as reasons for nonparticipation, there are individuals who have disassociated themselves from the labor force because they are in the "think they cannot get a job" category identified as such by the Department of Labor. These are the persons who constitute the "discouraged worker" group that have left the labor force in frustration. They are neither employed nor actively looking for work and thus do not meet the department's criteria for inclusion in the labor force. The evidence is that as job opportunities expand, the labor force grows primarily in response to decisions by persons who are not "discouraged workers," and who are not yet in the labor force, to become labor-force participants.

To a person who is about to enter the labor force, the prospect of finding employment in a reasonable period of time is as important as the market wage in determining his decision to participate. The overall rate of employment affects decisions because the higher the unemployment rate is, the lower is the possibility that a person will find employment. The job-search process will be examined in greater detail in Chapter 4, but it is obvious that job search is expensive in terms of transportation, personal grooming, and other expenses. Thus a high unemployment rate in the economy has a predicted negative effect on labor-force participation. This effect is usually referred to as the "discouragement effect."

The loss of employment by a household member who is regularly employed will also affect the participation decisions of other household members. It may encourage other household members to enter the labor force in order to at least partially replace the income lost. There is considerable controversy as to which effect is stronger, and whether they substantially offset one another. To the extent that the discouragement effect is greater than the additional-worker effect during a period of depression, there will be "hidden unemployment," i.e., unemployment masquerading as reduced labor-force participation. The formulation of public policy makes it important to determine whether the additional-worker or discouraged-worker tendency is stronger.

Both time-series and cross-section data have been used in an effort to identify whether the discouragement effect or the added-worker effect is stronger, or if they substantially offset one another.[14] Each type of data offers some advantages and disadvantages. Cross-section studies generally allow a wider choice of explanatory variables because of the availability of decennial census data. The major difficulty inherent in the use of time-series data derives from the lack of data available in this form to be used as variables, other than the unemployment rate and the labor-force-participation rate. Cross-section studies, on the other hand, cannot show the timing of a response to change. Similarly, differential-migration rates among employed and unemployed persons are typically ignored in cross-section studies.

Present-day controversy about the impact of the unemployment rate on labor-force participation stems from an early study by W. S. Woytinsky that, using time-series data, estimated that during the high unemployment years of the 1930s, the work force increased from 10 to 25 percent.[15] A later study by Clarence Long contradicted these findings. Their conflicting conclusions led W. Lee Hansen to undertake an additional study using gross-change data relating to the period 1954–1959.[16] His findings corroborate Long's; i.e., the labor force was not increased in consequence of increases in the level of unemployment on the basis of the data he examined for the postwar period.[17] Hansen suggested three factors that appeared to be relevant to his findings concerning the mid 1950s. One was that the postwar recession was relatively mild. A second was that large supplies of additional workers were relatively unavailable. Finally, the availability of unemployment compensation and/or of consumer-held cash assets appeared to influence the choice between market and nonmarket activity.

[14]Time-series data relate to a series of consecutive dates, e.g., weeks, months, years. Cross-section data reflect the experiences of different groups on a particular date or for a particular period, e.g., the year 1979.

[15]W. S. Woytinsky, *Employment and Earnings in the United States* (New York: Twentieth Century Fund, 1953).

[16]W. Lee Hansen, "Cyclical Sensitivity of the Labor Force," *American Economic Review* (June 1961).

[17]Clarence Long, *The Labor Force under Changing Income and Employment* (Princeton: Princeton University Press for the National Bureau of Economic Research, 1958), especially pp. 267–277.

A subsequent study undertaken by Jacob Mincer marshalled evidence that while some additional workers enter the labor force during recessions, more workers withdraw in discouragement.[18] These findings have been corroborated by the exhaustive studies undertaken by Bowen and Finnegan. Their analysis, which included married and unmarried males and females of all age groups, by color, is the most definitive study undertaken on the relationship between unemployment and labor-force participation. Their evidence is based on census data for 1960. Their results for the major age and sex groups are reported as *Economics in Action* 3:3.

ECONOMICS IN ACTION 3:3

The Relationship Between Labor-Market Conditions and Labor-Market Participation

The objective of the Bowen-Finnegan study was to determine whether differences among SMSA's in the labor-force participation rates of different groups can be explained by differences in labor-market conditions. The participation rate of prime-age males is examined in terms of three specific variables: (a) the unemployment rate in the local labor market, (b) an "industry mix" variable that reflects job opportunities for men, and (c) a measure of the average wage earned by men in the local labor market. The expectation is that the labor-force participation of males twenty-five to fifty-four years of age will be negatively associated with the unemployment rate and positively associated with the "maleness" of the job mix and the male wage rate.[19]

As a first step, the 1960 labor-force-participation rate of prime-age males in the 100 largest SMSA was calculated. The simple unweighted mean of these rates was 96.4. This vary high participation rate suggested that the effect of unemployment on the participation rate of prime-age males was too weak to be statistically significant.

This was not, however, the case when further analysis was done. There was a highly significant negative association between unemployment rates and the participation rate of prime-age males, which suggests that high unemployment *does* discourage some men for looking for

---

[18] Jacob Mincer, "Labor Force Participation and Unemployment: A Review of Recent Evidence," in R. A. and M. S. Gordon, eds., *Prosperity and Unemployment.* Mincer's paper also involves a methodological critique of a paper by Kenneth Strand and Thomas Dernburg, "Cyclical Variations in Civilian Labor Force Participation," the *Review of Economic Studies* 46 (November 1964).

[19] William Bowen and T. Aldrich Finnegan, *The Economics of Labor Force Participation, op. cit.,* Chapter 4.

work. Their finding is that a metropolitan area that is typical in terms of other variables but that has an unemployment rate one percentage point above the all SMSA average would be expected to have a labor-force participation rate for prime-age males that is about three-tenths of a percentage point below the all-SMSA average.

With a given unemployment rate, a representative prime-age male will have an easier time locating employment if the local labor market has an industry mix that is conducive to male employment. Specifically, a one-percentage-point difference among otherwise similar SMSAs in the ratio of male-to-female employment characteristics tended to be accompanied by a difference of approximately two-tenths of a percentage point in the participation rates of males aged twenty-five to fifty-four.[20]

While the wage rate influences the labor-force-participation rates of men aged twenty-five to fifty-four its impact is smaller than that of the unemployment-rate or the industry-mix variable. This finding supports the inference made on the basis of the data in Table 3-1 (above) that prime-age males are expected to and do work almost regardless of the wage rate. Their labor-force status is more strongly influenced by the state of the labor market than the wage rate.

The male unemployment rate is also expected to have an effect on female labor-force participation. For married women the expectation is that the discouraged-worker effect will predominate over the added-worker effect, although the relationship of unemployment to the labor-force participation of married women could be either positive or negative.[21] Analysis of the labor-force participation of women showed that, other individual and household characteristics held constant, wives with unemployed husbands are more likely to be in the labor force than wives whose husbands are employed. This is the "additional-worker effect." The important question is not whether this effect manifests itself but, rather, how strong it is when labor-market conditions are adverse and discourage the participation of wives as well as their husbands.

In addition to the unemployment rate, six variables are expected to cause intercity differences in the labor-force-participation rates of married women. These are "other income," husband's income, schooling (i.e., the median number of years of school completed by all females twenty-five and over), color (a percentage of married women who are nonwhite), net migration into and out of the area, and the presence of children. The signs in the parentheses indicate the direction of the effect that each is expected to have on labor-force participation: income of husbands (−); other income (−); schooling of wives (+); migration of

---

[20] Bowen and Finnegan, *op. cit.*, p. 78.

[21] Bowen and Finnegan, *op. cit.*, Chapter 6, especially pp. 178–190.

females (+); percent nonwhite (+); presence of children (−).

When these factors are held constant, in order to examine the separate effect of the unemployment rate on the labor-force-participation rate of married women the finding is that a metropolitan area having an unemployment rate of one percentage point above the average of the economy as a whole during the 1960 census week would be expected to have a labor-force-participation rate for married women ages 15−54, which is about one percentage point below the all-SMSA average. On balance, therefore, married women were considerably more responsive to the discouragement effect of higher unemployment than to the additional-worker effect.

Separate analysis was undertaken of the labor-force-participation rates of single women and six other groups. The participation rates for all three groups of single women (women never married, divorced women, separated women, and women with husbands absent) exhibit a consistently inverse association between the overall unemployment rate and labor-force-participation rates.[22]

The participation rates of older persons are extraordinarily sensitive to levels of unemployment in local labor markets.[23] High unemployment rates similarly had a marked negative effect on the labor-force-participation rates of young males. As expected, their sensitivity to the unemployment rate diminishes steadily as they approach age twenty-five.[24]

Further Controversy about Labor-Force Participation

Bowen and Finnegan found a smaller relationship between labor-force participation and unemployment on the basis of time-series data than on the basis of SMSA cross-section data. They maintain that the smaller response evidenced by the time-series data is caused by the lagged response of labor-force-participation rates, which is more accurately reflected in cross-section results. Another pair of investigators has expressed skepticism about their explanation of the difference between time-series and cross-section statistical results.[25] It is argued that the Bowen-Finnegan estimates are too large; there is a bias which results from the simultaneous determination of labor-force-participation rates and unemployment rates in local labor markets.

The Fleisher-Rhodes model is intended to test the hypothesis that

[22] *Op. cit.*, Chapter 8.

[23] *Op. cit.*, Chapter 9.

[24] *Op. cit.*, Chapter 14.

[25] Belton M. Fleisher and George Rhodes, "Unemployment and the Labor Force Participation of Married Men and Women: A Simultaneous Model," *Review of Economics and Statistics* (November 1976).

while the effect of aggregate demand on labor-force participation, operating through local labor-market unemployment rates, is substantial and negative, it is smaller than it was found to be in the Bowen-Finnegan study, which treated unemployment rates in each local labor market as a constant *independent* variable. Their statistical findings support their model and are offered in the belief that they help resolve the differences found by Bowen and Finnegan on the basis of time-series data and cross-section data in the relationship between unemployment and labor-force-participation rates.

A question that needs to be asked in evaluating the Fleisher-Rhodes findings is whether the premise of interdependence between labor-force-participation rates and unemployment is conceptually satisfying. The Bowen-Finnegan study treated the unemployment rate in each local labor market as an independent variable. The alternative assumption that the unemployment rate is a dependent variable that is interdependent with labor-force participation implies that the characteristics of the labor force in each local area (i.e., schooling, training, and commitment to market activity) exert a determining influence on both labor-force participation and unemployment rates. The implication is that the same set of personal characteristics that affect individual labor-force participation also affect workers' unemployment experiences. This premise is controversial and raises the whole question of the role of schooling and investment in human capital in determining labor-force behavior and the functioning of labor markets. This is a matter that will be addressed in Chapter 4 and again in Part III in connection with labor-market policy.

Hours of Work

The Long-Run Trend toward a Decreased Work Week

The secular decline in the amount of labor supplied by full-time workers, as reflected in the length of the full-time work week, is among the dramatic changes that have taken place in the American economy during the twentieth century. Between 1900 and 1940, the full-time work week declined approximately 35 percent. The simultaneous increase in permanent real wages and property incomes made it possible for successive generations to enjoy more commodities and also more leisure. The decline in hours, which is exhibited in Table 3-4, reflects both the reduction in the length of the work week that characterized industry as a whole and the shift away from industries such as agriculture, in which the work week has traditionally been long. H. G. Lewis has rationalized the secular decline in hours of work in terms of the work-leisure decisions examined in Chapter 2, and inferred that leisure is a

·TABLE 3-4   *Average Weekly Hours of Work, 1900–40*

Year	Nonagricultural Wage and Salary Workers[a]	Manufacture
1900	58.5	55.0
1905	57.2	54.5
1910	55.6	52.2
1915	53.4	50.4
1920	50.6	48.1
1925	49.0	47.9
1930	47.1	43.6
1935	41.7	36.4
1940	42.5	37.6

Annual rates of change 1900–40[b]

	−.009	−.010
	(.0004)	(.0003)

[a] These figures are based on establishment data, and reflect hours paid for by firms, rather than hours actually worked. Because paid leisure was not widespread until after 1940, this series is a reasonably accurate representation of hours actually worked by wage and salary workers during the prewar period.

[b] Standard errors are in parentheses.

SOURCE: For nonagricultural, John D. Owen, *The Price of Leisure* (Rotterdam: Rotterdam University Press, 1969), p. 67; for manufacturing, Ethel B. Jones, "New Estimates of Hours of Work per Week and Hourly Earnings, 1900–1957," *Review of Economics and Statistics,* Vol. 43, No, 4 (November 1963), p. 375; all in Thomas J. Knieser, "The Full-time Work Week in the United States, 1900–1970," *Industrial and Labor Relations Review,* Vol. 30, No. 1 (October 1976), p. 4. Reprinted with the permission of the *Review.* © 1976 by Cornell University. All rights reserved.

commodity for which the long-run income effect outweighs the substitution effect.[26]

The shortening of the work week has come about in a variety of ways. Besides the decline in the standard work week, workers typically have more holidays, shorter working days, more rest periods, and more "coffee breaks." In addition, many firms are experimenting with "four-day weeks" and alternative time schedules designed to provide even longer periods of free time for workers while maintaining or enhancing the efficiency requirements of their employers. These insti-

[26] H. G. Lewis, "Hours of Work and Hours of Leisure," reprinted in R. Marshall and R. Perlman, eds., *An Anthology of Labor Economics* (New York: John Wiley and Sons, 1972), pp. 203–209.

tutional changes suggest that leisure is a "normal" commodity, i.e., a commodity for which the long-run income effect outweighs the long-run substitution effect.

The Work Week since World War II

There is some disagreement about the long-term trend of hours in the period since World War II. While the general impression is that the historical downward trend in hours came to an end during the 1930s, Professor Rees contends that the reductions have, in fact, continued. They have, however, taken the form of increases in paid vacations and holidays that do not show up in official statistics that measure only hours and that treat an hour of paid vacation precisely the same as an hour of work.[27]

Rees's contention about the continuing decline in the number of hours in the full-time work week has recently been questioned. Knieser maintains that the work week has not changed significantly since 1940. Using the monthly survey of the nation's households conducted by the Census Bureau of the Department of Labor, which is reported as the "unadjusted" average in Table 3-5, Knieser maintains that the length of the average work week from 1956 to 1971 has remained virtually unchanged, after the unadjusted average is corrected to reflect the underreporting of vacations, holidays, and sick days.

The argument that the work week has continued to decline but that the decline has taken the form of more paid vacations and holidays that are masked in the published data is quite consistent with the traditional analysis of individual behavior in the labor market. As was discussed in Chapter 2, an individual maximizes utility (given the market prices of goods and leisure and nonlabor income) by allocating his budget between wage goods and leisure. Leisure is assumed to be a normal good, and the taste for leisure is assumed to be stable overtime. Thus, the supply of hours depends on tastes, the real-wage rate, and real-asset income. This model is quite consistent with the inverse relationship between real wages and the declining average length of the full time work week that was observed secularly up until World War II.

It does not, however, explain the stability in the full-time work week in the United States in the period since. An explanation for the failing of the traditional model in this regard is that it assumes tastes to be "given" and also treats labor-market behavior as an individual rather than a family decision. Recognition that the labor-supply decisions of husbands and wives are interdependent implies that a secular analysis of the full-time work week requires that the effect of increases in the average

[27]Albert Rees, *Work and Pay* (New York: Harper and Row, 1973), Chapter 2.

Table 3-5 *Average Weekly Hours of Work for Men 25–44, 1956–71.*[a]

Year	Unadjusted Average[b]	Adjusted Average[c]
1956	44.5	42.3
1957	44.3	42.1
1958	43.6	42.4
1959	43.9	41.6
1960	44.1	41.9
1961	44.4	42.3
1962	44.7	42.5
1963	44.9	42.6
1964	44.5	42.3
1965	45.3	43.1
1966	45.5	43.3
1967	45.0	42.6
1968	44.8	42.3
1969	44.8	42.2
1970	43.9	41.3
1971	44.0	41.4

Annual rates of change 1956–71[d]

	+.0007	+.0001
	(.0006)	(.0008)

[a] Average workweek figures for men 25–44 are unavailable for 1940–55.

[b] Average weekly hours of work, men age 25–44, unadjusted for those employed but absent from work during the survey week (household data).

[c] First column adjusted for absences.

[d] Standard errors are in parentheses.

SOURCE: U.S. Bureau of Labor Statistics Employment and Earnings (Washington, D.C., G.P.O., various issues), as tabulated by Thomas J. Knieser, "The Full-time Work Week in the United States," p. 5. Reprinted with permission from the *Review.* © 1976 by Cornell University. All rights reserved.

wage of women should be incorporated into the analysis.[28] Knieser's more complete labor-supply model, which incorporates both the effect of changes in female wages and the effect on the "taste" for goods associated with the secular increases in education, predicts the postwar stability of the average full-time work week more accurately than the simpler labor-supply model that omits these variables.

[28] Between 1899 and 1939 the weekly earnings of women in manufacturing increased from 54 percent to about 58 percent of the weekly earnings of males. This rate of increase became somewhat larger in the period since. See U.S. Bureau of the Census, United States Census of Population 1970: Industrial Characteristics: Victor R. Fuchs, "Recent Trends and Long-Run Prospects for Female Earnings," *American Economic Review* 64, 2 (May 1974): 236–42; and Victor R. Fuchs, "Differences in Hourly Earnings between Men and Women," *Monthly Labor Review* 93, 6 (June 1970): 10–18.

Concluding Remarks

The theory of household choice about the allocation of time between market and nonmarket activity provides a basis for our "expectations" about the way in which people actually behave. However, while empirical investigation has verified some expectations, it has also turned up some suprises. The decline in the length of the average work week up through the 1930s, as real-income levels rose, is completely expected and in perfect accord with the traditional labor-supply model. The finding that the work week has not continued to decline over the last thirty years is the result of careful arithmetic "sleuthing." These results are readily explained by means of an expanded labor-supply model that specifically recognizes the interdependence of the labor-supply decisions of husbands and wives and also allows for changing "tastes."

The insights provided by the Graduated Work-Incentive Experiment into the labor-force-participation behavior and hours of work supplied by family members receiving benefits were quite unexpected. The expectation was that such benefits would reduce labor-force partici- pation and also the number of hours worked. These expectations were not borne out by the experiment, which implies that static models require reexamination in a dynamic context if they are to shed light on human behavior in the real world.

A consensus appears to have been reached on the basis of empirical studies concerning the dominance of the "discouraged-worker effect" over the "added-worker" effect. But there is no consensus about the magnitude of the decline in labor-force participation that is likely to accompany a decline in aggregate demand. The Bowen-Finnegan model, in which the unemployment rate is an independent variable, predicts that a decline in aggregate demand is likely to be associated with a con- siderable number of "discouraged" workers and consequently with "hidden" unemployment which develops as workers withdraw from the labor market because they think there are no jobs available.

A more recent inquiry, as has been seen, maintains that the Bowen-Finnegan estimate of the number of discouraged workers is excessive and seeks to reconcile the discrepancy between the estimates based on time-series data and (higher) estimates based on cross-section data. The alternative model hypothesizes that unemployment rates and labor-force-participation rates are interdependent and that labor-force characteristics, such as schooling, training, and commitment to market activity, influence both the labor-force-participation rates and the unemployment rates of local labor markets to a degree that considerably reduces the effect of the level of employment (or unemployment) in the economy as a whole on labor-force-participation rates in local labor markets. The issues that this hypothesis addresses are extremely complex and can only be hinted at here, although they are, in a very real sense, at the heart of much of the controversy about labor-market behavior and the functioning of labor markets. The most obvious dimension of the controversy arises at the policy level. If the major cause of the negative relationship between labor-force participation and unemployment is attributable to forces other than aggregate demand, which affects adversely both labor-force participation and unemployment, the policy implication is that job creation alone may fail to increase employment among workers who lack characteristics, such as schooling, training, and labor-market commitments, that make them attractive employees. Policy to improve their employability by increasing the quality of the labor they supply may be necessary instead of, or in addition to, policy to stimulate aggregate demand.

The argument may be pursued further, for the premise of policy to enhance employability is that the choices that individuals, their families, and society make about schooling, training, and other forms of "investment in human capital" determine, in the final analysis, how well individuals and their families fare in the labor markets on which most are dependent for their wages and salaries. The mainstream view is that the theory of household choice, which was examined in Chapter 2, is properly extended to encompass various activities that improve the quality of the labor it supplies to the market by investing in what has come to be termed "human capital." Thus the full range of the issues raised by the hypothesis that labor-force participation and unemployment rates are interdependent cannot be done justice until the role of expenditures on schooling and training in improving the quality of the labor that is supplied to the market is examined. This is the task of Chapter 4.

Suggestions for Further Reading

H. G. Lewis. "Hours of Work and Hours of Leisure," reprinted in R. Marshall and R. Perlman, eds., *An Anthology of Labor Economics*. New York: John Wiley and Sons, 1972, pp. 203–209.

Jacob Mincer. "Labor Force Participation and Unemployment: A Review of Recent Evidence," in R. A. and M. S. Gordon, eds., *Property and Unemployment*. New York: Wiley, 1966.

Albert Rees. "An Overview of the Labor Supply Results." Symposium on the Graduated Work Incentive Experiment, *Journal of Human Resources* 2 (1974).

4 The Quality of the Labor Supply: Investment in Human Capital

The amount of effort individuals and households offer to the market is only one aspect of the labor-supply problem; the quality of that effort is equally important. Part of the differences among workers' physical and mental capabilities are inborn; others are the result of schooling, training on the job, learning while doing, and even health care. The common feature of these diverse activities is that they improve or maintain the market value of the services of persons who participate in the labor force. Job search and migration have a similar effect. Because the expenditures these activities involve are chiefly, if not exclusively, incurred to improve productivity and earnings, they are analogous to investment in physical capital.[1] Their intent is to earn a positive rate of return, precisely as is the case with physical capital.[2] Thus, the term "human capital" has come into use among economists, although it is undoubtedly still strange to those who have been taught to think of labor and capital as distinct factors of production.[3] A very large proportion of human-capital investment is the result of schooling. This chapter is concerned chiefly with examining the basis for household decisions to allocate resources to education and the effect that schooling has on earning and employment opportunities. It is, however, also useful to have some understanding about the origin of modern human-capital analysis as well the range of its micro- and macroeconomic applications and how they relate to the concerns of the labor economist.

[1] T. W. Schultz, "The Concept of Human Capital," *American Economic Review* 51 (March 1961), reprinted in M. Blaug, ed., *Economics of Education, 1 (1968)*.

[2] G. Becker, "Cost-Benefit Analysis of Educational Expenditure," reprinted in *Economics of Education,* pp. 183–184.

[3] But see H. G. Shaeffer, "A Critique of the Concept of Human Capital," in the same volume. Shaeffer argues that the concept of capital is not applicable to human beings precisely because such expenditures are not economically motivated.

Human-Capital Analysis and Its Relation to Labor Economics

Schooling and Economic Growth

Research undertaken during the post-World War II period made it apparent that the contribution of schooling and other forms of human-capital investment to economic growth had generally been underestimated. It became apparent that while additions to the stock of physical capital and the size of the labor force are the chief forces propelling an economy toward increases in its per capita output, there is some portion of growth that cannot be explained in these terms.[4] The "residual," which is the portion of growth that cannot be accounted for by increases in the number of workers and the stock of physical capital, has been attributed in part to technical progress and in part to improvements in human capital.

The importance of human capital in the growth process was reflected in the extraordinarily rapid recovery of countries whose plants and equipment were severely damaged or destroyed during World War II. Their experience also generated an interest in identifying the relative rates of growth of human and physical capital. Professor Theodore W. Schultz estimated that the annual rate of growth of human capital is approximately 4 percent, whereas the stock of physical capital is increasing at the rate of about 2 percent per year.[5] Much of the stock of human capital is represented by the education of persons in the labor force.

Educational improvements have also been identified as an important factor in generating economic growth in the United States and other countries. Table 4-1 summarizes Edward Denison's estimates of the increase (actual and projected) of national income in real terms and the percent of the growth rate attributable to quantitative and qualitative changes in the labor force. According to his estimates, education accounted for 12 percent of total growth between 1909 and 1929, and 23 percent between 1929 and 1956. He projects that it will account for 19 percent of total growth for the period 1960 to 1980.[6]

---

[4] Simon Kuznets, *Modern Economic Growth* (New Haven: Yale University Press, 1966).

[5] T. W. Schultz, "Rise in the Capital Stock Represented by Education in the United States, 1900–1957," in S. Muskin, ed., *Economics of Education* (Washington: 1962). See also Allen M. Cartter, "The Economic Value of Higher Education," in Neil Chamberlain, ed., *Contemporary Economic Issues* (Homewood: R. D. Irwin, 1969).

[6] A subsequent comparative study of nine countries, also by Denison, for the period 1950 to 1962 concluded that education did not account for more than 10 percent of the total rate of growth except in the United States, the U.K., and Belgium. See E. Denison, *Why Growth Rates Differ: Postwar Experience in Nine Western Countries* (Washington: 1967).

TABLE 4-1   *Growth of Output as Related to Education: United States*

Output and Education	1909–29	1929–56	1960–80
National output			
Growth rate	2.82	2.93	3.33
Percent owing to education	12.0	23.0	19.0
Output per employed worker			
Growth rate	1.22	1.60	1.62
Percent owing to education	29.0	42.0	40.0

SOURCE: E. F. Denison, "Measuring the Contribution of Education (and the Residual) Appendix to Economic Growth," *The Residual Factor and Economic Growth* (Paris: Organization for Economic Cooperation and Development, 1964).

There have been some criticisms of Denison's estimates, largely because education of the labor force is measured in terms of increases in the number of days of schooling, which does not necessarily reflect the amount of education received. Nevertheless, there is a consensus that education is a significant factor in the growth process even though its magnitude has so far eluded precise measurement.

Labor Economics and Human-Capital Research

Labor economists have generally had only a peripheral interest in the growth process, although they are well aware of its employment- and income-generating effects. Their chief microeconomic concern is to explain the *structure* of wages. Wage differences that are associated with age, sex, race, and occupation are related to differences in schooling, training, and labor-market experience. The labor economist is therefore concerned not only with examining individual and family decisions to acquire education, but also with employer decisions to provide "on-the-job training" and society's decisions to support education and training out of public funds.[7] These decisions are the chief supply side influences that underlie the wage structure that will be examined in Chapters 8–10.

The "new" theory of consumer behavior is another microeconomic spinoff of the human-capital analysis that is of peripheral interest to the labor economist. It has examined the role of education in the efficiency with which the family combines the goods and services purchased in the market with household resources to produce "final" commodities.

[7] Employer decisions are discussed in Chapter 7. The role of government in education is a policy question and is examined in Chapter 18.

Health and better family "background" for children, which gives them advantages in the labor market, are among the more important aspects of this research.[8]

On a macroeconomic level, labor economists are especially concerned with differences in the incidence of unemployment among groups and with differences in the distribution of personal income. Wages and salaries are the most important forms of personal income, and the families that experience poverty are typically labor-market failures. Table 4-2, which relates to the prosperous year 1970, provides some preliminary insight into the labor-market experiences of males with different levels of educational experience. The year 1970 is chosen for illustrative purposes because disparities are at a minimum during a prosperous year and because much of the census data available for that year are not available on an annual basis.

The data in Table 4-2 show that high-school dropouts had considerably lower rates of labor-force participation and a lower percentage of full-time workers than high-school and college graduates. High-school dropouts who are "blue-collar" workers bore the brunt of the increase in unemployment during that year. Their experience suggests that persons with higher levels of education are less likely to become unemployed. The incidence of poverty is also markedly lower among better-educated groups. Presumably this is because they are better able to adjust to the technological and demand changes that characterize a dynamic economy. New jobs are being created by changing production techniques and new patterns of demand. But these frequently have higher skill requirements; the result is that workers with

TABLE 4-2 *Education, Labor-Market Experience of Males 16 and Over, and Incidence of Poverty, 1970*

	High School Dropouts	High School Graduate	College Graduate
Typical occupational status	blue-collar	clerical	professional
Labor force participation	83.5%	90.1%	89.8%
Full-time workers	76.9%	83.9%	89.2%
Unemployment rate	8.0%	5.0%	2.0%
Average income	$7,600	$9,200	$14,400
Incidence of poverty*	30.9%	5.8%	2.0%

*U.S. Bureau of the Census

SOURCE: U.S. Department of Labor

[8] See Gary Becker and Robert T. Michael, "On the New Theory of Consumer Behavior," *Swedish Journal of Economics* (1973): 378–396.

limited skills who lose their jobs are often not able to respond to the new opportunities these changes generate. Further inquiry into the different impact of unemployment on different groups and its implications for the poverty problem is postponed to Parts II and III. The chief concern here is to further examine labor-supply decisions as they relate to labor "quality."

Education as an Investment

Education and Individual Earning Opportunities

Rates of labor-force participation and unemployment are generally reflected in earnings. All three are associated with levels of educational attainment. Table 4-3, Median Incomes of All Males by Age and Education, and Figure 4-1, whose "earnings-age-education profiles" display the tabulated information graphically, are based on 1970 census data.[9] Median income data are generally used as a proxy for earnings because wages, salaries, and other categories of earned income comprise the major portion of total income, except among those who are sixty-five and over for whom transfer payments bulk large.[10]

Several interesting and significant relationships, which are also apparent in previous census data and in comparable statistics available for other countries, are evident in the table and its accompanying figure.

TABLE 4-3   *Median Incomes of All Males by Age and Education—1970*

	Elementary School		High School	College	
Age	Less than 8 years	8 Years	4 Years	4 Years	5 or more years
25–34	5,699	6,749	9,451	11,553	12,932
35–44	7,040	8,503	11,312	17,480	19,672
45–54	6,834	8,436	11,774	19,414	21,096
55–64	5,844	7,722	10,987	17,202	21,345
65 and over	3,390	4,503	6,761	11,033	13,066

SOURCE: U.S. Bureau of the Census

[9] The median is the midpoint in an array of data arranged in ascending or descending order.

[10] A transfer payment is a current receipt that is not part of current earnings. Some examples are unemployment insurance, social-security benefits, and pensions. The Bureau of Census definition of "income," unlike the Department of Commerce's definition of "earnings," includes transfer payments. One problem that is avoided by utilizing data on median income by age and education is that it is not necessary to adjust those data statistically for different work-life expectancies.

FIGURE 4-1 *Earnings-Age-Education Profiles*

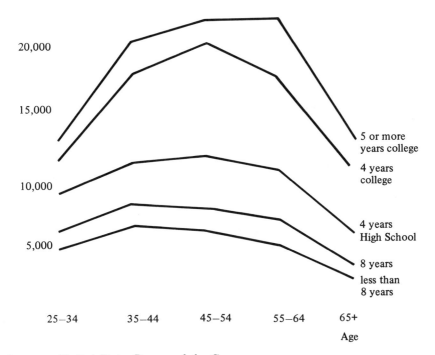

Income

SOURCE: United States Bureau of the Census

The most obvious is that earnings increase with age irrespective of the number of years of schooling acquired. The second is that earnings increase more rapidly and reach a higher level as the median number of years of schooling increases within an age group. The third is that a larger number of median years of schooling is associated with an earnings peak that comes later in life and declines less precipitously than that of those whose schooling is more limited.[11]

[11] The apparent tendency for earnings to decline well before retirement age warrants comment because it may be misleading. Age-earnings profiles derived from cross-sectional data are unable to reflect the secular increases in earnings associated with progress and increased capital accumulation. These factors would be apparent in longitudinal data spanning several decades, but cross-sectional data obscure the increase in earnings that is associated with the growth factor. Thus, the dollar earnings of an individual age 50 are likely to be higher than they were ten years earlier and, similarly, are likely to be higher at age 60 (assuming he is still in the labor force) than at age 50, though the *rate of increase* in his earnings is likely to be lower than it was during the earlier decades of his life.

While earnings-age-education profiles show a positive relationship between schooling and earning, they do not "prove" that schooling "causes" higher earnings. There are many other factors, among them training, experience, sex, race, ability, personal drive, and employment contacts that affect earnings at different ages and schooling levels. It is necessary to control for their influence to determine the separate effect of formal education on earnings. Considerable research effort has been directed to this problem, and, as will be discussed later in the chapter, there is a great deal of controversy about it among labor economists and others interested in education as an investment.

Educational Expenditures as a Family Decision

The relationship between education and earnings suggests that schooling has virtually become a prerequisite for employment. It further implies that expenditures for education are not purely consumption expenditures, because they improve the earning capabilities of the individuals who are schooled. This is increasingly the case when students enter their high-school years, i.e., grades nine through twelve. Preschool and elementary-school education is essentially a consumer good to children and their parents, although the attitudes, learning processes, and academic skills acquired at these levels become factors in determining both the demand for and the effectiveness of subsequent investments in education.

As is the case with labor-force participation, the family is viewed as an economic unit with respect to making investments in its members. Family members allocate their time between market and nonmarket activities on the basis of investments already made in schooling, training, and work experience. The choices made with respect to *current* investment in any family member tend to reflect the expected *future* allocation of his/her time.[12] Thus, investment in human capital is generally sex linked, as is the differential allocation of time within the household.

A study by the American Council of Education is enlightening about the relationship between investment in schooling and the expectation of future labor-force participation. About two-thirds of the male freshmen they surveyed and one-half of the female freshmen expressed the view that "the chief benefit of college is that it increases earning power." Their data, reflecting the concern of freshmen students with the

---

[12] Jacob Mincer and Solomon Polacheck, "Family Investments in Human Capital: Earnings of Women," *Journal of Political Economy* 82, 2 (March/April 1974): S76–S108.

economic implications of their college plans indicates that 77 percent of the males and 70 percent of the females expressed the view that they were going to college to get a better job.[13]

Expressed in the language of the economist, these responses imply that a college education is viewed as an investment whose value is to be judged on the basis of its expected returns, net of costs, in comparison with alternative investments that could be financed with the same commitment of money and time.[14] Investment in the schooling of a family member is thus comparable to a businessman's purchase of a machine, a building, or other earning asset. It follows that comparable information is needed to make a decision. It is necessary to know the costs of acquiring education as a earning asset and the returns this investment can be expected to yield over a working lifetime.

The costs of education and other forms of human capital investment are both direct and indirect. To express matters somewhat differently, the costs of investment in human capital are both monetary and nonmonetary. Tuition payments, fees for books, laboratories and materials, and dormitory and other living expenses specifically associated with school attendance, including transportation costs, are direct out-of-pocket expenses. Besides these direct expenses, a loss of earnings accompanies time away from the labor market. The money receipts an individual foregoes represents an income flow he can command without additional education. These may be zero or very low if the individual is not of legal age to work full-time or if employment opportunities are limited. In an actual calculation, it would seem appropriate to use the earnings of those of similar age and training. The relevant income stream is that expected to be forthcoming after the education contemplated is complete, and it is properly estimated net of the costs, direct and indirect, incurred in order to obtain it.

There is, of course, no way in which an individual can determine precisely the worthwhileness of investing in himself. But it is likely that

[13] American Council of Education, "The American Freshman: National Norms for Fall 1971." *Ace Research Reports,* Vol. 6, No. 6, 1971, pp. 27–28, 35–36; *The American Freshman: National Norms for Fall 1974,* University of California, Los Angeles: pp. 20, 32.

[14] While the labor economist is particularly interested in the monetary returns of investment, there are also benefits, such as the satisfaction of working at a particular job or profession, that cannot be evaluated in pecuniary terms. Education may also have "neighborhood effects" that confer benefits on other members of society for which they have not paid. An interesting discussion is to be found in M. Blaug, *An Introduction to the Economics of Education* (London: Penguin Press, 1968). There is also considerable interest in the benefits that households derive from education through improvements in the effectiveness with which households allocate resources. See, for example, Robert Michael, *The Effect of Education on Efficiency in Consumption* (New York: National Bureau of Economic Research, 1972).

students beyond the age of compulsory schooling make their educational choices partly by comparing the present earnings of individuals with varying amounts of education, even though they are uncertain about the probability of duplicating the experience others have had.

The Responsive-Supply Behavior of College-Age Youth

The educational and career decisions of young people and their families are critical in their impact on the labor market because they underlie the supply behavior of this very important group of market participants. The sensitivity of their decision making to such economic incentives as salaries and employment opportunities is, therefore, a determinant of the equilibration of the job market. Equilibration will be a more drawn-out process and have a greater impact on salaries if young-people's choices are only somewhat affected by economic factors. If, on the other hand, they are highly sensitive to changing career opportunities and salaries and alter their educational plans accordingly, then the equilibration process will be accomplished more quickly and with a smaller impact on salaries.

A recent careful study of the supply behavior of college-age males during the period 1951 to 1974 indicates that over 95 percent of the variation in the fraction of young men in college reflects their response to two measures of their future economic prospects: (1) the income of college graduates relative to other workers and (2) relative employment opportunities.[15]

Salaries offered to new graduates are a good indicator of the state of the college job market because they are set by the state of demand-and-supply forces rather than by collective bargaining, as is the case in unionized blue-collar markets. The search activities of prospective graduates and employers that take place every spring generate a particularly active job market for college graduates that is highly sensitive to demand-and-supply fluctuations. These changes have a rapid, and sometimes dramatic, impact on the market for new graduates. The openings offered new graduates are the "entry port" through which young people make the transition from school into the world of work. Changes are typically initiated in the starting salaries of these workers before they eventually are incorporated into the overall salary structure, which also affects older workers. Thus the active job market of the young provides the "margin of adjustment" to change in the college job market as a whole.

---

[15]Richard B. Freeman. *The Overeducated American* (New York: Academic Press, 1976), p. 53. This section is essentially based on Freeman's seminal research into the functioning of the college job market.

The availability of *job opportunities* is a further indicator of market change. Educated persons typically find employment. Thus the critical variable, along with starting salaries, is the availability of employment in the area for which the individual has been trained. The quality of the jobs available to new graduates reflects the nonprice aspect of market adjustment. Thus, changes in the employment status of new graduates are a "leading indicator" of the state of the college market. Changes in salaries and employment opportunities become reflected in college-enrollment figures and, with approximately a four-year lapse, in the number of new college graduates entering the job market. The sensitivity of college enrollments to expected market opportunities was very evident in the changing behavior of college-age youth during the 1960s and 1970s. The large graduating classes of the late 1960s and early 1970s reflect supply responses to the halcyon job market of the period that preceded it. Similarly, the deterioration of college enrollments during the mid-1970s and into the present reflects the softening of the college job market that became evident in the late 1960s and early 1970s.

The drop in college enrollments that began in 1969 was clearly associated with the declining job market. Elimination of the military draft, which undoubtedly encouraged enrollments in the preceding period, played some part in causing the initial decline. Rising unemployment and the reduction in real incomes in consequence of inflation were a contributing factor to the continuing decline in the mid 1970s. But the change in *market opportunities* was the critical factor to which young people responded, and which underlies the choices that the great majority made with respect to college enrollment.

The dynamic force to which the college job market responds is change originating on the demand side, which interacts with supply conditions in a *feedback process*. The feedback process, as will be examined shortly, generates an oscillating pattern that is characterized by alternating shortages and surpluses of college graduates every four or five years.

The demand-side change to which the market has been reacting over the last two decades, and which is expected to govern the changes of the future, is the shifting industrial composition of employment. Industries differ greatly in the opportunities they generate for college-trained people. In 1970, for example, more than 30 percent of those employed in finance had college degrees, whereas only 6 percent of those who worked in the automobile industry were college graduates. Changes in the industrial mix of jobs during the 1950s and 1960s brought about large increases in the demand for highly educated workers. In the period 1960 to 1969, employment grew more than twice as rapidly in college-intensive industries as in other industries. This reflects the great importance, during the period, of research and development (R and D), defense, and education, which are the three main college-manpower-intensive activities of the economy.

The industries that provide employment for large numbers of graduates are federal public administration, finance, insurance, realty, professional services including education, and certain manufacturing industries, among them ordnance, electrical machinery, aircraft, electronic computing, petroleum instruments, and chemicals. The manufacturing industries, along with transportation, communication, and agriculture, hire relatively few college graduates. Table 4-4 compares the rate of growth of college-manpower-intensive industries with other industries for the periods 1960 to 1969 and 1969 to 1974. During the period 1960 to 1969 employment in the college-intensive industries grew more than twice as rapidly as all other industries. In the period 1969 to 1974, employment in college-intensive industries declined relative to the previous decade, so that the demand for graduates in the college-manpower-intensive industries was only 0.8 percent greater than the demand generated by other industries. This compares with the differential rate of 2.4 percent per annum in the 1960 to 1969 period, as is underscored by Table 4-4. The relative decline in the demand for college-trained workers reflects the slower growth in the 1969 to 1974 period of the sectors of the economy that employ large numbers of

TABLE 4-4 *Compound Annual Percentage Change in Employment in College-Manpower-Intensive and Other Industries in the Periods 1960–1974 and 1969–1974*

Industries	1960–1969	1969–1974
College-manpower-intensive	4.4	2.8
Noneducational:	3.8	2.3
Professional services[a]	5.4	5.9
Federal public administration, except postal service	2.0	0.0
Finance, insurance, and realty	3.7	3.2
College intensive manufacturing[b]	3.6	−1.2
Education	6.2	3.9
All other[c]	2.0	2.0
National total	2.8	2.2

[a] Excludes educational services.

[b] Ordnance, chemicals, petroleum, professional instruments, aircraft, electrical machinery, and electronic computing machinery, with 1960 electronic computing machinery estimated.

[c] Agriculture included.

SOURCE: Richard Freeman, *The Overeducated American* (New York: Academic Press, 1976), p. 64. Reprinted with permission.

college graduates as contrasted with the preceding period, 1960 to 1969.

The change in the character of government activities has had a markedly destabilizing impact on the economic status of graduates. Federal policies have changed greatly in a short period of time. In particular, the research-and-development spending whose rapid acceleration during the early and mid-1960s generated a sharp increase in the demand for engineers and graduate scientists underwent a marked decline in the late 1960s and 1970s. This change contributed significantly to the collapse of the college job market. The defense industries similarly experienced pronounced cutbacks that, in turn, became reflected in demand-side forces.

The Cobweb Feedback System

The preceding discussion has already implied that the supply of college graduates in the current market is determined by the market conditions that prevailed four or five years earlier. Since it requires four or five years to "produce" new college graduates, the effect of a change in market conditions is not only delayed but also interacts with supply-side forces in a way that generates alternating periods of shortage and surplus in four- to five-year intervals. Figure 4-2 displays the nature of this cobweb dynamic in a particularly graphic way. It shows the impact of good employment opportunities and the shortage of graduates at the end of the 1960s, which was already noted in Table 4-4, on the supply side of the market. During the 1960s, college enrollments doubled so that there was a gain between 1960 and 1970 of 4.3 million persons.

FIGURE 4-2 *Cobweb Dynamics in the College Job Market*

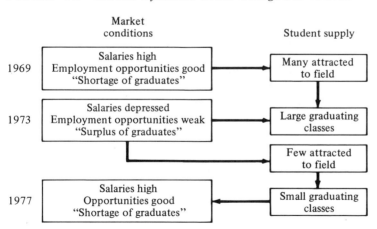

SOURCE: Richard Freeman, *The Overeducated American* (New York: Academic Press, 1976), p. 60. Reprinted with permission.

This large increase reflects both the influence of the baby boom of the post-World War II period, which increased the college-age population of the 1960s, and, more important, their responsive-supply behavior. It is not merely that the college-age population grew, but that the proportion of this age group that chose to enroll in college increased. This response "produced" the large graduating classes of 1973, with its attendant reduction in starting salaries, that reflected the surplus of graduates. This responsive-supply behavior, which reflects decision-making at the level of the household, is more important than demographic forces are in explaining the increase in the number of new college graduates during the first half of the present decade. Freeman estimates that only 30 to 40 percent of the enrollment change was owing to demographic forces and that the balance reflects market forces.[16] The decline in salaries in 1973 reduced enrollments, which, with the smaller graduating classes, resulted in the relatively improved 1977 and 1978 market for new graduates. The improvement so far is only moderate, and unless there is a sharp increase in demand in the future, the college-income premium that was available to the young in 1960s will not be restored.

Intergroup Differences in Declining Enrollment

The 1970s trend of declining college enrollments was disparate among groups. The data reveal, quite surprisingly, that the decline in enrollments was greatest among middle-class young people and least severe among those whose families are in the lower-income brackets. Part of this difference is undoubtedly the result of differentials in the availability of scholarship money and loans to those from lower-income background. Indeed, the number of young black men enrolled in colleges, a group that did not attend in substantial numbers until the 1960s, has continued to increase. This trend reflects in part the greater value of acquiring a college degree as a result of affirmative-action programs and the consequent reduction in discrimination. But it also suggests that young people from lower-income families, regardless of ethnic or racial background, are less discouraged by depressed market opportunities than those coming from more advantaged families, because they still view college as the best avenue for socioeconomic advancement.

The Rate of Return from Schooling

The Concept

A more precise way of evaluating the worthwhileness, from an economic point of view, of investing in education (or other investment

---

[16] Freeman, *op. cit.*, p. 69.

alternatives) is to estimate its "rate of return." The rate of return reflects the relationship among four key magnitudes: costs, returns (i.e., the monetary value of benefits), time, and the rate of interest in terms of which costs and returns are to be discounted. Discounting is the procedure of using an appropriate interest rate to establish the *present worth* of a dollar of expected future income or outlay. Just as interest is expected to be earned in the future on a sum of money invested today, so an income that is not expected to be earned until some future date must be discounted at the current relevant rate of interest in order to determine its present value. Thus, the present value (PV) of an investment is equal to

$$PV = \frac{Y_1}{(1 + i)} + \frac{Y_2}{(1 + i)^2} + \cdots \frac{Y_n}{(1 + i)^n}$$

where $Y_1 + Y_2 + \ldots Y_n$ is the stream of expected revenues minus the expected private costs, discounted at rate i, over n years. Each investment opportunity is associated with a separate stream of expected costs and receipts over a period of years.

An example will help clarify how the choice among options would be made. Assume a student age eighteen, about to graduate from high school, is considering (1) attending business school for a year and entering the labor market at age nineteen, or (2) attending college for four years and entering the labor market at age twenty-two. Either option can be financed with a bank loan whose rate of interest is 15 percent per year. The present value of either option can be computed using the present value equation as follows:

$$PV = \sum_{n=18}^{65} \frac{Y_n}{(1 + .15)^{n-18}}$$

where PV is the present value of the option at age eighteen and Y_n represents earnings net of costs for $65 - 18 = 47$ years of expected work life.

If he chooses option (1), Y_n will be negative for one year because of the earnings lost while he attends school. If he chooses option (2), Y_n will be negative for four years. His income stream net of costs will presumably be higher with a college education than without it, but he will start to earn three years later. Earnings that are postponed are worth less, because they are discounted over a longer period of time.

There is, of course, no way of determining which of the two options is the better choice unless we have information about the cost and income streams each alternative is likely to involve. It is, however, worth noting that the present value of any investment will be lower the higher the rate of interest. Further, the present value of an investment may be quite low or negative even if net earnings are expected ultimately to be high. Many professions yield high incomes but not necessarily high rates of return. If earnings begin fairly late in.life, an estimate of present value may involve discounting earnings over many more years than investment costs are discounted. The combination of high schooling costs and many years of lost earnings may cause investment costs to be effectively greater than returns which are discounted over fewer years. These are considerations that an individual needs to take into account in order to choose the option with the highest present value.

There is another way of formulating the choice problem posed above. One can think of the individual as seeking to identify the option that will yield the highest *internal rate of return*. This is the rate at which the costs and returns of an investment are exactly equal when they are discounted back to the present. An individual has an economic incentive to invest a sum of money in his future productivity, which he expects to yield an internal rate of return (r) equal to the interest rate (i) at which he can finance his investment. Investment is profitable as long as the internal rate of return exceeds the rate of interest.

If we relate this logic to our hypothetical high-school graduate, if he expects a rate of return in excess of 15 percent, it is profitable for him to invest in further education. Differently expressed, the internal rate of return is the rate at which the present value of the expected income stream is equal to the costs incurred to earn it. These costs, as noted before, properly include tuition and other school-related costs (but not usual living expenses) and the income lost by not working. Thus, the internal rate (r) equates the cost (C) and the present value (PV) of the expected income stream in the equation

$$C = PV = \sum_{n=18}^{65} \frac{Y_n}{(1 + r)^{n-18}}$$

The individual estimates r on the basis of the information he has about the costs of investing and the income stream he expects the costs to yield. By comparing r with the interest cost of i of financing, he can evaluate the worthwhileness of the investment he is considering. His decision-making procedure is thus based on essentially the same considerations as those guiding a businessman.

The Effect of Imperfect Capital Markets and Unequal Income Distribution

The generally accepted formula for estimating the return to education is, as has already been noted, to calculate the expected net-earnings stream on the basis of age-earnings-education data and to establish its present value at an appropriate rate of discount. Thus, two individuals who expect to earn equivalent incomes when they complete their educations will not necessarily undertake equal investments because the capital market with which they are confronted is not perfect. There is a wide spread in the rates at which different households are able to borrow. This implies that it will be quite rational for one individual to reject an additional year of schooling (and the utility of its prospective income) while another, who evaluates his earnings potential to be precisely the same and who attaches the same utility to this prospect, elects to continue his studies.

It has also been recognized that human capital is, in some respects, inferior to physical capital from the standpoint of its characteristics as an investment alternative. The characteristics of physical capital facilitate its being financed by private lenders, i.e., it can be jointly owned and legal title can be transferred by sale and inheritance.[17] Human capital, on the other hand, because it is embodied in human beings, is an inferior asset from the standpoint of a lender. Self-financing thus predominates as the method of payment for human capital, and family wealth is an important determinant of the discount rate.

The pattern of income distribution also exerts an influence on the allocation of resources to education. Fewer educational services are likely to be bought in the private market to service the children of poor families. Parents may not be ignorant of the potential gains to be derived from educating their children, but the difference in their ability to meet the direct and indirect costs of education implies that they will purchase fewer privately supplied educational services than will be purchased by those whose incomes are higher. The greatly limited resources of low-income families implies that they have higher discount rates than do higher-income groups. These impediments played a vital role, especially during the period of the 1960s, in encouraging governmental participation in the provision of education as an essential part of American manpower policy. They are also among the issues in the controversy about the role of schooling in relation to labor-market experiences.

Private and Social Rates of Return

There have been numerous empirical efforts to estimate private and total rates of return to schooling. One researcher undertook to calculate the present value of the different income streams associated with different amounts of schooling using alternative discount rates.[18]

[17] Assaf Razim, "Lifetime Uncertainty, Human Capital, and Physical Capital." Discussion Paper 74-40, Department of Economics, University of Minnesota (May 1974).

[18] B. Wilkinson, "Present Values of Lifetime Earnings for Different Occupations," *Journal of Political Economy* (December 1966).

Another calculated expected earnings by level of schooling.[19] The study by W. Lee Hansen, which is regarded as classic, is of special interest because it estimated rates of return on the basis of both private resource and total resource costs.[20] A later study by Taubman and Wales also estimated private and social rates of return.[21] Private rates of return may differ from social rates because some benefits accrue to individuals other than those who were educated. A differential also appears in the computations because private benefits are calculated after deducting income taxes from earnings and because social costs include total expenditures per student on education and not just average tuition. The chief value of estimating social returns to education is that it sheds light on the societal as well as the private gains from education. Although it is a rough measure at best, partly because it cannot include nonmonetary costs and benefits, this type of estimate provides information of the sort needed to guide public policy for deciding on the resource allocation that should be made to support schooling and training.

The NBER-TH Data

The problem of computing the rate of return to investment in education is greatly complicated by the difficulties inherent in identifying population groups that are comparable except in terms of their education. Mental ability and family background are particularly likely to bias the findings. A recent study by Taubman and Wales utilized a data source that seemed to circumvent some of these difficulties. These data were drawn from a World War II sample of 75,000 volunteers who passed the Aviation Cadet Qualifying Test with a score equivalent to that of the median of high-school graduates. A 1955 study utilized the results of tests administered to this group to predict the vocational success of a random sample of 17,000 of these 75,000 individuals.[22] The National Bureau of Economic Research conducted a further survey of men who responded to a 1955 questionnaire and compiled information about earnings from their initial jobs and jobs in 1955 and 1969. The NBER-TH average earnings are consistent with data by age and education in 1955 and 1968 with the current population reports.[23] The

---

[19] Giora Hanoch, "An Analysis of Earnings and Schooling," *Journal of Human Resources* (Fall 1967).

[20] W. L. Hansen, "Total and Private Rates of Return to Investment in Schooling," *Journal of Political Economy* 71 (April 1963).

[21] Paul Taubman and Terrence Wales, *Higher Education and Earnings* (New York: McGraw-Hill Book Company, 1974).

[22] For a more detailed description of the NBER-TH sample, see Paul Taubman and Terrence Wales, *op. cit.*, Chapters 1 and 5.

[23] NBER-TH is an acronym for National Bureau of Economic Research and researchers Thorndyke and Hagen, who collected the 1955 data.

1969 respondents are more heavily concentrated in the higher education and ability levels, but there is no success bias in reported earnings within ability and education groups. While this study is based on a population that is generally brighter and better-educated than the U.S. population as a whole, it utilizes a new and extremely rich data source that promises improved estimates of the private and social returns to higher educational attainment. The findings are examined as Economics in Action 4:1.

ECONOMICS IN ACTION 4:1

Earnings Differentials Due to Education

As summarized in Table 4-A the extra earnings associated with college education in 1955 and 1969 ranged between 11 and 31 percent higher than those obtainable with a high-school diploma at all educational levels. In 1969, persons with some college earned about 17 percent more than high-school graduates, while those with an undergraduate degree, some graduate work, and a master's degree received 26 to 32 percent more. Ph.D.'s, L.L.B.'s, and M.D.'s earned 27, 84, and 106 percent more, respectively, than high-school graduates of the same ability level.

A further important finding, which is also evident in Table 4-A, is that the returns to education are erratic in that each additional year or plateau does not add as much income as the previous one did. Except for the huge increase associated with the M.D. degree and the L.L.B. degree in 1969, increases in income beyond the "some college" level were small. Because of the nature of the sample, it was possible to calculate the returns to education given above with ability and other characteristics held constant.

TABLE 4-A   *Increases in Earnings by Education Level as a Percentage of High-School Earnings, 1955, 1969*

Education	1955	1969
Some College	11	17
Undergraduate Degree*	12	31
Some Graduate Work	15	26
Master's*	10	32
Ph.D.	2	27
M.D.	72	106
L.L.B.	19	84

*Those who did not teach.

SOURCE   Paul Taubman and Terrence Wales, *Higher Education and Earnings,* (New York: McGraw-Hill Book Company, 1974), p. 71. Used with permission of McGraw-Hill Book Company.

ECONOMICS IN ACTION 4:2

The Decline in the Economic Rewards of College in the 1970s

A matter of particular interest is to evaluate the extent of the decline in the economic rewards to higher education and determine whether the changing economic value of college training during the 1970s represents long-run or cyclic forces.[24] Insight into these matters is provided by the Current Population Survey (CPS) consumer-income tapes for 1969 and 1974. The 1969 tape records income data for 1968 and reflects a college market that was still strong, while the 1974 tape contains income data for 1973, which reflects a weakening market for college graduates.

Table 4-B summarizes the relevant data. Income or salaries, expressed in constant 1967 dollars, are recorded for full-time year-round workers ages twenty-five and over and ages twenty-five through thirty-four. The most important piece of information it conveys is that there was a marked decline in the premium that has historically been associated with a college education. The ratio of college to high-school incomes (line 3) dropped by 11.8 percent, and the dollar difference in income streams is down from $4,611 in 1969 to $3,190 in 1974. (Line 1 minus line 2).

Focusing on the twenty-five to thirty-four-year age group (line 4), in which the decline in relative income is expected on the basis of the active-market hypothesis examined above, there is a decline of 16.5 percent in the ratio of college to high-school graduates' incomes. In constant dollars, the difference in income streams was from $3,031 in 1969 to $1,260 in 1974. Declines in college starting rates by field of specialization are recorded on lines 7–14. These records of monthly college starting salaries highlight the concentration of the decline among younger men.[25]

Whether the depressed college market of the 1970s represents a unique development can be determined by comparing the change in the income of college and high-school graduates in that period with changes in previous periods. Data are available by age group for the periods 1963 to 1968 and 1956 to 1961. Both five-year periods are characterized by increasing unemployment and were periods during which college graduates experienced greater increases in income than did similarly aged high-school graduates. By contrast, the data for 1968 to 1973 show a

[24] Richard B. Freeman, "The Decline in the Economic Rewards to College Education," *Review of Economics and Statistics* 59 (February 1977): 18–21.

[25] The 1969 and 1974 March tapes on starting salaries for new female graduates show a decline in their occupational attainment but no deterioration in their income position. This is also in accord with the active-market hypothesis, because other workers hold relatively permanent jobs.

TABLE 4-B   *The Changing Income of Male College Graduates Relative to Other Workers, 1969–1974, '75*

	Incomes or Salaries (in 1967 dollars) and Income Ratios		
	1969	1974–'75[a]	Percentage Change
Annual Incomes of Full-time, Year-round Male Workers			
1. 4-year-college graduates, aged 25 and over	$13,361	$12,194	−8.7%
2. High-school graduates, aged 25 and over	8,750	9,004	2.9
3. Ratio	1.53	1.35	−11.8
4. 4-year-college graduates, aged 25−34	10,903	9,196	−15.7
5. High-school graduates, aged 25−34	7,872	7,936	0.8
6. Ratio	1.39	1.16	−16.5
College Starting Rates (monthly)			
7. Accounting	693	615	−11.3
8. Business-general	626	532	−15.0
9. Humanities and social sciences	607	494	−18.6
10. Engineering			
Chemical	773	751	−2.8
Electrical	752	678	−9.8
Mechanical	747	704	−5.8
11. Chemistry	706	604	−14.5
12. Mathematics	709	580	−18.2
Other, Wage or Salary Series			
13. Hourly average earnings Total private non-supervisory workers	2.77	2.81	1.4
Contract construction workers	4.36	4.49	3.0
14. Index of real compensation per man hour	105.2	108.9	3.5

[a]1974 for lines 1−6; 1975 for lines 7−14.

SOURCE: *Lines 1-6:* U.S. Bureau of Census, Current Population Reports, *Consumer Income Series* P-60 no. 75, table 47, p. 101; no. 101, table 58, p. 116. *Lines 7-14:* College Placement Council, Salary Survey, Final Report, July 1975, p. 4; June 1969, p. 4. Other wage or salaries from U.S. Bureau of Labor Statistics, *Monthly Labor Review,* July 1975, pp. 85, 88, 107−108, with May 1975 used for 1975; deflator for 1969 is 109.8, for 1974, 147.7; for 1975, 159.3. All in Table 1, Richard B. Freeman, "Economic Rewards to College Education," *The Review of Economics and Statistics* LIX, February 1977.

marked reversal of this pattern for the youngest groups. College graduates aged twenty-five through twenty-nine obtained much lower rates of increase than did high-school graduates, *which was an unprecedented development*. The downturn in the market did not simply represent a reduction of past upward trends for graduates, but also a significant deterioration in the economic position, which reflects the *countercyclic* movement in the college marketplace relative to other job markets. The deterioration in the relative position of college graduates

TABLE 4-C *Potential Future-Income Streams by Age, 1973–1978*

Age	Actual 1973 Earnings	Potential Earnings, 1978, Using			
		1973 Cross-Section	1968 Cross-Section	1968-73 Cohort Gains	1963-68 Cohort Gains
25-29 Years					
College	$10.242	$15,113	$13,579	$11,630	$15,949
High school	9,702	11,618	11,282	9,953	13,860
Ratio	1.06	1.30	1.20	1.17	1.15
30-34 Years					
College	15,113	17,684	17,540	18,375	21,166
High school	11,618	11,827	12,266	12,641	15,259
Ratio	1.51	1.50	1.43	1.45	1.39
35-39 Years					
College	17,684	18,265	17,214	19,134	22,936
High school	11,827	12,680	11,997	13,067	14,616
Ratio	1.51	1.44	1.44	1.46	1.57
40-44 Years					
College	18,265	18,806	19,067	20,903	22,171
High school	12,680	12,945	12,456	14,123	14,879
Ratio	1.44	1.48	1.52	1.48	1.49
45-49 Years					
College	18,806	18,194	18,887	19,946	21,398
High school	12,945	12,315	12,784	13,863	14,437
Ratio	1.45	1.48	1.48	1.44	1.48

SOURCE: *1973:* 1968 March CPS tapes. *1963–68 Cohort Gains:* U.S. Bureau of Census, Current Population Reports *Consumer Income Series* P-60 no. 92, table 19, pp. 66, 68, 46, 48. Sumarized as Table 6 in Richard B. Freeman, "Economic Rewards to College Education," *Review of Economics and Statistics* LIX, February 1977.

during the 1970s was exacerbated by cyclic adjustments.

These findings do not necessarily imply that the depressed college market of the 1970s reflects a long-term change in the job market. The range of possibilities with respect to future income streams is very wide. If the income experience of those graduating in the 1970s is like that of past graduates, part of their losses will be recouped. Table 4-C compares possible 1978 income for men in various age groups on the basis of alternative assumptions. If, for example, twenty-five to twenty-nine-year-old men experience earnings that are like those of the 1973 cross section, their incomes will increase sufficiently to yield a college–high-school differential of 30 percent in 1978. If, on the other hand, their experiences are like those represented by the 1968 cross section, college men will attain incomes that are only 15 to 20 percent above those of high-school men.

It is also possible to estimate the discounted lifetime earnings and internal rates of return for persons aged twenty-five to twenty-nine and 1974 using alternative assumptions to chart their future-income streams and CPS data on starting salaries. The computations show that the combined effect of the reduction in the college-earnings premium and the increased costs of college reduced the internal rate of return. The magnitude of the decline depends on the assumptions made. Under the most realistic assumptions, the private rate of return from a college education declines from 11 percent to 7 percent and the social rate from 12 percent to 9 percent.

Controversy concerning the Role of Schooling

Some Problems of Interpreting Rate-of-Return Estimates

While rate-of-return estimates are useful for understanding the supply of educated workers, there are certain features of these estimates that may be misleading. Specifically, the (census) income data that such studies employ include receipts from real property and other assets in addition to earnings. Since the ownership of such assets is likely to be functionally related to earnings, it probably tends to raise the income-education profile of better-educated groups.[26]

Further, income differentials cannot be unequivocally attributed to the quantity or quality of formal education. Education at home before formal schooling begins, family environment as well as "on-the-job training," and experience that is gained once a person is employed are

---

[26]E. F. Renshaw, "Estimating the Returns to Education," *Review of Economics and Statistics* 42 (August 1960): 318–24.

also causes of income differentials. Their impact cannot be separated easily from that of formal schooling. It is also not clear to what extent earnings differentials reflect differences in ability. There is some evidence that individuals of greater ability, whether the latter is measured in terms of scores on various standard examinations or rank in class, are the ones who typically pursue more education. There seems to be a self-selection process at work that results in earnings differentials that, in part, reward greater ability as well as greater investment.[27]

The availability of job opportunities, the state of one's health, individual psychological characteristics that enter into work-leisure preferences, and motivation are also important determinants of earnings differentials. It is, therefore, very difficult to assess what part of an individual's income stream is specifically attributable to education and what part is attributable to various other influences. These difficulties are among the reasons for heated controversy about the significance of investment in education for explaining earnings differentials. The issues of this controversy are an integral part of the conflict between those who attribute earnings differentials largely to differences in education and other forms of human-capital investment, and those who attribute them to institutional factors operating chiefly on the demand side of labor markets.

Is Schooling the Link between Productivity and Earnings?

Age-education-earnings profiles indisputably reflect the positive relationship between additional years of schooling and higher levels of income. Better-educated persons have higher labor-force-participation rates and tend to be employed in better-paying occupations. The inference has therefore been made that schooling develops the cognitive skills and work habits essential to worker productivity and employability. The presumption is that schooling is the link between productivity and earnings. This is, however, a presumption that not everyone will agree to. There is considerable disagreement as to whether differences in schooling explain differential employment and earnings experiences.

Controversy about the role of the educational system in teaching skills that are valuable in the marketplace has become widespread.[28]

[27] D. Wolfe, "Economics and Educational Values," in S. E. Harris, ed., *Higher Education in the U.S.: The Economic Problems* (Cambridge, Mass.: Harvard University Press, 1960), p. 178; also W. L. Hansen *et al.,* "Schooling and Earning of Low Achievers," *American Economic Review* 60 (June 1970).

[28] The current controversy reflects continued emphasis on the facts brought to light in the Coleman Report. See James S. Coleman *et al., Equality of Educational Opportunity* (United States Office of Education, 1966).

Skills differentials among American school children have been widely publicized, as have been the disparities among schools, as reflected in expenditures per child. There is, however, some evidence that differences in proficiency among students, as reflected in their test scores, is associated with differences in home environments rather than differences in their schools. Family income and educational levels, number of siblings, and other background characteristics have been identified as substantially more important in determining success in learning than the amount of public funds devoted to education. Some observers have inferred that schools perform a chiefly custodial function between the nursery and the world of work and that it matters little, in terms of their effect on pupil achievement, whether or not more money is spent to upgrade schools that are identified as being deficient.

The Jencks study was particularly skeptical of the role of schooling in facilitating individual success in the marketplace. Indeed, Jencks maintained that "economic success seems to depend on varieties of luck and on-the-job competence that are only moderately related to family background, schooling, or scores on standardized tests. The definition of competence varies greatly from one job to another, but it seems in most cases to depend more on personality than on technical skills."[29] None of the measurable variables—not parental education, income, test scores, or expenditures in school—exhibit a statistically significant relationship to individual earnings, according to Jencks's findings. Thus, the Jencks report imputes a negative role to schools in developing individual earning capacities. But it does so on very different grounds from the Coleman Report. The latter simply implies that schooling plays a lesser role in the learning process than the host of influences we can group together under the umbrella term "background." But it does not deny the relationship between achievement and earnings.

While neither Coleman nor Jencks is an economist, the questions raised by their reports (and other inquiries) have provoked extensive further testing to determine whether the income-schooling association is meaningful. Several studies have been undertaken that test earnings as functions of family background and measured ability. An early study finds that the contribution of schooling to earnings is reduced by approximately 12 percent when family background is standardized.[30] A more recent study by Griliches and Mason finds that the income

[29]Christopher Jencks *et al., Inequality: A Reassessment of the Effect of Family and Schooling in America* (New York: Basic Books, 1972), p. 8.

[30] F. T. Juster, ed., *Introduction and Summary in Education, Income, and Human Behavior,* 1 (New York: McGraw-Hill, 1975), pp. 1–43; and J. Morgan and M. David, "Education and Income," *Quarterly Journal of Economics* 77 (August 1963): 423–437.

contribution of schooling is reduced by as much as 25 percent when family background is controlled for.[31]

School *quality* and its effect on earnings is a more elusive element to measure. There is, however, at least one recent study by Finis Welch whose conclusions imply that the quality of schooling, judged in terms of expenditures per pupil, is, indeed, an important determinant of earnings.

ECONOMIC THEORY IN ACTION 4:3

Schooling and the "Vintage" Effect on Black Earnings

Questioning the Jencks argument that the quality of schooling has little effect on earnings, Finis Welch studied the returns to investment by blacks who attended school in the 1950s and 1960s.[32] Earnings data for 1959, classified by market experience for black and white urban males, were drawn from 1960 census data. Comparable data for 1966 were taken from the Survey of Economic Opportunity. In the 1959 data, blacks with one to four years of experience had earnings that increased relative to white earnings as the level of school completion increased. For persons with five to twelve years of experience, the black-white earnings ratio was insensitive to schooling, and for persons with thirteen to twenty-five years of experience the relative earnings of blacks fell as schooling increased.

Welch explains these differences in terms of differences in the *quality* of the schools they attended. Using expenditures per pupil as a proxy for quality differences, he maintains that persons with one to four years of experience attended schools that offered programs of better quality than those attended by persons who received their schooling in the 1920s and 1930s. The earlier educational programs produced human capital of a different "vintage" from that of later programs. Welch finds that the schooling of blacks who entered the work force during the 1960s is yielding more to blacks than to whites when comparisons are limited to recent vintages. He estimated that the ratio of black-white rates of return was between 1.03 and 1.41 for blacks who entered the labor force in the 1960s. Their annual earnings ratio approached 90 percent. A substantial earnings gap remains, but Welch's study implies that the vintage effect, coupled with the tight labor market of the 1960s, pushed black earnings toward parity. The study is also regarded as providing an

[31] Z. Griliches and M. Mason, "Education, Income, and Ability," *Journal of Political Economy* 80 (March/April 1972): 74–103.

[32] Finis Welch, "Black-White Differences in Returns to Schooling," in Orley Ashenfelter and Albert Rees, *Discrimination in Labor Markets* (Princeton: Princeton University Press, 1973).

important piece of evidence that the quality of education does have a measurable effect on earnings.

Schooling as a Credential

While the Coleman and Jencks reports stress the negligible influence of schooling on earnings, other investigators stress its positive role in providing credentials to those who attend and graduate. They emphasize the role of certificates, diplomas, and degrees in the employee-selection process. They contend that firms minimize their search costs by utilizing information about the type and level of schooling as a basis for selecting among applicants. "Pieces of paper" that denote successful completion of a course of study are generally interpreted as demonstrating some level of achievement, ability to get along socially, ambition, and so forth, all of which a firm will value in its employees.

Credentialism is clearly a screening device in that it separates those who have the necessary prerequisite of formal education from those who do not.[33] Does it do more than this? There are some who assert that it does—that credentialism is a technique for discriminating against those who have less formal education but who can perform the job equally well.[34] Thus, the issues of the schooling controversy are actually much more far-reaching than the role of schools per se. The controversy reflects criticism on various levels of the assumptions and predictions of the human-capital analysis with respect to the functioning of labor markets and the kinds of policy prescriptions that emanate from it.

Writers challenging the tenets of orthodox or "mainstream" theorizing about the relationship between education, labor productivity, and employment prospects do so for different reasons. Peter Doeringer and Michael J. Piore question the premise that individuals exercise much influence over the rate at which current earnings are sacrificed for future prospects.[35] They reject the view that a person's earnings over a lifetime are essentially the product of his own behavior.

As proponents of the dual-labor-markets view, they maintain that workers entering the labor market are judged on the basis of their educational credentials, race, and sex to determine their suitability for employment in the primary market or the secondary market. Jobs in the

---

[33] Taubman and Wales have verified statistically that education is being used as a screening device to present those with low educational attainment from entering high-paying occupations. However, they associate educational differences with productivity differences. See *op. cit.*, Chapter 9.

[34] Ivar Berg, *Education and Jobs: The Great Training Robbery* (Boston: Beacon Press, 1971).

[35] Peter Doeringer and Michael J. Piore, *Internal Labor Markets and Manpower Analysis* (Lexington, Mass.: D. C. Heath, 1971).

primary market are characterized by steady employment, with "on the job" training opportunities, fringe benefits, and, above all, promotion opportunities that provide wage increases and eventual supervisory responsibilities. Jobs in the "secondary" market are menial, poorly paid, and highly unstable.

Minorities, women, and white males who lack credentials are typically judged as having a limited productive potential. These judgments become the basis for negative employer attitudes about the provision of training opportunities that lead to job security and promotion. They are thus precluded from the primary market from the very beginning of their working lives. The experience their jobs provide adds virtually nothing to improve on the inferior credentials of those who were disadvantaged to begin with. Writers who interpret the institutional setting of labor markets as "dual," therefore, regard the school system as a participant in discrimination against those whose only options are to be found in the secondary labor market. This highly controversial argument is examined in depth in Chapter 12 below.

The Radical View of Schooling

The radical view of schooling interprets the existence and perpetuation of a segmented labor market within a Marxist framework.[36] According to this interpretation, the characteristics of labor markets are generated by the drive towards profit maximization in the capitalistic system. Thus, Marxist critics point to those firms, particularly in the service industries, e.g., restaurants, hospitals, laundries, and dry-cleaning establishments, that operate on very low profit margins. These firms cannot afford to hire efficient, motivated workers who expect permanent, well-paying employment with "prospects." The school system caters to their requirements for cheap labor by "legitimizing" a system of rewards that reproduces the capitalist order.

More specifically, radical economists view schooling (as well as training and child rearing) as performing dual economic functions. Schools are involved indirectly in the production process, and they also help perpetuate the economic and social order we associate with capitalism. This is accomplished partly by developing work-relevant personality traits in children. Dependability, respect for authority, and responsiveness to incentive mechanisms are traits that are inculcated and reinforced by the schools. These are characteristics that the Marxist identifies as essential to extracting surplus value from workers.

According to the radical view, the school system also contributes to

[36] Samuel Bowles and Herbert Gintis, "The Problem With Human-Capital Theory—A Marxian Critique," *American Economic Review, Papers and Proceedings* 65 (May 1975): 74–82.

perpetuating the capitalistic system by segmenting the work force.[37] By using IQ and other cognitive performance measures, the school system generates and perpetuates a meritocracy that stratifies and separates workers on the basis of formal credentials, race, ethnic origin, and sex. The system therefore militates against the development of a class-conscious body of wage workers who identify with one another and recognize that their interests are not served by the capitalistic system.

Concluding Remarks

Conflicting views about the role of schooling make it evident that human-capital analysis, which has become an integral part of the orthodox position, is very much in the eye of the storm. The more important aspects of controversy about the role of schooling have been presented in this chapter because they merit consideration in their own right, besides providing perspective for understanding the mainstream view of the role that schooling plays in determining the quality of the labor supply and the effect that the skills thus acquired has on future labor-market experience. Human-capital theorists identify schooling as the chief, though not exclusive, route toward the development of skills that eventually underlie wage differentials. They agree that ability, family background, and other factors contribute to the effectiveness of the investment process, but emphasize the paramount role of schooling in determining earning and employment opportunities.

There is an important parallel between the theory of labor-force participation and the theory of investment in education that merits emphasis. According to the mainstream view, households allocate their resources, including time, to maximize the real income of the family. Family members divide their time between market and nonmarket activities in accordance with this principle. Investment in the schooling of family members beyond that required by law and custom is made on the presumption that the return from future labor-market participation will justify the expenditure. Thus the quality of the labor supply, at least to the extent that it is associated with schooling, can be explained in terms of the theory of household behavior. Maximizing choices govern the allocation of time to the market and into investment in schooling. In short, decisions made on the supply side of the labor market at the level of the household exert a major influence on labor-market outcomes. This interpretation is an integral part of the mainstream view. In the chapter that follows this analysis is further extended to inquire into the role of choice in the allocation of the labor supply into occupations and jobs.

[37]Michael Reich, David M. Gordon, and Richard C. Edwards, "A Theory of Labor-Market Segmentation," *American Economic Review, Papers and Proceedings* 63 (May 1973): 359–365.

Suggestions for Further Reading

G. Becker. "Investment in Human Capital: Effects on Earnings," reprinted in J. F. Burton *et al.*, eds., *Readings in Labor Market Analysis*. New York: Holt, Rinehart and Winston, 1971.

G. Becker. "Investment in Human Capital: Rates of Return," reprinted in J. F. Burton *et al.*, eds., *Readings in Labor Market Analysis*. New York: Holt, Rinehart and Winston, 1971.

Ivar Berg. *Education and Jobs: The Great Training Robbery*. Boston: Beacon Press, 1971.

Mark Blaug. "Human Capital Theory; A Slightly Jaundiced View," *Journal of Economic Literature* 14:3 (September 1976): 827–855.

S. Bowles and H. Gintis. "The Problem with Human Capital Theory—A Marxian Critique." *American Economic Review* 65 (May 1975): 74–82.

Richard B. Freeman. *The Overeducated American*. New York: Academic Press, 1976.

Z. Griliches and M. Mason. "Education, Income and Ability." *Journal of Political Economy* 80 (March/April, 1972): 74–103.

T. W. Schultz. "The Concept of Human Capital," *American Economic Review* 51 (March 1961), reprinted in M. Blaug, ed., *Economics of Education* 1. 1968.

Paul Taubman and Terrence Wales. *Higher Education and Earnings*. New York: McGraw-Hill Book Company, 1974.

Finis Welch. "Black-White Differences in Returns to Schooling," in Orley Ashenfelter and Albert Rees, *Discrimination in Labor Markets*. Princeton: Princeton University Press, 1973.

5 The Allocation of Labor to Occupations and Jobs

Preferences, Education, and Changes in Occupational Distribution

Doctor? Lawyer? Indian chief? Individuals enter the world of work with preferences and capabilities for certain kinds of work. As has been seen, economists have devoted considerable attention to studying the effect of investment in education for identifying and developing capabilities. But there has been little interest in explaining the origin and shaping of occupational preferences. This problem has chiefly been a matter for inquiry by psychologists.

Psychologists hypothesize that occupational choice reflects a complex developmental process that starts in childhood and is related to the individual's concept of self. Time and experience mold both the individual's self-concept and his vocational preferences. The "final" choice, which may be revised many times over a working lifetime, reflects the individual's translation of his self-concept into occupational terms. The psychologists' chief concern has been the development of techniques for matching persons with jobs. These have been found useful by the military, by career-guidance counselors, and by the personnel departments of most establishments to varying degrees. However, these techniques tell us very little, if anything, about the process by which occupational choices are made.

Psychological theories about occupational preferences are not yet very useful to the economist. Unlike the psychologist, the economist takes preferences as given and directs his concern to explaining an individual's response to alternative economic opportunities and the monetary costs associated with them.

The alternative occupational opportunities that present themselves to individuals once they enter the labor market are very much dependent on the kind and amount of schooling they have acquired; most occupations have educational prerequisites. Table 5-1, which is based on the last census, shows that in 1970, almost 56 percent of those employed as professionals, or technical and kindred workers, had four or more years of college. More than half of all clerical workers had a high-school diploma. By contrast, a large proportion of individuals employed as farm laborers and foremen had only an elementary-school education.

TABLE 5-1 *Educational Level of Employed Persons by Occupation and Percentages, 1970*

Occupation	Elementary	High School		College	
	8 years and less %	1−3 years %	4 years %	1−3 years %	4 years and more %
Professional, technical, and kindred	1.8	4.4	17.5	20.5	55.8
Managers and administrators	8.9	13.7	34.1	19.9	23.3
Sales	9.5	21.5	38.2	1.9	11.8
Clerical	5.1	1.6	54.1	19.7	5.1
Craftsmen and kindred	23.6	25.7	39.8	8.8	2.3
Operators (except transport)	30.5	30.3	33.5	5.0	.8
Transport-equipment operator	29.3	3.1	32.4	6.3	.9
Laborers (except farm)	34.3	31.9	26.1	6.7	1.0
Farmers and farm managers	39.6	16.8	32.2	7.5	3.8
Farm laborers; farm foremen	50.2	24.7	18.3	5.3	1.4
Service	25.4	30.2	32.8	9.8	1.7

SOURCE: U.S. Bureau of the Census, United States Summary.

Secular changes in opportunities and their interaction with supply-side responses produced the remarkable change in the occupational distribution of the U.S. labor force that is reflected in Table 5-2. This table leaves no doubt that the labor force has displayed considerable occupational mobility over the last three and a half decades. Fewer than 40 percent were employed in goods-type occupations in 1970. By 1980 two-thirds of all workers are expected to be employed in service-type occupations, and the remaining third in goods-type occupations. This

TABLE 5-2 *Occupational Distribution of the U.S. Labor Force, Selected Years, 1930–80*

	1930	1960	1970	(Projected) 1980
Service-type occupations	36.5%	55.5%	60.7%	64.6%
Professional, technical, and kindred workers	7.1	11.4	14.2	16.3
Managers, officials, and proprietors (excluding farm)	7.7	10.7	10.5	10.0
Clerical and kindred workers	9.3	14.8	17.4	18.2
Sales workers	6.5	6.4	6.2	6.3
Service workers	5.9	12.2	12.4	13.8
Goods-type occupations	63.3	44.2	39.3	35.4
Craftsmen, foremen, and kindred workers	13.4	13.0	12.9	12.8
Operatives and kindred workers	16.4	18.2	17.7	16.2
Laborers (excluding farm and mine)	11.4	5.4	4.7	3.7
Farmers and farm laborers	22.1	7.8	4.0	2.7

SOURCE: *Historical Statistics of the United States* (Washington, D.C.: Government Printing Office, 1965), p. 76; *Manpower Report of the President* (Washington, D.C.: Government Printing Office, 1973), p. 225.

allocation will reverse almost exactly the occupational-deployment pattern of 1930. These occupational shifts have been accompanied by a rise in the median level of education among all occupational groups.

Economists have focused their attention on examining three routes via which workers become allocated among occupations and jobs within occupations. These routes are (1) formal schooling, (2) job search, and (3) on-the-job training and job experience. Each activity provides a link to the labor market. Secondary as well as postsecondary education may be vocational and/or academic and is increasingly associated with varying degrees of career counseling and planning. On-the-job training and labor-market experience provide skills beyond those acquired by formal schooling, typically in a work environment that is associated with job ladders and upward mobility. Work thus provides opportunities for continued investment in human capital. The job-search activities of new entrants and experienced workers are directed at locating alternative opportunities for earning wages and/or acquiring training. This chapter is concerned chiefly with examining how the supply responses of different groups shape the occupational and job allocation of the labor force through these alternative links to the labor market.

Market Conditions and Occupational Choices

The work ethic that underlies the behavior of much of the American labor force dictates responsiveness to financial rewards and upward mobility in terms of occupation. The assumption is that the occupational changes recorded in Table 5-2 reflect choices in response to the changing economic opportunities generated in a dynamic economy.

Participation in certain occupations is predicated on the gift of scarce natural talents. Professional athletes, artists, and actors are obvious examples of individuals who are often able to command average earnings that are significantly above those of individuals in occupations that require comparable training costs but less native ability. The earnings differential they enjoy is, in effect, a "rent" to their scarce natural talents. These differentials are identified as rent precisely because the scarcities they reward are generally not eliminated simply by training additional numbers of individuals. The talents of these relatively fortunate few are typically not reproducible. Thus, their owners are able to command scarcity rewards that are analogous to the rents earned by those who own choice parcels of land or other natural resources.

The size of these rents and, indeed, whether or not they will, on the average, tend to prevail depends on the extent of the optimism with which hopefuls in professions such as entertainment and sports evaluate their opportunities and on the number who stay, even if they prove to be unsuccessful. It is entirely possible that, on the average, the very high earnings of the fortunate few who enjoy extraordinary financial success is offset by the very low average earnings of those who are unsuccessful. Thus, the average earnings of people in occupations that require a high degree of native talent may, in fact, be less than that earned in other occupations in which native talent is less significant. This is notoriously true in the entertainment industry as well as in professional sports. The very high rewards of the successful few are, on balance, offset by the relatively low rewards of the unsuccessful.[1]

The conclusion that occupations that require unique talents probably do not, on balance, yield significant rents should not, however, cause us to dismiss the conception of wage differentials as scarcity payments. Indeed, at least as far back as classical times, economic theorists have explained occupational differences in wages in terms of differences in supply that are associated either with differences in natural endowments or differences in the cost of training. The modern human-

---

[1] For an interesting discussion of the recognition of the net advantages of employment opportunities by Adam Smith and other classical writers, see Simon Rottenberg, "On Choice in Labor Markets," republished in Burton, Benham, Vaughn, and Flanagan, eds., *Readings in Labor Market Analysis* (New York: Holt, Rinehart and Winston, 1971).

capital hypothesis had its beginnings in the classical theory of wage differences.[2]

Nonmonetary Factors and Alternative Choices

Workers are typically sensitive to the nonmonetary characteristics of alternative opportunities as well as to their wage-rate differences. For example, the safety and pleasantness of work, the timing of assigned work hours (e.g., a late shift), and vacations are among the many nonmonetary characteristics that are likely to be viewed as either advantages or disadvantages of a job opportunity. Employment opportunities with characteristics workers regard as disadvantages will normally have to be higher-paying (e.g., the late shift typically pays more than the regular one) than those that offer advantages. Equally efficient workers will feel indifferent toward alternative activities paying identical wage rates only if neither involves a discernible advantage or disadvantage. The net advantage of any employment opportunity reflects the net money income (i.e., gross income minus the cost of education, training, and moving) plus or minus the value the worker attaches to its *nonmonetary* advantages and disadvantages. People choose among different opportunities on the basis of their net advantages. If workers are free to move among occupations and locations, the choice mechanism tends to equalize the net advantage among different opportunities.

These tendencies are operative in all markets. However, they manifest themselves with particular clarity in the changes that take place in choices among entry-level jobs. Their impact on the occupational choices of college-age young people have been studied very closely because the information that is needed to examine them is readily available from college-enrollment data and student records.

Cobweb Effects and the Occupational Choices of College-Age Youth

The responsive-supply behavior of college-age youth, as reflected in their decisions about college enrollment, has already been emphasized. Their economic motivation is further evidenced by the career plans of entering freshmen; these are uniquely responsive to changes in market conditions. Table 5-3 compares the "probable" occupations of freshmen entering college in 1974 with those who entered in 1966. The choices of the latter reflect the strong market of the 1960s for elementary- and secondary-school teachers, engineers, and business professionals. By

---

[2] Adam Smith, *The Wealth of Nations*, Book 3, Chapter 10.

TABLE 5-3   *Changes in Freshman Career Plans in the Declining Market*
—Distribution by Probable Career Occupations

	Male		Female	
	1966	1974	1966	1974
Business	18.5	17.6	3.3	8.5
College professor	2.1	0.7	1.5	0.8
Doctor	7.4	6.9	1.7	3.5
Elementary, secondary-school teacher	11.3	3.8	34.1	11.9
Engineer	16.3	8.5	0.2	0.8
Farmer	3.2	6.2	0.2	1.3
Health profession, including nurse	3.2	5.8	11.9	22.7
Lawyer	6.7	5.3	0.7	2.3
Scientist	4.9	2.7	1.9	1.4
Other	15.8	24.5	31.0	26.9
Undecided	5.0	12.3	3.6	12.6

SOURCE: American Council on Education, "National Norms for Entering
College Freshmen—Fall 1966," *ACE Research Reports*, Vol. 2, No. 1,
pp. 6, 13; and (with University of California Graduate School of
Education, Los Angeles) *The American Freshmen: National Norms for
Fall 1974*, pp. 20, 32.

contrast, freshmen who entered in 1974 were planning in the midst of a
market decline, to which they responded with an increase in the number
preparing for work in the health sciences, farming, business, and "other"
jobs. A larger number also indicated that they were "undecided,"
presumably because they were uncertain about the kind of shift of
occupational choice that would be most advantageous in a declining
market. The occupational trend that emerged in the 1970s is clearly in
the direction of applied and business-oriented specialties rather than the
"pure" scientific and academic career choices that were being made
during the 1960s. Careers in medicine, especially, became relatively more
attractive as the encouragement to pure research declined during the
1960s and 1970s. Medicine is the only profession that has avoided the
cobweb fluctuations that characterized other occupations.[3]

Engineering, unlike medicine, exhibits a pattern of shortage-surplus
oscillations every four to five years. These produce corresponding swings
in starting salaries and in the number of students deciding to study (or

---

[3] The earnings of physicians have not only remained extraordinarily high but have
risen, relative to other professions. This is partly because of restrictionist policies that cut
the number of medical-school acceptances (medical schools are the only major segment of
higher education that did not expand rapidly in the post-World War II period) but also a
result of such institutional factors as the federal subsidization of medical services under
Medicare and Medicaid in the 1960s and 1970s.

not to study) engineering. The demand for engineering curricula increases when R and D spending increases and when the demand for engineers in durable-goods industries increases. It declines when large numbers of engineering students graduate and when earning opportunities are good in other occupations. It has been estimated that a 10 percent increase in the number of new B.S. engineers is associated with a 5 percent decline in enrollments in the short run and even more in the long run. The resulting oscillations tend to be dampened because of the lag structure of the adjustment process, unless the process is shocked by exogenous disturbances.[4]

The internal dynamics of engineering demand and supply are expected to generate a very different job-market picture for this occupation from the one associated with the overall college job market. Engineering enrollments were expected to peak in 1978, before declining and flattening out between 1982 and 1987.[5] Individual areas of engineering, as has been the case in the past, are expected to offer differing experiences. For example, metallurgical engineering was near the bottom of the salary scale in the 1960s, when aeronautical engineering was a booming specialty. At present, aeronautical engineering is among the lowest-paid specialties, while metallurgical engineering ranks among the highest-paying.

The law profession is similarly subject to the cobweb effect. As much as 90 percent of the variation in the supply of new lawyers and in legal salaries can be explained by the cobweb model. Freeman estimates that a 10 percent increase in legal salaries, given other wages and salaries, raises the number of first-year law students 10 percent the first year and 30 to 40 percent over the long run. This, in turn, increases the number of graduates and reduces the salaries paid to attorneys and first-year graduates.[6]

There was a major boom in the market for young lawyers in the late 1960s that was spurred by the slow increase in supply during the preceding period and the large backlog of cases. An exceptional growth in the number of new law-school applicants was recorded between 1969 and 1971 as the position of college graduates generally deteriorated. By 1975, the cobweb depressant effect of the labor market created problems for new law graduates, whose real starting salaries were lower than those of comparable graduates in earlier years. The economic situation of law graduates is expected to remain depressed until the end of the decade,

[4] Richard B. Freeman, "A Cobweb Model of the Supply and Starting Salary of New Engineers," *Industrial Labor Relations Review* (January 1976).

[5] Richard B. Freeman, *The Overeducated American* (New York: Academic Press, 1976), p. 116.

[6] Richard B. Freeman, "Legal Cobwebs: A Recursive Model of the Market for New Layers," *Review of Economics and Statistics* (May 1975).

when the large increase in new graduates is expected to diminish.

Business administration, like engineering and the legal profession, also experiences cobweb oscillations. This field was, however, in the midst of a cyclical upswing when the overall college job market was falling, which served to improve the position of managerial specialists relative to other college graduates. By the mid 1970s business administration was the largest single major for male students and attracted twice as many graduates as engineering, which was the second-largest field of specialization.[7] The rate of advance in the relative position of business graduates has already leveled off, which suggests that when the job market for new college graduates improves in the 1980s, the number choosing business careers as an occupation will also level off.

The Occupational Responses of Black Students

The occupational-supply responses of black students are related to the large-scale effort under Title III of the Civil Rights Act of 1964 to reduce job-market discrimination. Prior to this legislation, black graduates were virtually excluded from managerial and other high-paying jobs. Proportionately fewer blacks than whites attended college, and those who sought professional careers were concentrated in low-paying fields, such as the ministry and teaching. The impact of discrimination has historically been greatest among college-trained blacks, both in terms of salaries and in job opportunities.

Civil-rights legislation has had a dramatic effect on the economic status of new black college graduates who responded with extraordinary speed to the changed market situation, both in terms of college enrollment and altered career plans.[8] The increase in black enrollments was concentrated in the predominantly white schools and colleges.

Table 5-4, which records the starting salaries of black college graduates by field as compared to all male graduates for 1968 through 1970, indicates that this minority achieved parity or close to it in most fields and, in some instances (e.g., law graduates and M.B.A.'s), received better starting salaries than comparable white graduates.

Figure 5-1 displays the occupational improvement of black college graduates in an alternative way by showing the fraction employed as managers for the period 1959 through 1973. Whereas management jobs have traditionally been closed to blacks, Figure 5-1 shows that the proportion of male black college men who achieved managerial status was approximately tripled during the decade after the Civil Rights Act of 1964. Black college students moved into business, college teaching,

[7] Richard B. Freeman, *The Overeducated American*, p. 131.
[8] Richard B. Freeman, *Black Elite: The New Market for Highly Educated Black Americans* (New York: McGraw-Hill, 1976).

TABLE 5-4 *Comparable Starting Salaries of Black College and All-Male Graduates, by Field and College, 1968–1970*

	Average salary of black graduates	Comparable average national salary	Ratio
Howard (1968–1969), bachelor's degrees in:			
Civil engineering,	$800	$797	1.00
Electrical engineering	805	826	.98
Mechanical engineering	810	820	.99
Accounting	758	761	1.00
Other business fields	666	687	.97
Mathematics, chemistry, and physics	706	784	.90
Other liberal arts	644	667	.97
North Carolina A&T (1969–1970), bachelor's degree in:			
Engineering	800	873	.92
Texas Southern (1969–1970), bachelor's degrees in:			
Industrial engineering,	833	849	.98
Business	816	836	.98
Liberal arts	615	682	.98
Texas Southern Graduate, 1969–1970			
Law (J.D.)	1050	988	1.06
Business (M.B.A.)	1097	1026	1.07

SOURCE: Richard Freeman, *The Overeducated American* (New York: The Academic Press, 1976), p. 140. Reprinted with permission.

engineering, medicine, dentistry, law, and other fields traditionally closed to them. Young blacks, to an even greater extent than young whites, place great emphasis on economic factors in making their educational and career decisions. Consequently, the changes in the occupational distribution of blacks and of blacks relative to whites are largely the result of their supply behavior in response to economic factors.[9]

[9] Richard B. Freeman, "Changes in the Labor Market for Black America, 1948–1972," *Brookings Papers on Economic Activity* (Summer 1973).

FIGURE 5-1 *Fraction of nonwhite and white college graduates employed as managers, 1959–1973*

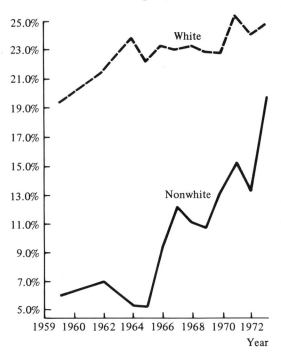

SOURCE: Bureau of Labor Statistics, *Educational Attainment of Workers*, Special Labor Force Reports, various years.

As is implicit in Table 5-5, the occupational status of all blacks generally improved. The percentage of those employed as farm and service workers has been dramatically reduced since 1960. By 1975 the proportion of blue-collar workers was only somewhat higher than the percentage of white workers. The most dramatic gain is thus in the white-collar occupations, with new college graduates enjoying the greatest gains. Older college-trained black men did not benefit as greatly as the younger group did from the decline in discrimination. They lacked both the training and experience to profit from the new opportunities and benefited from the new job market to a lesser extent than younger blacks did. However, black graduates on the whole continued to improve their occupational positions. The proportion of blacks in fields such as accounting, computer sciences, engineering, and labor relations continued to increase between 1970 and 1974. Nevertheless, the market

TABLE 5-5   *Occupational Distribution of Whites and Nonwhites, 1960–1975 (Percentages)*

Occupation	1960 Non-white	White	1965 Non-white	White	1975 Non-white	White
White-collar workers	16.1	46.6	19.5	47.9	34.2	51.7
Professional and technical	4.8	12.1	6.9	13.2	11.4	15.5
Managers, officials, proprietors	2.6	11.7	2.7	11.2	4.4	11.2
Clerical Workers	7.3	15.7	8.2	16.6	15.7	18.1
Sales workers	1.5	7.0	1.8	6.9	2.7	6.9
Blue-collar workers	40.1	36.2	41.0	36.4	37.4	32.4
Craftsmen and foremen	6.0	13.8	6.8	13.7	8.8	13.4
Operatives	20.4	17.9	21.5	18.4	20.0	14.6
Nonfarm laborers	13.7	4.4	12.6	4.3	8.7	4.4
Service workers	31.7	9.9	31.6	10.3	25.8	12.3
Private household	14.2	1.7	12.6	1.6	4.9	1.0
Other	17.5	8.2	19.1	8.7	20.9	11.3
Farm workers	12.1	7.4	7.8	5.4	2.6	3.6
Farmers and farm managers	3.2	4.3	1.8	3.3	.6	2.0
Laborers and foremen	9.0	3.0	6.0	2.3	2.0	1.5

SOURCE: *Employment and Training Report of the President*, 1976, p. 237.

decline of the mid-1970s caused the ratio of average weekly earnings of all black male graduates to drop from 79 percent in 1973 to 77 percent in 1975.

While the economic positions of white college-educated workers fell in the declining market of the recent past, that of black college workers relative to that of high-school workers improved. College-educated blacks, consequently, have a higher rate of return than do whites on their investment. Freeman's most conservative estimate implies a rate of return of 11 percent for black male college students as compared with 10 percent for white males during the mid-1970s.[10] Thus, for the first time in American history, the incentive for black men to go to college is greater than that for white men.

[10]Richard B. Freeman, *Black Elite, op. cit.,* Chapter 3.

The Occupational Distribution of Women

Educational Levels and Occupations

The disparity between the occupational positions (and incomes) of college women as compared with college men has historically been greater than that between black and white college men. The relative occupational position of women deteriorated in the period between 1930 and 1960. While the fraction of all workers who were women increased from 22.1 percent to 32.7 percent between 1930 and 1960, the fraction of professional workers who were women declined from 44.4 percent to 38.1 percent.[11]

Most of the occupations into which women have gravitated reflect the influence of culture and tradition. Thus, women predominate in teaching at the primary level, library work, nursing, sales, office work, and assembly work requiring finger dexterity. Women are underrepresented in many professions (law, dentistry, engineering, and architecture in particular), as well as in supervisory and managerial positions.

There are striking differences between the occupational categories of men and women even within an educational level. Specifically, as is evident from Table 5-6, only 4.8 percent of the women who were college graduates in 1970 were classified as managers, whereas 20 percent of the men were in this occupational group. More than 12 percent of college-educated women were attached to the "clerical and kindred workers" category, which is at a lower educational level, whereas only 4.9 percent of the male college graduates were in this category.

Similar disparities between education and occupation are apparent at the high-school level. Among female high-school graduates, only 1.8 percent are employed as craftsmen, compared with 26.4 percent of male high-school graduates. However, 11.4 percent are employed as "operatives," which is a lower-paying occupational category. Women tend to be "overeducated" for the jobs they hold, i.e., women with equivalent education are employed at lower occupational levels. There is also a greater concentration of women in particular occupations, e.g., 50.4 percent of female high-school graduates were in the "clerical and kindred worker" category. This has the effect of driving down wages relative to those earned by men with equivalent levels of education. Women's occupations are also typically associated with industries that are less profitable than those employing large numbers of men and that therefore tend to pay lower wages.

---

[11] R. Blitz, "Women in Professions, 1870–1970," *Monthly Labor Review* (May 1974): 34–39.

TABLE 5-6   *Ratio of Total Money Earnings of Civilian Women Workers to Earnings of Civilian Men Workers, Selected Years, 1956–71*

Occupational group	Actual ratios					Adjusted ratios	
	1956	1960	1965	1969	1971	1969	1971
Total	63.3	60.7	59.9	58.9	59.5	65.9	66.1
Professional and technical workers	62.4	61.3	65.2	62.2	66.4	67.9	72.4
Teachers, primary and secondary schools	(*)	75.6	79.9	72.4	82.0	(*)	(*)
Managers, officials, and proprietors	59.1	52.9	53.2	53.1	53.0	57.2	56.8
Clerical workers	71.7	67.6	67.2	65.0	62.4	70.0	66.9
Sales workers	41.8	40.9	40.5	40.2	42.1	45.7	47.4
Craftsmen and foreman	(*)	(*)	56.7	56.7	56.4	60.8	60.2
Operatives	62.1	59.4	56.6	58.7	60.5	65.4	66.6
Service workers, excluding private-household workers.	55.4	57.2	55.4	57.4	58.5	62.5	63.2

SOURCE: B. R. Chiswick and J. O'Neill, *Human Resources and Income Distribution* (New York: W. W. Norton, 1977), p. 652. Reprinted with permission.

The differential in earnings between men and women is partially attributable to differences in their occupational distribution. After allowing for the differential in hours worked, the money earnings of full-time year-round women workers amounted to 66 percent of the money earnings of males in 1971. The differential in earnings is evident for all educational levels, and, as is shown graphically in Figure 5-2, the differential increases with age. The female age-earnings profile is considerably flatter than that of men, and the median income of male high-school graduates who were full-time year-round workers was typically above that of full-time year-round working women who had four or more years of college.

Preferences and Women's Occupational Distribution

The factors that underlie the occupational and earnings differential between men and women are very complex. Discrimination by employers and fellow employees is clearly among the reasons for the differential. But the effect of discrimination has operated in tandem with the traditional role of women as producers of goods and services in the home. As a consequence, they obtain less labor-market experience and

FIGURE 5-2   *Annual Income by Age, for Male and Female High-School and College Graduates*

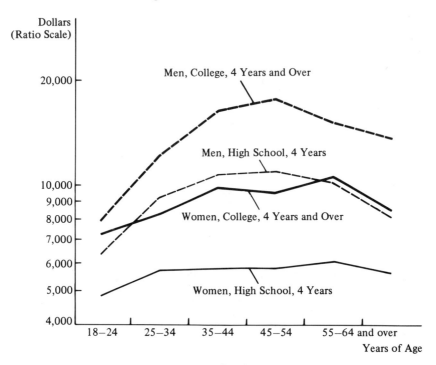

Men, College, 4 Years and Over

Men, High School, 4 Years

Women, College, 4 Years and Over

Women, High School, 4 Years

[1] Median income of full-time, year-round workers, 1971.
SOURCE: Department of Commerce

allocate less time to on-the-job training. However, the role of preferences in explaining occupational differences presents a problem. It is often reported that the majority of college-trained women have viewed their homemaking activities as their primary function and regarded career opportunities as secondary.[12] However, the evidence that the occupational distribution of women is chiefly a reflection of their preferences is not unequivocal.

The logic of the theory of choice in explaining the proportion of women in an occupation is that any factor that is negatively related to the proportion of intended supply should, in general, be positively related to the proportion of females who choose an occupation. Conversely, any factor that is positively related to intended labor supply

[12] J. Bernard, *Academic Women* (University Park, Pa.: Pennsylvania State University Press, 1964).

should, in general, be negatively related to the proportion of women choosing an occupation. It has, therefore, been suggested that the observed difference in the occupational distribution of women is consistent with their preferences only under the following conditions:[13] (1) if the more female-dominated occupations do, in fact, offer a higher wage than the male-dominated occupations for lower levels of participation; (2) if the women entering female-dominated occupations really intend to engage in less market activity than those who enter male-dominated occupations; and (3) if their intended participation rate is so low that it becomes relatively unprofitable for them to pursue a male-dominated occupation.

The objective is to test the proportion female of an occupation that reflects women's labor-supply *preferences*. A study that undertakes to determine the relationship between factors known to affect the labor-force participation of married women and the proportion female in the occupations they enter is examined in *Economic Theory in Action* 5:1.

ECONOMIC THEORY IN ACTION 5:1

Do Women Entering Female-dominated Occupations Intend to Supply Less Time to the Labor Market?

The factors known to influence the labor supply of married women are the wife's potential wage, her schooling, her husband's income and schooling, nonlabor income, her age, and the number and age of her children. The expectation is that there is a negative relationship between a wife's wage and the proportion female in the occupation she enters. Increases in nonlabor income are expected to increase the demand for leisure and reduce a wife's labor supply. An increase in a husband's permanent income, as represented by his educational attainment, is expected to have a negative influence on his wife's labor supply. A husband's transitory income, however, although also negatively related to a wife's labor supply, is expected to be negatively related to the proportion female of the occupation she enters. The premise is that a woman views her increased labor supply as temporary if it reflects a response to *transitory* income.

It is further expected that the number of preschool children and the number of children between six and eleven will be positively related to the proportion female in the occupation in which the mother is employed. However, the effect of neither age nor schooling on the

---

[13] Harriet Zellner, "Determinants of Occupational Segregation," in C. B. Lloyd, ed., *Sex, Discrimination and the Division of Labor* (New York: Columbia University Press, 1975), pp. 125–143.

proportion female can be predicted *a priori*. Age increases the relative productivity of a woman's time in the home, which generates both negative-substitution and positive-income effects on intended labor supply. The net effect depends on which is stronger, and cannot be predicted *a priori*. This is also the case with respect to the effect of schooling. More schooling may be associated with a stronger "taste" for market activity. On the other hand, it also increases nonmarket relative to market productivity. No prediction can, therefore, be made about the sign of the relationship between schooling and the proportion female in an occupation.

In order to estimate the relationships empirically, the proportion female of the occupation in which each of the married women in the sample was employed was statistically related to each of the above supply variables. The finding was that the variables generally acknowledged to exercise a positive influence on choice with respect to the labor-force participation of married women are *not* reflected in their occupational choices. It is acknowledged that there may be some supply-side influences that the model does not test, e.g., the wages that women can earn in male-dominated occupations are too low to make them attractive. However, the conclusion reached by the study is that prevailing differences in the occupational attachments of men and women reflect the influence of *demand-side* forces rather than female preferences operating on the supply side.

Changing Occupational Opportunities for Women

There has recently been a moderate increase in the proportion of women moving into traditionally male-dominated occupations. As shown in Table 5-7, there have been particularly large changes since 1960 in the number of women accountants, lawyers, life and physical scientists, university teachers, and managers.

The changing job market and the new occupational opportunities available for young female college graduates has had the effect of raising the return to investment in college. The premium that college women aged twenty-five to twenty-nine have been able to earn in comparison with high-school graduates reflects an increase in the pecuniary rewards of college education. Historically, the chief economic gain of their educations to college women was the likelihood that they would marry college men. The present deterioration in the earnings of young college men relative to college women now implies an increase for women in the monetary rewards of work relative to marriage.

Whatever the cause of observed differences between male and female earnings, it brings about a differential allocation of time between the sexes to job-market activities and the "occupation" of "household

TABLE 5-7 *Increasing Proportion of Women in Male-Dominated Professions*

Occupation	1960	1970	1974
Professional	38.4	39.9	40.5
Accountants	16.5	26.2	23.7
Architects	2.1	3.6	—
Engineers	0.8	0.6	1.3
Law	3.5	4.9	7.0
Life and physical sciences	9.2	13.7	15.9
Pharmacists	7.5	12.0	—
Doctors	6.9	9.3	9.3
Editors and reporters	36.6	40.6	43.6
Teachers, college and university	23.9	28.6	30.9
Managers	14.8	16.6	18.5
Salaried managers	13.9	16.1	18.4

SOURCE: Richard Freeman, *The Overeducated American* (New York: The Academic Press, 1976), p. 172. Reprinted with permission.

production." It is not economically prudent for a spouse who earns a higher market wage to devote as much time to household production as a spouse earning a lower wage. Higher male earnings imply that the normal economic response of women is to devote a larger proportion of their time to home production and to be geographically mobile in response to the career opportunities of their husbands.

Search, Experience, and Job Training

The Search Process

An individual exits from his formal education with given skills. Prospective employers do not, however, value these skills equally. The would-be employee is therefore confronted with the problem of acquiring information about the wage offers that different employers will make to him. Such information is not a free good. The cost of its acquisition reflects the value of the leisure time given up in order to search, or, if employment is foregone in order to search, the cost of information is reflected by the wages given up.[14]

---

[14] The seminal work investigating the costs and resources for search is George Stigler, "The Economics of Information," *Journal of Political Economy* (June 1961), and "Information in the Labor Market," *Journal of Political Economy*, Supp. 70 (October 1962): 94–105.

Different employers make different offers to a searcher. The wage offer that will be encountered on a particular day is, of course, unknown. But there is some probability distribution of wages whose parameters the worker "knows" (subjectively) or that he can infer from the information he acquires in the process of searching. Given the probability distribution, F, of wages the individual may be envisaged as undertaking the activity of searching for an acceptable offer.[15] The amount of search (and thus his period of unemployment if he is a full-time searcher) depends on (1) the probability distribution of wages F, (2) the opportunity cost c of searching, and (3) his reservation wage, W_r, which is the minimal acceptance wage. The first wage offer received will be accepted if it exceeds W_r, the reservation wage. Search will be continued if W_1 is less than W_r.

The individual's reservation wage is set at a level that equates the marginal cost of obtaining one more job offer with its expected marginal return. Since future income must be discounted in order to establish its present value, it follows that the reservation wage will decline over time as the search period is lengthened. The search period can, therefore, not be infinitely long.[16] The worker is envisaged as undertaking an optimal amount of serach, i.e., he equates the marginal cost of one more job offer with the expected marginal return of an additional search contact. Thus, he will search only as long as the value of the leisure time it requires to generate an additional wage offer is less than the discounted present value of the wage offer he thinks he can generate. A theoretical problem that arises in this context, which has important policy implications, concerns the effect of unemployment insurance in extending the duration of unemployment by an insured worker who had been laid off. The possibility of increased leisure is inherent in unemployment insurance, since benefits clearly subsidize nonmarket activity. The effect is to lengthen the period of search and extend the duration of unemployment. This important aspect of search activity is examined in Chapter 20. Our immediate interest is the relationship between search and labor-market experience. While it is possible for a worker to devote his time exclusively to search, this behavior typically is characteristic only for new entrants into the labor force or for those who have been laid off. Two national surveys provide information that suggests that the search process

---

[15] A probability distribution expresses the proportion of the time (or relative frequency) with which an event will occur in the long run. If the probabilities of obtaining mutually exclusive wage offers of $W_1, W_2 \ldots$, and W_r are respectively $P(W_1), P(W_2) \ldots$, and $P(W_r)$, then the mathematical expectation that a particular wage offer will be received in n trials is: $W_i \cdot P(W_1) + W_2 \cdot P(W_2) + \ldots + W_n \cdot P(W_n)$.

[16] If the discount rate is taken into consideration, the present value of an offer, y, is By, where $B \equiv 1/1 + r$ is the discount factor and r is the rate of interest. Thus the reservation wage is the solution to $W_r \equiv B[E_{max}(W_r, X_1) - c]$, which implies that discounting causes the searcher to limit his search activity.

is typically conducted by workers while they are employed and that quitting takes place only after another job has been lined up.[17] These surveys, conducted in 1955 and 1961, found that among workers who undertook only one job change during the year and changed jobs to achieve an improvement in status, about 80 percent did not experience unemployment.

Learning, Experience, and the Occupational Structure

Learning does not come to an end after graduation, and education is not produced only in schools and colleges. At some point it becomes economically advantageous to change the site of learning activity from the schoolroom to the marketplace. Investment in human capital proceeds more efficiently, beyond some point, when it takes place in conjunction with work experience.

Background skills are generally provided through formal schooling, but most of the specific skills that contribute to productivity are acquired after high-school graduation. Historically, apprenticeship was the typical training ground for the young. A boy would be taught his craft by a master workman, often living and working in his household in exchange for room and board and perhaps a small wage. Other arrangements might involve a monetary payment to the master, who was responsible for the boy's training until he qualified to become a journeyman. After the establishment of craft-type unions, apprenticeship programs typically came under their control.

Union-sponsored apprenticeship programs are, however, no longer the main source of training opportunities. Their place has been taken partly by the job-training programs provided by employers. Since an individual's opportunity to improve his earnings is associated with the acquisition of additional skills and experience, the opportunity for on-the-job training and upward mobility may well make a job that pays a lower starting wage more attractive than an alternative opportunity that pays a higher wage. Workers have a demand for learning opportunities and are willing to "pay" for them (in the form of lower wages) because they provide a chance to increase marketable skills, knowledge, and ultimately, future income. Work and learning are thus complementary; the market for jobs is a dual market in which firms supply learning opportunities as a by-product of their production activities.

The occupational structure that has developed in the economy may be interpreted as the outcome of a dynamic process in which workers move from one type of work activity to another over the course of their

---

[17] Gertrude Bancroft and Stuart Garfinkle, "Job Mobility in 1961," *Monthly Labor Review* 85 (August 1963): 897–906.

working lives.[18] If, at the time of their entry into the labor market, they become employed by a firm that provides a whole spectrum of jobs, workers go through a series of promotions in the firm as their skills and knowledge accumulate.

If there is more hiring at entry-level jobs than there are promotion opportunities further up the hierarchy, some workers will have to search elsewhere for the kind of work-learning experiences they are seeking, whereas workers who have reached their desired maximum skill, given investment opportunities and costs, will be "stayers" rather than "movers." Clearly, variations in learning capacity and in levels of schooling are associated with corresponding and opposite variations in the real costs of learning, which affect individual incentives to accumulate knowledge and skill.[19] Thus, the maximization of an individual's wealth over a lifetime can be viewed as a problem of optimum capital accumulation. Optimization requires the choice of a sequence of work activities such that at any age the discounted marginal return is greater than or equal to the marginal cost of the investment.[20] This view implies that there is an optimum sequence of work activities over a working lifetime and that individual choice simultaneously determines earnings as well as the occupation patterns of workers over their lifetimes. In this sense the labor market is a mechanism for "trading" in lifetime incomes and wealth.

General versus Specific Training

Whether on-the-job training is of the informal "learning by doing" sort whose orientation is to the requirements of a worker's new assignment or a more formal program providing either general or specific training, the result is that the activity enhances the worker's productivity. If the training he receives is "general" in that it is transferable to a variety of job opportunities, it is likely that the employee will bear the cost of the training himself. It has been shown that the cost of providing general "on-the-job training" will not be borne by employers.[21] Employees pay the cost of general training themselves by receiving current wages which are less than their current productivity. Their market wages, after the training period, will reflect the productivity increases that result from training.

[18] Sherwin Rosen, "Learning and Experience in the Labor Market," *Journal of Human Resources* VII (Summer 1972): 326–342.

[19] This is the case whether schooling is a real producer of knowledge or serves only to establish credentials.

[20] Sherwin Rosen, *op. cit.,* pp. 333–334.

[21] Gary Becker, *Human Capital* (New York: Columbia University Press, 1964), Chapter 2, pp. 7–29.

The reason why employees typically bear the costs of general training is not difficult to understand. A profit-maximizing firm would not pay for training that is equally valuable to many firms because it would sustain a "capital loss" each time a trained worker left its employ. The only way an employer would collect a return on training he provides to a worker is by paying a wage that is less than the value of the marginal product. This is, however, generally not possible. No firm confronted with a competitive labor market will long be able to retain a trained worker at a wage below the value of his marginal product, because alternative opportunities for earning a higher wage are readily available to the worker.

Completely specific training, on the other hand, does not increase worker productivity to other firms. The willingness of firms (and workers) to pay specific training costs is closely related to the likelihood of labor turnover. Were the worker to bear the training cost, a layoff would represent a loss that he could not recoup through earnings elsewhere because his productivity (and wages) would be less in alternative opportunities. Were the employer to bear the training cost, the loss imposed by a worker who quits could not readily be offset by hiring a substitute who would not be equally productive until he too went through a training period, which would require additional costs. Thus, it is likely that both the costs and returns of specific training will be shared by employers and employees.[22]

While the choice between jobs is frequently based on the relative opportunities they provide for continued self-investment, there is evidence that formal education is often a prerequisite for more specialized on-the-job training. A study by Jacob Mincer established that on-the-job training opportunities are very limited for persons having low educational levels, whereas it is very significant at upper levels.[23] The opportunity to accept employment that offers training for advancement is often contingent on being a high-school or even a college graduate. Employers search for workers for whom they make training opportunities available just as workers such for opportunities that provide training. The value of information to an employer is the present value of the savings he makes by hiring workers of a given quality at a lower wage rate. The greater the amount of search undertaken by workers, the higher the cost to employers of a given quality of labor. The institutional characteristics of the market determine how the cost of investment in information is shared between employers and employees.

---

[22] Becker, *op. cit.*, pp. 19–20.

[23] Jacob Mincer, "On-the-Job Training: Costs, Returns, and Some Implications," *Journal of Political Economy* LXX (October 1962).

Concluding Remarks

The concern of this chapter has been to examine the role of choice in the allocation of the labor supply among occupations. Census data show that major shifts have taken place in the occupational deployment of the labor force during the last several decades. The inference that is made on the basis of economic principle is that these changes are consistent with maximizing behavior on the part of labor-force participants. According to the supply-oriented theories of mobility that this chapter has examined and that reflect the majority view of the way in which labor markets function, job mobility is stimulated by changes in the expected income associated with alternative opportunities.

Freeman's empirical studies verify that supply-side responses take place in cobweb fashion among college graduates—male and female, black and white—to demand-side changes. The enrollment of college and professional-school students is a response to entry-level salaries whose variations are consistent with a competitive market.

While Freeman's findings lend support to the hypothesis that competitive market pressures are in evidence (except in medicine) in the ups and downs of starting salaries, there is no consensus that the wage structure as a whole reflects competitive forces. Doubt about the pervasiveness of competitive market pressure, except at the entry level, is related to the impact that firm-specific on-the-job training has on employment practices and wages.

Employees with specific training are less likely to quit and are less likely to be laid off or fired than employees with no training or general training. Economic principle also suggests that rational firms pay specifically trained workers a higher wage than they could receive elsewhere, whereas this is not the case for generally trained workers. The effect of specific training on wages is to raise them above those paid to generally trained workers, because firms that have paid part of worker training costs are willing to pay workers a premium in order to forestall turnover. Employers have more incentive to retain workers with specific training, and the latter have an incentive to remain with the firms that trained them. After workers' initial employment in entry-level jobs, on-the-job training and experiences become the prerequisites for their upward mobility in the firm. To the extent that individuals work for promotions and raises within the organizations that employ them (and there appear to be strong incentives for both employees and employers toward this pattern), the firm becomes an "internal labor market" that is more or less insulated from the competition of the external market. "Entry ports" to an internal labor market are typically limited to lower-level jobs that serve as the first rung on a promotion ladder. Employees who have reached higher-level jobs through internal promotion thus tend to be insulated from the direct influence of external labor-market competition.

The pervasiveness and signifance of internal labor markets in our economy is a matter of great controversy. Mainstream economists, among them Gary Becker and Walter Oi, have examined the implication of "on-the-job training" within the framework of the competitive model. However, the proponents of the dual-labor-markets hypothesis maintain that the competitive model is rendered irrelevant for explaining the structure of wages when internal labor markets become pervasive in an economy. To understand the issues between them, it is necessary to proceed to an examination of the demand side of the labor market. This is undertaken in the following two chapters.

Suggestions for Further Reading

Gary Becker. *Economic Theory*. New York: Alfred A. Knopf, 1971, Lecture 34, pp. 166–169.

Gary Becker. *Human Capital*. New York: Columbia University Press, 1964, Chapter 2, pp. 7–29.

Richard B. Freeman. *The Overeducated American*. New York: Academic Press, 1976.

Jacob Mincer. "On-the-Job Training: Costs, Returns, and Some Implications." *Journal of Political Economy* 70 (October 1962).

Sherwin Rosen. "Learning and Experience in the Labor Market." *Journal of Human Resources* 7 (Summer 1972).

Mary H. Stevenson. "Relative Wages and Sex Segregation by Occupation," in C. B. Lloyd, ed., *Sex, Discrimination, and the Division of Labor*. New York: Columbia University Press, 1975, pp. 175–200.

George Stigler. "The Economics of Information." *Journal of Political Economy* (June 1961).

George Stigler. "Information in the Labor Market." *Journal of Political Economy*, Supplement 70 (October 1962).

Harriet Zellner. "Determinants of Occupational Segregation," in C. B. Lloyd, ed., *Sex, Discrimination, and the Division of Labor*. New York: Columbia University Press, 1975, pp. 125–143.

6 The Employment Decisions of "Price-Taking" Firms

We have already noted the changes in the allocation of labor resources that have accompanied the shift to a service-oriented economy. This information is enlightening, but it does not further our understanding of the demand for labor by individual firms in the various sectors of the economy. The question that concerns us in this chapter, therefore, as part of our inquiry into the microeconomic aspects of the labor market, is the examination of employer decision-making about the amount of labor that will be employed.

Just as the supply side of the labor market reflects the utility-maximizing behavior of households, so the demand side reflects the employment decisions of business firms. Economists are not of one mind concerning the demand side of the labor market any more than they are with respect to examining the supply side. Much depends on their perception of the basis on which firms make their employment decisions and the constraints they encounter in making them. The essential constraint is the position of the firm as a "price taker" or "price maker" in the commodity and labor markets in which it operates.

The classification of market structures according to the position of firms in commodity and factor markets as "price takers" or "price makers" is among the results of inquiries by Joan Robinson and Edward Chamberlin into the functioning of imperfect markets.[1] One of their findings is that a firm would not experience the infinitely elastic sales (i.e., demand) curve of a "price taker" (or "pure competitor") if it is (a) a single seller (monopoly), (b) one of a few sellers (oligopoly), or (c) if it "differentiated" its product by advertising or otherwise distinguishing its

---

[1] Joan Robinson, *The Economics of Imperfect Competition* (London: Macmillan and Company, 1933); E. Chamberlin, *The Theory of Monopolistic Competition* (Cambridge, Mass.: Harvard University Press, 8th edition, 1962).

output from its competitors, in which case the firm is a "monopolistic competitor." It was also established that a firm's employment decision is uniquely related to the degree of market power it commands both in selling its product and in employing its factors. These observations led to a classification of markets as being purely competitive, monopolistically competitive, oligopolostic, or monopolistic.

While the preceding market classification has become standard it is somewhat cumbersome and not necessary for our purpose. Thus, we opt for the simpler terminology of "price takers" and "price makers." A firm is a "price taker" in its commodity market if it is a relatively small firm that can vary its own output without changing the price established in the market through the interaction of demand-and-supply forces. This type of market situation, which is commonly described by the term "pure competition," still exists in the production and sale of primary raw products and some services. If the firm is similarly unable to affect the wage rate at which it hires its workers, then it is a "price taker" in the labor market as well as in the commodity market.

What considerations govern the employment decision (i.e., the demand for labor) of a firm that is a price taker in its commodity and factor markets? It is reasonable to presume that under these circumstances a firm's demand for labor (or any other factor) will reflect the choices it makes to "channel" or allocate the factors it employs among alternative uses in order to maximize its profits (or minimize losses). Profit maximization implies that the costs of hiring workers and other factors are weighed against the revenues that are earned from the sale of their output. Entrepreneurial profit-maximizing behavior thus parallels that which takes place on the supply side of the market as a result of the maximizing choices of households. The marginal-productivity principle is central to such behavior on the demand side of the factor market.

The Marginal-Productivity Principle

The Production Process

When profit maximization is a major objective of business firms, it follows that labor and other productive factors are employed only because they are expected to contribute to achieving this goal. In considering the employment of an additional worker at a given wage, an employer attempts, first, to evaluate how much another employee is likely to add to his total product and, second, how much the added product will contribute to total revenue. The addition to total product by an additional worker is what the economist terms *marginal physical product* (MPP). More specifically, marginal physical product is $\Delta Q / \Delta N$ where ΔQ is the change in output associated with the employment of an additional worker, ΔN. Marginal revenue is the money value of the additional product, i.e., $MR = MPP(p)$ where p is the price at which the additional product can be sold.

Employers are also concerned with average worker productivity. An example will help to clarify the distinction between average product (Q/L) and marginal product $(\Delta Q/\Delta L)$. Table 6-1 assumes that the firm in question has a given complement of capital equipment, plant, land, and managerial talent and that labor is its only variable input. This assumption corresponds to the economist's conception of "the short run" during which variations in output are constrained by the firm's fixed inputs. Without troubling to show fixed inputs in the table because they are assumed to be constant throughout, we can develop an example to illustrate the change in total product as labor inputs change by one unit.

TABLE 6-1   *Hypothetical Input, Output, and Product Data: The Case of a*
                "Price Taker"

(1)	(2)	(3)	(4)	(5)	(6)	(7)
Labor		APP_n	MPP_n			
Inputs (L)	Output (Q)	(2):(1)	(ΔQ)	$P = MR$	MRP_n	ARP
5	110	22.0	*25	.50	$12.50	$11.00
6	125	20.8	15	.50	7.50	10.40
7	135	19.3	10	.50	5.00	9.65
8	143	17.9	7	.50	3.50	8.95
9	149	16.5	6	.50	3.00	8.25
10	152	15.2	3	.50	1.50	7.60

*Implies that 4 labor input units yield 85 units of output.

To avoid the problem of distinguishing between the number of persons and the number of hours worked, it is assumed that labor's productivity depends only on the number of persons hired to work with a given complement of plant and and equipment and not on the length of the work week. Total output Q, which is a function of labor inputs L and fixed inputs K, increases as additional labor units are added, as is recorded in Table 6-1. It is also reflected in the slope of the production function $q(L,K)$, which is shown in the upper portion of Figure 6-1. This curve shows that total product increases at an increasing rate (i.e., marginal product increases) as long as additional variable inputs can be combined with increasing effectiveness with a given stock of fixed factors. But variable factors cannot be added without eventually encountering diminishing returns and rising average and marginal costs

FIGURE 6-1 *Production with One Variable Input*

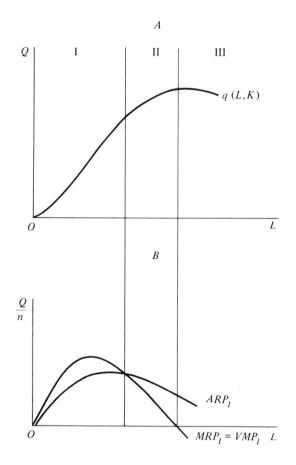

of production; if a firm changes its short-run output by varying the "mix" of its factor inputs, it experiences a U-shaped cost curve. In the hypothetical example of Table 6-1, diminishing returns take place after five labor inputs are employed. Thereafter labor's marginal product falls, eventually becoming zero. If still more labor inputs are added, marginal product will eventually become negative. Total product, q, increases only as long as the marginal product is positive, and it is a maximum when the marginal product of the variable factor is zero.

It is characteristic of production processes that the average physical product of labor q/L (or any other factor) declines less rapidly than its marginal product $\Delta q/\Delta L$. Thus, in Table 6-1, q/L is still rising when the sixth man is hired although marginal product declined with the addition of the fifth worker. The average product of labor is equivalent to the slope of a line drawn from the origin (O) to any point on the production function. The marginal product of labor $\Delta q/\Delta L$ is equivalent to the slope of a tangent to the production function at any point along its length.

The output zones I, II, and III that are identified in Figure 6-1 have important economic significance. The average productivity of the variable factor is rising throughout Zone I, which indicates that fixed factors of production are not being fully utilized. It is therefore not profitable to operate in this range but rather to expand output and operate in Zone II. The alternative is to abandon part of the fixed factor in order to utilize the remainder more fully so as to reach the top of the *ARP* curve.

Zone III is similarly unprofitable. Operation in this zone is uneconomical because the marginal product of labor is negative in this stage. A reduction in the number of labor units employed will increase production and lower the cost of operation. Thus, a firm's hiring decisions with respect to labor relate to its decisions to vary output within Zone II. Within this range of production the marginal product of labor is declining (but is still positive and less than its average product).

In principle, the decision rule that guides a firm is quite simple. Given the selling price, p, of its product, the firm evaluates a worker's physical product in terms of its money value, i.e., in terms of the market price of its output. Two magnitudes are important: *marginal revenue product* and *average revenue product*. The marginal revenue product of labor (MRP_l) is its marginal *physical* product multiplied by the *marginal revenue* his output yields.[2] The average revenue product of labor (ARP_l) is the worker's average physical product multiplied by the selling price of his output.

The MRP_l and the ARP_l associated with various labor inputs can be represented graphically as in the lower portion of Figure 6-1. Dollar receipts are measured on the vertical axis and the number of labor units hired are measured on the horizontal axis. The downward slope of the MRP_l curve, when additional labor inputs are added at lower wage rates, tells us that it represents a firm's demand curve for the factor. It does not, of course, tell us *how many* units of a particular type of labor a firm would hire if it were confronted with such a demand curve. To determine this, it is necessary to know the money wage rate at which workers of a particular type can be hired. Given this information, the profit-maximizing level of employment for the firm can be determined.

[2] It is sometimes useful to distinguish between the marginal revenue product of labor and its marginal value product (VMP). VMP_l is the marginal product of labor multiplied by the *market price* of his output. If a firm is a price taker, marginal revenue equals price, i.e., $MMP_l(p) = MRP_l = VMP_l$, as in Column 6.

If we recall that a firm maximizes profit (minimizes losses) by producing the output at which marginal cost (i.e., the added cost of producing one more unit of output) equals marginal revenue, it will be readily understood that when labor is the only variable input, this profit-maximizing rule is simply applied to its labor inputs. Thus, *at any given money wage rate*, a firm will maximize its gain (minimize its losses) if $w = MRP_l < ARP_l$. That is, at a given wage rate and with a given selling price for its product, a profit-maximizing firm will hire that number of workers at which the money wage rate it must pay its workers is equal to labor's marginal-revenue product, where the latter is equal to or less than the average revenue product. This is consistent with operating somewhere in Zone II.

In the example given in Table 6-1, seven labor units would be hired if the hourly wage rate is five dollars. If fewer than seven persons were being employed at that wage rate, $MRP_l > w$, and net proceeds could be increased by hiring more labor. The most profitable volume of employment at an hourly wage of seventy dollars and fifty cents would be six persons. At four dollars per hour, however, it would be profitable to hire eight persons. Thus, the points on the MRP_l curve, *after labor's marginal product has started to diminish,* trace out the firm's demand curve for labor. Given the money wage rate with which the firm is confronted, it is this curve that determines what the profit-maximizing (loss-minimizing) volume of employment will be. In making a decision to hire on this basis, the firm is simply applying the same profit-maximizing rule it follows in determining its output to deciding the amount of the particular kind of labor it will employ.

It is important to note at this point that while the employer is confronted with hiring workers at a particular money wage, he is not indifferent to the value of the money wage in real terms. The real wage he pays a worker reflects the ratio w/P where P is the general price level of all goods and services. If the general price level has risen and the price of his product reflects this rise while the money wage rate an employer needs to pay his workers remains the same, the real wage has, in effect, fallen. On the other hand, if the price level has fallen, money wages remaining the same, the real wage rate has, in effect, risen. The individual firm will then find it less profitable to hire the same number of workers as previously at a given money-wage rate. By the same reasoning, an employer will find it profitable to hire more workers at a lower money-wage rate *only* if the general price level is not also falling. In short, in representing the individual firm as moving down its labor-demand curve as the money-wage rate is reduced, the presumption is that the general price level is unchanged. In general, this is a reasonable assumption to make in examining the decision-making process of an individual employer. The decisions he makes at the level of the firm have no impact on the general price level. Assuming that the wage rate at which labor can be hired is given to the firm, which is the case when it is a "price taking" employer, the firm's demand for labor depends on the marginal product of its labor and the price that it receives for its output. The profit-maximizing rule is that the firm will hire labor up to the point at which the additional output produced by the last worker employed just equals the money wage that must be paid.

Substitution among Inputs

While an increase in labor's wage rate from five dollars per hour to seven dollars and fifty cents in the hypothetical example posed above reduces the most profitable employment level from seven persons to six, it does not follow that it will be profitable for the firm to reduce output. If the profit-maximizing output is 135 units, then an increase in the wage rate may well mean that another input will be substituted for the labor inputs involved in order to maintain a constant rate of output. The substitute input may be capital or a different kind of labor. The input combination that will be chosen is that which will produce the desired output at a minimum cost. Given the cost of capital, r, and the wage rate, w, a firm will minimize the cost of a given level of output if the ratio of the marginal product of capital to the marginal product of labor is equal to the ratio of their input prices. The firm's equilibrium input of labor and capital is thus consistent with the condition that

$$\frac{MP_l}{MP_k} = \frac{w}{r}$$

If this equilibrium condition is satisfied and wages subsequently rise, as hypothesized above, the relationship between the marginal product of labor and the wage rate changes. Thus,

$$\frac{MP_l}{w} < \frac{MP_k}{r}$$

The marginal product of an additional dollar's worth of labor is now less than the marginal product of an additional dollar's worth of capital. The firm could thus reduce its expenditure for labor by one dollar while increasing its expenditure for capital by less than a dollar, and achieve the same output at a lower cost. When it is possible to substitute one input for another, each will be used until the ratio of their marginal-revenue products is equal to the ratio of their prices. It is profitable to continue the substitution of capital for labor as long as the above inequality persists. Eventually MP_l/w will become equal to MP_k/r

because the marginal productivity of labor increases as its employment diminishes, while the marginal productivity of capital will decrease as the input of capital is increased.

Scale Effects and the Long-Run Labor-Demand Curve

The preceding discussion of substitution among inputs makes it clear that a change in the wage rate of labor has a different impact on the demand for it in the short run than in the long run. In the short run, output is produced and employment decisions are made within the constraint of a given stock of capital. In the long run, *scale effects* may come about as changes in the price of labor alter the quantity of capital as well as the quantity of labor. Thus, in Figure 6-2 a rise in the wage rate from w_o to w_1 causes an employer to move leftward along his demand curve MRP_l from point A to B, at which he hires a smaller number of workers than before. However, the short-run effect of reduced employment may not carry over into the long run. In the long run the firm can expand (or contract) its capital stock. If the rise in the wage rate has made labor expensive relative to capital, the firm may increase the size of its plant. Each worker will now be assisted by a larger capital component. This implies that the same number of workers will produce a larger output than previously. Thus, labor's marginal-revenue-product curve will shift upward to the right to MRP_l'.

Assuming the wage of labor remains at W_1, the firm will maximize

FIGURE 6-2 *The Long-Run Demand Curve for Labor*

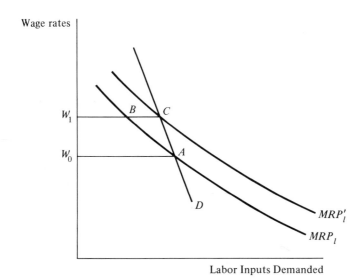

Labor Inputs Demanded

profits by hiring an amount of labor represented by point C in Figure 6-2. While its short-run labor-demand curve is denoted by the distance from B to A in Figure 6-2, the long-run demand curve is the steeper line running from C to A. This illustrates that the elasticity of the demand for labor, which will be examined in detail below, depends on the substitutability between labor and other inputs and on the effect that substitution has on labor's productivity.

Factor Substitution and Isoquants

The essential conclusion that derives from the marginal-productivity principle is that the demand for labor or other factors of production is downward-sloping. This conclusion about the demand for labor by a firm is premised on three assumptions. These are (1) that the firm's behavior is governed by the object of maximizing its profits (or that it seeks to minimize losses), (2) that the firm alters its capital-labor "mix" in response to changes in the relative prices of labor and capital, and (3) that the wage at which labor is employed is given to the firm; i.e., the firm is a "price taker" in its factor market. That the downward-sloping demand curve for labor by a firm is predicated on these assumptions can be established more rigorously with the aid of an analytical tool known as an *isoquant*.

An isoquant is a graphic representation of the relationship between two types of factor inputs and their output. Assume that labor (L) and captial (K) inputs lend themselves to being combined in different porportions to yield the *same* output. Figure 6-3 is a map in which each isoquant represents a given quantity of output, which can be produced by varying combinations of labor and capital. An isoquant is thus a "production indifference curve" and is analogous to the indifference curves that have been found useful in analyzing household behavior. Just as an indifference curve shows the various combinations of two alternatives (e.g., work and leisure) that yield equal satisfaction to a household, so an isoquant (or substitution curve) shows various combinations of two factor inputs that yield the same total quantity of a given output.

Because the marginal rate of technical substitution falls as labor is substituted for capital, isoquants must be concave from above. Concavity is a reflection of a diminishing marginal rate of technical substitution between factors. If, for example, capital inputs are decreased in specific amounts, proportionately more labor must be added to maintain the same output level. In Figure 6-3, inputs of labor are measured along the horizontal axis and inputs of capital along the vertical. Q_1 represents a given quantity of output that can be produced with various input combinations. Q_2, which lies above to the right of Q_1 and Q_o, which lies below and to the left, represent larger and smaller outputs than Q_1.

FIGURE 6-3   *Typical Isoquants*

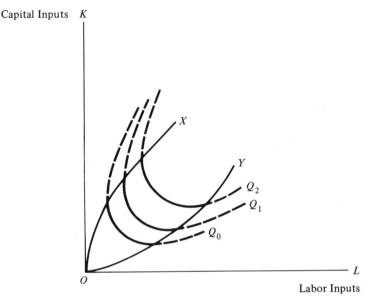

The slope of an isoquant at any point measures the marginal rate of technical substitution between two factors in the production of a particular output, Q. The marginal rate of substitution of one factor for another in producing the same output may be either positive or negative. However, rational producer behavior rules out a positive substitution ratio because it implies that employment of more of *both* inputs yields the *same* output. It is clearly unprofitable for a firm to use more than the minimum factor input required to produce a particular volume of output. This is shown in Figure 6-3, in which ridge lines X and Y are drawn to mark off the limits of rational factor employment. Those portions of the isoquants that lie outside the ridge lines X and Y, as shown by the broken lines in Figure 6-3, are uneconomical-factor combinations and are therefore not relevant to production decisions.

In order to determine the optimum combination of factors for producing a given output, it is necessary to know the prices at which the factors can be employed and the budget that has been allocated for employing them. Assume that the wage of labor is w_1 while the interest rate on capital is r, and that the budget \$$B$ has been allocated to employ them. Thus in Figure 6-4 the firm can employ any combination of labor and capital that lies on the line connecting \$$B/_r$ to \$$B/w_1$. This line is the constant outlay or isocost curve. Each point on it represents an expenditure of \$$B$ to employ a different combination of labor and

FIGURE 6-4 *Derivation of a Labor-Demand Curve*

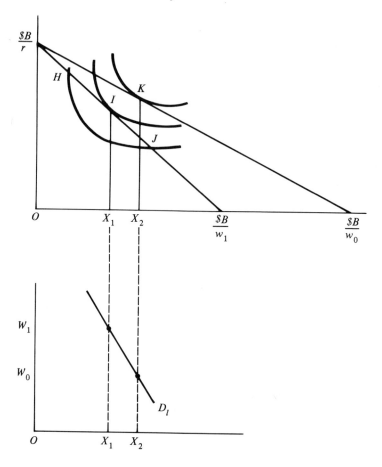

capital. The isocost line is analogous to the budget constraint confronting a household. The position of the isocost line in Figure 6-4
indicates that the firm could employ any combination of labor and
capital lying on it; e.g., it could employ combinations H, I, or J. But the
best combination is I, because this combination enables the firm to
achieve the biggest output it can with a given factor input. The tangency
of the isoquant and the isocost line at I means that the ratio of the
marginal rates of substitution between labor and capital is equal to the
ratio of their wage and interest costs. I is therefore the optimum combination of labor and capital with respect to output Q_1, given the budget
allocation $\$B$, the rate of wages, and the rate of interest. If the input
combination I is not the one that is chosen, it would be possible to increase total product (or reduce the cost of the present output).

If the price at which a factor can be employed becomes changed, the optimal input combination will also change because it alters the ratio of their costs. It is possible, on the basis of this principle, to derive a demand curve for a factor and verify more rigorously the reason for its downward slope. The typical downward slope of a firm's demand curve for labor can be demonstrated with the aid of a family of isoquants and various assumed budget constraints. Given its budget constraint, the amount of labor that a hypothetical firm would hire at a wage of w_1 is OX_1. The wage-quantity relationship represented by OX_1 and w_1 in the lower portion of Figure 6-4 is one point on the firm's labor demand curve, D_l. This curve can be established by assuming another wage rate, either higher or lower than w_1 in order to identify the amount of employment that will be offered at a different wage.

Assume that the wage falls to w_0. Given its budget, the firm can now hire its inputs along the new budget constraint, which is identified by drawing a line from point $\$B/r$ on the vertical axis to $\$B/w_0$ on the horizontal axis. The optimum factor combination now is K, which is comprised of a larger amount of of labor, OX_2, and also a larger amount of capital.[3] The larger quantity of labor that is employed reflects the substitution of labor for capital as the wage rate is lowered. The coordinate of OX_2 and wage rate w_0 provides a second point on the graph in the lower portion of Figure 6-4; together with the point representing the coordinate between OX_1 and wage w_1, it provides the information required to derive the demand curve D_l.

The Elasticity of the Demand for Labor

The responsiveness of the demand for labor to changes in the wage rate requires further examination. While the quantity demanded of some inputs is not very sensitive to price changes, the quantity demanded of others is very sensitive. Economists use the term *price elasticity* to express the sensitivity of the demand for an input (or a commodity) to a change in its price. A simple and rather direct way of determining the elasticity of the demand for a factor to a price change is to compute the change in the budget allocated to its employment if its price changes. If the amount spent to employ a particular type of labor is the same regardless of wage increases or decreases, the elasticity of the demand for it is said to be *unitary*. If an increase (decrease) in wages results in a larger (smaller)

---

[3]In this case the fall in the wage rate causes an income effect as well as a substitution effect. The substitution effect results because the fall in the cost of labor relative to capital causes a substitution between them. Additionally, the fall in wages increases the firm's real budget, which enables it to hire more capital as well as more labor.

wage bill, the demand for that type of labor is *inelastic*. Analogously, if an increase in wages (decrease) results in a smaller (larger) budget allocation, the demand for it is *elastic*. Thus, returning to the example given above, in which the demand for labor was reduced from seven to six persons when the hourly wage rate increased from five dollars to seven dollars and fifty cents, the demand for labor is *inelastic*. This is the case because the wage bill for six persons at seventy dollars and fifty cents per hour amounts to forty-five dollars, whereas at a wage of five dollars it will only be thirty-five dollars per hour because not more than seven persons will be hired.

The price or wage elasticity of the demand for labor can be defined and measured more precisely. The percentage change in the quantity of any input, say, labor, L, is defined as 100 ΔL divided by L. For example, if the quantity demanded increases from ten to twenty units, the percentage rise in $L = 100\Delta L/L = 1000/10 = 100$ percent. Similarly, the percentage change in the wage of labor, w, is given by the expression $100\Delta w/w$. Therefore the wage elasticity of the demand for labor is:

$$e = -\frac{100\Delta L/L}{100\Delta w/w}.$$

Dividing the numerator and the denominator by 100 results in:

$$e = -\frac{\Delta L/L}{\Delta w/w}.$$

Thus, the elasticity of the demand for an input to a change in its price is the percentage change in the quantity employed, which results from a 1 percent change in its price. Alternatively, the price elasticity of the demand for input x

$$= -\frac{\text{percentage change in the quantity of } x \text{ demanded}}{\text{percentage change in the price of } x}$$

The minus sign that precedes the fraction requires a word of explanation. It is inserted to make the elasticity number positive. Because of the negative incline of the demand curve, a rise in wages will bring about a fall in the quantity demanded, so that the numerator and the denominator of the elasticity fraction will be of the opposite sign. The fraction will therefore be a negative number. Thus, to make the elasticity coefficient a positive number, a minus sign is inserted into the elasticity formula to facilitate linguistic convenience.

Returning to the preceding example, if wages rise from five dollars to seven dollars and fifty cents and employment declines from seven labor units to six, the wage elasticity of demand is:

$$e = - \cfrac{-\dfrac{\Delta L}{L}}{\dfrac{\Delta w}{w}} = \cfrac{\dfrac{-1}{7}}{\dfrac{2.50}{5.00}} = \cfrac{\dfrac{1}{7}}{\dfrac{1}{2}} = \dfrac{2}{7} = .285$$

The coefficient .285 implies that in this hypothetical case, the demand for labor is *inelastic*, i.e., an increase in wages of 1 percent reduces employment by only .285 percent. If the coefficient is greater than 1, it means that the demand for labor is *elastic* with respect to the wage rate. That is, a 1 percent increase in the wage rate will reduce employment by more than 1 percent.

The great English theorist Alfred Marshall identified four conditions under which the derived demand for labor will be relatively inelastic.[4] These are (1) if it is technologically difficult or impossible to substitute other inputs for labor, (2) if the demand for the product labor produces is itself price inelastic, (3) if the ratio of labor cost to total cost is low, and (4) if the supply of a substitute or complementary input is relatively inelastic.

The first condition implies that if labor is essential in a firm's production function, then other inputs are unlikely to be substituted for labor, even if there is a substantial increase in its wage.

The second condition results because the demand for labor is derived from the product it helps to produce. The elasticity of the demand for a product is reflected in the demand for the factor inputs that produce it. Thus, the greater the price sensitivity of the demand for a commodity, the greater the elasticity of demand for the labor (and other factor inputs) used to produce it. Conversely, if the demand for a commodity is relatively inelastic, the demand for the inputs that are used in its production also tend to be relatively inelastic.[5]

Marshall's third condition implies that the demand for labor is more elastic the greater the ratio of labor cost to total cost. If wages are a very small part of total cost, even a large wage increase is likely to have a small effect on the price of the product; it will, therefore, have a similarly small effect on sales and employment. For example, if the wages of

---

[4] Alfred Marshall, *Principles of Economics*, 8th edition, Book V, Chapter 6.

[5] J. R. Hicks noted an exception to the general rule that the demand for labor is more elastic the greater the elasticity of demand for the product. If the elasticity of substitution between factor inputs (as stated in the first condition) is greater than the price elasticity of demand for labor, then an increase in the relative cost of labor will reduce the elasticity of demand for labor. See John R. Hicks, *The Theory of Wages*, 2nd edition (London: Macmillan Co., 1963), p. 245.

plumbers represent 1 percent of the total cost of a new house and there are no substitutes for their services, an increase of 50 percent in their wage would add only one-half of 1 percent to the total price of a house. Thus, even if the demand for houses is quite elastic (say a 1 percent increase in the price of a house decreases construction by 2 percent), the effect of a large percentage increase in the wage of plumbers on the volume of construction would be negligible (e.g., a 50 percent wage increase would reduce construction by only 1 percent).

The fourth condition relates the sensitivity of the demand for a factor to the *supply* sensitivity of other inputs with which it is used jointly or for which it is a substitute. Take, for example, the case in which two types of labor are complementary to one another and the supply of one of them is quite elastic with respect to its wages. An increase in the prevailing wage for this type of labor would then cause the demand for the other labor input with which it is used cooperatively to be minimally affected even if its price rises. If, however, two types of labor are substitutes for one another and labor of the first type is relatively elastic in its supply, an increase in the wage rate of labor of the first type is likely to have an adverse effect on the demand for labor of the second type, because of the possibility of substitution between them.

Marshall's laws of derived demand have great practical significance because they largely determine the net gain to its membership (given that a wage increase may have an adverse effect on employment) that a union can achieve as a result of its bargaining. These implications will be explored in more detail in Chapter 8.

Empirical Evidence Concerning the Demand for Labor

Data that will enable us to verify on an empirical level whether the demand curve for labor (or other factors) is downward-sloping is not readily available. Testing this proposition requires information about the firm's production function that tells us how output behaves as input combinations are varied in response to a change in one factor price, while other input prices and the demand for the product *remain constant.* One study that undertook to ascertain the elasticity of demand for production man hours in a group of two-digit manufacturing industries reports results that are consistent with the theoretical expectations examined above. That is, a change in the total cost of hiring production workers was associated with an inverse change in their employment. Similarly, a change in the cost of capital was associated with an inverse change in the demand for production-worker hours. These findings, which are reported as *Economics in Action* 6.1, provide some interesting empirical evidence about factor substitution in response to changes in their costs of employment.

ECONOMICS IN ACTION 6:1

The Elasticity of Demand for Production Manhours in Selected Industries

Quarterly data for the period 1954–64 for seventeen industries having a two-digit Standard Industrial Classification Code were used to determine the elasticity of demand for production-worker man hours with respect to their total hourly cost and the cost of capital.[6] The study is premised on the assumption that the firms' objective is to maximize profits (π) and that the industries are price takers. Thus,

$$\pi = PQ - W_1L_1 - W_2L_2 - \text{qd}K - \text{rq}K$$

where P is the price of output Q, W_1 is the total hourly cost of production-worker man hours L_1, W_2 is the total hourly cost of overhead-worker man hours L_2, q is the price of capital goods K, d is the rate of replacement of capital goods, and r is the rate of interest. The term $\text{qd}K$ is to be interpreted as the cost of replacing depreciated capital goods, while $\text{rq}K$ is the cost of holding an amount of money in the form of capital stock.

Data relating to W_1L_1 and W_2L_2 were generated on the basis of information taken from Standard Industrial Classification studies and the Bureau of Labor Statistics. The wholesale price index of durable manufactures was used as a proxy for the price of capital goods, q, and the interest rate, r, was represented by Moody's Aaa corporate bond rate. The rate replacement of capital was taken to be 0.025 (quarterly).[7]

It was ascertained that the elasticity of demand for production-worker man hours is highly variable from industry to industry. Other factor prices remaining constant, a 1 percent increase (decrease) in the total cost of a production-worker hour in a nondurable manufacturing industry resulted in a reduction (an increase) in employment of as little as 0.276 percent in the printing industry and as much as 1.527 in the case of petroleum production. The average value of this elasticity in the nondurable manufacturing sector was 0.405. In durable-goods-manufacturing industries a 1 percent increase (decrease) in the total cost of a production-worker hour lead to a reduction (an increase) in the demand for production-worker hours ranging from 0.120 percent in the furniture

[6] Roger N. Waud, "Man-hour Behavior in U.S. Manufacturing: A Neoclassical Interpretation," *Journal of Political Economy* 76 (May/June 1968).

[7] This value was estimated by Dale W. Jorgenson in "Capital Theory and Investment Behavior," *American Economic Review* LII (May 1963).

industry to as much as 2.366 percent in the case of fabricated metals. The average value of this elasticity is 1.507.

The number of man hours employed are also sensitive to the cost of capital. It is estimated that a 1 percent increase (decrease) in the cost of capital, i.e., in $q(d + r)$ will result, other things remaining constant, in an increase (a decrease) in the demand for production-worker hours of as low as 0.084 percent in the petroleum industry to as high as 0.675 percent in the rubber and plastics industry; the average value of this elasticity in the nondurable-goods sector is 0.234. For the durable-goods-manufacturing sector the elasticity of demand ranges between 0.317 percent in the case of fabricated metals to as much as 0.995 percent in the case of machinery. The average value of the elasticity coefficient in this sector is 0.53. These estimates of the elasticity of substitution between capital and labor identify substantial differences from one industry to another. Most estimates, however, fall in the range of 0.8 to 1.2.[8] Thus it is generally believed that for the economy as a whole the elasticity of substitution between capital and labor approximates unity.[9]

Some Problems Concerning Demand at the Level of the Firm and the Industry

While the preceding study yielded results that are consistent with a downward-sloping demand curve for labor in the specific industries it included, the findings relate only to the demand for production-worker hours in markets in which participants are "price takers." This is not an unimportant finding, for there are some such markets, in spite of the pervasiveness of firms that have "price making" capabilities. The demand for workers in the secondary market is quite sensitive to wage changes, but it cannot be inferred that the demand schedules for labor in other types of markets are similarly downward-sloping.

There are also problems that arise on a theoretical level about the relationship between the demand for labor at the level of the firm and at the level of the industry. Since the firm's demand curve reflects the quantities that will be hired at various wage rates, given the possibility of substituting less expensive (or alternatively more productive) factors for

[8] This is consistent with the conclusion reached by Ziv Griliches, "Production Functions in Manufacturing: Some Preliminary Results," in Murray Brown, ed., *The Theory and Empirical Analysis of Production* (New York: Columbia University Press, 1967), pp. 275–322. See also Ernst Berndt, "Reconciling Alternative Estimates of the Elasticity of Substitution," *Review of Economics and Statistics* 58, 1 (February 1976): 59–68.

[9] The empirical findings of an elasticity of substitution between labor and capital that approximates 1 is often interpreted as supporting studies, which will be examined in Chapter 17, that find the relative income shares of labor and capital to be historically constant.

it, it seems reasonable at first glance to sum up the labor-demand curves of particular firms to arrive at a labor-demand curve for the market as a whole. However, there is a technical problem that is likely to arise in performing this aggregation.[10] The problem arises because the selling price of the product is likely to change as the output levels of individual firms vary, which makes it impossible to aggregate them. Thus, to represent a market-demand curve for labor, we must proceed either by assuming that the product price remains constant or, alternatively, that we are summing up individual firms' labor-demand curves on the assumption that they have taken into account any change in selling price that they are likely to encounter. This limits our capability for determining demand curves for labor on an industry basis. However, leaving aside this technical difficulty and aggregating the labor-demand curves of all firms employing a particular (i.e., homogeneous) type of labor will yield a market-demand curve for labor that is a decreasing function of the real wage rate. It is the interaction of this market-demand curve with the labor-supply curve that sets the wage of labor in markets in which employers as well as workers are price "takers."

Wage Determination in Price-Taking Markets

The labor-supply curve with which the market-demand curve interacts is the outcome of the labor-supply decisions of households. Given their wealth endowments, the prevailing rate of money wages, and the price level, each worker will choose to supply that number of hours of labor that will yield the most preferred combination of market and nonmarket activity. The supply curve of labor to the market as a whole can be obtained by adding up individual supply curves, as was shown in chapter 2.

Figure 6-5A thus depicts demand-and-supply curves for a labor market in which employers and employees are price takers. None of the participants has the capability of influencing the going wage rate, W, by altering either the amount of labor that is offered to the market or the amount of labor that is demanded. Each household takes the going rate as "given" and maximizes by making whatever allocation of time it considers appropriate. Each firm maximizes by employing labor until its MRP_l is equal to the wage rate, as in Figure 6-5B.

An important analytical conclusion emerges from this examination of the firm's employment decision. The firm can employ all the labor it wishes to hire at the going market wage rate. Its labor-supply curve is

---

[10]For a discussion of this point and its implication for the aggregate demand for labor, see Sidney Weintraub, *An Approach to the Theory of Income Distribution* (Philadelphia: Chilton Co., 1958), Chapter 1.

FIGURE 6-5 *Wage Determination in Price-Taking Markets*

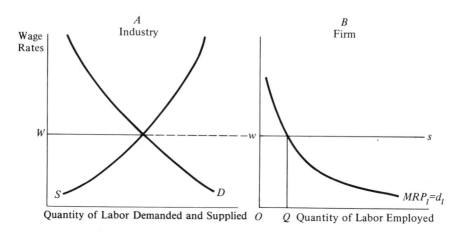

Quantity of Labor Demanded and Supplied O Q Quantity of Labor Employed

infinitely elastic at the going wage rate. It can employ labor along the supply curve *ws* in Figure 6-5B without encountering any upward pressure in the price it must pay as a result of its own demand for labor inputs.

Concluding Remarks

The conclusion that a firm that is a price taker in its labor-market encounters an infinitely elastic labor-supply curve means that, from the point of view of the firm, its labor supply is infinitely large. This observation suggests that the workers that comprise this supply are likely to have only the minimal skills that are characteristic of persons who are employed in the secondary labor markets of the economy. These workers are readily replaceable if they quit or if the firm lays them off because of a decline in demand. Furthermore, since their skill requirements are minimal, employers are unlikely to have an incentive to offer them job training or retain their services if the demand for their product declines. Labor services that are nonspecific can be performed by equally low-skilled replacements who are easily hired, if the demand for their product or service increases. The inference is that employment decisions are governed by different considerations when the labor supply curve is not infinitely elastic. The circumstances under which a firm's labor-supply schedule is *upward-sloping* and the impact that this has on its employment decisions are examined in Chapter 7.

Suggestions for Further Reading

Allan M. Cartter. *The Theory of Wages and Employment.* Homewood, Illinois: Irwin, 1959, Chapters 2–4.

Richard A. Lester. "Shortcomings of Marginal Analysis for Wage-Employment Problems." *American Economic Review* 36 (March 1946): 63–82.

Fritz Machlup. "Marginal Analysis and Empirical Research." *American Economic Review* 36 (September 1946): 519–554.

F. M. Scherer. *Industrial Market Structure and Economic Performance.* Chicago: Rand McNally, 1970, Chapter 3.

Roger N. Waud. "Man-hour Behavior in U.S. Manufacturing: A Neoclassical Interpretation." *Journal of Political Economy* 76 (May/June 1968).

Sidney Weintraub. *An Approach to the Theory of Income Distribution.* Philadelphia: Chilton Co., 1958, Chapter 1.

7 The Employment Decisions of "Price-Making" Firms

The preceeding chapter undertook to examine the employment decisions of firms that are "price takers" in their commodity and labor markets. Using the principle of diminishing marginal productivity, it was established that under these conditions the demand curve for labor for the firm and for the industry is downward sloping, i.e., there is a negative relationship between the wage rate and the volume of employment offered by price-taking industries and their constituent firms. The interaction of the market-demand curve that price takers generate for a particular kind of labor with the labor-supply curve that is generated through the work-leisure choices of household members sets the prevailing wage rate. Employing firms can hire whatever quantities of labor they conceive to be consistent with their goal of maximizing profits at that wage rate.

While there are some markets in which firms are price takers in both their commodity and labor markets, there are many markets in which firms have price-making power. Price-making power in the labor market occurs in its extreme form under conditions of monopsony, that is, where a single employer of labor provides all the available jobs in a given geographical locale. One-company towns, in which a single employer provides virtually the only opportunity for employment, are, however, largely a thing of the past. They have been eliminated by the mobility of modern workers and the greater tendency toward industrial diversification. But there are still some small communities in which several employers "cooperate" in matters relating to personnel policy. There are also some workers, among them nurses and schoolteachers, whose employment options are limited to the relatively few hospitals or school districts in an area. One concern of this chapter will therefore be to investigate the effect of a monopsony in the labor market.

While the monopsony case is interesting and has some real-world relevance, contemporary interest in price-making markets centers principally on oligopolistic firms in large-scale manufacturing industries. Their short-run production functions are fundamentally different from those encountered by price-taking firms because they are characterized by "fixed coefficients." Furthermore, given their large productive capacity, oligopolistic firms are typically such large employers of labor in their local markets that they confront an upward-sloping labor-supply curve rather than the infinitely elastic curve of the small employer. Oligopolists thus make employment decisions that are different from those of a price taker, and their employees are, in effect, attached to different labor markets from those in which the employees of price-taking firms find work. After its inquiry into the nature and effect of monopsony this chapter will examine the employment decisions of oligopolists and how they are related to oligopoly wage and price policy.

The Employment Decision under Monopsony

One of the important conclusions of Chapter 6 was that in a labor market in which firms are price takers, each has the opportunity to hire as many units of equally efficient labor as it finds profitable at the competitively established wage rate. That is, its labor-supply curve is infinitely elastic at the going wage rate. In practice, however, it far more likely that an individual firm's labor-supply curve will reflect the shape and elasticity of the market supply curve.[1] The presence of "monopsony" or buyer's monopoly in hiring labor is one case in which a firm's short-run labor-supply curve will be upward-sloping rather than infinitely elastic. This is illustrated in Figure 7-1. Inputs of labor are measured along the horizontal axis, and the related money values are measured on the vertical axis.

Since the firm is assumed to be a price taker in its commodity market, even though it is a monopsonist in its labor market, its demand curve for labor is derived from its marginal-revenue product curve and is identified as $D_1 = MRP_1$. Unlike his "price taking" counterpart, a monopsonistic buyer of labor does not have an infinitely elastic labor-supply curve like $AC_1 = MC_1$. His labor-supply curve slopes upward; in order to attract additional workers, he must offer higher wages. The average cost of labor, AC_2, will therefore be rising, and the marginal cost, MC_2, rises more rapidly.[2] The effect of an upward-sloping

---

[1] It will be recalled from Chapter 2 that the market labor-supply curve is upward-sloping in response to the preferences of labor-force participants for market and nonmarket activities.

[2] See Joan Robinson, *The Economics of Imperfect Competition* (London: Macmillan and Company, Ltd., 1934), Chapter 26.

FIGURE 7-1   *The Employment Decision of a Monopsonist Compared with That of a Price-Taking Employer*

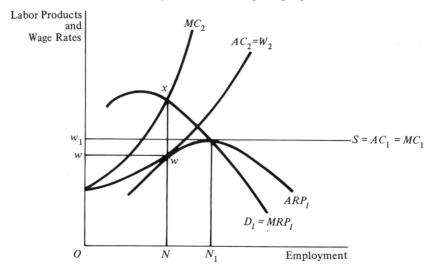

labor-supply curve is that it causes a firm to employ a smaller quantity of labor than it would if it were a price taker, and pay a wage that is less than labor's marginal-revenue product.[3]

Referring to Figure 7-1, one can see that an employer hiring at a "price taker's" wage of w_1 will hire ON_1 units of labor. But a monopsonistic employer whose upward-sloping supply curve is like MC_2 will hire only ON workers and pay a wage of Nw, which is equivalent to labor's average-revenue product. As can be seen from Figure 7-1, the firm imposes "monopsonistic exploitation." The extent of this exploitation is wx, i.e., it is equal to Nx, the value of the marginal product of ON workers, minus Nw, the wage it is paying.

As has already been observed, there are few examples of monopsony in today's labor markets because "one-company towns" are largely a thing of the past. Nevertheless there are some workers who do confront conditions that approximate monopsony. Until the recent change in the rules governing contractual arrangements between ballplayers and their teams, a player in organized baseball became subject to monopsonistic exploitation as soon as he signed his first contract.[4] This situation has been remedied. But there are still some examples of monopsony in the labor market. The professional attachment of schoolteachers, coupled

[3] Robinson, *op. cit.*, p. 250.

[4] Simon Rottenberg, "The Baseball Player's Labor Market," *Journal of Political Economy* (June 1956).

with their geographic preferences, causes their salaries to be negotiated under conditions that approximate monopsony. A case study of their employment experiences is examined as *Economic Theory in Action* 7:1.

ECONOMIC THEORY IN ACTION 7:1

Monopsony in the Market for Public-School Teachers

The availability of alternative-employment opportunities for public-school teachers is a function of the number of districts in a local area. Given the supply of newly qualified persons who can be attracted to a region, the competition among districts causes each to be confronted with an upward-sloping labor-supply curve. The expectation is that the larger the number of comparable districts in a growing public-school system, the higher the entry wage that must be paid to attract additional teachers.

This hypothesis was tested empirically on the basis of cross-sectional data for 136 school districts for the period 1966–67.[5] The study had the intention of explaining statistically the behavior of the district's contractual salary for the beginning teacher. The presumption was that beginning salaries would depend chiefly on the number of school districts in the county. The expectation was that variations in beginning salaries would be positively related to percentage variations in the number of districts. Other variables that were expected to affect beginning salaries are per capita income, the percentage of school revenues derived from local sources, and the district's property-tax rate. These were presumed to reflect the ability and willingness of the district to pay salaries.

The 136 districts were subdivided into three subsamples, in which sixty-nine districts had enrollments of 25,000 to 50,000, forty-three districts had enrollments of 50,000 to 100,000, and twenty-four districts had enrollments greater than 100,000. For districts with fewer than 100,000 students, the degree of competition in the labor market was shown to be an important determinant of the entry-level salary. Teachers' salaries varied inversely with the number of bargaining units in the relevant labor market. The implication is that consolidation of school districts would increase the bargaining power of administrators. Conversely, decentralization of school districts would increase the number of bargaining units and strengthen the bargaining position of teachers.

Is it possible for workers to escape a monopsonistic employer's power over the wage rate? Clearly, the more closely workers are "locked

[5]John H. Landon and Robert N. Baird, "Monopsony in the Market for Public School Teachers," *American Economic Review* (December 1971): 996–971.

into" an area or tied to an occupation, the greater the employer's power. Unionization or the establishment of a minimum wage may provide a counterforce. If, for example, a union can negotiate a wage of $\bar{w}$ as in Figure 7-2, the labor-supply curve, S, becomes horizontal at the bargained wage. The intersection of S with the demand curve at x results in employment, $O\bar{N}$, which is larger than ON at wage w. Thus, it may be possible to increase *both* the wage rate and the level of employment in a monopsonistic situation. There is, however, a limit. In Figure 7-2, the wage cannot be raised above $\bar{w}$ without decreasing employment. If the wage were raised as high as w^*, employment would be no greater than the previous monopsonistic level, ON.

FIGURE 7-2   *The Effect of a Union on Monopsony Wages and Employment*

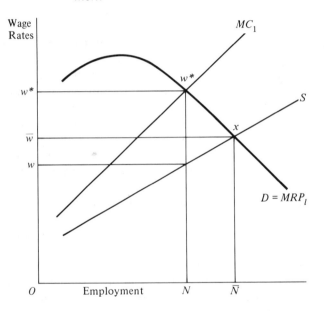

Other Reasons for Individual-Firm Upward-Sloping Labor-Supply Curves

Labor Availability in the Local Market

Many firms are sufficiently large employers of labor in their local labor markets to exert a significant influence over the level of wages at which they hire their personnel. They then face an upward-sloping labor-supply curve even though they are not monopsonists. If, as in

Figure 7-3, the wage rate prevailing is (say) *ow*, at which there remains
a pool of unemployed workers from which a firm can continue to hire, it
will be possible to expand employment from *OX* to *OY* as demand
increases from *DD* to *D'D'* without the necessity of raising the rate.
Once the reservoir of unemployed persons approaches exhaustion, the
firm will find it necessary to offer a higher wage than *ow* to attract
workers from competing employers.[6] Thus the firm will be confronted
with a labor-supply curve whose configuration is like *ww' S*, the "kink"
at *w'* reflecting the necessity for paying higher wage rates to attract additional workers if demand continues to increase to *D''D''*.

FIGURE 7-3   *The Upward-Sloping Labor-Supply Curve of an Oligopolist*

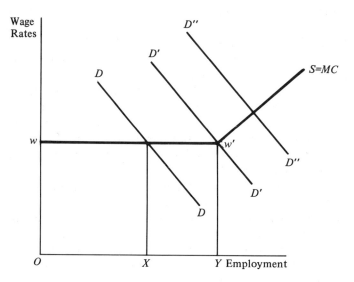

The elasticity of the supply curve, i.e., the upward change of the
wage rate required to attract a given increase in the firm's supply of
labor, depends, of course, on the extent to which the other firms similarly
raise their wages in order to retain or increase the number of workers in
their employ. If the wages that other firms have to pay in the face of a
labor shortage are not increased, the upward slope of the labor-supply
curves of all employers will be less sharp than it would be if firms respond to one another's increased wage offers by duplicating (or exceeding) them. However, large employers of labor are never able to hire
workers along an infinitely elastic labor-supply curve, as is the case when

[6]Lloyd G. Reynolds, "The Supply of Labor to the Firm," *Quarterly Journal of
Economics* 60 (May 1946).

price-taking firms in product markets confront a labor market in which their demands for workers have no effect on the wage rate. The oligopolistic firms that dominate in much of the large-scale manufacturing segment of the economy are very large employers of labor and are confronted with upward-sloping labor-supply curves. This upward slope of their labor-supply curves is among the reasons why their employment decisions differ from those of a price-taking firm. There are, however, other reasons why labor markets function differently in the presence of oligopoly from the way they do when markets are dominated by price-taking firms. Some other important factors are examined next.

The Labor-Market Behavior of Oligopolists

While the upward slope of their labor-supply curve distinguishes the labor-market behavior of an oligopolistic firm, this is not the only contributing factor. The fact that oligopolistic firms have fundamentally different cost-of-production experiences than those that characterize price-taking firms is also important. In addition, oligopolistic firms have price-making power in their commodity markets. These characteristics underlie their employment decisions and are reflected in their behavior in the labor market. Thus it is necessary to have some degree of understanding about the cost-of-production experiences of price-making firms and the nature of their pricing policy as a basis for understanding their employment decisions.

A detailed investigation of oligopoly is beyond the scope of this book, particularly because interpretation of some of the findings that have been investigated extensively in the literature dealing with industrial organization are still a matter of controversy. This literature is, nevertheless, a promising basis for making inferences about the functioning of labor markets in the presence of oligopoly that are more realistic than those that are derived from conventional price theory. It is, however, appropriate to note that the theory of the employment decisions of price-making firms is still in embryonic form.[7]

The Cost Experience of Oligopolists Contrasted with That of Price Takers

Studies in the field of industrial organization suggest that a fruitful way of examining the differences in the employment decisions of

---

[7]Important insights into the labor-market behavior of oligopolies have been derived from studies undertaken by specialists in the fields of organization theory and business finance. See in particular the works of Frederick M. Scherer, *Industrial Market Structure and Economic Performance* (Chicago: Rand McNally, 1970), and Alfred Eichner, *The Megacorp and Oligopoly* (Cambridge: Cambridge University Press, 1976).

"price-making" and "price-taking" markets is to consider the unique characteristics of their representative firms. The representative "price-taking" firm is a sole proprietorship or partnership operating a single plant that produces a small portion of a fairly standardized product in a market served by a large number of other producers, each of whom has a productive capacity that is small relative to the industry's total output. Confronted with a given selling price for its product, each "price taker" determines the profit-maximizing (loss-minimizing) output by equating marginal cost to marginal revenue, as was seen in Chapter 6. In the short run they accomplish changes in output by varying their inputs of labor and raw materials. Their capital-labor ratio thus changes as output varies. Depending on the quantity of output they decide to produce in order to maximize their profits, firms will hire labor at the market wage rate until $w = MRP_l$. Beyond some point, output will increase at a decreasing rate so that average variable and average total costs rise. This causes price-taking firms to be characterized by cost curves which have a U-shaped appearance. U-shaped average total cost curves necessarily accompany the experience of diminishing average (and marginal) productivity that occurs as additional variable inputs are added to fixed inputs to increase output. As was also seen in Chapter 6, the experience of diminishing returns to labor as a variable input also accounts for the downward-sloping marginal-revenue-product curve of labor that underlies the downward-sloping labor-demand curve that is experienced by price-taking firms.

The distinguishing characteristics of the representative "price making" firm are very different from those of a "price taker." Firms that have price-making capabilities characteristically are corporate organizations, i.e., the stockholders constitute the ownership interest, but the management function, which encompasses decisions about output, employment, pricing, investment, and future growth, is performed by a professionally trained executive group. Price-making firms also have productive capacities that are large enough, relative to the demand for the product, to limit the number of competing sellers to a few large firms. Their market is therefore "oligopolistic" and "concentrated." The degree of concentration of power is most commonly measured in terms of a "concentration ratio," which expresses the percentage of total sales made by the leading four firms.[8]

The large oligopolistic firm has a fundamentally different short-run cost experience from that of a price-taking firm because it operates

---

[8] Concentration ratios are also published in the leading eight, twenty, and fifty firms among U.S. manufacturing industries. See U.S. Bureau of the Census, Annual Survey of Manufacturers, Concentration Ratios by Industry.

numerous plants, each of which is characterized by fixed technical coefficients per unit of output.[9] These fixed technical coefficients derive partly from engineering standards and partly from work rules. Engineering standards established for combining inputs prescribe specific proportions between factors, e.g., a certain number of workers to be used in conjunction with equipment or machinery. Once established, these standards are readily applied by production managers, even if the nature of the technology being used actually does permit variations in factor proportions. Typically these standards become part of the work rules observed by workers in a plant and are incorporated into collective-bargaining agreements. Engineering requirements therefore tend to make the labor requirement per unit of output a "quasi-fixed" factor in the short run.

The presence of labor as a quasi-fixed factor of production to the firm in the short run has several important implications. One is that the demand curve for labor will no longer be downward-sloping. It will be recalled from Chapter 6 that a downward-sloping demand curve for labor reflects the diminution in the marginal productivity of labor that takes place as additional labor inputs are combined with a given amount of capital. It is only when a firm's production function lends itself to altering the "mix" of labor and capital that it is possible to identify the marginal product of labor that underlies the downward-sloping demand curve. Furthermore, it is only when the "mix" of labor and capital can be varied that the firm experiences a U-shaped cost-of-production curve.

Since its production coefficients are fixed in the short run (i.e., the labor-capital "mix" cannot be altered), the typical oligopolistic firm makes its adjustments to changes in demand partly by management of its inventories and partly by starting up or closing down one or more of its many plants or plant segments to alter its rate of production. An oligopolistic firm, in order to maintain its share of the market, must have sufficient productive capacity in reserve to meet unexpected demands for its product. Thus, it typically produces below 100 percent of its engineer-rated capacity. Empirical evidence confirms that oligopolistic firms typically operate at levels that are between sixty-five percent and ninety-five percent of engineer-rated capacity and that average variable and marginal costs are constant over this range of output.[10] Unlike

[9] Alfred S. Eichner, *The Megacorp and Oligopoly* (Cambridge: Cambridge University Press, 1976), Chapter 2.

[10] See J. Johnstone, *Statistical Cost Analysis* (New York: McGraw-Hill, 1960), pp. 136–48, 168; also Alan A. Walters, "Production and Cost, an Econometric Survey," *Econometrica* 31: 1–66; Bela Gold, "New Perspectives on Cost Theory and Empirical Findings," *Journal of Industrial Economics* 14: 164–89; L. S. Zudak, "Labor Demand and Multiproduct Cost in Semi-Continuous and Multiprocess Facilities," *Journal of Industrial Economics* 19: 267–290.

price-taking firms, oligopolistic firms are typically able to vary their output over a considerable range while experiencing constant average variable costs.

Labor as a Quasi-Fixed Factor in an "Internal" Market

A further factor contributes toward fixed coefficients of production in the short run, especially in large firms. Labor tends to be a "quasi-fixed" factor of production because of the "employment" costs a firm incurs in hiring its labor inputs.[11] There are expenditures for recruiting, interviewing, processing payrolls, and for supplements such as unemployment compensation. These costs are closely related to the number of new workers a firm hires. Once these costs have been incurred, a firm will prefer not to lose the workers on whom they have been expended as a result of either quits or layoffs.

In addition to hiring costs a firm incurs training expenses. As was noted in the discussion of "on-the-job training" in Chapter 5, rational behavior by a firm suggests that it devote its expenditures for training chiefly to *specific* training. Specific training does not improve the alternative product of a worker in other employments. It thus reduces the likelihood that a trained worker will quit to seek other employment.

Many firms attempt to reinforce this relationship by adopting pension and profit-sharing plans and paying wage premiums to induce longer employment tenure. They may also promote only or chiefly from within the firm, so that the large firm becomes an "internal" market for its employees.[12] Its employees typically have little contact with the external labor market as they progress up the job ladder of a firm. It is not unusual for firms to adopt hiring policies that preclude workers who do not possess characteristics likely to lead to long-term employment records. The same logic that governs a firm's behavior in hiring guides them in trying to avoid quits and layoffs among workers on whom hiring and training costs have been expended. A firm will be reluctant to respond to a decline in the demand for its product (or an increase in wages) by laying off workers.

The elasticity of the demand for labor is thus likely to be

---

[11] Employment costs are particularly emphasized by Walter Oi in "Labor as a Quasi-Fixed Factor," *Journal of Political Economy* (December 1962): 538–555.

[12] It has been suggested that reliance on internal promotion and the association of wages with jobs rather than with individuals is an efficiency device from the standpoint of the firm. The correspondence between wages and marginal productivity at ports of entry is likely to be imperfect, but over time, an improved correspondence can be expected between wages and job assignments in the internal-labor-market hierarchy. Oliver E. Williamson, Michael L. Wachter, and Jeffrey E. Harris, "Understanding the Employment Relation: The Analyses of Idiosyncratic Exchange," *Bell Journal of Economics* 6, 1 (Spring 1975).

significantly less the greater the employment costs that are associated with its hire. This reenforces the conclusion reached earlier, in connection with on-the-job training, that workers with more specific training are less likely to experience layoffs than are those with general training. A study by Jacob Mincer provides empirical support for the hypothesis that employers have greater incentive to retain workers with specific training and that the latter have an incentive to remain with the firms that trained them.[13] Another study of employer layoff behavior, which included the industry-concentration ratio among the variables governing layoffs of workers in whom firm-specific investments had been made, established that layoff rates are negatively correlated with the industry-concentration ratio.[14] The implication is that concentrated industries do not adjust their work forces in strict proportion to output changes over short periods. Overhead personnel, in particular, are likely to be retained in order to avoid the costs of rehiring and retraining when business conditions improve.[15] These findings are consistent with the conclusion that workers who become associated with large firms that, in effect, operate internal labor markets have more stable employment experience than those whose high rate of turnover brings them into frequent contact with the external labor market.

Concentration and Labor Earnings

There are a number of reasons for the inference that firms having market power in their commodity markets pay higher wages than do firms that are price takers. One basis for this inference is that firms with high profit might choose to use part of their profits to pay higher wages; there is thus an element of "monopoly rent" in the wage payments they make.

Another basis for the inference that oligopolists pay high wages is that industries with high profits, whether owing to market power in their commodity markets or other causes, are more likely to become unionized. High wages might then be the result either of successful bargaining by the union or of the "threat effect," to which management reacts by paying higher wages.[16]

It is also possible that concentration and unionization are related to industry-labor-force variables that affect earnings. Specifically, labor earnings are likely to be larger if high percentages of the labor force are

[13] Jacob Mincer, "On the Job Training: Costs, Returns, and Implications," *Journal of Political Economy* 70 (Supplement, October 1962): 50–79.

[14] However, strong support has not established the related hypothesis that concentrated industries accept more disguised unemployment during a recession than do price-taking firms. See F. M. Scherer, *op. cit.,* pp. 309–314.

[15] Donald O. Parsons, "Specific Human Capital: An Application to Quit Rates and Layoff Rates," *Journal of Political Economy*.

[16] The role of the threat effect on the wage structure is examined in Chapter 9.

(a) male, (b) skilled, (c) white, and (d) located in an urban labor market in a high-wage region. Even if earnings are higher in concentrated or heavily unionized industries, high wages do not reflect monopoly rents if they can be wholly accounted for by the personal attributes of their recipients.

The hypothesis that concentrated industries pay more for the services of their workers than these might earn in alternative employment is difficult to test because many of the other variables that bear on the determination of wages are correlated with industry structure. In particular, concentration and unionization are closely related, and their separate effects must be "unscrambled." One well-known study, which used a sample of nineteen industry groups established that there was a relationship between the percentage of workers employed in manufacturing establishments operating under collective-bargaining agreements and the weighted average-concentration ratios of the sample.[17] It is possible, in the light of this finding, that the relationship between wage increases and concentration is spurious, and that union power (which is also associated with concentration) is the principal cause of the higher earnings of workers in concentrated industries.[18] In order to identify the separate effects of concentration on wage policy, it is relevant to test the hypothesis that firms with market power are willing to share their monetary gains with labor instead of retaining them all in the form of higher profits. The methodology and results of such a study are reported as *Economics in Action 7:2*.

ECONOMICS IN ACTION 7:2

Concentration and Labor Earnings

The chief hypothesis under investigation is whether concentrated industries pay higher annual rates for labor attached to particular occupations. The objective is to identify the effect of concentration on earnings as distinct from unionization.[19] The second hypothesis seeks to establish whether the high earnings of workers in concentrated industries can be accounted for by the "quality" characteristics of the labor employed.

Weiss' study proceeded by using the wage and salary income reported in 1959 by individuals in the 1/1000 sample of the 1960 census. Holding constant industry characteristics (e.g., unionization, changes in employment levels, plant size, durability of product, and skill requirements),

[17] William G. Bowen, *Wage Behavior in the Postwar Period* (Princeton: Princeton University Industrial Relations Section, 1960), p. 70.

[18] This hypothesis is examined further in Chapter 8.

[19] Leonard Weiss, "Concentration and Labor Earnings," *American Economic Review* (March 1966): 96–117.

it was found that total annual earnings are positively and significantly related to concentration. One specific finding relates to male semiskilled workers. They were found to earn 16 percent more than similar workers employed by price-taking industries when unionization was weak but only 11 percent more when unionization was strong. This representative finding suggests that when other variables are disregarded, the high wages observable in concentrated industries are chiefly attributable to concentration rather than to unionization.

The second part of the study introduced a group of additional variables that related to the personal characteristics of individuals in the sample. These included weeks worked since 1959, hours worked per week, age, education, family size, race, and region of the country. When these characteristics were taken into account, in roughly half of the occupations the net effect of concentration turned out to be negative. The inference is that the high profits associated with concentration are shared with labor, but that labor's high earnings are chiefly accounted for by the personal characteristics of the labor employed. Concentration thus appears to be correlated with some of the personal-characteristic variables, which consequently reduces the explanatory power of the concentration variable with respect to labor earning.

Oligopoly and Wage-Cost Markup Pricing

The relationship between wage policy and price policy in oligopolistic markets is another subject of controversy. Oligopoly price policy reflects the interdependence of the product-demand curves of competing sellers. Each firm has a large enough productive capacity to have an impact on the industry, and unileratal price changing invites retaliation, which can lead to a price war. A firm that cuts its price in the hope of increasing its sales will find its competitors adopting the same policy in order to maintain their share of the market. The pricing decision is thus typically to "follow" the pricing decision of the largest producer who assumes the role of the ''price leader''; price leadership is essential to joint profit maximization.[20] There appears to be a consensus that the price leader will set his commodity price by adding a "markup" to his wage cost. Thus, his price per unit is $p = w + k$ where w is the wage cost and k is the "markup," to cover other production costs (including

---

[20] R. A. Gordon, *Business Leadership in a Large Corporation* (Washington: Brookings Institution, 1945), p. 327. The relevance of the profit-maximization assumption to oligopoly pricing is a highly controversial issue. The view that this assumption is not appropriate to oligopoly situations is expressed by Herbert Simon, "A Behavioral Model of Rational Choice," *Quarterly Journal of Economics* 39: 99–118. See also Richard M. Cyert and James G. March, *A Behavioral Theory of the Firm* (Englewood Cliffs, N.J.: Prentice Hall, 1963); R. J. Manson and Anthony Downs, "A Theory of Large Managerial Firms," *Journal of Political Economy* 73: 221–236; and Alfred Eichner, *op. cit.*

depreciation) and profit.[21] Oligopoly prices tend to remain constant for long periods of time as firms follow the announced price of the "leader."

This type of pricing policy is very significant with respect to the labor-market decisions of oligopolistic firms. Since price stability in the commodity market is essential to long-run oligopoly goals—especially the goal of maximizing long-run growth—oligopolistic firms have a particular interest in establishing wage rates that remain stable for considerable periods of time. Their requirement for stable wages is thus quite compatible with the objective that unions have to use collective bargaining to remove the wage rate from the authority of the market-place insofar as possible. Union goals to insulate wage rates against declining demand are thus quite compatible with the oligopolist's goal of keeping product prices rigid.[22] This rigidity is facilitated by the existence of multiyear labor contracts. It is relevant to note in this connection that the first multiyear contract was a *corporate* innovation initially offered in conjunction with a productivity wage increase. General Motors offered the auto workers a wage increase tied to productivity increases in order to secure a five-year contract guaranteeing not only labor peace, but also an agreed-upon rate of increase in wages. The principle of the productivity wage increase is now broadly accepted in manufacturing industries, although the matter of *how much* productivity has advanced in the recent period is an area of controversy. This issue is critical for, as will be examined in greater detail in Chapter 9, multiyear wage contracts tend to be negotiated in "patterns," which many observers associate with inflationary pressures in the economy.

Concluding Remarks

The introduction of the upward-sloping labor-supply curve at the level of the individual firm is a major step in the direction of extending the "price-taking" model of Chapter 6 to conditions in price-making markets. Equally important, however, is the insight into the labor-market behavior of price-making firms that derives from the recognition that they operate large plants considerably below their engineer-rated capacity and are thus able to expand output without experiencing increases in

---

[21] Among the large number of writers who have adopted this formulation we particularly note M. Fleming, *Introduction to Economic Analysis* (London: Allen & Unwin, 1969), pp. 91–95; Sidney Weintraub, *Price Theory* (New York: Pitman, 1949); Paul Davidson, *Money and the Real World* (New York: John Wiley, 1972), Chapter 3; Douglas Vickers, *Financial Markets in the Capitalist Process* (Philadelphia, Pa.: University of Pennsylvania Press, 1978), pp. 29–33; Donald J. Harris, "The Price Policy of Firms, the Level of Employment and the Distribution of Income in the Short Run," *Australian Economic Papers* 13 (1974); and Alfred S. Eichner, "A Theory of the Determination of the Markup under Oligopoly," *Economic Journal* 83 (December 1973).

[22] The relationship between concentration and the prevalence of trade unions is examined in Chapter 8, which follows.

their average variable costs. The fixed production coefficients imposed by engineering standards have become reflected in management practices and the rules of the work place, which cause labor inputs to be treated as "quasi-fixed" rather than as variable factors. The labor-demand curves of firms that are price makers in their commodity markets therefore do not exhibit the downward slope that characterizes the labor-demand curve of price-taking firms.

The trend toward the development of an internal labor market has been intensified by the enormous rise in research and development that has taken place. This has created a new class of professional and technical workers and expanded automation processes, which facilitate the upgrading of skilled workers. Once hired at an entry-level job, a worker moves within a labor market that is internal to the firm employing and training him. Even if they are laid off, most workers are at least somewhat isolated from the external market, for the usual practice is to recall them back to work, usually at the same wage rate as was earned before the layoff. One might say that the *proletariat* is being replaced by a *salariat*. The demand-and-supply forces that operate in the external market are, therefore, less relevant for explaining prevailing wages, except in entry-level jobs, than are the forces operating in the internal markets of specific companies. The bargaining power of unions is among these forces. The chapter that follows examines how union power affects wage-rate determination and the employment decision.

Suggestions for Further Reading

Alfred S. Eichner. *The Megacorp and Oligopoly*. Cambridge: Cambridge University Press, 1976, Chapters 1–3.

Bela Gold. "New Perspectives on Cost Theory and Empirical Findings." *Journal of Industrial Economics* 14: 164–189.

J. H. Landon and Robert N. Baird. "Monopsony in the Market for Public School Teachers." *American Economic Review* (December 1971): 966–71.

Jacob Mincer. "On the Job Training: Costs, Returns, and Some Implications." *Journal of Political Economy* 70 (Supplement, October 1972).

Walter Oi. "Labor as a Quasi-Fixed Factor." *Journal of Political Economy* (December 1972).

Joan Robinson. *The Economics of Imperfect Competition*. London: MacMillan and Company Ltd., 1934, Chapter 26.

Simon Rottenberg. "The Baseballer's Labor Market." *Journal of Political Economy* (June 1956).

Leonard Weiss. "Concentration and Labor Earnings." *American Economic Review* (March 1966): 96–117.

8 *The Impact of Bargaining Power on Wages and Employment Decisions*

It has thus far been assumed that employees interact with their employers as individuals on a one-to-one basis. In fact, however, it is typical in approximately one-quarter of American labor markets for the terms and conditions of employment to be the outcome of interactions between employers and trade unions. In the United States economy, the labor union is, in a basic sense, an agent for the individual worker and his household. In contrast with the greater involvement of the labor movements of other countries in political activity, unions in the American economy are chiefly concerned with issues relating directly to job activity—wages, hours, benefits, and working conditions in the plant. Unionization is thus an alternative to competition among workers. The chief objective of "market" or "collective bargaining" unionism is to insulate labors' wage rates from the vagaries of the marketplace.[1]

This objective raises several interesting questions. Specifically, why is the extent of unionization only about one-fourth of the labor force? In which industries and regions have unions met with success, and what reasons can be offered for the distribution of unionism?

On a somewhat different level of inquiry from the factual one implicit in the foregoing questions, it is also relevant to ask what precisely is the nature of a union as an institution in the American economy. Does it, so to speak, have a "life of its own" with organization interests and requirements that may differ from the interests and

---

[1] It is beyond the scope of this book to examine the evolution of unionism in this country from its early days as a social movement, guided by ideological precepts, into market or collective-bargaining unionism, which is guided by economic precepts. For a classic study of the history of unionism in America, see John R. Commons, *History of the Labor Movement in the United States*, 4 vols., (New York: Macmillan Company, 1918), and Selig Perlman, *A History of Trade Unionism in the United States* (New York: Macmillan Company, 1937).

objectives of its members? There is no consensus about the answer to this highly controversial question. On the one hand, there is the institutionalist view that unions have altered the basic nature of the labor market to such a degree that economic analysis is no longer useful or relevant in explaining the wage-determining process.[2] According to this interpretation, wages are set by institutional forces and are properly incorporated into economic models as exogenous constants. The prevailing wage rate cannot be explained as the outcome of an endogenous process taking place within an economic model.

There is, on the other hand, the alternate view that market forces function through the institution of collective bargaining in essentially the same way as in nonunion labor markets. This view holds that, normally, union impact on wage rates is not large. The alternative goals that they might pursue can be incorporated into economic models to demonstrate that wage determination is amenable to economic analysis even in the presence of trade unions.[3] The essence of this argument, which reflects the position of mainstream thinkers, is that economic analysis is applicable to examining the behavior of labor organizations and that it yields better predictions about the functioning of labor markets than an institutionally oriented approach does. This chapter examines both views, beginning with the neoclassical position that union behavior is amenable to economic analysis and that wage rates are explainable in terms of economic models.

The Extent and Distribution of Unionism

Since the union serves as the employees' representative in bargaining with employers and safeguards his day-to-day interests on the job, one would expect most workers to become union members. But this has, in fact, not happened, as is evident in Figure 8-1. Approximately one-quarter of the total labor force is presently unionized. In percentage terms, unions were at their peak membership during the mid-1940s and again in the mid-1950s. Over a third of nonagricultural employees and about one-quarter of the total labor force were union members in the mid-1940s. The 1950s was a period of declining union membership, partly because of the shift of the work force into white-collar occupations and into the service industries. Typically, workers in the service industries and white-collar jobs are not attracted into unions. This is partly because they are generally better-educated than manual workers,

---

[2] See, for example, Arthur M. Ross, *Trade Union Wage Policy* (Berkeley: University of California Press, 1965), esp. pp. 1–8, 11–16.

[3] John T. Dunlop, *Wage Determination under Trade Unions* (New York: Augustus M. Kelley, 1950).

FIGURE 8-1   *Union Membership as a Percent of Total Labor Force and of Employees in Nonagricultural Establishments, 1930–74*

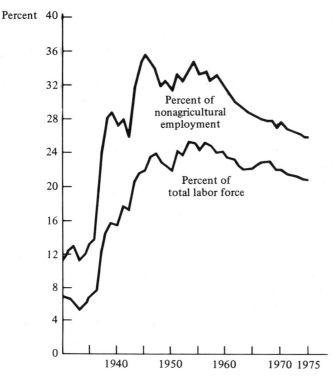

SOURCE: *Directory of National Unions and Employee Associations* (1975).

and also because white collar workers more readily identify with management in terms of the jobs they aspire to achieve.

In absolute numbers, union membership reached a peak of 17.9 million members in 1966. The expansion of manufacturing employment during the Vietnam War years and the organization of government employees facilitated the increase in union membership so that it exceeded the 15 million-member mark set in the mid-1940s and the peak of 17.5 million members that was reached in 1956.

Looked at in terms of membership by industry group, approximately 45 percent of union members are employed in the manufacturing sector, 45 percent in nonmanufacturing, and 9 percent in government.[4] However, the distribution is quite unequal within those sectors; four basic industry groups, namely, metals (including steel-fabricated metals,

[4]Bulletin 1596, U.S. Bureau of Labor Statistics, p. 62.

machinery, and electrical equipment), transportation equipment (i.e., automobiles and aircraft), construction, and transportation represent about half of all union members.

In geographic terms, the pattern of unionization is similarly disparate. About one-half of all union membership is concentrated in the five states of New York, California, Pennsylvania, Illinois, and Ohio, which also lead in terms of total population. The extent of organization is least in North Carolina, South Carolina, South Dakota, Florida, and Mississippi.[5] Union weakness in the South is not, however, uniformly distributed; unionization is weak in the textile, clothing, lumber, and furniture industries, but in the automobile and steel industries, southern plants are as well organized as those located elsewhere. Similarly, longshore workers in southern ports are typically organized, and many construction workers are union members.

The experience of individual unions is, as might be expected, often quite different from that of the union movement as a whole. For example, unions in railroading, textiles, marine transport, and shoe-making have lost members over the last ten decades, while unions in government service, printing, construction, retail trade, and trucking have gained. This is largely the result of changing industrial patterns. But it is also a matter of union leadership and the extent of union jurisdiction over industrial groups. Figure 8-2 reflects the membership experiences since 1950 of the six largest unions in the private sector and that of AFSCME, the American Federation of State, County and Municipal

FIGURE 8-2   *Membership of Seven Largest Unions, 1951-1976.*

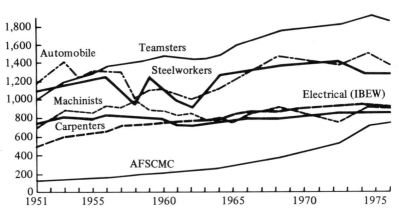

SOURCE: *Directory of National Unions and Employee Associations* (1976).

[5] Bulletin 1596, *op. cit.*

Employees, which is the largest union in the public sector. The three largest unions, the Brotherhood of Teamsters, the United Steelworkers, and the United Automobile Workers, have over a million members each. These three represent only 2 percent of the total number of unions, but account for about 20 percent of union membership. The top ten unions represent 45 percent of the total union membership but constitute only 6 percent of the number of national unions. The union scene is thus one of concentration, which parallels the concentration that characterizes product markets.

Economic Models of Trade-Union Behavior

Some Problems of Model Building

Formal models of the wage-employment bargaining in which unions participate are necessarily predicated on a wide range of possible assumptions. This is partly because employers and unions typically have differing perceptions about future market conditions that become reflected in the wage-employment stance they adopt. For example, unions may expect market conditions to improve sufficiently to provide a basis for their wage demands, while employers may be pessimistic in their evaluations of the future market. Consequently, the predictions of the model are likely to be quite imprecise with respect to particular situations.

An even more basic reason why models of union behavior in the bargaining process are likely to be imprecise is that rank-and-file members and union leaders may differ in their conception of union goals. This makes it difficult to identify the proper assumptions on which to model trade-union behavior. Individual members are particularly interested in wage rates, job security, working conditions, and fringe benefits. Union leaders, on the other hand, may be concerned chiefly with expanding the membership of an internally stable organization. This goal is typically part of the personal objective of a leader to be reelected by his membership.

Needless to say, incumbents are not always protected against replacement. There are union leaders who have retained leadership for long periods of time, notably George Meany and Walter Reuther. But David MacDonald and Philip Carey lost support in the national elections held by the United Steelworkers and International Union of Electrical Workers. Union leaders are confronted with the possibility of replacement when they negotiate agreements with management that the membership votes down. This sharing of power between union members and their leadership makes it difficult to construct a formal model of union behavior paralleling the model of the profit-maximizing firm.

However, in spite of the difficulties that are posed in depicting conflicting goals of union behavior within the confines of a formal model, many models have been constructed in the hope of providing insight into the nature of the wage-employment bargain.

Since our objective is to isolate the impact of the union on wages and employment, we begin with the initial simplifying assumption that the demand side of the market is characterized by large numbers of competitive employers who are without influence in setting the terms of employment. This inquiry is relevant because several highly successful and powerful unions, among them the United Mine Workers, the Teamsters, and the Building Trades Union, operate in industries that are highly competitive, or would be so in the absence of unions and government regulations prohibiting price competition. Later, we shall examine the alternative case of "bilateral monopoly," in which a strong labor union negotiates with an employer who also has substantial power.

Union Impact on a Competitive Labor Market

Figure 8-3 is drawn on the assumption that an individual employer, whose demand curve for labor is $MRP_l = d_l$, is confronted with a wage rate, OW, established in a competitive labor market through the interaction of demand-and-supply forces. The firm can employ all the labor it wishes at this competitive wage rate; i.e., its labor-supply curve is *ws*, which is perfectly elastic at the going wage rate of Ow. It will hire ON workers from the total supply being offered in the market.

Suppose now that the workers in this market organize a union that acts on their behalf to establish the wage rate (and other conditions of employment). How will the presence of a union alter the relationships depicted in Figure 8-3? Assume to begin with that the union negotiates a

FIGURE 8-3   *Union Impact on a Competitive Labor Market*

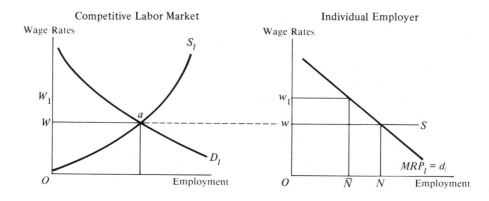

wage rate of OW, which is the same rate previously established in the market. The supply curve of labor to the firm is then perfectly elastic at the bargained rate, and the market-supply curve of labor is WaS_l. Given its demand curve for labor, the individual firm will continue to hire ON workers as before.

The situation will, however, be different if the union is able to negotiate a wage rate that exceeds that previously established in a competitive market. Suppose, for example, that the negotiated wage rate is at the higher level Ow_1. The individual firm whose demand curve for labor is $MRP_l = d_l$ will now offer employment to $O\overline{N}$ workers rather than ON workers as before. The effect of union bargaining is thus to raise the wage rate but reduce the level of employment. Workers who are able to retain their jobs benefit from the wage increase, but those who become unemployed are clearly worse off. Given the labor-supply curve, the amount of unemployment experienced as a result of union efforts to raise wages depends both on the elasticity of the demand for labor, i.e., on the sensitivity of the firm to the increase in the wage rate, and on the elasticity of the demand for the product that labor produces.[6] To recall the theory of derived demand examined in Chapter 6, four conditions that typically cause the demand for union labor to be relatively inelastic are (1) that there is no readily available substitute for that type of labor in the production function, (2) that the demand for the final product is inelastic, (3) that the ratio between the cost of union labor and the total cost of the product is small, and (4) that the supply of substitute or complementary factors of production (e.g., nonunion labor) is relatively inelastic.[7] In short, the extent of the unemployment that will result from union efforts to raise wages depends both on the elasticity of the demand for the product and on the elasticity of the demand for labor. If the labor involved can readily be replaced by other nonunionized workers or by capital, the amount of unemploymnet among unionized workers will be increased, i.e., the demand for union labor will be relatively elastic. The more inelastic the demand for unionized labor, the smaller will be the reduction in the demand for their labor services in consequence of union efforts to raise wages.

If the demand for labor is inelastic, a union might be able to negotiate a shorter work week and maintain employment at or close to its previous level in spite of a higher wage rate. Employees would then

---

[6] The extent of the unemployment effect also depends on the shape of the labor-supply curve. If, for example, there is a backward-bending labor-supply curve, workers prefer to work fewer hours at higher wage rates, which lessens the employment impact of union-set wages.

[7] When there is oligopoly in its product market a union may benefit when wages represent a large rather than a small proportion of total costs. See p. 160 below.

receive a higher wage rate (per hour, day, or week) but would be employed for a shorter work period. This alternative would not, of course, be possible if the demand curve for labor is elastic; an increased wage rate coupled with an elastic demand for labor would preclude spreading the benefits of a higher wage rate, as is possible if the demand for labor is relatively inelastic.

In summary, the implications for employment of union-wage bargaining in an otherwise competitive labor market are several. First, unless wages are a small part of total costs, there will invariably be some unemployment when a union raises its wage above the competitive level. Second, the extent of this unemployment depends on the elasticity of the demand for the final product as well as the demand for labor.[8] The latter depends, in part, on the availability of nonunion labor. This suggests that to be really effective in raising wages, a union must organize the entire labor market. Failing this, union workers are continuously threatened by other workers who might be willing to work at a lower wage rate. Third, the extent to which individual workers benefit from a higher negotiated wage rate depends not only on the degree of inelasticity that characterizes the demand for labor, but also on the extent to which this gain might be offset in consequence of a shorter work week. *Economics in Action 8:1* reviews some empirical evidence that is relevant to verifying the validity of this theoretical argument.

ECONOMICS IN ACTION 8:1

The Employment Effect of United Mine Workers Wage Policies during the 1950s

H. Gregg Lewis undertook to estimate the effect of the wage policies of the United Mine Workers during the 1950s.[9] He noted that the average number of men employed on "active mine days" declined by almost two-thirds between 1947 and 1961. In terms of "man days," employment declined by three-fifths, and in terms of "man hours" it declined by three-fourths. The hypothesis is that the large postwar increase in union-wage demands were a critical factor in the decrease of employment.

The first step in the study was to compute the ratio of average hourly earnings and average hourly compensation for bituminous-

---

[8]Hicks also noted the importance of the elasticity of substitution between inputs and its relationship to the elasticity of the demand for the product. See above Chapter 6, p. 162n5.

[9]H. Gregg Lewis, "Relative Employment Effects of Unions," *American Economic Review* Supplement vol. 54 (May 1964).

coal-mining wage earners and compare them to corresponding figures for production workers in manufacturing. It was established that the impact of unionism on the relative wage position of bituminous coal miners was close to zero in 1945. Between 1957 and 1959, which was a period of declining employment, the relative average hourly earnings of bituminous-coal workers were 28 percent above the 1945 level. While the falling demand for coal was undoubtedly a factor in declining employment, there was also some degree of substitution between capital and labor. Lewis's computations establish a substitution effect in the range of 15 to 25 percent. The decline in employment in the bituminous-coal industry, which the union accepted in order to achieve its wage demands during the 1950s, was two to three times as large as that experienced in other heavily unionized industries. The choice that union leaders made to sacrifice employment in order to achieve wage goals was rationalized in terms of the aging labor force of the industry. The expectation was that the attrition of the work force as a result of retirement would offset at least part of the decline in the demand for their services, which is attributable to the shrinking demand for the coal.[10]

Market Unionism and Product-Price Fixing

The experiences of unionized coal miners bears out the conclusion, reached on the basis of economic principle, that a union has to be very mindful of the likely employment effects of its wage demands before pressing them on employers. In the case of the mine workers, as already suggested, the decision to sacrifice employment was a conscious one based partly on the premise that the industry would experience an offsetting attrition in its work force as older workers retired and younger ones sought employment elsewhere.

Their wage demands were also coupled with measures to fix the price of coal. This is something that the mine owners were unable to achieve, but the miners' unions, aided by legislative price fixing that dated back to the Guffey Coal Act of the early New Deal period, enforced a basic price floor throughout the entire industry. This was accomplished partly through outright production restriction by limiting tonnage, as in the Pennsylvania anthracite mines, and by keeping the mines open for only three days a week. Periodic strikes further reduced

---

[10] While the elasticity of substitution between capital and labor in bituminous-coal mining was apparently larger than in other unionized industries during the 1950s, Lewis hazards the guess that the substitution effect, together with the effect on employment of the welfare-contribution component, nevertheless accounts for less than one-half of the postwar decline in employment in bituminous-coal mining. The balance is attributable to shrinking demand.

coal surpluses. These measures are consistent with the aim of market unionism to eliminate wages as a factor in competition.

While the pattern of union impact on commodity prices differs from industry to industry, it appears clear that unionism is incompatible with commodity markets in which firms are price takers. The decline of the American textile unions is a case in point; the power of the union has been substantially undermined as a result of its inability to control product prices. Its experience is thus quite unlike that of the International Ladies' Garment Workers Union, which has successfully limited the number of contractors who can sew and finish dresses for a single manufacturer. They have also stopped firms from moving out of a fixed geographic area (New York City's "garment district") and restricted new ones from entering. Thus, the ILGWU has successfully policed the garment industry and established a series of price lines and grades for men's clothing and women's dresses.

The construction trades have similarly worked out a system for controlling prices in the product market in order to achieve control over wages. Union power resides in the function they perform as a "work contractor" for builders and construction firms. Very few firms that bid on heavy construction work, such as dams, roads, and power stations, maintain a permanent work force. The union thus serves as their labor-force recruiting agent. It is virtually impossible for a contractor who does not deal with the union to win a bid or be supplied the labor he requires, if he wins one, unless he deals through the union.[11] Employers' associations rather than individual contractors engage in wage bargaining with construction unions. Since wages are a very large element in construction bids, unions effectively control the bids that can be tendered by controlling wages. The experiences of the construction industry, together with those of the coal and garment industries, make it quite clear that their success in industries that are normally "price takers" depends on limiting the authority of the market over the price that prevails in the commodity market.[12]

The Case of Bilateral Monopoly

Since the employees of oligopolistic firms are typically unionized, it is relevant to analyze the effect on wages and employment that results if a union bargains with an employer who is sufficiently strong to counter

[11] It is, however, also relevant to note that there has been a rapid growth of nonunion construction since the increase in the relative wage of unionized construction workers since the late 1960s. The challenge of that nonunion sector now appears to be restraining most union-wage settlements in construction.

[12] In some cases government legislation and regulation further promote restriction on commodity prices. For example, ICC regulations preclude price competition among carriers. The Davis Bacon Act and a variety of state laws limit price competition in the building trades.

the effect of the union. The case of "bilateral monopoly" provides useful insights, even though the firms in an actual market situation are likely to be oligopsonists (i.e., one of a few large employers) rather than monopsonists. A variety of models have been developed to describe the outcome of employer-employee relationships when the power of a monopsonistic employer is offset by the counterbalancing power of a union. No single model of bilateral monopoly commands general acceptance, because every model is necessarily predicated on a specific set of assumptions. The predictions of one model are therefore not relevant to situations that require different assumptions.

Among the assumptions that have been made as a basis for constructing models of union behavior we may note the assumptions that (1) the union's objective is to maximize either its wage rate or the level of employment, (2) that its objective is to maximize the net return or, alternatively, the wage bill, and (3) that its objective is to maximize the size of its membership. The success with which a union will be able to pursue any of these objectives depends, of course, on the relative strength of the two parties to the wage-employment bargain.

Union Goals concerning Wage Rates

It is useful to approach the problem of alternative models of union behavior by recalling the importance of money wage rates in the choice between market and nonmarket activity. A fall in *money* wages is likely to cause workers to withdraw their labor from the market. Unions will therefore resist most attempts by employers to make downward revisions in their money-wage rate. Their resistance has important implications for the level of employment in the economy as a whole during periods of declining economic activity, as will be examined in depth in Chapter 14. For the present, we note the unique importance to unions of maintaining the current money-wage rate. Maintenance of money-wage rates is sometimes the chief goal even if this policy makes severe increases in unemployment unavoidable. It is only under special circumstances that a union will be amenable to a money-wage reduction in order to protect employment opportunities. While it is rare, a more likely concession to an employer with whom a union has had good relations is to assist him in improving worker productivity.

It is also important to note that union-wage demands are not made in a vacuum. All wage earners make comparisons between themselves and other groups, and union members and their leaders are no exception. Employees generally expect to maintain historical parities or differentials between themselves and other wage earners. If their own wages get out of line through upward adjustments that have been made elsewhere, union attention tends to become quickly focused on restoring the previous relationship.

While a union is likely to be quite zealous about protecting its current money wage, increases in the wage rate will not be a viable goal if large increases in unemployment are likely to result. The experience of the Amalgamated Clothing Workers and the Amalgamated Association of Street, Railway and Motor Coach Operators since World War II are two well-known instances in which unions have had almost no measurable effect on earnings even though they have organized virtually all the companies in their jurisdictions. Both unions had a significant influence on their members' earnings in earlier years, but their more recent experience reflects the impact of the decline in the demand for their final product. Substantial declines in their product markets appear to have made these unions somewhat hesitant to aggregate the worsening employment situation by an aggressive wage policy. Their concerns are compounded by the increasing average age of union members, which has increasingly reduced their options in the labor market and their mobility in relation to alternative job opportunities. Employment security has become relatively more important than higher wage rates, particularly since reduced employment is likely to generate a reduction in union membership. Maximization of the wage rate is thus unlikely to be a goal that a union will pursue singlemindedly; by the same token, maximum employment is also unlikely to be its singleminded objective. Clearly, no union will ever seek wage rates or employment levels as exclusive goals. Rather, it is the *best combination* of wage rates and employment levels that will be sought. This suggests that a more reasonable union goal is to maximize the *net return* that it can realize.

The Case of the Indeterminate Wage Rate

The notion of a union seeking to maximize its net return envisions a behavior pattern that is analogous to that of a business monopoly. Recall the principle that a profit-maximizing firm achieves its objective by producing an output at which marginal cost equals marginal revenue. A seller whose market is imperfect has a downward-sloping marginal-revenue curve. Analogously, a union that considers its "business" to be the sale of labor will maximize its net return by equating *its* marginal revenue curve, *MD*, with the labor-supply curve as in Figure 8-4. As before, the labor-supply curve, S_l, reflects the wage rates that must be paid to call forth different amounts of labor, and $MRP_l = d_l$ is the employer's labor-demand curve. The curve *MD*, which is marginal to the MRP_l, indicates the change in the union's revenue (viewing the union as a seller of labor) as it offers different quantities of labor. The union that behaves as a monopolistic seller of labor will be maximizing "profits" by equating *MD* with S_l and will seek a wage of OW_u, as in Figure 8-4. This wage is equivalent to the marginal-revenue product of *ON* workers. This is the

FIGURE 8-4   *The Case of an Indeterminate Wage Rate*

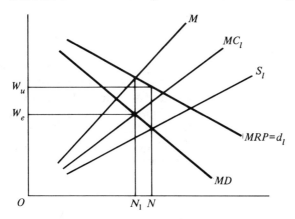

number of workers who will be employed *provided* that the union's demand for a wage of OW_u is agreed to by the employer.

If, however, the employer is as strong as the union, he will view the relevant supply-of-labor curve as being MC_l rather than S_l. MC_l, the marginal cost of labor schedule, is marginal to S_l (the schedule that reflects worker preferences concerning market and nonmarket activity) and therefore lies above it. It follows that an employer who views MC_l as his labor-supply curve will be guided in his employment decisions by M, the curve that is marginal to MC_l. A strong employer will seek to equate M to $MRP_l = d_l$, his labor-demand curve. If he is successful, he will employ ON_1 units of labor as in Figure 8-4 and offer to pay a wage of W_e, which is consistent with the supply price of that quantity of labor and below the union demand for W_u.

If an employer is not sufficiently strong to press this wage offer on his employees, the wage will be indeterminate, i.e., it will emerge somewhere *between* W_u, the union wage demand, and W_e, the employer's wage offer. Employment will correspondingly be between ON and ON_1. The stronger the union, the closer the wage will tend to gravitate toward W_u. A weaker union implies that the wage will move closer to W_e, the wage that the employer would offer if he were in a position of greater relative strength. We cannot, however, predict precisely what wage and employment level will result but only that the compromise wage will be somewhere between W_u and W_e and that the employment level will be adjusted accordingly.[13]

---

[13] J. T. Dunlop, *Wage Determination under Trade Unions*, p. 33. It has been suggested that it is the joint return of the monopsonist and the union that will be maximized in an actual bargaining situation. See S. Siegel and L. Fouraker, *Bargaining and Group Decision Making: Experiments in Bilateral Monopoly* (New York: McGraw-Hill, 1960).

Maximization of Membership

It is possible that maximization of union membership is the chief goal of a union. If this is the case the membership function becomes the relevant supply curve of labor. This curve reflects the appraisal by the leadership (of the union) of the amount of labor that will join the union at each wage rate. Thus, in Figure 8-5, *MF* identifies the willingness of workers to associate themselves with the union at various wage rates. It is likely to lie to the left of S_l, the curve expressing their market-nonmarket preferences, which is the traditional labor-supply curve. Needless to say, if there is a union shop, so that workers must join the union as a condition of maintaining employment, the membership function and the supply function converge.

FIGURE 8-5 *Maximizing Union Membership*

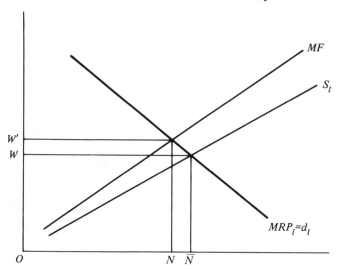

The union will maximize its membership by equating *MF*, its membership function, to the demand curve for labor. In Figure 8-5 the wage rate that will maximize membership is OW'. This is the same rate as OW_u in Figure 8-4. Since the membership function lies to the left of the supply function, the union is not able to provide as much employment as it could obtain at the lower wage rate OW. $O\bar{N}$ represents the amount of employment consistent with work-leisure choices at a wage of OW. This is the market wage that tends to be reached if the union is weak relative to the employer.

Given alternate assumptions about the relative strength of an employer *vis à vis* a union and about union objectives with respect to maximizing wages, union membership, or employment, the most significant conclusion that derives from the bilateral-monopoly model is, as has already been suggested, that it is impossible to predict a unique wage rate. There may be a tendency toward a unique level of employment, but the most that can be concluded with respect to wage rates (apart from the obvious point that they are likely to exceed the level that would prevail under competition) is that they will tend to be set within limits that correspond to the highest wage demand that is consistent with union membership and employment objectives and the lowest wage offer employers find it practical to make, given their labor requirements (and those of competing employers) and the market-nonmarket preferences of prospective employees.[14]

Concentration and Wage Increases

It was noted in Chapter 7 that when oligopoly prevails in a market the price leader(s) establishes a price, $p = w + k$, where k is a markup to cover nonwage costs including profit. The expectation in an oligopolistic market is that wage increases can be "passed through" to commodity prices. Thus, one would expect a positive relationship between market-concentration ratios and wage increases. Empirical studies lend support to this inference. Some of the more important ones are summarized as *Economics in Action* 8:2.

ECONOMICS IN ACTION 8:2

Concentration Rates and Wage-Rate Increases

An early study of wage changes in thirty-four manufacturing industries between 1923 and 1940 utilized concentration ratios to measure market power. The concentration ratio is the percentage of total

[14] A. M. Cartter has developed the concept of the "union-wage-preference path," which attempts to delimit the range of the wage indeterminacy associated with the bilateral-monopoly model. His analysis postulates various possible levels of labor demand and develops an indifference map of various wage-employment combinations. Cartter's logic is that if a union is concerned, there are alternative union wage-employment indifference curves as well as alternative employer-demand curves, from which it is possible to trace out a "wage-preference path." Each point on this path identifies alternative combinations of wage-employment levels with which a union would be equally well satisfied. Thus the wage-preference path sets the upper limit to the wage-employment bargain, while the labor-supply curve sets the lower limit. It is Cartter's conclusion that as the demand for labor increases, unions tend to favor wage increases rather than expansion of employment. Conversely, if the demand for labor declines, the tendency will be to reject wage reductions even at the expense of considerable unemployment. See A. Cartter, *Theory of Wages and Employment* (Homewood: R. D. Irwin, 1959), pp. 86–106.

industry sales made by the leading four U.S. manufacturing firms. Garbarino's study established a strong relationship between concentration ratios and wage increases for the period being studied.[15] A later study, which examined data relating to the period 1953–1959, also identified a strong relationship between wage-rate increases and concentration ratios in a sample of eighty-one four-digit manufacturing industries.[16] A more pronounced relationship was identified after 1952 than for the years preceding it. The sum and substance of these studies is that there has been a strong positive relationship between industrial concentration and rates of wage increase.

The reasons for the observed relationship between industrial concentration and wage increases are not difficult to perceive. Monopoly profits are compatible with wage increases that are not accompanied by reductions in employment. Similarly, oligopolies that are characterized by product- and labor-demand curves that are inelastic at prevailing prices are unlikely to reduce employment in consequence of wage increases that raise their costs. If, as in Figure 8-6, an oligopolistic firm maximizes it profits at price p and output OX, it will not choose to alter its output if it is confronted with a wage increase. The greater elasticity of its demand curve to the left of the kink at X^1 indicates that to increase its commodity price because wages have increased would reduce profits. In such a case a union might be able to raise wages within the limits of the discontinuity in the marginal-revenue product curve without generating unemployment.

If an oligopolistic firm is operating on an inelastic segment of its demand curve, e.g., $X'Y'$, it is conceivable that they will offer less resistance to a union effort to increase wages because they are able to shift the increase to consumers in the form of higher prices. Oligopolies that raise prices by the same *percentage* amount as they increase wages may, in fact, profit from a wage increase, depending on the ratio of wage costs to total costs and the elasticity of the demand for the final product.

When there is oligopoly in its product market, a union may be in an advantageous position if the wages of its membership represent a *substantial* rather than a small part of total cost. This is the case if there are relatively few good substitutes for union labor in the production process and the demand for the final product is highly inelastic.[17] Under these conditions employment is not adversely affected by an increase in wages. An inelastic product demand, coupled with limited substitution

[15] J. W. Garbarino, "A Theory of Industry Wage Structure Variation," *Quarterly Journal of Economics* (May 1950).

[16] William Bowen, "Wage Behavior in the Postwar Period" (Princeton: Princeton University Industrial Relations Section, 1960).

[17] J. R. Hicks, *The Theory of Wages* (London: Macmillan and Co., 1935), pp. 241–246.

FIGURE 8-6 *A "Kinked" Product Demand Curve*

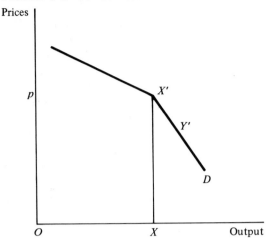

possibilities between union labor and other factors, causes firms to raise their prices when they are confronted with having to pay higher wages, instead of reducing the number of workers they employ.

Controversy about Modeling Trade-Union Behavior

Inadequacy of Economic Analysis

There is considerable controversy between mainstream economists and their institutionalist critics about the impact that unions have on wage determination. The most important conclusion to emerge from trade-union models that hypothesize alternative union goals as a basis for analyzing their impact on the wage-employment bargain is that economic principle can explain wage-rate determination. There is, however, no consensus that this conclusion is well founded. A number of well-known and highly respected economists, among them Clark Kerr, maintain that institutional forces *negate* the primary influence of the marketplace in the determination of wage rates as well as of the income share going to labor. Economic variables (e.g., profits and employment) influence the wage-determination process, but institutional forces blur their operation to a degree that makes it impossible to explain wage rates in terms of any economic model. Institutional forces are seen as introducing a number of noneconomic variables that significantly dilute the impact of the forces on which traditional wage analysis is predicated.

Kerr's well-known description of these forces maintains that "the institutional market is distinguished by the substitution of institutional rules for frictions as the principal delineator of job-market limits; of institutional and leadership comparisons for physical movement as the main basis for the interrelatedness of wage markets; and of policies of unions, employers, and government for the more traditional action of market forces as the significant source of wage movements.''[18] His conclusion is that wage rates are established by institutional forces. The basis for this view, which runs counter to the mainstream view, warrants examination and appraisal.

Much of the disagreement between mainstream and institutional economists turns on the validity of the assumptions made in the traditional analysis. Specifically, the trade-union models that were examined above assume that there is a fundamental identity of interests between the union and its members. It was further assumed that unions act to maximize the economic position, however identified, of its members. Finally, it is assumed that the union "sells" labor and that it is, like all sellers, concerned about "profits", i.e., about volume (i.e., employment) as well as price.

Institutionalists maintain that these assumptions fail to provide a rational explanatory basis for many union actions. Consider the phenomena of strikes: why do unions strike and why do employers accept strikes when the consensus is that strikes don't pay and that both sides would gain financially if strikes were settled early so that their monetary costs could be avoided on both sides? Yet it is not infrequent that unions and their employers will remain deadlocked for protracted periods, even when the parties are separated by relatively small differences.

Along the same lines, why do unions often seem to ignore the employment effects of their wage demands? (Witness such cases as that of the United Mine Workers Union, which was reviewed above, and which could be reinforced with other examples.) Why are unions more concerned with *changes* in the level of wages than in the level itself, and why are relative wages viewed as more critical than absolute wages if unions aim to maximize the workers' position? Moreover, why do unions prefer industry-wide bargaining when the practice of closing down a whole industry actually decreases the unions' ability to conduct a strike? When an entire industry is shut down, it removes the threat to individual employers of losing business to competitors and thus undermines, at least somewhat, their incentive to settle on the union's terms. At the same time, an industry-wide strike is more likely to awaken public enmity

---

[18]Some proponents of the view that union behavior can be analyzed in terms of economic principle have, however, conceded that given the diversity of union and membership goals it is probably not possible to construct a generalized model of trade-union behavior. McConnell suggests that labor-market theorists forego, temporarily at least, general explanations of wages and concentrate on analyzing specific situations. See Campbell R. McConnell, "Institutional Economic Trade Union Behavior," *Industrial and Labor Relations Review* 8, 2 (April 1955).

against the union rather than against employers. Observations such as these are the basis for the contention that a realistic model of the trade union requires recognition that there are not two but three parties involved in labor-management negotiations: the management, the union leadership, and the union rank and file. They thus maintain that the behavioral assumptions that are required for a meaningful inquiry are different from those that are traditionally used. Specifically, it is necessary to recognize

1. that unions' goals are not identical with those of their members. Indeed, "membership requirements" may actually be in conflict with "union requirements." For example, union members are typically impeded from joining a rival union that they believe would serve their interests better.
2. that the union's goal is to preserve its own sovereignty and extend its power. This goal may be in conflict with the traditional goal of wealth maximization and may take precedence over it when "the chips are down."
3. that the union is not engaged in selling labor. Labor is "sold" by individual workers, and the union is essentially a price-fixing institution that may have only limited concern with the employment effects of its price-fixing policies.

The conception of a union as a political entity requires recognizing that the union is confronted with diverse pressures. Its own membership, rival unions, rival leaders within the union, its own employer, other employers, government, and even consumers impose varying degrees of pressure. It is the overwhelming impact of these pressures that, in the view of institutionalist writers, makes it fruitful to study union behavior in terms of political rather than economic models.[19]

The Rebuttal

Writers who defend the relevance of economic analysis for explaining union behavior contend that the argument concerning lack of identity between the unions and their constituents is not well grounded. They maintain that because trade unions are among the more democratic institutions of our society, a union will undermine its support and ability to function successfully if it fails to act in a manner that is consistent with the interests of its constituents. It is reasoned that every relevant economic goal can be satisfied to some degree. While unions sometimes make concessions to government, the public, and business

[19]McConnell, *op. cit.*

enterprise, it does not follow that these are inconsistent with the basic aims of unionism. Policies that seem inconsistent with economic objectives in the short run may be entirely compatible with long-run objectives.

Moreover, it is argued, it is possible to serve the objectives of the union and its membership simultaneously, particularly in the long run. The union's survival and growth is dependent on its ability to satisfy the wants of its membership. The fact that a union has survived over a long period of time reflects a successful blending of its own and its members' objectives. Thus, the alleged conflict between union and membership requirements is viewed as an insufficient basis for "casting aside the orthodox approach to the labor market."[20]

It is also relevant to recognize that most orthodox theorists have discarded the bilateral-monopoly model of trade-union behavior, and instead of ignoring the effects of union bargaining for wages on employment, they are interpreting union wage policy as a response to the *ex ante* effects of its wage policy on employment and other strategic variables. Thus, the employment effects of particular policies are interpreted as becoming reflected in *future* wage policy, i.e., they are interpreted as responding to the effect of wages on employment with a lag. Employment effects are particularly taken into account in industries that are not fully organized and that are characterized by strong competition in the product market.

Concluding Remarks

The preceding discussion made the simplifying assumption that the bargained wage rate is "the" wage rate. Thus, the question of the wage structure was temporarily ignored and must now be integrated to take note of the management practice (already noticed in Chapter 5) of identifying work assignments in terms of job classifications. A single industrial plant may have thousands of job classifications. Most of these are linked to certain other classifications either by (1) their technological characteristics, (2) their relationship to the administrative organization, or (3) common social customs with respect to wage making.

Typically, the wages established for work assignments within a job cluster are more closely related to one another than they are to those that relate to other clusters. Thus, the wage structure of a plant is comprised of the rates that are established for its various job clusters, each of which has a number of rates.

Ordinarily, a job cluster is associated with a key wage rate (or rates), which typically relates to jobs that are quite standardized with respect to

[20]McConnell, *op. cit.*

job content and for which there is a counterpart in other firms. Thus, the key rate may be that paid in the highest job classification, the entry-level rate, or the rate that relates to the job classification employing the largest number of workers. Other wage rates prevailing in a plant tend to move with the rate for key jobs, and it is these rates that unions and managements typically have in mind when revisions in the internal wage structure are being considered. The changes that are made in the wages relating to key jobs alter the entire wage structure.

Key job rates are also the wage rates that tie the internal rate structure of individual firms to the rates that prevail in the external market. The external market cannot operate directly on the rates prevailing internally for a myriad of jobs that are only somewhat differentiated from one another. The key wage rates of an internal wage structure are not insulated from the external market, although they are not equally affected. However, to the extent that they are, the adjustments that are made in them, whether in response to institutional or market forces, are transmitted cluster by cluster to other rates within individual plants.

When wages are exogenously established, i.e., set by institutional forces, they tend to exhibit rigidity in the face of changes in demand and/or supply forces, particularly in a downward direction. Their ability to perform the market-clearing function that is traditionally attributed to them is thus impaired. In a tight labor market, the gap between labor supply and demand becomes closed by means of wage increases, lower hiring standards, and new job descriptions. But in a situation of excess labor supply, institutionally set wage rates imply a labor-market disequilibrium that may not be readily corrected, for reasons that will be explored in Part II.

The question whether wages are exogenously established by institutional forces rather than by the outcome of internal market forces arises in a broader context when the problem of the wage *structure* is considered. The central importance of the "key" wage rate within a cluster of jobs serves to alert us that to focus on "the" wage rate is a gross oversimplification. The key wage rate singles out one (or more) key job rate(s) within the internal wage structure of a firm or plant as a basis for examining changes in the rates prevailing for a cluster as a whole. The rates associated with a cluster of jobs are indicative that an occupational or skill hierarchy has emerged with increasing industrialization. Whereas the wage structure of an agricultural economy is largely undifferentiated by skill and product-market differences, industrialization has created numerous new occupations and job operations that are associated with differential wages. Wage theory cannot, therefore, content itself with explaining a single wage rate; it is necessary to explain the wage differences associated with various skills and occupations.

Occupational differentials are only one among the several types of wage differences that prevail in the economy. There are also industrial differentials, regional differentials, and differentials between union and nonunion workers, white and nonwhite workers, and male and female workers. The latter two, i.e., differentials between white and nonwhite and between male and female workers, are sometimes different from other types of wage differences because they reflect *wage discrimination.* Wage differentials are discriminatory when they are not related to efficiency differences in the performance of essentially similar jobs in similar work environments. Each of these types of wage differential poses the question whether they can be explained in terms of the theoretical principles of economics or whether they are the outcome of institutional forces. The chapter that follows examines the matter of the structure of wage rates principally in terms of the union role in wage interdependency.

Suggestions for Further Reading

Orley Ashenfelter. "Discrimination and Trade Unions," in Albert Rees and Orley Ashenfelter, eds., *Discrimination in Labor Markets.* Princeton: Princeton University Press, 1971.

William Fellner, "Prices and Wages under Bilateral Monopoly" *Quarterly Journal of Economics*, LXI, (August 1947) pp. 503–532.

Milton Friedman. "Some Comments on the Significance of Labor Unions for Economic Policy," in John F. Burton, Jr., *et al., Readings in Labor Market Analyses.* New York: Holt, Rinehart and Winston, Inc., 1971.

G. E. Johnson. "Bargaining Theory, Trade Unions and Industrial Strike Activity." *American Economic Review* (March 1969): 35–46.

H. G. Lewis, "Unionism and Relative Wages in the United States," reprinted in John F. Burton, Jr., *et al., Readings in Labor Market Analyses.* New York: Holt, Rinehart and Winston, Inc., 1971.

Alfred Marshall. Principles of Economics, 8th ed. London: Macmillan and Co. Ltd., 1924, pp. 518–538.

Melvin Reder. "Unions and Wages: The Problem of Measurement." *Journal of Political Economy* (April 1965): 118–196.

9 *The Union Role in Wage Interdependency*

All commodity and factor prices are interdependent with one another. Interdependencies among wage rates are particularly difficult to explain because they involve both the *structure* and the *level* of wage rates. The problem of explaining the structure of wages (i.e., the relationship of one wage rate to another) is among the most complex and controversial matters to which the economist must address himself. Two issues, in particular, come to the forefront. One concerns the relationship between wages in the nonunion sector and wages negotiated in the union sector. The matter of interindustry and interregional differentials also lends itself to being addressed in this context. The popular presumption is that unions are capable of raising the wages of their membership and that the wage structure is dominated by the institution of unions as opposed to market supply-and-demand forces.

The second issue concerns the interdependence among the wage bargains struck by different unions and the possibility that a "spillover" or imitation effect may develop in nonunion markets. Wage changes in the union sector will then tend to "spill over" into the nonunion sector and exert an effect on the *level* as opposed to (or in addition to) the structure of wages. The problem of the wage level (and also the general price level) is a macroeconomic problem. However, the prevalence of wage interdependencies implies that microeconomic and macroeconomic inquiry into the behavior of labor markets cannot be rigidly compartmentalized.

The Relationship between Union and Nonunion Wages

We know intuitively that the impact of unionism is related to the degree of unionization. If 50 percent of the workers eligible for unionization are actually unionized, and a union negotiates to raise the relative wages of workers in the group by 10 percent, which has the effect of lowering the relative wage of nonunion workers by 2 percent, the net impact of unionism on the wages of unionized workers is plus-4 percent. While the impact of unionism on their relative wages is clearly larger the higher degree of unionization, there are other less apparent linkages between union and nonunion labor, which are examined below.

In order for unions to affect the structure of wages it is necessary that either (1) the wage increases they secure have the effect of lowering the wage rates of nonunionized workers elsewhere in the economy or (2) the wage increases they secure are experienced to a lesser extent by nonunion workers. Clearly, the first effect will produce a greater impact on the wage structure than the second.

Milton Friedman has argued that the expectation, in general, is that "any rise in the wage rates secured by unions for certain classes of workers would tend to lower the wage rates of other workers."[1] The presumption is that the supply of labor in the nonunion sector is increased because of layoffs in the union sector in response to the relative decline in nonunion wages. According to Friedman's reasoning, nonunion wages will be driven down if wage increases are secured by union workers elsewhere in the economy. He thus concludes that union efforts to raise wages are likely to affect the *structure* but not the *level* of wages.

Two alternative lines of reasoning that lead to a different conclusion are possible. One maintains that the effect of a differential between union and nonunion wages poses a possible threat that nonunion workers will organize and that they will be granted similar wage increases in order that employers may avoid this. The second possibility is that union wage increases cause the prices of union goods to rise, which, in the case of an elastic demand for them, is likely to stimulate the demand for goods produced by nonunion workers. This will limit the effect of the increased supply of nonunion labor on nonunion wages.

These counterarguments to Friedman make it clear that his conclusion rests on two implicit assumptions. These are that (1) there is no significant "threat effect" and (2) the wage increases achieved by unions are accompanied by sufficient unemployment to exert a downward pressure on wages in the nonunionized sector. Given the extent of unionization, the possibility that the second condition (i.e., unemployment) will prevail is governed by the principle of derived demand. Since labor is used cooperatively in the production process, along with other factors, and the demand for it is traditionally thought to be derived from the demand for the final product, it follows that a wage demand pressed

[1] M. Friedman, "Some Comments on the Significance of Labor Unions for Economic Policy," in D. McCord Wright, *The Impact of the Union* (New York: 1951), pp. 215–16.

by a union is least likely to have an adverse effect on its members' level of employment if the employer's demand for their labor is inelastic and if the demand for the final product is also inelastic.

The experience of the United Mine Workers that was reviewed in Chapter 8 above is one of the more dramatic examples of the possible adverse employment effects of union wage policies.[2] However, unions have found it possible to limit these negative experiences by such devices as share-work or make-work rules and output restrictions. The introduction of institutional constraints such as work sharing implies that a net exodus of workers from the union sector need not follow in consequence of union-won wage increases. Indeed, there may even be a net *influx* of workers from the nonunion sector into the union sector if make-work rules limit excesses in the labor supply and therefore the tendency of nonunion wages to fall.

Make-work rules (e.g., rules concerning the ratio between auxiliary and/or supervisory and production workers), which require employers to hire larger numbers of workers than they would normally be willing to hire at the union rate, have the effect of making wage costs into fixed cost items. Not all unions will be able to enforce these rules to the same degree, because elastic product demands are clearly not compatible with substantial enforcement of make-work rules. However, as was emphasized in Chapter 7, the large price-making firms that dominate the manufacturing sector of the economy are typically confronted with both inelastic product-demand curves and an inelastic demand for labor. When such inelasticities exist, union-won wage increases are less likely to result in adverse employment experiences.

The "Threat" Effect and Anticipatory Wage Increases

The prediction of economic theory about the effect of union wages on nonunion wages is not unequivocal. On the one hand it may be argued that any effort by unions to force up the union wage must decrease employment in that sector, so that there is an increase in the supply of labor in the nonunion sector. This will, presumably, generate downward pressure on the nonunion wage.

An alternative line of reasoning about the likely effect of a union-nonunion wage differential introduces the possibility of future organization by nonunion workers. While Friedman expects the wage increases secured by unions to be offset by declines elsewhere in the economy, nonunion workers are sometimes also given wage increases in the hope of impeding their unionization. Indeed, nonunion employers encouraged company unions during the 1930s and gave them substantial

---

[2] See *supra*, Chapter 8, pp. 203–204. See also *Economics in Action* 9:1 below.

wage increases. This suggests that wage increases in union firms may have the effect, especially during periods of considerable union growth, of raising nonunion wages above the levels that would otherwise prevail.

The premise is that a profit-maximizing employer is always likely to determine his own optimal-wage offer in light of the level of the union wage rate. Interviews with nonunion employers confirm that the threat of unionism is generally an important factor in the determination of nonunion wages and that they keep careful track of union contracts at other plants.[3] If the quality of an industry's labor supply is positively related to its wage rate, nonunion firms will be forced to raise their wages if union wages rise, if they are not to experience a decline in average labor efficiency. Both the morale and productivity of nonunion workers is likely to suffer if the differential between the union and the nonunion sector becomes very large.[4] This suggests the possibility that nonunion wages will reflect the influence of union "pushfulness" as well as market forces. *Economics in Action* 9:1 reports an effort to test this hypothesis empirically.

ECONOMICS IN ACTION 9:1

Trade-Union Power, Threat Effects, and Nonunion Wages

Empirical study of the effect that the threat of unionization may have on the wages paid to unorganized workers is handicapped by data limitations that preclude identification of union and nonunion workers on an individual basis. Bureau of Labor Statistics surveys of establishments in urban places were thus utilized as a basis for information about union membership. Workers were identified as union members if more than one-half of all workers in an establishment were covered by a collective-bargaining agreement.[5]

The study used mean-wage data from the 1958 Census of Manufactures in conjunction with population data from the 1960 census to compute average hourly earnings for production workers. The objective was to predict the effect of the threat of unionism on the wages paid by nonorganized firms.

The finding was that the greater the threat of unionization, the more effective the nonunion wage will be in countering the threat. Wage push

[3] Albert Rees and George P. Schultze, *Workers and Wages in the Urban Labor Market* (University of Chicago Press, 1970), p. 45.

[4] H. Slichter Sumner, "Do the Wage-Fixing Arrangements in the American Labor Market Have an Inflationary Bias?" *American Economic Review* 55 (1954): 322–346.

[5] Sherwin Rosen, "Trade Union Power, Threat Effects and the Extent of Union Organization," *Review of Economic Studies* 36 (1969): 185–196.

by unions eventually spreads to the nonunion sectors of their industries through threat responses. The threat effect is more likely to raise nonunion wages if the history of unionism has been brief.

A rise in nonunion wages may, in turn, produce second-order effects on union wages that are negotiated, in the first instance, on the basis of a presumed differential between the union and the nonunion wage.[6] The premise is that given the demand for union labor, an internal trade-off will be made between wage increases and employment losses. The structure of wages will then be substantially unchanged, i.e., the original union-nonunion wage relationship will be restored. However, the *level* of union and nonunion wage rates may be raised. Thus, unions may play an important role, which will be examined in more detail in Chapter 16 in generating cost-push inflation. It is, however, relevant to examine some evidence about the effect of unions on the *structure* of wages before approaching the matter of the level of wages. We shall consider interregional and interindustry differentials and then the union-non-union wage structure as a whole.

Unions and the Structure of Wages

Unions and Geographical Wage Differentials

The relationship between wages in the northern and in the southern regions of the U.S. economy is an interdependency that has invited many efforts to measure and explain the differences.[7] The southern wage picture is very mixed. Average wages in the south are approximately 20 percent less than those of the rest of the nation. The exception to this generalization is apparent in industries that have a local-market character. Specifically, the differential between southern and northern wages in the construction industry is larger than it was four decades ago. Wages in southern paper mills are also above the level that prevails in the north, although they were historically 15 percent lower. In part, this is owing to the fact that the older, higher-cost mills of the north have been tolerated by the unions as an alternative to forcing them out of business as a result of the higher standard wage. It is also partly owing to the rapid expansion of employment in southern mills, which necessitated some increase in southern wage rates in order to facilitate the transfer of papermakers from the north to the south.

[6] O. R. Ashenfelter, E. E. Johnson, and J. H. Pencavel, "Trade Unions at the Rate of Change of Money Wages in United States Manufacturing Industry," *Review of Economic Studies* 39 (1971).

[7] See in particular Lowell E. Galloway, "The North-South Wage Differential," *Review of Economics and Statistics* (August 1963), and H. M. Douty, "Regional Wage Differentials: Forces and Counterforces," *Monthly Labor Review* (March 1968): 74–81.

In other industries, among them coal mining, basic steel, the automobile industry, and other heavy-manufacturing industries, geographic wage differentials have been reduced or eliminated. The wage differential between northern and southern textile mills is smaller than it has been historically. The southern textile industry has expanded relative to that in the North, and active competition for labor has exerted an upward pressure on wage rates that has narrowed the north-south differential. Union mills, which are in the minority in the textile industry, are located mainly in the North and cannot be forced to pay more than the increasing wage minima legislated under the Fair Labor Standards Act without being pressured out of the industry. Essentially the same pattern prevails in the clothing, furniture, and hosiery industries.

Part of the continued differential between the North-South *average* wage level is owing to differences in industry composition and the cost of living.[8] But a more fundamental reason for the difference is the fact that the South has had a relative labor surplus. The region has a high natural rate of population growth, which is an important factor in explaining the lower capital-labor ratio and the lower average wage than that prevailing in the North.

There are, however, important counterforces at work that are operating to further narrow the North-South wage differential. A particularly important counterfactor is that southern industry has grown at a more rapid rate than other sections of the country. This is partly the result of the region's high natural rate of population growth. There has also been a significant redistribution of unskilled labor from agricultural to urban areas and a substantial net migration of labor out of the South, while capital has been attracted into the region. Thus, market forces appear to be operating to further narrow the disparity between northern and southern wages.[9]

Unions and Relative Wages

Efforts to quantify the wage differential between union and nonunion workers have proceeded in two quite different ways. One is to use cross-section data that compare the wages of union workers with those of nonunion workers in other occupations and areas at one point in time.[10] One can then determine, after controlling for other variables

---

[8] P. R. R. Coelho and M. A. Ghali examine the part of the North-South wage differential that is attributable to cost-of-living differences in "The End of the North-South Wage Differential," *American Economic Review* 61, 5 (December 1971).

[9] Nevertheless, Douty has expressed the view that "it is unlikely that the southern wage differential, however measured, will disappear in the near future."

[10] One such study is H. G. Lewis, "The Effects of Unions on Industrial Wage Differentials," Conference of National Bureau of Economic Research (April 1960).

which affect wages, such as sex, age, education, region, and size of the community, whether wage rates exhibit a systematic relationship to unionization. A second way to measure the wage impact of unions is to utilize time-series data for a group of unionized workers that go back sufficiently far in time to include a period prior to unionization.[11] Both types of studies present formidable difficulties. The most ambitious of the studies undertaken to date is that conducted by H. Gregg Lewis, which is summarized as *Economics in Action* 9:2.

ECONOMICS IN ACTION 9:2

Unionism and Relative Wages in the U.S.

Reviewing the estimates of more than two dozen researchers who estimated the effect of unions on the relative wages of their members, H. Gregg Lewis notes an extraordinarily large range of effects.[12] The impact of unions on relative wages in the bituminous-coal industry were computed as being from zero to over 100 percent. The relative wages of miners in unionized mines appear to have been more than twice as high as they would have been in the absence of unionization during the deflationary period after 1920–21. In contrast, near the end of World War II, the relative wages of unionized miners were found to have been no higher than they would have been in the absence of unionization. But neither extreme was of long duration. By the mid-1920s the estimated relative wage of unionized miners was only half as much as it had been in 1921–22. Similarly, the relative wage of unionized miners in 1956–1957 was about the same as in 1924–1926.

The large impact that unions had on relative wages in the coal industry is unique. Studies of other industries examined by Lewis yielded estimates of the impact of unions on relative wages that did not exceed 40 percent. Only three of the estimates found relative wages to be higher by more than 25 percent. Specifically, the relative wage of skilled building craftsmen may have been slightly in excess of 25 percent in 1930–1934. Relative wages in the manufacture of men's and boys' coats and suits ranged between 30 and 39 percent above nonunion wages in the period between 1928 and 1932, while the relative wages of commercial-airlines pilots in 1956 was between 21 and 34 percent above that of their nonunion counterparts.

Lewis's estimates of the effect of unionism on the average wage of

---

[11] See, for example, S. P. Sobatka, "Union Influence on Wages: The Construction Industry," *Journal of Political Economy* (April 1953).

[12] H. G. Lewis, *Unionism and Relative Wages in the United States* (Chicago: University of Chicago Press, 1962).

all union labor relative to that of all nonunion labor at key dates during the last forty years is summarized in Table 9A. Column 1 is the average extent of unionism in the economy as a whole; Column 2 is the average relative wage of union relative to nonunion labor. These averages are used to compute Column 3, which measures the wages of union labor relative to all labor. The corresponding figures for nonunion labor are given in Column 4.

TABLE 9-A   *Summary of Estimates of Average Relative Wage Effects of Unionism in Selected Periods (Percent)*

		Average Relative Wage Effect of Unionism		
Period	Average Extent of Unionism in the Economy (1)	Union Labor Relative to Nonunion Labor (2)	Union Labor Relative to All Labor (3)	Nonunion Labor Relative to All Labor (4)
1923–29	7 to 8	15 to 20	14 to 18	−1
1931–33	7 to 8	>25	>23	<−1
1939–41	18 to 20	10 to 20	8 to 16	−4 to −2
1945–49	24 to 27	0 to 5	0 to 4	−1 to 0
1957–58	27	10 to 15	7 to 11	−4 to −3

SOURCE: H. Gregg Lewis, *Unionism and Relative Wages in the United States* (1962).

Lewis's estimates imply that the question whether unions have altered the wage structure by raising the rates earned by their members relative to those received by nonunion members must be answered within the context of particular time periods and particular unions. The evidence is that the relative wage impact of unionism was greatest near the bottom of the depression of the 1930s and least during the periods of inflation and low unemployment that followed the two World Wars.

Unions have historically been reluctant to accept wage cuts during periods of deflation because of the possibility that deflation might not continue. Contrarily, the impact of unions is lessened during prosperous periods, which expand the demand for labor generally and raise wages without the need for union pressure. Lewis's findings are that in the 1931–33 period, unionism may have raised the average relative-wage position of union labor in excess of 23 percent and lowered that of non-union labor by somewhat more than 6 percent. In the inflationary period following World War II, unions appear to have had little effect on the relative wages of union and nonunion labor. Since that time, it is estimated that unionism has raised the average relative wage of union labor by about 7–11 percent and reduced the average relative wage of nonunion labor by approximately 3 or 4 percent.[13] On the whole, therefore, the evidence is that the effect of unions on the differential between union and nonunion workers has been quite modest. It is, however, relevant to examine also the relationship between unions and interindustry differences in wages.

Unions and Interindustry Differences

A study by H. Gregg Lewis that is no longer new but that remains relevant provides a useful perspective about the extent to which interindustry dispersions in relative wages are attributable to the degree of unionization in an industry. He computed the relative average compensation per wage and salary worker among approximately seventy industries as reported by the U.S. Department of Commerce for the period 1929–1958. For the period as a whole, the wage structure was quite stable, though the amount of relative wage dispersion was quite large; the thirty-year average was 30.1 percent. On the basis of these data, it may be asked to what extent the relative wage dispersion among industries is the result of unionization.

Lewis developed an index to reflect the impact of unions on relative wages. He estimates that in the period examined, the value of R (as he designates his index) was only between 0.04 and 0.06. This calculation implies that the level of relative wage dispersion must be accounted for chiefly in terms of factors other than unionism. Lewis concluded that in 1963 the impact of unionism on relative wage inequality among all workers was small and, furthermore, that the direction of the effect is ambiguous.[14] Lewis's findings imply that interindustry wage differentials are not attributable to the influence of unions. Indeed, causality may run in the other direction: *viz.*, unions may be more successful in securing wage increases for their members in industries in which the product market is characterized by price-taking firms.

This interpretation of the relationship between wage differentials and concentration is consistent with Galbraith's argument that when unions deal with oligopolies, they are able to "capture" part of the profits that arise in the product market. In this context, union power is interpreted as a response to oligopoly, i.e., union power is a "countervailing" rather than an original power.[15] As has already been noted, there are several statistical studies that show a strong relationship between

[13] H. Gregg Lewis, *Unionism and Relative Wages in the United States.*

[14] H. Gregg Lewis, "Unionism and Relative Wages in the United States," in John Burton, Jr., *et al., Readings in Labor Market Analysis* (New York: Holt, Rinehart and Winston, Inc., 1971), pp. 458–476.

[15] J. K. Galbraith, *American Capitalism: A Theory of Countervailing Power* (New York: Houghton Mifflin and Co., 1952), p. 515.

concentration in the product market and wage increases.[16] However, the interaction between concentration, unionization, and wage gains is extremely complex. The difficulties inherent in identifying the separate effects on wages of unionization and concentration are complicated by the relationship between concentration and plant size. Larger plants typically pay higher wages than smaller ones. Thus the wage impact of unions, which is often attributed to concentration, may actually reflect the influence of large plant size.[17] There is evidence that for a given level of unionization the union-wage impact is not significantly greater in concentrated industries.[18]

There is, however, the possibility that the wage increases won by unions in the large, concentrated industries tend to "spill over" into other industries. Recent studies of wage determination in what is termed the "key" group of industries have examined the role of the bargaining process in determining wage changes that are subsequently transmitted to other industries via institutional forces that generate imitation or "spillover" effects. If this is the case, the impact of wage interdependency is chiefly on the *level* of wages. Once again, a central issue in connection with these studies is whether wage changes are attributable to the institutional forces reflected in union pushfulness or to market forces to which unions are responding.

Pattern Bargaining

Key "Groups" and Wage Determination

It has been observed that the wage structure in many industries is affected by wage agreements that are negotiated by a relatively few large unions in the "heavy" industries.[19] The wage rates that have become

[16] See Chapter 7, pp. 184–187.

[17] Stanley H. Masters, "Wages and Plant Size: An Interindustry Analysis," *Review of Economics and Statistics* (August 1969): 341–45.

[18] Leonard Weiss, "Concentration and Labor Earning," *American Economic Review* (March 1966): 96–117. However, it is worth noting that other researchers have reached different conclusions. Stafford's comments on Weiss' paper (*American Economic Review,* March 1968) maintains that the differential attributable to unions is about 15 percent. Adrian Throop ("The Union-Nonunion Wage Differential and Cost-Push Inflation," *American Economic Review,* March 1968), estimates that the union-nonunion wage differential was 22.3 in 1950 and 26.0 in 1960, but he recognizes that his results may have an upward bias. But, Melvin Reder in his review of Lewis's study suggests that the data are so faulty that "one cannot reject the null hypothesis that the relative wage effect of unionism has been zero for most of the period since 1920." See Melvin W. Reder, "Unions and Wages: The Problem of Measurement," *Journal of Political Economy* (April 1965): 188–196.

[19] Otto Eckstein and Thomas Wilson, "The Determination of Money Wages in American Industry," *Quarterly Journal of Economics* (August 1962): 379–414; Y. P. Mehra, "Spillovers in Wage Determination in U.S. Manufacturing Industries," *Review of Economics and Statistics* 63 (August 1967): 300–312.

established in a broad group of two- and three-digit industries, specifically, metals production, rubber, stone, clay, glass, machinery, transportation equipment, and instruments, exhibit a pattern. These industries are geographically clustered in the Midwest and are dominated by large industrial corporations that frequently have input-output relations. They are also characterized by strong industrial unions and high wages and have generally similar requirements with respect to skill. The political relationships among unions in "heavy" industries are close because some unions are bargaining agents in several industries. Geographic proximity, including the proximity of some large plants, makes members of different unions aware of each other's settlements. This suggests that they bring pressure on their own leaders to achieve as good settlements as the rest of the group obtained. These industries are thought to be "key" industries in the sense that there is a wage pattern among them that is reflected in the interdependence of the wage settlements that they conclude. For example, settlements in the cement and aluminum industries typically follow wage settlements concluded in the steel industry, while those in the rubber and plate-glass industries tend to follow the auto-industry settlement. Their geographic proximity and the fact that some unions bargain on behalf of several industries implies that union members are usually aware of settlements concluded in other industries and, consequently, tend to bring pressure on their own leadership to achieve similar outcomes.

The contract negotiated between a union and its employers specifies the wage rates that will prevail for the period of the contract, which typically extends for one to three years. This institutional arrangement is particularly important because it inevitably means that the economic conditions that prevail at the time of contract negotiations, or that are expected to prevail, exert a major effect in the determination of wages. Thus, it may be asked, "What is the impact of institutional forces in determining wage changes as opposed to the classical supply-and-demand analysis that maintains that only the conditions in the labor market determine wages?" In the hope of resolving the issue, a statistical analysis of wage changes was undertaken on the premise that they reflect institutional as well as economic forces that operate in the product and labor markets. This study is examined as *Economics in Action* 9:3.

ECONOMICS IN ACTION 9:3

The Process of Wage Changes in Key Industries

The model which was formulated to examine the process of wage determination in the United States economy identified unemployment as the critical variable in the labor market and the profit rate as the critical variable in the product market.[20] The latter variable appeared appropriate on several grounds: (1) the profit rate is representative of short-run conditions that affect bargaining; (2) it is representative of the long-run structural characteristics of the market, such as the degree of monopoly power; and (3) it reflects the union aim of maintaining labor's share of the industry's income and its consequent insistence on large wage increases when profits are high. The relationship between wage changes and productivity levels was also investigated.

These variables were examined empirically in order to ascertain the process of wage determination in key industries and their effect elsewhere in the economy. Specifically, what was investigated was the *rate of increase* of wages in the key group for a series of five wage "rounds" that were experienced between 1948 and 1960. These rounds reflect the chronologies of the contract settlements that were negotiated during the postwar period. Each round ranged from one to four years with the pattern for the round being set in the early key bargains, which determined wage movements in the succeeding months or years, until the next "round" commenced and started a new series of negotiations and settlements. Thus, the wage movements in the key industries in 1958 were largely determined by the economic circumstances that prevailed in 1955–1956. The hypothesis is that the wage agreements reached in the key groups produced subsequent "spillover" effects during which the changes in the former became "mirrored" in similar wage changes in industries outside the key group.

Investigation of the rate of increase in wage rates in the key group proceeded by examining the relationship between the annual rate of increase of straight-time hourly earnings in the key group and profits (π) and unemployment (U) for the five wage rounds that occurred between 1946 and 1960. Both profits and unemployment were identified as highly significant independent variables for explaining wage-rate changes. Profits were identified as accounting for 57 percent of the change in wage rates, while unemployment accounted for the other 43 percent. This result was interpreted as being compatible with the hypothesis that institutional factors in the product and factor market are important in wage determination. Additional time-series analysis of wages in individual industries verified the key-group hypothesis, i.e., profits and unemployment were the significant independent variables for explaining wage-rate changes.

---

[20]Otto Eckstein and Thomas Wilson, "The Determination of Money Wages in American Industry," *op. cit.* The importance of key groups has also been noted by John E. Maher on the basis of his detailed analysis of contract terms. See his paper "The Wage Pattern in the United States 1946–1957," *Industrial and Labor Relations Review* 15 (October 1961).

The relationship between productivity and wages was also examined empirically. Productivity did not appear to be an important independent variable in wage determination. In particular, the industries with the most impressive long-run productivity gains, among them chemicals, tobacco, textiles, and lumber, did not receive large wage increases. No relationship was identified between interindustry productivity gains and the size of the wage increases received. Furthermore, there was only limited evidence that consumer prices played a major role in determining wage behavior, except during periods of extreme price change.

The relevance of profit-employment variables with respect to the wage changes in eleven industries outside of the key group was also subjected to examination. Key wages were found to be statistically significant in explaining wage changes in industries outside the key group in eight out of eleven cases. This suggests that wages in other industries reflect a "spillover" from the key group. As a result of this relationship, it is maintained, there is an important nexus between the process of wage determination in key groups of industries and the *rate of change* in wages in the economy as a whole. What the economy is experiencing at the microeconomic level of the firms that comprise its key groups is seen as affecting in an important way what it will experience with respect to wage (and presumably price) levels in the economy as a whole.[21]

The Rebuttal to the "Key Wage" Hypothesis

The Eckstein-Wilson study of wage interdependence has been criticized on several levels. An early critique maintained that their methodology does not "resolve the problem of distinguishing between institutional imitation and spillover effects and neoclassical labor-supply forces operating through the mobility of labor at the margin."[22] The study was evaluated as being "ambiguous" because it is unable to provide unequivocal guidance in determining whether wage changes are the product of institutional or of economic forces. The profit and unemployment rates which Eckstein and Wilson use as variables to statistically "explain" wage-rate changes can be interpreted as reflecting the determining influence of *either* market or bargaining variables.

A basic problem that arises in connection with testing the above propositions concerns the kind of data on which the conclusions are based. It has been argued that the study of wage interdependence

---

[21] These interrelationships are examined in depth in Part II, Chapters 15 and 16.

[22] Timothy W. McGuire and Leonard A. Rapping, "The Determination of Money Wages in American Industry: Comment," *Quarterly Journal of Economics* 81 (November 1967).

requires the use of data that separate contractual wages from wage drift. Wage drift reflects overtime and merit payments as well as contractual wages and is, therefore, misleading with respect to the impact of institutional versus market forces. Accordingly, an analysis of effective annual-wage changes by union affiliation was undertaken in order to test the hypothesis of wage interdependence.

ECONOMICS IN ACTION 9:4

An Alternative Test of the Interdependence Hypothesis

An alternative examination of the effect of unionism on money-wage changes utilizes separate time series of union and nonunion wage changes in the U.S. economy that are taken from the Survey of Wage Developments in Manufacturing compiled by the U.S. Bureau of Labor Statistics.[23] These data about effective wage changes for union and nonunion workers in manufacturing for the 1961–1975 period show that the union workers received wage increases amounting to as little as zero and as much as 10 percent in the early part of the period and, more recently, that wage increases ranged between zero to over 13 percent. It is thus inferred that a union's first-year settlement (in a multiyear contract) is responsive to labor-market conditions, just as nonunion wages are.

The finding that first-year settlements are sensitive to market conditions does not rule out spillovers, but implies that current wage adjustments among organized workers do not always rigidly follow one another, as they appeared to do in the early postwar years. With respect to nonunion wage changes in manufacturing, the finding is that the dispersion around the median wage increase of nonunion wage changes exceeds the dispersion of union wage changes. This is consistent with the greater wage interdependence among groups of unionized workers, but the test is not considered to be a strong one. There are strong tendencies toward imitation via wage drift, but the rate of change in negotiated union wage rates exhibits significant variation and, in some years, does not differ substantially from the dispersion of changes in nonunion wages. A response in the pattern to unfavorable economic conditions was found even within the jurisdiction of the United Automobile Workers and the United Steelworkers, although these deviations occurred only in the smaller plants and were more frequent in fringe benefits and work-rule enforcement than in wages.[24] Wage contagion

[23] Robert Flanagan, "Wage Interdependence in Unionized Labor Markets," *Brookings Papers on Economic Activity* 3 (1976).

[24] Robert Flanagan, *op cit.*

among negotiated union wage rates thus appears to be less stringent than the limitation, via wage drift, of earnings.

Further study was undertaken in order to ascertain more specifically the role of the duration of labor-market contracts as an influence in delaying the effect of market changes on union wages. The study examined annual changes in nonunion, "current" union, and "effective" union wages for the period 1960–1975. Effective union-wage changes represent current wage changes plus deferred increases plus cost-of-living adjustments. Comparison of effective union-wage changes with nonunion changes established that nonunion firms are more responsive to labor-market pressures than are union firms. There is a difference in the average wage responsiveness of the union and nonunion sectors, but it is attributable to the prevalence of multiyear contracts in unionized manufacturing industries. Only 1 percent of the labor agreements covering at least 1,000 workers have a duration of one year or less. A comparison of the effect of labor-market pressure on current and effective union-wage changes is the basis for the conclusion that the limited responsiveness of union wages to market conditions is mainly the by-product of the duration-of-labor agreements. First-year negotiated wage changes are almost as sensitive to labor-market pressures as nonunion wages are. Also, union-wage movements in different industries vary considerably. More important, union-wage movements in different industries were not found to "leak out" into the nonunion sector, where wages are lower and more flexible.[25]

There is also reason for expecting that many wage patterns would exist without unions. Wages are expected to be similar in the locally and regionally competitive product markets that characterize hotels, restaurants, and wholesale trade. A similarity of wage movements would also be expected in many oligopolistic industries, among them the automobile, aerospace, meat-packing, and rubber industries, even in the absence of unions.[26] There are wage patterns in these industries that would emerge when similar economic conditions affect firms in the same or related industries. But such patterns do not imply that there is a "key" negotiation that, once concluded, essentially determines wage changes for major sectors of the organized economy.

Concluding Remarks

The study of money wages in American industry by Eckstein and Wilson concludes that "the influence of labor- and product-markets

---

[25] See in particular Harold M. Levinson, "Pattern Bargaining: A Case Study of the Automobile Workers," *Quarterly Journal of Economics* 74 (May 1960): 296–317.

[26] Robert Flanagan, *op. cit.*, p. 673.

conditions on wages can be identified clearly once the institutional reality of spillovers and long-term contracts is recognized in the statistical design ...."[27] When examined in a statistical framework, wages in the key group are "explained" by the profit rates and the unemployment rates in the group. Wages in other industries outside this group are "explained" by "spillover" effects emanating from the key group.

The most valuable insight derived from the Eckstein-Wilson study is its empirical verification of "pattern" bargaining. While the profit and unemployment levels that "determine" the key wage may be proxies for economic forces operating in the product and labor markets, it is also important to recognize that the relationship the authors identified is *statistical*. No theoretical hypothesis was developed to link wage-rate changes to profits and unemployment levels in a causal way. Thus, the controversy between the theoretical and institutional approaches to wage interdependency is not resolved by their study. The controversy is critical, for *if* wage determination reflects the institutional environment, wages emerge as an *exogenous* magnitude that cannot be explained as being endogenously determined by an economic model.

If wages are exogenously established, i.e., set by institutional forces, they will necessarily exhibit rigidity in the face of changes in demand and/or supply forces, particularly in a downward direction. Their ability to perform the market-clearing function, which is traditionally attributed to them, will thus be impaired. In a tight labor market the gap between labor supply and demand tends to close because of wage increases, lower hiring standards, and new job descriptions. But in a situation of excess labor supply, institutionally set wage rates imply a labor market disequilibrium that may not be readily corrected, for reasons that will be explored on a theoretical level in Part II and in a policy context in Part III. The important point at this juncture is that wage interdependencies may affect the *level* of wages as well as the *structure* of wages.

The central importance of the "key" wage rate within a cluster of jobs serves to alert us that to focus on "the" wage rate is to oversimplify. The key wage rate simply singles out one (or more) key job rate(s) within the internal wage structure of a firm or plant as a basis for examining changes in the rates prevailing for a cluster as a whole. The rates associated with a cluster of jobs are indicative that an occupational or skill hierarchy has emerged along with increasing industrialization. Whereas the wage structure of an agricultural economy is largely undifferentiated by skill and product-market differences, industrialization has created numerous new occupations and job operations that

[27] Eckstein and Wilson, "Comment," *Quarterly Journal of Economics* 81 (November 1967): 668.

are associated with differential wages. Wage theory cannot, therefore, content itself with explaining a single wage rate; it is necessary to explain the wage differences associated with various skills and occupations. The chapter that follows examines the structure of wage rates principally in terms of occupational differences.

Suggestions for Further Reading

H. M. Douty. "Regional Wage Differentials: Forces and Counterforces." *Monthly Labor Review* (March 1968): 74–81.

Otto Eckstein and Thomas Wilson. "The Determination of Money Wages in American Industry." *Quarterly Journal of Economics* (August 1962): 379–414.

Robert J. Flanagan. "Wage Interdependence in Unionized Labor Markets." *Brookings Papers on Economic Activity* 3 (1976).

Milton Friedman. "Some Comments on the Significance of Labor Unions for Economic Policy," in David McCord Wright, ed., *The Impact of the Union*. New York: Harcourt Brace Jovanovich, 1951.

Lowell E. Galloway. "The North-South Wage Differential." *Review of Economics and Statistics* (August 1963).

H. G. Lewis. "Unionism and Relative Wages in the United States," reprinted in John Burton, Jr., *et al., Readings in Labor Market Analysis*. New York: Holt, Rinehart and Winston, Inc., 1971.

Y. P. Mehra. "Spillovers in Wage Determination in U.S. Manufacturing Industries." *Review of Economics and Statistics* 68 (August 1967): 300–312.

Melvin Reder. "Unions and Wages: The Problem of Measurement." *Journal of Political Economy* (April 1965): 188–196.

Sherwin Rosen. "Trade Union Power, Threat Effects, and the Extent of Organization." *Review of Economic Studies* 36 (1969): 185–196.

10 *The Wage Structure: Occupational Wage Differences*

In the days when the union scene was dominated by the American Federation of Labor (AFL) which organized workers along craft lines, union efforts were principally aimed at raising the relative wages of skilled workers. With the advent in 1935 of the Congress for Industrial Organization (CIO), which organizes workers along industrial lines and irrespective of skills, raising the wages of "blue collar" relative to "white collar" occupations became a major union objective. Subsequent to the merger of the AFL and the CIO, after their last separate conventions in 1955, the objective of unionism became, on the one hand, to improve the relative wages of all union members and, on the other, to move in the direction of greater equity, largely in acquiescence to political pressure from within unions, by pursuing a "standard wage rate." This appears to be the case particularly where the pattern has been toward industry-wide bargaining. There are nevertheless, occupational wage differences that persist even within the framework of the standard wage rate. This chapter is concerned chiefly with examining short-run, cyclical, and secular changes in the occupational wage structure.

The Theory of Wage Differentials

A useful preliminary to examining the theoretical basis for wage differentials is to recall the observations made in Chapter 5 about the choices that prospective workers make among alternative opportunities. It was noted there that people respond to both the nonmonetary and the monetary characteristics of alternative employment opportunities. The nonmonetary characteristics of alternative opportunities tend to become reflected in wage differentials among them. The tendency is for *different* wage rates to be established *even under competition* if the activities involve advantages or disadvantages. Given the demand for labor to fill particular kinds of job vacancies, economic principle implies that wage rates will be in equilibrium when the net advantages of different employments among which people can move are equalized for equally efficient individuals. Thus it is possible and indeed likely that wage differentials will persist between homogeneous types of labor and perform the function of "equalizing" the net advantage of alternative opportunities. Economic principle does not maintain that freedom on the part of workers to move among occupations and locations will equalize wages. Rather it maintains that there is a tendency to equalize the net advantages among alternative employment opportunities when workers are free to choose among them. The net advantage of any employment opportunity, it will be recalled, reflects its net money income (i.e., the gross income minus the cost of education, training, and moving, plus or minus the value attached by the worker to its nonmonetary advantages). Thus, the expectation is that occupational wage differentials will be closely related to their educational and training requirements. A backward glance to Table 5-1 in Chapter 5 is useful at this juncture, to reconfirm the fact that differences exist in educational attainment among persons attached to various occupations. The expectation is that these differences will be mirrored in earnings differentials that reflect differentials in skill.

Short-Run Fluctuations in Skill Margins

Wage differences that reflect skill margins are altered relatively little during "normal" periods, but there is considerable basis for the view that they narrow sharply during economic expansions. This is particularly the case during overtime when the differentials are quickly generated. Expansions bring about an imbalance in the labor market that is associated with a high job-vacancy rate. The number of unfilled job vacancies is a measure of the magnitude of excess demand in the labor market at a particular moment in time. A "tight" labor market is characterized by a large number of unfilled job vacancies.

The relative scarcity of available job applicants can be met by raising wage offers or by reducing the quality standards that govern hiring or by introducing some combination of both these methods. Melvin Reder advanced a "job vacancy" hypothesis that emphasizes the role of variations in the quality of the labor supply that result from upgrading workers relative to the jobs they are to fill. He views quality variations as a basis for explaining the narrowing of wage differentials between skilled and unskilled workers in periods when the labor reserve is substantially reduced by increases in aggregate demand.[1]

[1] Melvin W. Reder, "The Theory of Occupational Wage Differentials," *American Economic Review* 44, 5 (December 1955).

Employers are most concerned with maintaining quality standards for the new employees they hire when incompetence poses a danger to lives and property. When this is not a prime consideration, they are likely to respond to labor shortage by providing supplemental training in order to upgrade workers.[2] Supplemental training is likely to be the rule when the skill differential is large and the necessary skill can be acquired in a relatively short time. The effect of this response is to facilitate upward mobility among occupations within a firm. Workers, in effect, "move up" occupationally as they acquire additional skills. This response to a high vacancy rate therefore does not alter the wage structure; it facilitates granting smaller wage increases in a tight labor market.

Several advantages accrue to employers from upgrading workers in order to meet shortages where possible. One is that the increased compensation paid to a worker who has improved his skills needs to be paid only to promoted workers and not to others, as is generally the case when wage rates are increased. Second, the process of shifting workers and reclassifying jobs can be undertaken as a more or less continuous process that is not subject to changing wage rates, which, typically, is done only periodically. (Changes in job classifications also incur less protest than do wage reductions.)

The job-vacancy hypothesis suggests that the occupational wage differential is likely to become wider in a labor market in which there is unemployment. When there is a general slackening of demand, employers are less likely to lay off skilled workers than unskilled workers. Chapter 7 emphasized that this is especially the case when investments have been made via "on-the-job training." Thus, the job-vacancy model suggests that while labor shortages tend to narrow skill differentials, periods of excess labor supply are likely to be characterized by larger wage differentials. That is, the wages of unskilled and/or inexperienced workers are likely to be more sensitive to labor-market conditions than are the wages of those who are more skilled and experienced.

It also explains why the narrowing of occupational wage rates that occurs during wartime shortages is only partially reversed afterward. Wartime demands stimulate the relative supply of skilled workers, and the added skills tend to be reinforced by "experience differentials," i.e., wage differentials associated with the length of service in a given firm or organization. A study that examines the salaries of starting engineers as compared with experienced engineers has provided empirical verification for these inferences.

[2] Others besides Reder have noted reliance on upgrading. See P. B. Doeringer and M. J. Piore, in *Internal Labor and Manpower Analysis* (Lexington, Mass.: D. C. Heath and Co., 1971). This process was observed earlier by L. Reynolds, in *Structure of Labor Markets* (New York: Harper and Brothers, 1951), p. 139.

ECONOMICS IN ACTION 10:1

The Salaries of Starting and Experienced Engineers during Periods of Changing Demand

Monthly salary data for engineers, classified by years of experience, were examined for selected years between 1894 and 1953.[3] It was found that during periods of rapidly increasing demand for the services of engineers, the ratio of the salaries of starting engineers to those of experienced engineers increased rapidly. The salaries of less experienced engineers also increased relative to those earned by more experienced workers. For example, during the World War I period, the increase in the earnings of engineers at the starting level and of those with between one and ten years of experience increased 60 to 80 percent between 1914 and 1916 and between 1919 and 1921. By contrast, the increase in wages for engineering graduates with ten to twenty years of experience ranged between zero and 20 percent. Essentially the same pattern of differential increases is in evidence during the World War II period and during the Korean War.

Average monthly salaries during the Korean War for research engineers and scientists holding a B.S. degree are recorded in Table 10-A in terms of percentage changes by years of experience. The differential rate of wage increase enjoyed by engineers with zero or one year of experience is apparent in the percentage changes in their average monthly salaries in 1951–1952 and 1952–1953.

TABLE 10-A *Percentage Changes of Engineering Salaries, by Years of Experience*

	0	1	9	10	11
1948– 9	−3.2	−0.3	2.8	1.1	0.9
1949–50	1.8	1.7	2.0	3.5	3.2
1950–51	6.9	5.0	7.6	6.7	6.9
1951–52	11.3	12.7	8.2	9.4	8.1
1952–53	6.8	6.7	3.8	4.0	4.4
1953–54	3.7	5.5	1.6	2.1	3.4
1954–55	7.2	5.0	16.6	8.9	8.0

SOURCE: Blank and Stigler, *The Demand and Supply of Scientific Personnel* (New York: National Bureau of Economic Research, 1957), Table A-15, p. 141. Reprinted with permission.

[3] D. M. Blank and George Stigler, *The Demand and Supply of Scientific Personnel* (New York: National Bureau of Economic Research, 1957).

The demand for engineers in the postwar period was accompanied by a decline in the salaries of inexperienced engineers.[4] Moreover, during periods of severe recession, like that which characterized the 1930s, the decline in the salaries of the inexperienced was relatively greater than that of those who had more years of experience. Although depression years are not included in Table 10-A, the median salary of those with one year's experience declined 26.5 percent between 1929 and 1932, as compared with 18.7 percent for all engineers.

Between 1929 and 1939, the median salary for beginning engineers declined 14.1 percent as compared with a decline of 4.2 percent for all engineers. This study suggests that in a tight labor market it is more profitable, given the initial differences in their salaries, to train the inexperienced and promote them to senior positions. Conversely, it is more profitable to hire those who have more experience when labor-market conditions ease.

The chief difference in the two types of market situations derives from the cost of recruiting and hiring in a tight labor market. The search costs of locating experienced engineers already in someone else's employ and the cost of "pirating" causes the marginal cost of hiring additional experienced workers to rise more or less substantially when the labor market tightens. But since these costs are not applicable to new graduates, the marginal cost of recruiting inexperienced workers is lower. Thus, it was found that in a tight market, given the supply of inexperienced engineers, the cost differential of hiring experienced versus inexperienced workers tends to increase the demand for those with less experience, which drives up their wages.

Conversely, it is easier to hire an experienced worker (e.g., engineers) from among those who are currently looking for a job when the market loosens. The marginal cost of hiring an experienced engineer falls when the overall demand for engineers falls. The shift in demand .from those who are less experienced to those who are more experienced results in a tendency for the demand for and wages of those who are inexperienced to decline.

An Alternative Hypothesis: The Impact of Institutional Forces

Reder's hypothesis maintains that the relatively greater upward pressure on unskilled compared with skilled wages reflects market forces. However, the narrowing of skill differentials during boom periods has also been attributed to institutional rather than to market forces. A fairly

---

[4]Similar evidence is provided by Robert Evans for clerical workers in the Boston area. See "Worker Quality and Wage Dispersion: An Analysis of a Clerical Labor Market in Boston," *Proc. of Industrial Relations Research Association* (December 1961): 250–251.

long history is attached to the hypothesis that there are institutional pressures which raise the wages of less skilled workers proportionately more during periods of rapidly rising prices than to raise those paid to high-priced workers. The premise is that inflation places an inequitable burden on workers who are most poorly paid.[5]

Clearly, there is no way to decide between the job-vacancy and the institutional hypotheses on any but an empirical basis. Unfortunately, the data that are available to support theoretical speculation and thereby minimize controversy are very few. The studies that have been undertaken do not appear to provide a definitive answer concerning which of these hypotheses best accounts for the reduced skill differential that characterizes inflationary periods. It is, nevertheless, enlightening to review the findings of a study by Robert Evans that undertook to examine data pertaining to the Civil War and the periods of the first and second World Wars.

ECONOMICS IN ACTION 10:2

Institutional Forces and the Narrowing of Wage Differentials during Inflation

There appears to be a real wage level below which workers, especially adult males, will not work. Custom and social attitudes appear to have sanctioned such minimums even before money-wage minimums were established by statute or union wage policy. This implies that in periods of rising prices the money wages of those who were least skilled were raised in order to maintain the social minimum in real terms. What support is there for this hypothesis?

Evans's study utilized data from the Civil War and both world wars to establish a simple rank-order correlation between the skill margin and various measures of excess demand. These were unemployment, labor loss, the ratio of skilled to unskilled workers, and the labor-force-participation rate. He also established a statistical relationship between the skill margin and real compensation, the skill margin and money compensation, and the skill margin and the Consumer Price Index.[6] He utilized the data compiled by Wesley Mitchell on the ratio between the wages of skilled handicraftsmen and unskilled laborers as a measure of the skill margin during the Civil War. For the world war periods the

---

[5] Wesley C. Mitchell, *A History of the Greenbacks* (Chicago: University of Chicago Press, 1933), p. 303. Also, Gerhard Bry, *Wages in Germany 1871–1945* (Princeton: Princeton University Press, 1960), pp. 83–85.

[6] Robert Evans, "Wage Differentials, Excess Demand for Labor and Inflation: A Note," *Review of Economics and Statistics* 45 (February 1963): 95–98.

skill margin is represented by the ratio of union-wage scales of journeymen to those of laborers in the building trades.

Since a tight labor market is an essential aspect of Reder's job-vacancy hypothesis, Evans particularly examined the behavior of key relationships in those periods when unemployment was 4 percent or lower. It is evident from Table 10-B that there was a closer correspondence between rising prices and the decreasing skill margin than between the latter and the various labor-market variables that are also correlated with the skill margin.

TABLE 10-B *Percentage Changes in Excess Variables and Inflation (Years of 4 Percent Unemployment)*

Year	Skill Margin	Unemployment Rate	Labor-Loss Rate	Ratio of Actual to Potential Labor Input	Labor-Force-Participation Rate	Real Compensation	Money Compensation
1917–18	−4.20	− 70.0	..	..	..	+12.4	+31.9
1918–19	−1.70	+ 61.9	..	..	..	− .7	+14.3
1919–20	−7.80	+ 70.5	..	..	..	− 2.8	+12.5
1942–43	−.7	− 63.6	+38.1	..	+5.9	+ 7.4	+12.8
1943–44	− .7	− 42.9	− 1.2	..	+1.2	+ 6.3	+ 7.6
1944–45	−2.6	+ 56.0	0.0	..	−2.0	− 1.2	+ .9
1945–46	−4.6	+112.0	−17.3	..	−7.6	− 1.9	+ 6.6

SOURCE: Robert Evans, "Wage Differentials, Excess Demand for Labor and Inflation: A Note," *Review of Economics and Statistics* 45 (February 1963): 95–98.

A similar finding characterizes the experience of the Civil War. Major movements in the skill margin occurred in 1862–63 and 1863–4, which are also years of maximum price increase. Thus Evans concludes that, in terms of aggregate movements, institutional pressures to keep up with changes in the wage differential between skilled and unskilled workers during the three wartime periods were more important than any measure of excess demand in the labor market.

Secular Changes in Skill Differentials

Education and Skill Differential

Assuming that it is reasonable to use the median number of years of schooling as a proxy for the improvement in the quality of labor force attributable to education, Table 10-1 provides some insight into the increasing supply of more qualified labor since the 1920s. Since the theory of household choice leads us to the conclusion that individuals will invest in education if the present value of the returns they expect to earn over their working lifetime is greater than or equal to the sum of the direct and indirect costs expended in its acquisition, the inference is that wage differences among occupations will be consistent with differences in educational levels. The expectation is that persons classified as "professional, technical and kindred workers" and "managers, officials, and proprietors" will have higher earnings than persons in occupational groups that have lower educational requirements.

TABLE 10-1 *Median Number of Years of Schooling by Males at Specified Dates*

Age at Specified Date	1920	1930	1940	1950	1960	1970
1) 25−29	8.4	8.7	10.1	12.0	12.3	12.5
2) 45−54	8.1	8.2	8.4	8.7	10.0	12.0
3) (1)−(2)	0.3	0.5	1.7	3.3	2.3	0.5

SOURCE: U.S. Bureau of the Census, Current Population Characteristics Series, P-20, pp. 6–7.

This expectation is borne out by Table 10-2, which presents ten occupational groups identified by the United States Department of Commerce and the median earnings, by occupation, of year-round, full-time male civilian workers for 1939, 1958, 1968, and 1975. Since earnings reflect the number of hours per week and weeks worked per year as well as the wage rate, data on earnings are not precisely equivalent to wage rates. However, the spread among occupational categories provides a reasonably good picture of occupational differences among wage rates.

In order to faciliate the identification of occupational differentials, earnings have been converted into an index that sets the earnings of the category "laborers, except farm" equal to 100 percent. The index numbers recorded in Table 10-2 compute the ratio of the wages of the most skilled to that of the least skilled (i.e., the extremes of the wage structure). This technique measures the skill differential among them. Changes in the index over time reflect changes in the skill differential. The index for 1975, which is the last year for which data are presently available, reflects a narrowing of the skill differential in comparison with that of 1968. While the highest incomes are those earned by "profes-

TABLE 10-2 *Median Earnings of Year-Round, Full-Time Male Civilians by Occupation, 1939, 1958, 1968, 1975*

Earnings in Dollars

Occupational Group	1939	Index	1958	Index	1968	Index	1975	Index
Professional, technical, and kindred workers	$2,100	211.9	6,513	177.4	9,960	239.1	15,555	170.3
Farmers and farm workers	430	43.4	490	13.3	3,734	89.2	2,547	27.9
Managers, officials, and proprietors	2,254	227.5	6,431	175.1	9,765	234.5	16,598	181.7
Clerical and kindred workers	1,564	157.8	4,839	131.8	7,034	168.9	12,138	132.9
Sales workers	1,451	146.4	5,332	145.2	7,367	176.9	13,787	150.9
Craftsmen, foremen, and kindred workers	1,562	157.6	5,365	146.1	7,705	185.0	12,917	141.4
Operatives and kindred	1,268	128.0	4,460	121.5	6,209	149.1	11,106	121.6
Service workers	1,019	102.8	3,898	106.2	4,820	115.7	9,592	105.0
Farm laborers and foremen	365	36.7	1,406	38.3	2,073	49.8	5,300	58.0
Laborers, except farm	991	100.0	3,672	100.0	4,165	100.0	9,134	100.0

SOURCE: U.S. Department of Commerce, Bureau of Census, Current Population Reports: Income of Persons in the United States, 1958, Series P-60, no. 33, p. 51; Statistical Abstract of the United States, 1970.

sional, technical, and kindred workers" and "managers, officials, and proprietors," their relative position has deteriorated in comparison to what it was at the end of the 1960s, although this group has fared relatively better than "professional, technical, and kindred workers." Except for the considerable improvement in the relative position of "farmers and farm managers" and "farm laborers and foremen," the index for 1968 approximates that of 1958, which in all but a few categories reflects a narrowing of the skill differential since 1939.

An alternative way of measuring changes in interoccupational wages is to identify changes in the dispersion of the whole wage structure. The results of a study that utilized a composite sample of many occupations in many industries to identify the long-term trend of the skill differential are reviewed as *Economics in Action* 10:3.

ECONOMICS IN ACTION 10:3

The Narrowing of the Skill Differential, 1900–1956

The relative dispersion of hourly wages was compared for the years 1903 and 1956 using a composite sample of many occupations in many industries in order to identify secular changes in the skill differential.[7] The years 1903 and 1956 were chosen to measure the trend of wage differentials because they were presumed to be years during which wages could reasonably be taken to exhibit a similar cyclical relationship. Using the reference cycles of the National Bureau of Economic Research, the year 1903 was identified as a peak year of the cycle. Since the trend of wages was continuously upward from 1945 to 1956, wage data from 1956 were selected as the terminal date of the study.

Changes in the coefficient of variation (i.e., the standard deviation exhibited by the data divided by the arithmetic mean), which is considered to be a good measure of structural changes, are recorded in Table 10-C. While the same occupations that were highly paid in 1903 were also highly paid in 1956, it was found that the coefficient of variation using either 1903 or 1956 occupational weights fell by approximately one-third, i.e., skill differentials narrowed. Does this experience reflect the influence of market forces, or is it primarily attributable to institutional forces that served to reduce wage differentials between blue-collar and white-collar workers? The next several sections focus on this question.

TABLE 10-C *Changes in Coefficient of Variation, 141 Occupations, 1903–1956*

	1903	1956	Percent Changes
1903 and 1956 weights, respectively	0.515	0.234	−54.6
1903 weights	.515	.341	−33.8
1956 weights	0.369	0.234	−36.6

SOURCE: Paul Keat, "Long Term Changes in Occupational Wage Structure, 1900–1956," *Journal of Political Economy* 68, (December 1960). Reprinted by permission of the University of Chicago Press.

Becker's Hypothesis about the Narrowing Differential

While there is no question that the overall level of schooling has increased and that the relative supply of better-educated labor has increased along with it in response to market forces, there is no consensus on the way in which schooling has operated to narrow the wage differential.

Gary Becker has argued that the narrowing wage differential is the consequence of a secular growth in productivity and that increased schooling is a *responsive* rather than an autonomous force. His argument

[7] Paul Keat, "Long-Term Changes in Occupational Wage Structure, 1900–1956," *Journal of Political Economy* 68 (December 1960). Herman P. Miller has also noted the comparison of earnings differentials. See *Income of the American People* (New York: John Wiley and Sons, 1955), Chapter 9.

rests on the assumption that technological advances have been neutral (i.e., progress leaves the ratio of the marginal products of all factors unchanged) and that the demand for investment in human capital is "tied" to the demand for physical capital.

Becker's assumption of neutral technological advance implies that the increase in demand for skilled and unskilled labor has been proportionate so that their *relative* wages would be expected to remain the same. However, a proportionate rise in all wages also implies that the *absolute* difference between skilled and unskilled wages has widened. Thus, the rate of return on investment in education relative to that of physical capital has increased. In Becker's view, therefore, the increase in the median level of schooling has been a *response* to factors that raised the returns to schooling.[8] In short, investment in schooling in the human-capital model is an *endogenous* response to improvements in the relative rewards from education.

The Possible Influence of Institutional and Demand-Side Forces

While Becker's hypothesis is a very ingenious explanation of the narrowing of wage-rate differences in terms of an internal-response mechanism that governs investment in education, it is possible that the secular increase in the relative number of skilled workers reflects a change in relative demand and not in supply. It is also possible that the reduction in the skill differential is owing to institutional rather than market forces operating on the supply side.

One of the greatest classics in economics noted that the "supply of labor in a trade in any generation tends to conform to its earnings not in that but in the preceding generation."[9] Recent studies verify empirically that increases in the level of education may reflect a response to relative changes in the demand for educated labor.[10] A key reason for the lag of supply behind demand is that there is typically an information delay as well as a decision delay.[11]

To the extent that the increase in education reflects increases in the consumption of a superior or luxury good that accompanies a rise in income, demand-side forces have been at work in changing the supply of educated workers. However, a substantial part of increased schooling at the high-school level (and it is with schooling through grade twelve that we are chiefly concerned) reflects the effect of compulsory-school-attendance laws.

[8] Gary Becker, *Human Capital*, National Bureau of Economic Research (1964): 52–55.

[9] Alfred Marshall, *Principles of Economics*, 5th ed. (New York: Macmillan and Co., 1936), p. 571.

[10] See above, Chapter 5, pp. 121–127.

[11] George Stigler, "The Economics of Information," *Journal of Political Economy* 69 (June 1961): 213 ff.

The change in immigration policy has also been a major institutional factor in causing the relative decline in the supply of unskilled labor. As noted in Chapter 2, only a small portion of the American labor force is derived from legal immigration.[12] However, before the first world war, unskilled and relatively uneducated European immigrants came in such large numbers that significant occupational-skill differentials were generated and maintained. The Immigration Acts of 1921 and 1924 sharply reduced total immigration and gave preference to those with skills. This institutional change in the supply of unskilled labor contributed to the narrowing of skill differentials that has taken place. Legal regulation of child labor further contributed to the reduction in the supply of unskilled labor. Thus, institutional as well as market forces were at work in narrowing long-term wage differentials. But in the absence of more definitive empirical evidence, the relative importance of institutional and market forces cannot be established.

Concluding Remarks

The long-term narrowing of the skill differential from about the turn of the century in the United States is also apparent in foreign data.[13] Cyclically, the differential tends to narrow in boom periods and widen in depression. It is not clear whether market or institutional forces were responsible for the narrowing of wage differentials between occupations and skill levels during the postwar period. While certain forces exerted a powerful influence to keep the wages of skilled workers high, equally powerful institutional forces raised the relative wages of the unskilled. A major factor in maintaining high wages for skilled workers is to be found in the technological revolution of the last several decades, which has generated an increased demand for skilled workers. The demand is not being met readily, because of high training costs and high returns on alternative investments.

While market forces have kept the wages of skilled workers high, institutional forces have raised the relative wages of the unskilled. Minimum-wage legislation has exerted considerable upward pressure on the wages of the least skilled. There has also been general support for equalizing increases in wages, both in response to social forces and inflationary pressure. Market forces tend to be ignored as workers are given flat wage-rate increases to meet cost-of-living increases. A fall in

---

[12] The role of illegal immigration has been stressed chiefly by proponents of the segmented-labor hypothesis. They interpret it as a major factor in accounting for the exploitation of secondary workers.

[13] M. P. Fogarty, "Portrait of a Pay Structure," in J. L. Meij, ed., *Internal Wage Structure* (Amsterdam: North Holland Publishing Co., 1963).

real wages is generally regarded as a more serious matter for low-wage than for high-wage groups.[14]

Although wage-rate differentials between occupations and skill levels have narrowed during the postwar decade, differences in pay between male and female workers and white and nonwhite workers have persisted for a long period. It is only in the recent past and largely as a by-product of the civil-rights movement that these differences have become a public issue and prompted the attention of economists. Chapter 11 examines recent theoretical and empirical work on the matter of wage differences by sex and race.

Suggestions for Further Reading

Robert Evans. "Wage Differentials, Excess Demand for Labor and Inflation: A Note." *Review of Economics and Statistics* 45 (February 1963).
Paul Keat. "Long-Term Changes in Occupational Wage Structure, 1900–1956." *Journal of Political Economy* 68 (December 1960).
Melvin W. Reder. "The Theory of Occupational Wage Differentials." *American Economic Review* 44, 5 (December 1955).
Simon Rottenberg. "On Choice in Labor Markets," in Burton, Benham, Vaughn, and Flanagan, eds., *Readings in Labor Market Analysis*. New York: Holt, Rinehart and Winston, 1971.

[14] J. R. Hicks, "Economic Foundation of Wage Policy," *Economic Journal* 65 (September 1955).

11 *The Wage Structure: Discriminatory Differentials*

A relevant preliminary to an examination of discriminatory wage differentials is to note that there are types of discrimination other than market discrimination. Segregation in private clubs, institutions, and housing opportunities is manisfested as a refusal to associate with particular groups of persons rather than in differential pricing. This type of discrimination is nonmarket in nature. In contrast, *economic* discrimination is reflected in the structure of wages (and/or commodity prices).

Recent studies provide a basis for believing that economic discrimination against minorities has lessened. Specifically, the annual-earnings ratio of black workers who entered the labor market in the 1960s to their white counterparts has improved and now approaches 90 percent.[1] Comparable studies have been made that provide evidence concerning the improved earnings status of women. Nevertheless, substantial earnings gaps persist that cannot be accounted for in terms of schooling, experience (including on-the-job training), occupation, industry, or union membership.

Table 11-1 records median-income data for year-round full-time white and black workers, male as well as female, from 1967 to 1975. Income data are used in preference to wages because total-income differentials are much larger than differentials in earnings. The latter represent income derived from labor-market activity, whereas the former also includes income derived from accumulated wealth, e.g., stocks, bonds, and other income-yielding property. The information presented in Table 11-1 indicates that the median income of all workers—white, black, male and female—increased in terms of current dollars. The ratio

---

[1]A study by Finis Welch was examined as an example of *Economic Theory in Action* in Chapter 4, pp. 34–35.

TABLE 11-1 *Median Income for Year-Round Full-Time Workers by Race and Sex: 1967 to 1975 (in Current Dollars)*

| | MALE | | | FEMALE | | |
	White	Black	Ratio of Black to White	White	Black	Ratio of Black to White
Year						
1967	$7,505	$4,831	.65	$4,360	$3,248	.74
1968	8,047	5,370	.67	4,687	3,561	.76
1969	8,953	5,917	.66	5,182	4,126	.80
1970	9,447	6,435	.68	5,536	4,536	.82
1971	9,902	6,771	.68	5,767	5,092	.88
1972	10,918	7,373	.68	6,172	5,280	.86
1973	11,800	7,953	.67	6,598	5,595	.85
1974	12,527	8,883	.71	7,235	6,677	.92
1975	13,459	9,848	.73	7,737	7,392	.96

SOURCE: *Current Population Reprints* Series P-60, 105 (June 1977).

of black and white incomes for males remained substantially unchanged from 1967 to 1973 and has improved since that time. The relative position of black women exhibits a striking improvement of approximately twenty percentage points between 1967 and 1975. The relatively greater improvement in the position of black women, when compared with black men, suggests that differences in the ownership of property are greater between white and nonwhite men than they are between white and nonwhite women.[2]

A comparison of the mean income of males twenty-five years of age by educational attainment, by race for 1969 (U.S. Bureau of the Census), is displayed in Figure 11-1. It shows that, on the average, a black college graduate has a mean income that is no more than a white high-school graduate's, while a black high-school graduate had a lower mean income than a white high-school dropout did. The improvement in the relative position of black males is most clearly evident in the mean income of male college graduates. Figure 11-2, which shows black earnings as a percentage of white earnings for different levels of schooling, reflects the greatly improved position of black college graduates in a different way.

Much the same kind of earnings disparity that exists between black and white males exists between white males and females. Figure 11-3, Mean Incomes by Educational Attainment by Sex (1969), is a compan-

[2]Cited by O. Ashenfelter in "Changes in Labor Market Discrimination over Time," *Journal of Human Resources* (Fall 1970): 403–410.

FIGURE 11-1   *Mean Incomes of Males Twenty-Five Years of Age and Over, by Educational Attainment, by Race—1969*

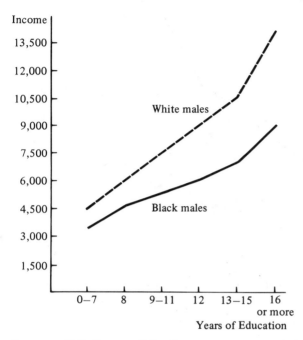

SOURCE: U.S. Bureau of the Census.

FIGURE 11-2   *Black Earnings as a Percentage of White Earnings*

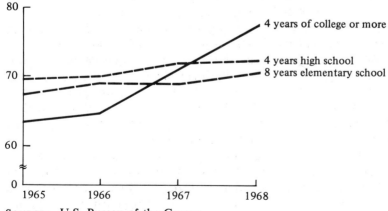

SOURCE: U.S. Bureau of the Census.

FIGURE 11-3   *Mean Incomes, by Educational Attainment, by Sex (1969)*

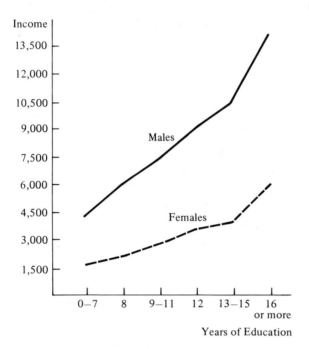

SOURCE: U.S. Bureau of the Census.

ion to Figure 11-1. It shows that on the average, women college graduates earn only slightly more than men who complete eight years of schooling. Indeed, the average male dropout earned almost $7,300 in 1969, which is equivalent to the average earnings of women who have gone to graduate school. Thus, the last Census showed that the magnitude of the disparity in earnings between males and females is even greater than that which exists between blacks and whites.

Assuming that it is reasonable to interpret equivalents of educational attainment as representing equivalent productivity, earnings differentials among workers who are homogeneous except in terms of race or sex (or ethnic background) reflect the presence of discrimination. Such differentials imply that the market has accorded a value to personal characteristics that are *unrelated to productivity*.

The magnitude of these differentials has been assessed for two cohorts of men aged forty-five to fifty-nine and fourteen to twenty-four using National Longitudinal Survey Data for 1966. The gross (i.e., unadjusted for endowment characteristics) racial hourly-wage-rate differential was estimated to be 41 percent in the older cohort and 28 percent in the younger. After an adjustment was made for differences in endowment (other than occupation), the racial hourly-wage-rate differential was estimated to be 13 percent in the older cohort and 7 percent in the younger cohort. These are the differentials that are attributable to the difference in the wage received per unit of endowment, i.e., they result from market discrimination. In short, approximately one-third of the racial hourly-wage-rate differential has been identified as being attributable to the racial differences in the prices paid for productive characteristics.[3]

In common with most of the other phenomena investigated in this book, efforts to "explain" discrimination have proceeded, on the one hand, in terms of demand-and-supply hypotheses and, on the other, in terms of institutional forces. The most widely held theory builds on the work of Gary Becker and is based on neoclassical assumptions of utility and profit maximization.[4] Alternative theoretical analyses have been offered by Kenneth Arrow, Edmund Phelps, and Barbara Bergman. Meanwhile, proponents of the dual-labor-markets view, as well as writers associated with the "new left," emphasize the fundamental role of institutional and political influences.

The Utility Theory of Discrimination

Discrimination by Other Employees

Becker's approach to examining discrimination assumes that an economic agent has a set of "tastes" that includes a preference for associating with a particular group, say white workers, W, and avoiding association with black workers, B. It further assumes that he is both able and willing to pay for the positive valuation of W and/or the negative valuation of B. Thus, white employers, employees, or consumers are conceived as being willing to sacrifice profits, accept lower wages, or pay higher prices in order to satisfy their preferences to avoid association with the group (say black workers) that is being discriminated against. The case of discrimination by other employees will be examined first.

Discriminatory tastes on the part of white workers against other racial or ethnic groups is particularly likely when the skills of the groups differ, as is typical between skilled and unskilled workers or supervisors and subordinates. A negative attitude on the part of whites toward a supervisor of a different race is likely to be stronger and more persistent than toward co-workers or subordinates of a different race. It would probably be very expensive for employers to compensate white workers

[3] Robert Flanagan, "Labor Force Experience, Job Turnover and Racial Wage Differentials," *Review of Economics and Statistics* 56, 4 (November 1974): 528.

[4] Gary Becker, *The Economics of Discrimination* (Chicago: University of Chicago Press, 1959).

for their dislike of being supervised by a nonwhite. The likelihood, therefore, according to Becker, is that supervisory workers will be white, and that the labor of subordinates and co-workers will be either all white or all black.[5] Profit-maximizing firms will pay white and nonwhite workers equally, but if there are discriminatory attitudes on the part of white workers against nonwhite co-workers, the preferences will produce *segregation* between them rather than discriminatory wage differentials.

Employer Discrimination: The *d* Coefficient

Becker has also examined the case of discrimination by employers. He maintains that it is likely to be less prevalent in competitive industries and, furthermore, if it does occur, it will lead to *wage differentials* between white and nonwhite workers rather than to their segregation.

To follow the logic of his argument, assume a market in which several firms are producing the same product with the same production function. In the short run, with capital given and two kinds of labor, W and B, which are perfect substitutes for one another, output reflects the marginal productivity of white labor and black labor. With given "tastes" for hiring W as opposed to B workers, employers "trade off" profits against the number of W and B employees. That is, they are conceived as behaving as though they are maximizing a utility function $U(\pi,W,B)$. The general equilibrium condition is that W and B workers are both fully employed and that the wage difference between them reflects the discriminatory tastes of employers.

Following the logic of employer-maximizing behavior that was investigated in Chapter 6, each employer will equate the marginal productivity of W labor and B labor to their price. The "price" of B labor is the market wage W_b plus d_b which is the differential or "discrimination coefficient" the employer is willing to pay, in terms of lower profits, for the satisfaction of reducing the number of B workers by one. The discrimination coefficient, d_b, is positive if the marginal utility is negative.[6] Thus an employer who discriminates will hire B labor only if its price is lower than W labor. The maximizing relationship between productivity and wages for black and white workers is

$$MP_b = W_B + d_B \tag{1}$$

and

$$MP_w = W_w + d_w \tag{2}$$

[5] Becker, *op. cit.*, pp. 56–58.

[6] The discrimination coefficient, d_b, is the negative of the marginal rate of substitution between profit and labor.

where d_w is zero if the employer has no preference for white workers and negative if he does. Since $W_B + d_b > W_w + d_w$, it follows that, in equilibrium, W wages will exceed B wages, and B workers are paid less than their marginal product. White workers gain (or do not lose) because d_w is zero or negative.

The magnitude of the differential between W wages and B wages (or between the wages of whites and other minority groups) depends chiefly on the number of black workers seeking employment. This principle can be illustrated with the aid of a supply-and-demand diagram that differs from the conventional one only in that the vertical axis measures the *ratio* between black and white wage rates. Thus, in Figure 11-4, the demand schedule for black labor

$$D_b = f \frac{(W_b + d_b)}{(W_w + d_w)}$$

represents the number of black workers offered employment at lower wage ratios; $W_w + d_w$ is a constant while $W_b + d_b$ becomes successively lower as the ratio of black to white workers increases.[7]

FIGURE 11-4 *The Ratio of Black-White Wages under Different Supply Conditions*

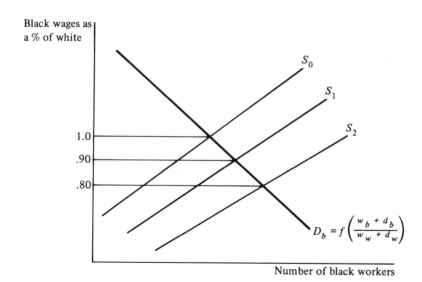

7 Remember, d_b is *negative*.

If the supply of black workers seeking employment is represented by the curve S_1, the ratio of black to white wages is higher than would be the case if the larger supply, S_2, is seeking employment. This analysis indicates that black wages will equal white wages only if the number of blacks seeking employment is sufficiently small, say S_0, so that the supply curve intersects the demand curve sufficiently far to the left for the ratio

$$\frac{(W_b + d_b)}{(W_w + d_w)} = 1.$$

But if the relevant supply curve of black labor is S_1 or S_2, $d_b > 0$ and black wages will be lower than white wages. Ashenfelter has given interesting empirical verification to this conclusion.

ECONOMICS IN ACTION 11:1

The Effect of Supply on Minority-Wage Differentials

Data supplied by the United States Equal Employment Opportunity Commission were evaluated to determine what are the employment patterns among minority groups in the United States.[8] The study focused on the distribution of employment by occupation, industry, and region.

Data on average earnings by occupation are not collected through the EEOC reporting form. Thus, it is necessary to infer the average earnings of particular minority groups from information about employment and occupation. An index was computed for this purpose for each group. The procedure for its computation was to multiply the proportion of each group's employment in each of the nine occupational categories by the average earnings for that occupation for all groups and then sum the resulting nine figures. The index is thus expressed in dollars and may be interpreted as reflecting the average salary for a particular minority group. In effect, the index measures the average money value of the occupational distribution for each group.

Expressed in terms of this index, the average money value of the Negro-male occupational distribution is only 77 percent of the Anglo male occupational distribution. This compares with indices for Spanish

---

[8] Orley Ashenfelter, "Minority Employment Patterns, 1966," prepared for U.S. Equal Employment Opportunity Commission and the Office of Manpower Policy Evaluation and Research of the United States Department of Labor. This study is particularly valuable for its evaluation of the data collected through the EEOC reporting system. These data are found to be particularly valuable because they allow a high degree of disaggregation by ethnic group.

American males, American Indian males, and Oriental males, which are 83 percent, 89 percent, and 101.3 percent of the Anglo index. The money value of the Oriental occupational structure was slightly more than 1 percent higher than that of the Anglo occupational structure because there is a heavier concentration in professional and technical employment; approximately 13 percent of Anglo males are professional and technical workers, whereas 30 percent of Oriental males are in these occupations.

There is, however, a significant variation in the occupational distributions of minority groups from region to region that reflects the numerical importance of the minority group in the region. Specifically, Orientals are concentrated in the West, where their employment comprises 2.5 percent of the totals. By contrast, they represent less than .2 percent of employment in the North and .1 percent of employment in the South. American Indians and Spanish Americans are similarly more concentrated in the West. The money value of their occupational distributions in each region is consistent with the magnitude of their population concentration. Thus, in comparison with their national position, there is a substantial deterioration in the occupational structure of Orientals and American Indians in the West. In the North and South the money values of the Oriental-male occupational structure is 12 percent above the national value, whereas in the West it is 4 percent below the national value. Moreover, the Oriental-male index is approximately 13 percent above the Anglo index in the North and the South, while it is 6 percent below the Anglo index in the West. Similarly, the indices for male American Indians are 1 percent and 4 percent higher in the North and South than their national values, but 4 percent lower in the West. Thus, EEOC data appear to substantiate the theoretical conclusion that disciminatory pay differentials are likely to be larger, the larger the number in the region of the population subgroup.

Competition, Monopoly, and Discrimination

Employers who discriminate are "trading off" between profits, π, and the number of B and W employees. That is, they are seeking to maximize a utility function $U(\pi,B,W)$. Their utility depends not only on profits but also on the ratio of W to B workers. However, profitability is itself dependent on the ratio of W to B workers because discrimination shifts an employer's demand to white labor, which is a more costly input than equally productive black labor. In terms of economic principle, therefore, competitive enterprises that are less discriminatory are more profitable than those which are more discriminatory.

Competition in the product market also has employment implications. If competitive industries discriminate less, on the average, than monopolistic ones, relatively more black labor will be employed in competitive industries than in monopolistic industries. Becker maintains that this analysis explains the difference in the number of nonwhite male employees in competitive and noncompetitive industries in eight census occupational categories in the South in 1940.[9] Industries are classified as monopolistic on the basis of "Nutter's Index" of the degree of monopoly.[10] An industry is classified as monopolistic if the four leading firms in an industry (measured in terms of value of total output) employ 50 percent or more of the workers in the industry. Among the thirty-eight industries, ten were identified as monopolistic and twenty-eight as competitive. It was then established that the relative number of nonwhite workers was greater in competitive than in monopolistic industries for seven of the eight categories. Nonwhites were relatively more numerous among "other service workers, laborers and operators." The only category in which more nonwhites were employed in monopolistic industries was that in which the supply of nonwhites was greater than the supply of whites.

Becker's findings that competitive industries discriminate less than do monopolistic ones has invited further examination. His argument is that firms with the smallest d values have the lowest unit costs and therefore eventually will produce the industry's entire output if other employers choose not to reduce their taste for discrimination. He inferred that monopolistic industries, which do not face competitive pressure to reduce their taste for discrimination, employ fewer blacks. Since his conclusion that racial discrimination is a function of monopoly is closely related to his classification of industries into competitive and monopolistic categories, it is relevant to review his methodology.

ECONOMIC THEORY IN ACTION 11:2

Market Structure and Discrimination

Becker's finding that competitive industries discriminate less is, as already noted, based on his utilization of Nutter's Index to classify industries as competitive or monopolistic. A critical shortcoming, it has been argued, is the aggregation of ten industries into a monopolistic group, and twenty-eight others into one competitive group.[11] One result of this grouping is that the existence of a few large competitive industries

[9] Gary Becker, *The Economics of Discrimination* (Chicago: University of Chicago Press, 1957, 1971), Chapter 3, pp. 47–50.

[10] G. W. Nutter, *The Extent of Enterprise Monopoly in the United States, 1899–1939* (Chicago: University of Chicago Press, 1951).

[11] Raymond Franklin and Michael Tanzer, "Traditional Microeconomic Analysis of Racial Discrimination: A Critical View and Alternative Approach," in David Mermelstein, ed., *Economics: Mainstream Readings and Critiques* (New York: Random House, 1970).

which employ a high proportion of blacks may greatly influence the final results. Lumping twenty-eight industries into one competitive group may obscure the presence of other competitive industries that are extremely discriminatory. Thus, Franklin and Tanzer argue that in order to evaluate more accurately the relationship between racial discrimination and competitive market structure, it is necessary to use a measurement process that will not be subject to distortion in consequence of aggregation. Accordingly the relationship between competitive structure and racial discrimination was tested by a ranking procedure.

When southern industries were ranked in order of degree of monopoly and in order of percentage of all male employees who are black, the relationship between them was found to be insignificant. A comparison of the degree of monopoly and discrimination against black females in southern industry similarly showed an insignificant relation. On this basis the study rejected Becker's market-structure hypothesis as an explanation of industrial discrimination against blacks.[12]

Statistical Theories of Discrimination

Imperfect Information

An alternative approach to interpreting employer discrimination is to view employer preferences for white rather than black (or male rather than female) employees as reflecting perceptions of worker productivity rather than a "taste" for nonassociation.[13] Employers who believe that black workers (or females) are less effective employees than white workers (or males) are willing to hire them, but only at lower wages.

The presumption of this approach is that employers lack information for evaluating workers' productivity potentials at a reasonably low cost and therefore rely on surrogate information. External characteristics such as color and sex, and other readily available "sorting devices," such as schooling and experience, therefore serve as proxies for precise information, which is very costly. An employer cannot know for certain whether a given worker is qualified. The tendency is thus to rely on the probability that a random black or white worker is qualified for a skilled job (and is likely to warrant the expenditure of the training and personnel costs that his or her employment will entail). Employers assign

---

[12]It also seems relevant to call attention to a study examining the effect of unionization on black wages. See Orley Ashenfelter, "Discrimination and Trade Unions," in Albert Rees and Orley Ashenfelter, eds., *Discrimination in Labor Markets* (Princeton: Princeton University Press, 1971).

[13]Kenneth Arrow, "The Theory of Discrimination," in Albert Rees and Orley Ashenfelter, eds., *ibid.*, p. 18. See also Edmund Phelps, "The Statistical Theory of Racism and Sexism," *American Economic Review* 62 (1972): 659–661.

a lower *subjective probability* (for whatever reason) that there will be a successful outcome when a worker is selected from a pool of blacks rather than from a pool of whites. Blacks are therefore hired at lower wages than whites are; this is not a reflection of preferences but rather of employer expectations concerning the productivity of blacks in comparison with whites.

Discrimination and Cyclical Unemployment

It has been observed that the relative labor-market position of blacks and women varies in the same direction as the level of business activity.[14] Thus, blacks experience relative income gains in tight labor markets. The Arrow-Phelps model of employer behavior interprets this behavior pattern in terms of the expected utility to be derived from alternative racial pools. The cyclical pattern of black/white employment is "explained" by adding two additional assumptions to the information-theoretic model. The first is that the expected utility of hiring a worker is a function of the expected delay in locating a suitable candidate; the second is the subjective probability that a random black or white worker from the available pool is qualified. The presumption is that as full employment of white males is approached, their hiring-delay period is lengthened. Thus, the expected utility of hiring an additional worker from the pool of black and/or female workers rises relative to hiring from the white pool, while the cost of holding out for white males only increases.[15] This may lead to sampling from the pool of black applicants.

If sampling shows that prejudgment about the expected utility of hiring blacks was erroneous, the presumption is that minorities will achieve permanent advancement. Each period of labor shortage should be accompanied by a relative advance in their relative earnings, and a ratchetlike effect would be expected to preserve previous gains. However, a glance back at Table 11-1 suggests that there is some basis for skepticism about the presence of a ratchet effect. Part of the relative-earnings gains of full-time black workers was lost after the recession of the early 1970s. In part this reflects racial differences in the distribution of employment. Because blacks are disproportionately employed in

---

[14]See Melvin Reder, "Wage Structure and Structural Unemployment," *Review of Economic Studies* 31 (October 1964), and H. Gilman, "Economic Discrimination and Unemployment," *American Economic Review* 55 (December 1965).

[15]While this model offers a rationalization of the apparent difference in the availability of job opportunities among groups, an essential element of this model is its assumption that black and female wages are sufficiently rigid relative to that of white males to permit a relatively greater employment response to business conditions. But this assumption poses the problem of explaining the differential in terms of racially different costs and returns to wage flexibility.

occupations in which employment is cyclically sensitive, their employment falls relative to that of whites during a recession.

The Relevance of Supply-Side Influences

The Becker-Arrow-Phelps hypotheses, which explain discrimination in terms of "tastes" and employer perceptions of the productivity probabilities of minority workers, direct their attention only to demand-side influences on the relative rates of pay for services that are otherwise homogenous. This approach neglects the supply of labor, in terms of both its quantity and its quality, as a relevant factor in explaining relative rates of compensation for black and female workers.

If, for example, black workers have identical supply functions as white workers, but employers will not hire black workers unless the wage is at least d cents per hour less than the wage of white labor, the adverse effect of discrimination on the wage rate is understated if the reduction in the quantity of black labor supplied is not taken into account. That is, the theory of choice concerning the allocation of time (Chapter 2) suggests that the extent of nonmarket activity among black workers will be greater if $W_b + d < W_w$. The wage impact of discrimination is not adequately measured as a function of the difference between their equilibrium-wage rate and that of comparable white workers who are not discriminated against. The equilibrium-wage differential among homogenous workers is affected by the impact that the discrimination coefficient has on the wage elasticity of the labor supply.[16] Price-quantity interactions can be ignored in estimating the impact of the "taste for discrimination" only if the wage elasticity of the labor supply of those discriminated against is zero.[17] Since this is unlikely to be the case, some economists, among them Barbara Bergman, have sought to explain the relatively lower wage rates of blacks and women in terms of hypotheses that emphasize supply-side factors as the source of wage differentials in excess of the costs and benefits associated with education and training.

The "Crowding" Hypothesis of Labor-Market Discrimination

Barbara Bergman has argued that blacks and women are "crowded" into relatively few occupations.[18] The fear of white males of sustaining

[16] Melvin Reder, "Comment," in Albert Rees and Orley Ashenfelter, eds., *Discrimination in Labor Markets*.

[17] While price-quantity interactions need to be taken into consideration, it is not clear how they operate cyclically to account for the relatively greater discrimination experienced by blacks and women in periods of business contraction. A neoclassical model would attempt to explain the differential in terms of racially different costs and returns to wage flexibility. See Melvin Reder, "Comment," *op. cit.*

[18] Barbara Bergman, "The Effect of White Incomes on Discrimination in Employment," *Journal of Political Economy* 79 (March/April 1971).

financial losses is advanced as the rationale for limiting the employment of blacks and women to relatively few occupations. Certain occupations have become associated with particular types of individuals, e.g., women becomes nurses, secretaries, clerks, and salespersons; blacks become household workers and laborers, while white males become professional, technical, and managerial employees. Because their supply is large relative to the demand for their services, persons in minority groups command wages that are lower than those earned by white males in occupations in which labor supplies are relatively smaller.

The "crowding" hypothesis is consistent with the relationship posited by the marginal-productivity principle concerning the interaction between labor supply, labor productivity, and wages. The productivity at the margin of workers in a "crowded" occupation will be lower than that of workers in a less crowded one. Thus, the wage differential that results is a consequence of occupational segregation rather than of discrimination in Becker's sense of the term, i.e., in the sense of the practice of paying different wage rates to equally qualified workers performing the same work.

The crowding hypothesis is fully compatible with the hypothesis that wage differentials reflect differences in investment in human capital. Specifically, it may be argued that skill differentials tend to become self-perpetuating partly because individuals who expect to encounter occupational segregation have little motivation to commit resources to acquiring higher types of skills. Furthermore, their low level of wages in crowded occupations may make it financially impossible for them to invest in themselves.

The crowding hypothesis poses two interesting and important empirical questions: first, what is the effect on relative incomes of crowding blacks into a limited number of occupations; second, how much would integration alter the respective incomes of blacks and whites? The answer to the first question clearly depends on the size of the black labor force that is being excluded. The answer to the second, which presumably would reallocate labor to more productive uses, depends on the increase in national income that improved efficiency is likely to yield.

ECONOMICS IN ACTION 11:3

The Effect on Black/White Incomes of Discrimination in Employment

The Census Bureau's Current Population Report on Consumer Income for 1967 was used to estimate money income by race, sex, and education for those who worked full-time during the year.[19] An estimate

---

[19] Barbara Bergman, *op cit.*

of the change in the wage levels of white and black workers in response to the desegregation of employment was computed for three values of the elasticity of substitution for groups having different levels of education. The chief finding is that even though national income is little

TABLE 11-A   *Postintegration Changes in Income:* Percentage Change, Income of Year-Round Full-Time Workers*

			School Years			
Sex						16 or
Sex	0–7	8	9–11	12	13–15	More
Elasticity of Substitution=0.25; Percentage Change in National Income=0.16						
Male:						
White	− 8.9	−2.3	−4.6	−2.2	−.1	−0.5
Negro	40.4	51.2	55.8	58.4	†	†
Female:						
White	−14.0	−5.2	−6.4	−2.3	−1.5	−0.7
Negro	45.6	49.2	38.0	34.6	†	†
Elasticity of Substitution=1.00; Percentage Change in National Income=0.59						
Male:						
White	− 7.9	−1.9	−3.9	−1.8	−1.4	−0.4
Negro	42.0	51.7	57.0	59.0	†	†
Female:						
White	−12.3	−4.5	−5.7	−2.0	−1.3	−0.7
Negro	48.5	50.3	39.0	34.9	†	†
Elasticity of Substitution=3.00; Percentage Change in National Income=1.41						
Male:						
White	− 5.8	−1.3	−2.6	−1.1	−0.9	−0.2
Negro	45.3	52.7	59.1	60.1	†	†
Female:						
White	− 8.7	−3.1	−4.2	−1.5	−1.0	−0.6
Negro	54.6	52.5	41.2	35.6	†	†

*The Income figures used to make these estimates include nonlabor income.
†No estimates made; see text for explanation.
SOURCE: Barbara Bergman, "The Effect of White Incomes on Discrimination in Employment," *Journal of Political Economy* 79 (March/April 1971).

affected by the inefficiencies induced by discrimination, considerable improvement could be made in the rate of remuneration of blacks at the expense of relatively small losses for most white males and only moderate losses for others.

The greatest loss would be experienced by white males who did not finish elementary school; the potential loss following integration was estimated at between six and nine percent for white males and between nine and fourteen percent for white women. Estimates of postintegration changes on the incomes of various educational groups computed separately for three values of the elasticity of substitution are recorded in Table 11-A.

A subsequent recalculation was undertaken in order to take into account that part of the black/white income differential that derives from the larger holdings of capital assets by whites in the upper educational groups. This lowered the overall estimate of the change in claims on income as a result of integration by 40 percent, although the estimates of white/black incomes in the lower educational groups were affected only slightly. A recalculation was also undertaken to reflect the possibility that blacks and whites of equivalent education are not perfect substitutes for each other. When it is assumed that half of the blacks in any educational class compete with whites (and other blacks) one class down, the damage, in terms of income, is increased from 9 to 23 percent for white males in the lowest educational class. However, the generalization that the incomes of most whites will be affected only trivially remains valid. This suggests to Bergman that whites' fears that they will sustain financial losses as a result of integration are generally not well founded except in the lowest educational group.

The Impact of Affirmative-Action Programs

The Contract-Compliance Program

While the Bergman study provides some insight into the likely effects of integration on the respective incomes of blacks and whites, it does not address itself to examining the effects of an affirmative-action program or to assessing the sources of the minority economic progress that has been achieved. The most important institutional changes that have promoted minority progress stem from Title VII of the Civil Rights Act of 1964 and the Equal Pay Act of 1963. The latter amended the Fair Labor Standards Act to require the fair-employment-practice (FEP) legislation of nonsouthern states and the Office of Federal Contract Compliance (OFCC) Department of Labor to require equal pay for equal work. The OFCC has authority to invoke various sanctions against employers who have government contracts if they fail to develop and implement affirmative-action programs.

Assessment of the effectiveness of the contract-compliance program for reducing discriminatory wage differentials is complicated by the multiple influences that have been at work in bringing about minority progress. One of these influences is the change that has taken place in the quality of the nonwhite labor force. The narrowing of the black-white earnings differential is partly a reflection of the "vintage effect"; quality improvements have occurred at a more rapid rate for blacks than for whites.[20] This may account for the narrowing of the black-white wage differential (and for the more rapid increase in rates of return on education to blacks).

The second factor that complicates assessment of the effectiveness of the contract-compliance program is the influence of general economic conditions. The relative income gains experienced by blacks in a tight labor market are partly a reflection of changes in the distribution of employment, i.e., blacks experience upward mobility in their occupations when labor markets tighten.

Since quality improvements and tight labor markets have had a narrowing effect on black-white earnings differentials, it is relevant to undertake a study that will isolate the impact of the contract-compliance program. Such a study would take the progress of the late sixties as given and assess the *marginal* effect of the contract-compliance program. That is, it would seek to identify the change in the relative economic status of blacks, during the sample period, that would have occurred in the *absence* of the contract-compliance program. One finding that results from such a study is that firms having government contracts posted larger increases in the employment of black workers relative to white workers than did firms without government contracts.[21] Another study identified significantly greater relative occupational gains for the blacks employed by government contractors.[22] These studies suggest the usefulness of assessing the potential impact of requiring all firms to be subject to the antidiscrimination requirements now imposed on government contractors. The findings of a study that undertook to identify the maximum potential impact of a contract-compliance program under alternative assumptions is reported as *Economics in Action* 11:4.

[20] Finis Welch, "Black-White Differences in Returns to Schooling," *American Economic Review* 63, 5 (December 1973): 893–907.

[21] Orley Ashenfelter and James Heckman, "Measuring the Effect of Antidiscrimination Programs," in Orley Ashenfelter and James Blum, eds., *op. cit.*

[22] George Burman, "The Economics of Discrimination: The Impact of Public Policy," Ph.D. Dissertation, University of Chicago, 1973, cited by Robert Flanagan, "Actual vs. Potential Impact of Government Anti-discrimination Programs," *Industrial and Labor Relations Review* 29 (July 1976): 501–502.

ECONOMICS IN ACTION 11:4

The Potential Impact of a Contract-Compliance Program under Alternative Assumptions

It is relevant to note that a federal contract-compliance program is intended to address only those wage differentials that reflect discrimination, i.e., that are attributable to racial differences in the prices paid for equivalent productive characteristics. Only about one-third of the racial hourly-wage differentials that exist are therefore amenable to being corrected through affirmative-action programs.

If all firms in the economy were to become subject to antidiscrimination regulations similar to those now imposed on government contractors, the maximum potential effect of the program in reducing the wage differential that is due to discrimination would also reflect the narrowing of differentials that are attributable to racial differentials in training and experience opportunities.[23] The OFCC explicitly requires information about the training opportunities made available to minorities. If equal-training opportunities were universally required, and if availability requirements could be enforced, so that blacks would improve their endowments and, consequently, their access to experience,

TABLE 11-B *Maximum Potential Impact of Contract-Compliance Program under Alternative Assumptions concerning Coverage and Nature of Impact. (Percentage of total racial-wage-rate differential)*

(Percentage of total racial-wage-rate differential)

Effect of Compliance Program	Younger Males		Older Males	
	Full Coverage	60 Percent Coverage	Full Coverage	60 Percent Coverage
1. Eliminates market discrimination $(ll_b - ll_b)$	25	15	32	19
2. Eliminates market discrimination and training differentials	29	17	35	21
3. Eliminates market discrimination, training, and firm-experience differentials	39	24	38	23

SOURCE: Robert J. Flanagan, "Labor Force Experience, Job Turnover, and Racial Wage Differentials," *Review of Economics and Statistics* 56, 4 (November 1974).

[23] Robert Flanagan, *op. cit.*

the wage differential that is attributable to discrimination could be further narrowed. Table 11-B provides an estimate of the percentage of the total wage-rate differential that could, conceivably, be eliminated if the antidiscrimination program were universally applicable. The finding is that a comprehensive program that equalizes opportunity for minorities might directly eliminate about 30 to 40 percent of the hourly-wage-rate differential in each cohort. The potential impact of the program is likely to be constrained by the unemployment experiences of black as compared with white workers.[24] The latter may not be significantly improved by a universal contract-compliance program. Some aspects of this aspect of minority progress are examined next.

Narrowing Wage Differentials and Employment

The net effect of measures to constrain racial wage-rate discrimination on the economic progress of minority groups depends partly on the impact of equal-pay-for-equal-work legislation on employment and unemployment rates. Investigation has shown that for the period 1968–1973, there was a trend increase in black (but not white) unemployment, after adjustment for cyclical and seasonal influences.[25] This suggests the possibility that employers have adjusted to constraints on wage discrimination by practicing discrimination in employment.

Aggregate data do not, however, tell the whole story. Decomposition of the 1968–1973 trend to reflect the demographic composition of the black labor force makes it possible to identify significant secular increases in the "new entrant into the labor force" rate among black teenagers of both sexes. Virtually all of the recent trend increase in the unemployment of black males reflects the experience of this labor-force group.

Their experience suggests that one effect of an antidiscrimination program is on expectations about the relative rewards of market and nonmarket activity. Thus, many individuals who previously were inclined toward nonmarket activity (e.g., teenagers) may become attracted to the labor market. The relevance of this inference appears to be borne out by the increase in the racial-unemployment differential of the sixteen to nineteen-year-old group. The racial-unemployment difference among experienced workers *fell* in response to greater equality of opportunity. It is because this decline was offset by the rise in unemployment among new labor-force entrants that the aggregate racial-unemployment ratio remained stable at a time when other indicators registered improvements in the relative position of blacks.

[24] These differentials are examined further in Chapters 13 and 14.

[25] Robert Flanagan, "On the Stability of the Racial Unemployment Differential," *Proceedings, American Economic Association* (May 1963): 302–308.

Concluding Remarks

Well over a century ago John Stuart Mill and other classical economists recognized that wage differentials tend to be eliminated only if labor-market participants have both knowledge that differentials exist and freedom to act on their knowledge. Mill thus emphasized the emergence of noncompeting labor groups that reflect the interrelationship between occupational choice and socioeconomic class. The children of lower-class workers almost inevitably work at unskilled, low-paying jobs because they come from poorly educated families who are in turn unable to educate their children to enable them to rise above their social class in the labor market.

Almost a century after the English classicists wrote about noncompeting labor groups, Francis Edgeworth expressed the view that women earn lower rates of pay because they are crowded into a comparatively small number of occupations. Edgeworth's emphasis on institutional barriers to the erosion of discriminatory wage differentials has become an integral part of contemporary criticism of mainstream theorizing. Bergman's hypothesis that wage rates in "Negro" and "female" occupations are below those of similarly educated white males because social factors "crowd" them into a relatively small number of "suitable" occupations is predicated on Edgeworth's observation. Her hypothesis poses a fundamental challenge to the competitive hypothesis because it deputes the assumption that occupational-labor supplies are typically wage elastic.

While Bergman's theory is neoclassical in its reliance on differences in productivity at the margin to explain occupational-wage differentials, it is firmly rooted in the present institutional setting, which precludes interclass mobility in response to wage differentials. Its explicit introduction of the role of barriers to mobility establishes a degree of kinship between Bergman's theory and the thinking of those who espouse the view that the labor market is divided into segments that are rooted in the separate subcultures of different socioeconomic classes. Their interpretation of labor markets maintains that the industrial structure and other "demand side" variables have greater explanatory power than have educational attainment and other "supply side" variables in predicting individual earnings. The challenge to neoclasscism posed by proponents of the view that labor markets are stratified or "dual" is examined in the chapter that follows. It serves to draw together and elaborate into a cogent whole the criticisms to mainstream thinking about the labor market and wage-rate determination that have previously been noted as aspects of the challenge currently being directed at neoclassical theorizing.

Suggestions for Further Reading

Kenneth Arrow. "The Theory of Discrimination," in Orley Ashenfelter and Albert Rees, eds., *Discrimination in Labor Markets*. Princeton: Princeton University Press, 1973.

Gary Becker. *The Economics of Discrimination*. Chicago: University of Chicago Press, 1959.

Barbara Bergman. "The Effect of White Incomes on Discrimination in Employment." *Journal of Political Economy* 79 (March/April 1971).

Robert Flanagan. "Racial Discrimination and Employment Segregation." *Journal of Human Resources* 8 (Fall 1973).

Robert Flanagan. "On the Stability of the Racial Unemployment Differential." *Proceedings, American Economic Association* (May 1976): 302–308.

Robert Flanagan. "Actual vs. Potential Impact of Contract Compliance Programs." *Industrial and Labor Relations Review* 29 (July 1976).

H. Gilman. "Economic Discrimination and Unemployment." *American Economic Review* 55 (December 1965).

Edmund Phelps. "The Statistical Theory of Racism and Sexism." *American Economic Review* 62 (1972).

12 *The Challenge to Orthodox Labor-Market and Wage Theory*

Neoclassical Theory in Review

The heterodox challenge to the body of theory that mainstream economists have developed to explain the labor-market phenomena underlying the wage structure has been anticipated at numerous junctures throughout the preceding chapters. The critics of orthodox theory have not simply proceeded in terms of generalities but have addressed themselves to most of the "building blocks" of the neoclassical tradition. It therefore seems useful to provide perspective about their criticisms by reviewing the essentials of the analysis from which they dissent.

Neoclassical theorizing in all its aspects, including analysis of labor markets and the wage structure, is predicated on the assumption that the relationships being examined arise out of the exchange of commodities (labor being among them) for money, and that all market participants are "maximizers." Thus, as was seen in Chapter 2, households are envisaged as making decisions about the allocation of time to participate in the labor market. The (generally) upward-sloping supply curve for labor as a whole is developed on the basis of the choices made by persons of labor-force age between market and nonmarket activity. The supply of labor is interpreted as a positive function of the real wage rate, at least up to that rate at which leisure is viewed as a superior good.

The maximizing premise is also conceived to underlie individual time allocations to the educational and training processes that determine the "quality" of the labor supply. Chapter 3 analyzed these supply-side decisions concerning investment in "human capital" as being closely related to occupational employment opportunities. The choices that individuals make among jobs are interpreted as being related to the opportunities they provide for continued self-investment, and empirical research has established that formal education is often a prerequisite for more specialized "on the job" training.

Maximizing behavior is also seen as governing the demand side of the market. Employers are envisaged as ranking employees (and prospective employees) along a queue that reflects an estimate of their respective marginal productivities. The training expenditures that employers are willing to make on employees is also explained by neoclassical theorists in terms of maximizing principles. A profit-maximizing firm is typically willing to bear only the costs of specific training, i.e., of training that does not increase the productivity of the persons they hire to other possible employers. The pattern that is described is usually of workers who become employed at entry-level jobs that serve as portals to on-the-job training and experience that qualifies them for upward mobility in the firm. The view that labor inputs are quasi-fixed rather than completely variable factors of production is thus compatible with recent developments in neoclassical thinking. The incentive of firms to recoup their investments in employees, coupled with the latters' interest in secure employment and promotion opportunities, has facilitated the emergence of the firm as an "internal labor market" that is more or less insulated from competition with the external market.

The presence of unions and their objectives with respect to maximizing the wage bill or the number of members must be taken into account in determining the outcome of the wage-employment bargain. It is the neoclassical view that while unions alter the outcome of the wage-employment relationship from what it would be under competitive conditions, the same market forces operate through the institution of collective bargaining in union markets as in those that are nonunion. Thus, they maintain that alternative union goals can be incorporated into economic models and that the process of determining key wage rates is amenable to economic analysis even in the presence of unions. The argument is that the market processes of capitalistic economies resemble the competitive model closely enough that it remains valid to view the world "as if" (as Friedman puts it) workers' wages equal their marginal productivities.[1] Alternatively, as Thurow expressed it, "The distribution of marginal products is identical with the distribution of earned income."[2] Thus, orthodox theorists see employers demanding what workers supply—namely, stocks of capital embodied in individual workers. The implication with respect to the problem of poverty and underemployment is that "if an individual's income is too low, his

---

[1] Milton Friedman, "The Methodology of Positive Economics," in M. Friedman, *Essays in Positive Economics* (Chicago: University of Chicago Press, 1953).

[2] Lester C. Thurow, *Poverty and Discrimination* (Washington, D.C.: The Brookings Institution, 1969), p. 20.

productivity is too low. His income can be raised only if his productivity can be raised."[3] The premise here is that an increase in a worker's productivity will be associated with an improved demand for his services and thus in his earnings.

Like the analysis of behavior on the supply side of the market, neoclassical analysis of the demand side reflects the market exchange framework of orthodox theory. The functioning of labor market is analyzed in parallel fashion with the analysis of commodity markets. As Friedman expressed it, demand and supply "are the two major categories into which the factors affecting the relative prices of products or factors of production are classified."[4]

Heterodox Criticism of Neoclassical Theorizing

The Attack on Assumptions

The most vigorous criticisms being directed against the neoclassical interpretation of the functioning of labor markets and the determination of the wage structure come from the proponents of the "dual" (or "segmented") and radical theories of the labor market. These theories re-echo some of the challenges of earlier critics of conventional theory, although they are more specifically the product of the social-reform movements of the 1960s. Many of the shortcomings of conventional theory that they address are shared by writers whose interests are not specifically in the field of labor.

In common with other critics of neoclassical theorizing, the critics of mainstream labor economics address themselves to the inadequacies of the assumptions on which these analyses are based. The maximizing assumption and its related marginalist technique is a particular basis for dissent. Most fundamental, perhaps, is the view of human nature that is implicit in the economic models of household behavior. As it is expressed by one critic, these models "rely on a caricature of human beings who continuously and consciously balance costs and benefits at the margin, whether in deciding on another year of schooling, whether or when to marry or be divorced, how many children to have and when, or whether and when to commit a crime."[5] Furthermore, the notion that households allocate time among market and nonmarket activities in order to maximize present or future income streams implicitly assumes that an increment of income has essentially the same value at the margin

---

[3] Thurow, *op. cit.*, p. 26.

[4] Friedman, *op. cit.*, p. 8.

[5] R. A. Gordon, "Rigor and Relevance in a Changing Institutional Setting," *American Economic Review* (March 1976): 3.

for a poor household as it does for a rich one. Reliance on a neutral concept such as "maximizing" diverts attention from the behavioral impact of differences in income. The theory of household choice takes the distribution of income and wealth as given. It also assumes that individuals are able to "choose" between employment and nonmarket activity. The conventional assumption, as was noted in Chapter 2, which dealt with the supply of labor, is that particularly among prime-age males "the inclination toward labor-force participation is ... uniformly strong."[6] But, phenomena such as the decline in black-male labor-force participation rates, even among men in the prime-age group, does not square well with the assumption about the universality of market-nonmarket preferences.

The maximizing assumption is closely related to the assumption of the essential competitiveness of the economy as well as to the assumption of the inherent harmonizing tendency of the social system. Radical thinkers, as well as those who conceive of the labor market as being segmented, interpret discrimination against black and other ethnic groups as being indicative of the irrelevance of competitive theories. The prediction of neoclassical theory that discriminatory wage differentials will tend to be eliminated has not been realized. As Kenneth Arrow (who is himself a neoclassicist) commented, "Since, in fact, racial discrimination has survived for a long time, we must asume that the model . . . [has] some limitations."[7]

The persistence of discrimination is a particularly critical basis for dissent from traditional thinking. The chief concern of the segmented market and radical theorists is about empirical findings such as the near-constant ratio of black to white average male income between 1950 and 1967. These data, and those of the period since, are interpreted as implying that the relative position of black males did not improve. There is recent evidence that the earnings of those black males who are highly educated are rising as rapidly as or, in some cases, more rapidly than those of white males.[8] However, these improvements are associated with evidence provided by cross-section studies of an earnings gap between black and white males which is widening with age and which suggests more severe discrimination against older males, e.g., with respect to on-the-job training.[9] The critics of orthodox theory maintain that these and similar experiences are indicative that competition does not operate in most

[6]William Bowen and T. Aldrich Finnegan, "Labor Force Participation and Unemployment," in A. M. Ross, ed., *Employment Policy and the Labor Market* (Berkeley: University of California Press, 1965), p. 126.

[7]Kenneth Arrow, "The Theory of Discrimination," *op. cit.*, p. 10.

[8]Richard Freeman, "Changes in the Labor Market for Black Americans, 1948–1972," *Brookings Papers on Economic Activity* 1 (1973).

[9]Richard Freeman, *op. cit.*, also Finis Welch, "Education and Racial Discrimination," in O. Ashenfelter and A. Rees, eds., *op. cit.*, pp. 43–81.

labor markets; the primary market is sheltered from competition both as a result of the large-scale presence of oligopolistic enterprises and the counterveiling power of unions. Competitive forces rule only in the unprotected sectors of the labor market from which disadvantaged workers are typically unable to escape.[10] Thus, they are destined to comprise a permanent group of low-wage earners in "poor" jobs. Because low-wage workers are without prospects, they "learn" negative attitudes and have poor work habits. Mainstream theorists interpret these attitudes and habits as given. The contrary view of their critics is that these attitudes and habits are *endogenous* to the operation of the labor market. Thus, it is among the tasks of the labor economist to explain how the attitudes and habits of low-wage workers emerged and why they are perpetuated.

The Relationship between Earning, Education, and Marginal Productivity

Criticism is also directed at the efforts of neoclassical theory to explain qualitative differences among labor-force participants. The conventional presumption is that earnings differences originate in differential human-capital investments among persons. The questions raised in Chapter 4 concerning the relationship between human-capital investment and the quality of the labor supply needs to be pursued further, for educational achievement is not clearly related to expenditures for schooling. At the intensive margin, variations in test scores among students are more clearly associated with differences in home environments. The consensus appears to be that there is not a significant positive relationship between educational expenditures and educational achievement, holding the number of years of schooling constant.[11] In the absence of interdependence between the effectiveness of resources for education and earnings differentials, the argument that productivity and education are related is difficult to support. It is only at the extensive margin (i.e., more years of schooling) that there is a positive relationship between educational input and schooling.

Furthermore, the role of schooling in determining individual success in the marketplace is also a matter of considerable controversy. Some researchers, as noted in Chapter 4 (e.g., Christopher Jencks), take the extreme position that there is no statistically significant basis for linking schooling and individual earning capacity. A milder stance (e.g., Grilich and Mason) is that there is an identifiable income-schooling relationship

---

[10] R. E. Hall, "Why Is the Unemployment Rate So High at Full Employment?" *Brookings Papers on Economic Activity* 3 (1976).

[11] Fred Mosteller and Daniel Moynihan, *On Equality of Educational Opportunity* (New York: Vintage Books, 1972).

but that it is considerably reduced when family background is controlled for.

A related observation that also bears on the issue of the positive relation between earnings and education relates to the use of education as a screening device by employers. Diplomas and degrees enable employers to identify, in an inexpensive way, who among their applicants has such desirable characteristics as punctuality and perseverance, which are school-related. The critics of neoclassicism associate credentialism more specifically with discrimination than with providing information about productivity-related characteristics.

Competing Alternative Hypotheses about Labor Markets

There are at present three other hypotheses that have been offered to rebut the neoclassical theory of labor-market behavior. Lester C. Thurow's "job competition" model is the interpretation that is closest to the traditional model. It is predicated on the view that the labor market is primarily a market that allocates *training opportunities* among different workers. This approach contrasts with the orthodox view that the labor market is primarily a market in which existing skills are sold. One aspect of the job-competition model is that it conceives of employers as repressing wage competition because of the training function of the labor market. Wage competition and job competition coexist as mechanisms for clearing labor markets. Thurow maintains that there is a continuum between wage and job competition in the American economy and that the "real world" is somewhere between these extremes.[12]

The basic hypothesis of those who view the labor market as being "dual," segmented, or "stratified" is that certain workers are economically disadvantaged because of their attachment to the lower tier of the secondary sector. Proponents of this view interpret the division of the labor market as being related to lower-, working-, and middle-class subcultures.[13]

---

[12] Lester C. Thurow, *Generating Inequality* (New York: Basic Books, 1975), p. 76.

[13] Michael Piore, "Notes for a Theory of Labor Market Stratification," in R. C. Edwards, M. Reich, and D. M. Gordon, *Labor Market Segmentation* (Lexington, Mass.: Lexington Books, D. C. Heath and Co., 1978), pp. 126–7. Earlier expositions of the segmented-labor-markets view associated employment instability chiefly with the character of the job. Instability on the job appears to be a more serious cause of ghetto unemployment than lack of skill. See P. B. Dorringer *et al.*, "Urban Manpower, Programs and Low Income Labor Markets: A Critical Assessment" (U.S. Department of Labor, January 1969.) More recent expositions (e.g., M. Piore, "Notes for a Theory of Labor Market Stratification") emphasize the influence of worker characteristics quite as much as the influence of job characteristics in producing employment instability.

The third group of nonneoclassical thinkers is working chiefly through the Union for Radical Political Economics and is especially concerned with explaining ghetto employment problems within the framework of Marxian economics. They have retained much of classical Marxist methodology and made revisions to accomodate current realities. A leading proponent of radical economic theory notes that "much of the analysis has not yet even been precisely formulated, much less published; it continues to flow through conversations, letters, and unpublished notes."[14] Thus, the still undeveloped state of radical economic theory suggests that it is appropriate to limit inquiry into alternative hypotheses to the job-competition and "dual" or "segmented" labor-markets theories.

The Segmented-Labor-Markets Theory

The "Subculture" of Class and Labor Supply

It will be recalled from Chapter 4 that the basic hypothesis of those who view the labor market as being "dual," "segmented," or "stratified" is that certain workers are economically disadvantaged because of their attachment to the lower tier of the secondary sector. The job opportunities that this sector makes available are characterized by instability, low pay, and the absence of fringe benefits, status, and opportunity for promotion and training. Such jobs are typically filled by urban minorities.

The opportunities in the upper and lower tiers of the primary sector present a sharp contrast to those of the secondary sector. The upper sector is distinguished by high pay, status, security, promotion opportunities, and personal freedom. Education is the essential requirement for this type of employment. Jobs in the lower tier of the primary sector typically pay well, provide promotion and training opportunities, and are secure. Workers tend to be regarded as quasi-fixed factors by virtue of the job training they receive.

Proponents of the segmented-labor-markets view interpret the division of the labor market into primary and secondary sectors as related to lower-, working- and middle-class subcultures. These subcultures contrast sharply with one another. The lower-class subculture is described as being characterized by attitudes toward schooling, work, and relationships that predispose toward erratic employment. In this sense the subculture of the lower class is adapted to the employment patterns that characterize the secondary labor market. That is, the

---

[14]David M. Gordon, *Theories of Poverty and Underemployment* (Lexington, Mass.: Lexington Books, D. C. Heath and Co., 1972), p. 53.

premise of the segmented-labor-markets view is that any given job tends to draw people from particular schools, neighborhoods, and family backgrounds.

The critical distinction between the primary and secondary sectors is that the mobility chain of the former represents a "career ladder" for upward progress in terms of pay and status, whereas the jobs in the latter are held in random fashion and do not provide opportunity for upward mobility. Mobility chains also reflect individual worker traits and the process through which they are acquired and changed by learning and the behavior of the social group.

The supply of secondary workers is drawn from among the youth of all three family backgrounds and those adults who are unable to make a transition to the working class subculture as they leave adolescence. Recent migrants, whether they are from Europe, Latin America, or the black South, are most likely to fail to complete the transition, which is characterized by family formation, stabilization of employment patterns, and association with a peer group with like characteristics. Migrants typically leave home at about the time they are passing into adulthood and fail to make the transition into a working-class life-style. Not only does their separation process attenuate the stabilization of life-styles but, in addition, reorientation difficulties obstruct the opportunity for stable employment. Thus, the lower-class subculture is partly the product of the migration process.[15]

As a given stream of migrants ages and the proportion of recent migrants declines, the working-class culture of the racial and ethnic group is restored. However, proponents of the segmented-labor-markets hypothesis believe that there is a critical difference between today's poor population and that of those who were poor in an earlier period. Most of these "made the transition at a time when the penalties for unstable work habits were more severe. Public-welfare programs have since reduced the costs of a life without work."[16] Thus, job stability develops and unemployment experiences diminish among older workers with dependents; the stabilizing influence of age is not, however, discernible until workers are in their thirties.[17] The rate at which the process of transition for migrants and youths proceeds depends on the effect that technology has in generating primary and secondary jobs. The segmented-labor-

---

[15] Michael Piore, "Notes for a Theory of Labor Market Stratification," in R. C. Richards, et al., eds., Labor Market Segmentation (Lexington, Mass.: D. C. Heath and Co., 1975).

[16] David Y. Gordon, Theories of Poverty and Underemployment (Lexington, Mass.: Lexington Books, D. C. Heath and Company, 1972), p. 48.

[17] P. B. Doeringer, et al., "Low Income Labor Markets and Urban Manpower Programs," Department of Economics, Harvard University (January 1969).

markets view thus conceives of the supply of labor as being rooted in the subculture of class while labor demand is rooted in technology.

Technology and the Demand for Labor

Proponents of the view that present labor markets are segmented regard the steel industry as the prototype of the technology that has shaped the job structure. The mechanization of the 1870s, which broke the power of the Amalgamated Association of Iron, Steel and Tin Workers, generated a requirement for a new class of semiskilled machine operator. The new process required neither the heavy workers nor the highly skilled craftsmen of the past. The mechanization of plants downgraded skilled workers and upgraded the unskilled.[18]

A dramatic decline in earnings was one consequence of the diminished importance of skilled workers. The effect of the new technology was to "homogenize" the work force and create a new class of workers.[19] On the other hand, the hourly rate for unskilled labor was raised. Thus, the historical sliding scale of wages for skilled workers and the contract system for paying helpers became outmoded. Between 1900 and World War I, piecework and various premium plans that encouraged production characterized the wage-payment system, in spite of worker opposition to productivity-oriented wage payments.

The new technology diminished the skill requirements for virtually all jobs, and the distinction between skilled and unskilled work became blurred. The solution to the problem of worker discontent in consequence of dead-end jobs was to rearrange the jobs themselves into "job ladders" along which workers could progress. This provided a work incentive while giving employers greater control and scope for maintaining worker discipline. Proponents of the segmented-labor-markets view observed that as early as 1900 *Iron Age* advised employers to hire only to fill the lowest job levels and to fill higher levels by promotion.[20] These writers also emphasize the bureaucratic character of large organizations, in opposition to neoclassical writers, who typically proceed within the framework of a competitive model.

While the mechanization of production virtually eliminated the traditional skilled worker, most industries still required new types of skilled workers capable of performing specific tasks, although they

---

[18] Katherine Stone, "The Origins of Job Structures in the Steel Industry," in R. C. Edwards, *et al., Labor Market Segmentation* (Lexington, Mass.: D. C. Heath and Company, 1973).

[19] Stone, *op. cit.,* p. 38.

[20] "Developing Employees," *Iron Age* (June 14, 1900). Some technological developments virtually eliminated skill requirements, Stone maintains that job ladders were developed to solve a labor problem rather than a production problem, *op. cit.*: 49.

lacked general knowledge of the production process as a whole. To fill this need, employers set up training systems that became alternatives to the union-controlled apprenticeships of the past. According to the segmented-labor-markets view, firms now invest in the "human capital" of their employees in order to insure that their capital equipment will be efficiently used. Thus, the relatively high wages earned even by those in the lower tier of the secondary market are partly explained by their high productivity. But most proponents of the segmented-labor-markets theory prefer a more institutional explanation. Specifically, they maintain that the economic power that underlies the profits that enable employers to make productivity-enhancing investments also enables them to pass along a share of their wage (and other) cost increases to consumers; specifically, "their oligopoly position permits them to maintain nonpoverty wage levels without seriously eroding their profit margins."[21] This encourages the job stability employers want. The stability of the work force also feeds back into the wage-bargaining process, according to proponents of the segmented-labor theory. Stable workers are more easily organized, and unionization, in turn, supports worker stability and an above-poverty wage structure to which workers who are discriminated against are unable to aspire.

The Low Wages of the Secondary Market

As was noted in Chapter 4, the importance of formal education in determining worker productivity is questioned by proponents of the segmented-labor-markets view. In support of their position they emphasize that even ghetto blacks are closing the educational gap between themselves and the average American. In 1970, the gap in the median number of years of schooling between young blacks and whites had fallen to less than half a year. Attributing the lower earnings of minority workers to their dearth of "human capital" is, therefore, less convincing than it was when the educational gap was more substantial. The alternative explanation of their low wages offered by segmented-labor theorists emphasizes the absence of economic power, the low profit margins, and the antiquated capital of secondary firms. Lack of market power by secondary market firms, as well as low worker productivity, contributes to the low wages of the workers they employ.

These factors are interdependent in secondary markets. Marginal firms that are unable to provide much in the way of complementary capital and that pay workers low wages discourage them from developing attitudes and work habits that enhance productivity and increase the

---

[21] Bennett Harrison, "The Theory of the Dual Economy," in B. Silverman and M. Yanovitch, eds., *The Worker in the Post Industrial World* (New York: The Free Press, 1971), p. 274.

firms' capacity to pay wages. Employers in the secondary labor market, unlike their counterparts in the primary market, have no reason to value or encourage stable work behavior. They cannot afford, nor do their technologies require, investments in specific training. The technology of secondary industries generates jobs that are quickly and easily learned. Thus, they rely on the general training that is provided free in the public schools. Since they themselves benefit from the instability of their work force they encourage—or at least do not discourage—casual work attitudes. Work tenure and wage rates are thus seen as being related chiefly to institutional forces and only weakly to the educational attainments of workers.[22]

The Neoclassical Response: Point and Counterpoint

Segmented Markets and Efficiency

Writers who conceive of the labor market as being segmented into primary and secondary markets, each with various "tiers," emphasize the dominant role of sociological factors in establishing a dichotomy among its various sectors and governing the interactions between workers and their relationship to management. The factors they emphasize have traditionally not been incorporated into neoclassical models. But as was recognized in Chapter 7, which introduced the concept of the internal labor market within the context of the neoclassical model, many of the observations that the proponents of the segmented-labor-markets view make concerning the internal labor market can be reinterpreted within an efficiency context. The nonneoclassical view is that custom and other institutional factors, rather than efficiency considerations, determine the wage structure and promotion pattern of the primary sector.

The counterargument of neoclassical writers is that while "the dual literature is a rich and provocative set of loosely connected empirical hypotheses about labor-market behavior ... its novel empirical findings can be integrated into a traditional model and indeed are more easily understood in such a context."[23] While the segmented-labor-markets point of view maintains that upward mobility is determined by sociological factors, e.g., seniority rather than efficiency,[24] neoclassical writers note that senior workers are also those who have acquired the

[22] P. B. Doeringer, "Ghetto Labor Markets—Problems and Programs," Discussion Paper No. 35, Program on Regional and Urban Economics, Harvard University (May 1968): 10–11.

[23] Michael Wachter, "Primary and Secondary Labor Markets: A Critique of the Dual Approach," *Brookings Papers on Economic Activity* 3 (1974): 680.

[24] Michael J. Piore, "The Impact of the Labor Market for the Design and Selection of Productive Techniques Within the Manufacturing Plant," *Quarterly Journal of Economics* 82 (November 1968): 602–620.

training that qualifies them for promotion along particular internal-promotion ladders. As they interpret the functioning of the internal labor market, the structure of relative wages, even if it is not competitively determined, promotes internal efficiency by giving workers the incentive they need to make them willing to acquire the training required for promotion. They emphasize the efficiency function that the promotion ladder performs in the internal labor market; its differential wage structure induces workers to absorb the training required for the internal efficiency the firm requires and the promotion the worker covets.

The neoclassical interpretation of the functioning of internal labor markets appears to be supported by a recent study by the Bureau of Labor Statistics that confirms that worker performance on the job, and not simply seniority, is important in explaining promotions.[25] The implication is that the internal market may well help firms to minimize losses by providing continuous screening rather than automatic mobility up the promotion ladder, i.e., "the internal labor market may well be the most efficient apparatus for analyzing and collecting data on individual performance."[26] Thus, the concept of an internal labor market is not incompatible with the view that efficiency considerations determine its functioning.[27]

Job Criteria and Job Mobility

A critical aspect of the segmented-labor-market hypothesis is that only "bad" jobs are available to workers in the secondary market who are precluded from upward mobility and thus from "good" jobs in the primary sector. This hypothesis is difficult to verify, because job characteristics such as good pay, good working conditions, advancement opportunities, and job stability do not necessarily divide jobs neatly into "good" and "bad" categories. For example, longshoring is unstable, hazardous work but pays high wages. Also, firms and industries that are chiefly in the high-wage sector may also be employers in secondary markets. In the absence of an operational definition of "good jobs" and "bad jobs," the segmented-labor-market hypothesis is difficult to test empirically. Nonetheless, an effort has been made to identify empirical evidence of labor-market segmentation by testing for upward mobility among young workers.

---

[25] U.S. Bureau of Labor Statistics, "Major Collective Bargaining Agreements: Seniority in Promotion and Transfer Provision," Bulletin 14, 25–11 (1970), p. 5.

[26] Wachter, *op. cit.*, p. 648.

[27] Oliver Williamson, Michael Wachter, and Harris particularly emphasize the efficiency-oriented response of the internal labor market but view the response as being to market forces rather than to institutional forces that govern the functioning of labor markets. See their "Understanding the Employment Relation: The Analyses of Idiosyncratic Exchange," *Bell Journal of Economic and Management Science* (1975).

ECONOMICS IN ACTION 12:1

Labor-Market Segmentation and Intersectoral Mobility

Proponents of the segmented-labor-markets view maintain that members of minority groups (including women) and lower-class whites are disproportionately allocated into secondary jobs at the outset of their work careers irrespective of ability and potential productivity. They are envisaged as being virtually precluded from upward mobility, regardless of education and training. Even if there is an increase in the aggregate demand for labor, it is maintained that workers from the secondary labor market are not moved upward along the hiring queue and into vacant jobs in the primary sector.

Data from the National Longitudinal Survey of young men were examined in order to test two related hypotheses. First, is there an impenetrable boundary between the primary and secondary sectors of the labor market, and second, does more investment in human capital, i.e., more education and training, improve intersectoral mobility?[28] The sample selected for analysis is a subset of a national probability sample of the civilian noninstitutional population of males fourteen through twenty-four years of age in 1966. These respondents had completed twelve or fewer years of schooling and were not enrolled in school between 1966 and 1968. They were classified as nonagricultural wage and salary workers on the basis of their first job after leaving school. The time frame of the analysis is the period from the first job to the 1968 job, a period of at least two years but longer for those youths who entered the labor market prior to 1966. The premise was that the study would serve as a relatively severe test of the dual-market theory, since young men select their first jobs in an unsystematic way and are highly mobile with respect to settling into career patterns. It was the further expectation that by limiting the universe to youths with twelve or fewer years of schooling, the study would facilitate inquiry into the work experiences of youths vulnerable to labor-market disadvantage.

The operational definition of primary and secondary jobs was a first step. Using 1960 census records of median earnings for three-digit occupational and industry codes, jobs were defined as "primary" or "secondary" on the basis of median earnings for the industry and the entire male labor force. A job was considered primary if (1) the occupation had median earnings greater than or equal to the median of the entire male labor force and the industry was one with median earnings of at least \$4,687, or (2) the industry was one with median

[28] Paul Andresani, *An Empirical Analysis of the Dual Labor Market Theory* (Columbus, Ohio: The Ohio State University Center for Human Resource Research, 1973).

earnings greater than or equal to the median of the entire male labor force and the occupation was one with median earnings of at least $4,687. Jobs paying less than these amounts were classified as secondary. This classification produced categories of jobs that appeared to be quite consistent with what most writers conceived to be the difference between primary and secondary employment situations.

Investigation of the likelihood that a youth's first job will be in the primary sector, on the basis of his socioeconomic status, educational attainment, mental ability, and the level of aggregate demand at the time of initial labor-market entry, is marked by a considerable degree of randomness. However, the statistical analysis indicates a *higher* likelihood that the first job will be a primary job for white youths than for black youths, in a tight labor market. Race is significantly related to the likelihood of a primary-sector first job.

With respect to the question of upward mobility between the secondary and primary sectors, the findings of the study were that the probability of *movement* is greater than that of confinement to employment in the secondary sector. Furthermore, among youths with no more than a high-school education, confinement to secondary-sector jobs did not appear to result from insufficient schooling or training. Support for the dual-labor-market hypothesis, at least on the basis of this study, is therefore limited. White youths who have graduated from high school are more likely to find employment in the primary sector in their first job. In the secondary sector, white youths appear able to move further ahead in the queue if they are more educated, more experienced, and married. For both groups, however, the probability of confinement to secondary-sector jobs is smaller than the probability of upward mobility. There is no evidence of an "impenetrable boundary" between market sectors.

While the study did not support the argument of the labor-market-segmentation hypothesis concerning mobility from the secondary sector into the primary sector, the findings also do not support the human-capital view of the relationship between education and employment in the primary sector. Levels of educational attainment are systematically related to the likelihood that white youths will enter primary-sector jobs. However, additional education did not significantly affect the probability of mobility between the secondary and primary market for either group.

Information "Externalities," "Feedback" Effects, and "Bad" Jobs

While empirical support for the hypothesis that workers in the secondary labor market are precluded from upward mobility into primary-sector jobs has not been established, there is evidence of racial differences in the probability of entry into and confinement within the secondary sector. White youths were more than two and one-half times as likely to enter the labor market in primary jobs, and nearly twice as likely to advance from the secondary to the primary jobs.[29] Neoclassical theorists argue that the fact of good workers being "locked into" bad jobs can be explained in terms of imperfect information, which upsets the normal ordering of workers and jobs. Skilled individuals may also find themselves in "bad jobs" because their finite life spans preclude new decisions about education, training, and career choices.[30] These "life-cycle effects" are compatible with neoclassical theory. The neoclassical model predicts that the wages of members of a particular cohort depend chiefly on such variables as education and training, but recognizes that in a dynamic economy particular cohorts may not have time to correct errors in their initial choices.

Proponents of the segmented-labor-markets view maintain that neoclassical writers introduce the role of information into the models in order to "salvage" their theories. As they see matters, information and training explanations do not facilitate an understanding of the inter-action between economic processes and worker preferences or tastes.[31] Preferences and tastes are, as has already been noted, viewed by neoclassisists as "given" and are therefore exogenous to their models. What is necessary, according to the critics of neoclassical theory, is to go beyond neoclassical theory and build an economic model that generates tastes (as well as technology).[32] Thus, proponents of the segmented-labor-markets view maintain that unstable employment in "bad" jobs encourages individuals holding them to develop "bad" work habits, which render them less skilled and also less trainable than those who are employed in the primary market. Their emphasis on the negative-feedback mechanism provides insights into the "tastes" that neoclassical writers assume to be given.[33] Indeed, they maintain that institutional

---

[29] Paul Andresani, *op. cit.*

[30] Michael Wachter, "Primary and Secondary Labor Markets: A Critique of the Dual Approach," *op. cit.*, p. 664.

[31] M. J. Piore, Comments on Wachter's paper, *op. cit.*, p. 685.

[32] As Piore expresses it, "The thrust of my approach is to make both technology and tastes integral parts of the economic process and to understand labor-market structure as the product of that integration." See Comments, *op. cit.*, p. 685. Similarly, labor unions need to be considered as a result of the system and explained in terms of an endogenous theory, instead of being examined only as a force operating on the system, *op. cit.*, p. 692.

[33] M. J. Piore, "Jobs and Training," in S. H. Deer and R. E. Barringer, eds., *The State and the Poor* (Cambridge, Mass.: Winthrop, 1970). Kenneth Arrow and Edmund Phelps, both of whom are of neoclassical persuasion, have also recognized the self-perpetuating syndrome of poor working habits emphasized by Piore. See K. Arrow, "The Theory of Discrimination," in "Discrimination in Labor Markets," in Orley Ashenfelter and Albert Rees, eds., *op. cit.*, pp. 3–33; and Edmund Phelps, "The Statistical Theory of Racism and Sexism," *American Economic Review* 62 (September 1972): 659–661.

conditioning goes far beyond the work environment of the secondary job market. Thus, the feedback mechanism should be extended to investigate also the influence of family background and neighborhood housing conditions and other aspects of the cultural environment during workers' preschool and school years.[34]

Employment Instability, Utility Maximization, and "Structuralism"

According to the segmented-labor-markets view, the unstable pattern of employment that characterizes the secondary market is closely related to its characteristic feature of offering only "bad jobs" to workers whose skills and work habits are inferior. Mainstream thinkers maintain that employment instability is explainable in terms of the neoclassical model. The essence of this model, it will be recalled, is that households allocate time to maximize family real income. The income of a family depends on the prevailing wage rate, the time family members allocate to labor-market participation, the availability of transfer payments, and their level relative to the wage rate. As noted in Chapter 2, which examined the neoclassical theory of labor supply, Mincer's finding was that the net economic gains and losses experienced by secondary workers is sufficiently small to account for their erratic employment behavior.[35] Studies examining the labor-force participation of married women are also important in this connection; Mincer's study established their tendency to enter the labor force when favorable labor-market conditions reduce search costs, and to leave it when labor-market conditions deteriorate. Similar behavior patterns are observable among secondary workers generally and, according to the neoclassical view, are explainable in terms of the maximizing behavioral assumptions of traditional theory.[36]

Proponents of the segmented-labor-markets view maintain, on the contrary, not only that the maximizing assumption is an unsatisfactory behavioral assumption but moreover that unstable employment derives chiefly from choices that emanate from the *demand* side of the labor market. They maintain that employers in the secondary labor market, unlike those in the primary sector, have no incentive for encouraging employment stability and, indeed, may have reasons for discouraging it. This argument was subsequently joined to their negative stance on the

[34] Thomas Vietorisz and Bennett Harrison, "Labor Market Segmentation: Positive Feedback and Divergent Development," *American Economic Association Proceedings* (May 1973). Neoclassical writers are now also developing treatments of endogenous taste change. See R. A. Pollack, "Habit Formation and Dynamic Demand Functions," *Journal of Political Economy* 18, Pt. 1 (July/August 1970): 745–763.

[35] *Supra*, Chapter 2, pp. 25–26.

[36] Wachter, *op. cit.*, p. 666.

probable effectiveness of policies for raising aggregate effective demand as an antipoverty weapon. It coincided with the finding that the incidence of unemployment during the 1960s and early 1970s had shifted to the disadvantaged groups, who are most likely to seek employment in the secondary market.[37]

The anomaly of higher-than-average unemployment in certain sectors of the economy led macrotheorists to the notion of "structural" unemployment. The observation that some sectors and groups appeared to be unable to participate in the general prosperity of the nation, because imbalances often accompany growth and change in a dynamic economy, implied that these specialized problems were not amenable to being dealt with via traditional fiscal and monetary stimuli. It was argued that these measures would not only fail to help alleviate the unique problems of particular groups but would also exacerbate the inflationary pressures that, during the late 1950s, were increasingly being attributed to internal changes in the structure of demand in an economy characterized by wages and prices that are flexible upward but not downward.[38] Thus, the changing nature of unemployment and its associated poverty problems became the basis for some measure of commonality in the analytical and policy concerns of the "structuralists" and the critics of neoclassical labor-market theory. Further detail on this aspect of "point and counterpoint" between neoclassical thinkers and their critics will be given in Part II, which investigates the macro-economic aspects of the economy.

Concluding Remarks

While there is substantial content in the writings of the critics of neoclassical labor-market theory, it seems fair to conclude that the challenge they offer continues to be more formidable in its critical aspects than in the alternative theories offered. Thus far, proponents of the segmented-labor-markets hypothesis have made the greatest progress in articulating a theoretical model to replace the one they are criticizing. But a great deal of additional refinement is required to facilitate further empirical testing. Even such a fundamental matter as distinguishing the primary sector from the secondary sector empirically still has received no definitive resolution.[39]

---

[37] George L. Perry, "Unemployment Flows in the U.S. Labor Market," *Brookings Papers on Economic Activity* 2 (1972).

[38] Charles L. Schultze, "Recent Inflation in the United States," Study Paper No. 1, Joint Economic Committee, Study of Employment, Growth and Price Levels (Washington, D.C., 1959).

[39] Commenting on Andresani's study (see Economics in Action 12:1), Glenn Cain suggests that his initial classification of dual and primary jobs predetermines some of his conclusions. However, Cain considers feasible an empirical test of the descriptive accuracy

While relatively little has thus far been accomplished in the realm of empirical testing, enough has been said on both sides between mainstream thinkers and their critics for the theoretical issues between them to emerge. Conventional analysis of labor-market behavior at the microeconomic level is particularly concerned with analyzing the role of choices made on the supply side of the market. The choices workers make with respect to labor-force participation, the number of hours allocated to market and nonmarket activity, and decisions to acquire additional education or training are thought to alter the supplies of labor in specific markets in response to changing demand conditions. The interaction of demand-side and supply-side forces is conceived to establish a wage structure within firms and among occupations, industries, and regions that, ideally, performs the function of allocating labor among alternative users and clears separate markets. It is recognized that information gaps, factor immobilities, and other "frictions" impose severe limitations. But the expectation is that wage-rate changes typically perform the function of eliminating excess demand or supply in particular markets.

In opposition to this conventional conception of labor-market forces, the critics maintain that demand-side forces are fundamental in the process of allocating jobs. Explicitly or implicitly, they dispute that there is a relationship between worker productivity and the demand for labor. They see the production process as being interrelated with a complex social process in which individual output is not separable from the output of the organization as a whole. The demand for labor is dictated by the requirements of the organizational structure. The firm's wage structure is tied to the various job slots the organization needs to fill and is set by a collective-bargaining agreement or by custom.

No precise relationship between the number of workers the organization employs and their individual productivities is plainly discernible. Thus, the critics of conventional theory conclude that the demand curve for labor cannot be represented as negatively sloped under modern conditions of production and organization. They also doubt that the kinds of maximizing decisions that conventional theory conceives to be at work on the supply side of the labor markets are relevant in determining either the composition or the length of the queue.

---

of the segmented-labor-markets thesis. He maintains that longitudinal data of the sorts used by Andresani are useful for testing hypotheses about mobility, while cross-sectional data would reveal more about the "structure" of occupations. His conjecture is that when an occupational distribution of jobs by sector is identified, it will resemble the distribution of wage and salary incomes, which, in turn, is similar in shape to the approximately log normal distribution of income. This shape implies support for the human-capital hypothesis. See Glenn C. Cain, "The Challenge of Dual and Radical Theories of the Labor Market," *American Economic Review Proceedings* 65 (May 1975).

The behavior of labor markets is thus interpreted as reflecting a demand-side response to a wage structure that is institutionally determined.

Demand-side influences are especially in evidence in connection with discrimination. Neoclassicists themselves agree that this aspect of their theorizing is particularly unsatisfactory. It is difficult to explain the pervasiveness of different rates of compensation for the same work (wage discrimination) and the assignment of jobs to equally qualified workers (job discrimination) except in terms of institutional forces operating on the demand side. The phenomenon of discrimination compounds the difficulties of explaining the emergence of the wage structure as endogenous to a labor-markets model. While the critics of orthodox theorizing view the neoclassical preoccupation with supply-side influences as inappropriate for explaining wage differentials, neoclassical writers have pressed their inquiry into supply-side influences even further and focused on pre–labor-market discrimination in the form of lesser schooling, lesser training, poorer health, and other investments that enhance productivity even before workers enter the labor market.

But the essential issue in neoclassical theorizing about labor markets and that of their critics is more fundamental than the matter of the relative importance of demand-side and supply-side influences. After all, neoclassicists from the time of Alfred Marshall have argued that it is the *interaction* of demand and supply forces that governs factor prices as well as commodity prices. "The nominal value of everything, whether it be a particular kind of labor or capital or anything else, rests, like the keystone of an arch, balanced in equilibrium between the contending pressures of its two opposing sides; the forces of demand press on the one side, and those of supply on the other."[40] Demand and supply together determine the price, which performs the function of clearing the market of the entire supply offered at the going price. Marshall reasons that in the short run the adjustment of the demand for and the supply of labor may be very imperfect. But he expects that in the long run the supply of particular types of labor will respond to wage differentials that "bear an indirect and complex relationship to the cost of rearing and training."[41] The rate of wages that emerges for each grade of labor depends on the amount of that grade demanded and supplied at a wage that tends to approximate (although it is not determined by) the worker's marginal-revenue product. It is precisely this aspect of neoclassical theory that its critics are particularly concerned to challenge.

The essential gap between the thinking of neoclassical writers and their critics attaches to the conception that the rate of wages is explainable in terms of supply-and-demand responses to market forces. Even if we regard all of the alternatives to neoclassical theory that have

[40]Alfred Marshall, *Principles of Economics*, 8th edition, p. 526.
[41]Marshall, *op. cit.*, p. 577.

thus far been offered as less than satisfactory, which is the case, the argument of the critics that the rate of wages is largely determined by institutional forces is highly persuasive. Furthermore, this view has a longer history than is evidenced by contemporary controversy.

The initial dissent from the neoclassical view that labor markets function in essentially the same way as commodity markets do came from J. M. Keynes, who, in his *General Theory of Employment Interest and Money* (1936), confronted the issue of the ability of labor markets in the economy as a whole to clear in response to a general cut in money wages. He maintained that strong institutional forces make money wages rigid downward. For reasons that will be explored in Chapter 14, he argued that if money wages could be reduced during periods of declining aggregate demand, the economy's labor resources would, nevertheless, experience involuntary unemployment. Writers who describe the labor market as functioning via "job competition," labor queues, internal labor markets characterized by job ladders and internal wage structures, and secondary markets characterized by underemployment are echoing Keynes's reservations about the imperfections of the wage-clearing mechanism, even though they do not typically express their dissent in terms of a model like Keynes's, in which money wages are exogenous and the economy's level of employment is governed chiefly by forces operating on the demand side. Keynes's analysis made it clear that the behavior of labor markets with respect to the level of wages and employment must be examined from a macroeconomic point of view, in addition to the microeconomic point of view that has been our focus thus far. The analysis of Part II, therefore, is directed toward examining the macroeconomic aspects of labor-market behavior.

Suggestions for Further Reading

Eileen Appelbaum. "Post Keynesian Theory: The Labor Market." *Challenge* (January/February 1979): 39 47.

Glenn C. Cain. "The Challenge of Dual and Radical Theories of the Labor Market." *American Economic Review Proceedings* 65 (May 1975).

David Gordon. *Theories of Poverty and Underemployment.* Lexington, Mass.: Lexington Books, D. C. Heath and Co., 1972.

Bennett Harrison. "The Theory of the Dual Economy," in B. Silverman and M. Yanovitch, eds., *The Worker in the Post Industrial World.* New York: The Free Press, 1971.

Michael Piore. "Notes for a Theory of Labor Market Stratification," in R. C. Edwards, *et al., Labor Market Segmentation.* Lexington, Mass.: D. C. Heath and Co., 1975.

Lester C. Thurow. *Poverty and Discrimination.* Washington, D.C.: The Brookings Institution, 1969.

Michael Wachter. "Primary and Secondary Labor Markets. A Critique of the Dual Approach." *Brookings Papers on Economic Activity* 3 (1974).

PART II

The Macroeconomic Aspects of Labor Markets

13 *The Structure of Labor Markets: Their Relationship to the Microeconomy*

The Scope of Macroeconomic Concerns

While labor economists have generally had a particular interest in the microeconomic aspects of labor-market behavior, they share the macro-economists' concern about the level and distribution of employment and unemployment, the level of wages (as distinct from the structure), the level of prices, and the distribution of income. The field of labor economics is no longer exclusively applied microeconomics; it is, at present, becoming increasingly macroeconomic in its orientation. The focus of the present chapter is on the structure of labor markets and how it relates to the level and distribution of employment and unemployment.

Concern about the level of employment and unemployment requires little explanation. Low employment imposes the hardship of unemployment on large numbers of families while depriving the economy of the output that would have accompanied their employment. The Full Employment and Balanced Growth Act of 1978 makes it the obligation of the federal government to "translate into practical reality the right of all Americans who are able, willing, and seeking work . . . ." The policy objective of achieving maximum or "full" employment presents a number of important questions and problems, which are the focal point of this chapter. The measurement of unemployment is basic among them. This is a problem that is empirical as well as theoretical. A second problem concerns the need for a criterion for identifying full employment. A third and related matter concerns the need to distinguish among types of unemployment and identify their causes; all unemployment is not essentially the same, and its incidence is distributed very unevenly across population groups. Since knowledge about the structure of labor markets provides perspective for approaching all these matters, we begin with a brief inquiry into the continuous flow of workers into and out of the labor markets of the U.S. economy.

Workers move into the market as they graduate from school, leave nonmarket activities (e.g., housekeeping, volunteer work, etc.), are laid off, or quit their present employment. They move out of the labor market as a result of retirement, death, return to school, or other nonmarket activities or discouragement related to unsuccessful search. Thus, the labor market is in a constant state of flux as it responds to changing economic conditions.

Since the labor market is characterized by a continual movement of workers into and out of employment, it is useful to conceive of the processes involved in terms of stocks and flows. As shown in Figure 13-1,

FIGURE 13-1 *Labor-Market Stocks and Flows*

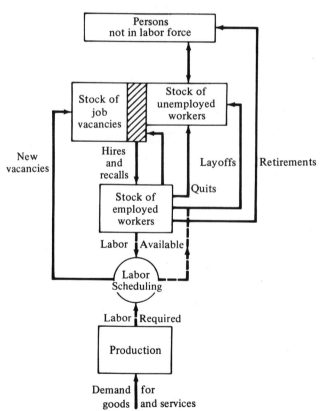

SOURCE: Adapted from C. C. Holt, "Improving the Labor Market Tradeoff between Inflation and Unemployment," *American Economic Review* (May 1969).

the number of employed workers and the number of unemployed workers is changed by the rate at which workers enter and leave the labor market and by the volume of job vacancies that are being generated as a result of quits and increases in the demand for new hires. Workers flow out of employment as a result of quits and layoffs; they return to employment as a result of recalls and new hires. The fact that the stock of unemployed workers is replaced within the short time of one month provides perspective about the speed of the flow. The stock figure reflects both the rate at which persons enter and leave the labor market and the volume of job vacancies that are generated by quits and demands for new hires. If gross inflows and outflows are approximately equal, the aggregate number of employed and unemployed workers remains relatively unchanged, even though the number of persons who have experienced unemployment during a particular period is substantially larger than the aggregate number employed at a particular time.

Figure 13-2, Annual Average Labor Flows in Manufacturing, represents the relationship between the flows associated with quits, layoffs, hires (accessions), and separations in another way. Accessions, separations, quits, and layoffs are shown as flows rather than as stocks. Statistical research has shown that labor-market stocks and flows are typically interrelated by a negative feedback. For example, when the labor market is tight, the stock of unemployed workers is low and the level of job vacancies is high. But this state tends to be accompanied by higher quit rates, which occur as workers feel encouraged to engage in more search activity. The stock of unemployed workers is thereby increased.

FIGURE   13-2   *Accessions, Separations, Quits, and Layoffs: Annual Average Labor Flows for U.S. Manufacturing*

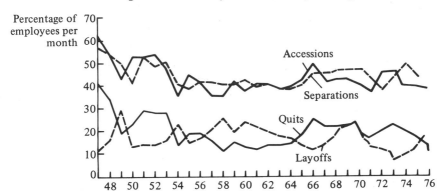

SOURCE: *Employment and Earnings,* U.S. Department of Labor.

Conversely, at high levels of unemployment the stock of unemployed workers is large in consequence of layoffs that occur because their services are no longer needed. But because jobs are harder to find when layoffs are high, the quit rate generally declines when unemployment levels rise. The flow averages between one-third to one-half of the total labor force on an annual basis. Alternatively expressed, the average duration of a job is between two and three years.[1]

Types of Unemployment and Their Measurement

"Counting" the Unemployed

Our critical concern in this chapter is to distinguish among types of unemployment and develop a basis for understanding what determines the economy's level of employment and unemployment, which is addressed in Chapter 14. The terms "employment" and "unemployment" require careful definition. Since labor markets are continuously in a state of flux, there will always be some unemployed workers. There are always some workers who are in the process of changing jobs or who have just entered the labor market after terminating nonmarket activities, such as schooling. Others are experiencing temporary layoffs as a result of seasonal changes, material shortages, and demand shifts that have increased the demand for some types of workers while reducing that for others. Their unemployment is "frictional" in that it is associated with imperfections in the operation of labor markets that produce periods of temporary unemployment for individual workers. Perceived on an individual basis, their unemployment is usually terminated by recalls and successful job search, although, in the aggregate, there are always persons who are temporarily unemployed as a result of frictions. This type of unemployment must be taken into account by the techniques used to measure unemployment statistically.

The Bureau of Labor Statistics definition of unemployed persons identifies those "who did not work at all during the survey week, were looking for work, and were available for work during the reference period."[2] Thus, in order for a person to be officially classified as unemployed, he must have engaged in some type of job-search activity within the preceding four-week period and be awaiting the results during the survey week. Job-search activity consists of specific actions such as registering with a public or private employment agency, writing letters of application, and meeting with prospective employers. If a person has not

[1] Charles C. Holt and M. H. David, *The Concept of Vacancies in a Dynamic Theory of the Labor Market: Measurement and Interpretation of Job Vacancies* (New York: National Bureau of Economic Research, 1966).

[2] *BLS Handbook of Methods*, U.S. Department of Labor, Bureau of Labor Statistics, 1911 (1971), p. 8.

been actively seeking work during the last four weeks he is not counted as employed or unemployed but is classified as "not in the labor force." Persons are also classified as unemployed if they are not presently working but are (1) waiting to be called back to a job from which they have been laid off, (2) are waiting to report to a new job within the next thirty days, or (3) would have been searching for work except that they were temporarily ill. The criteria for determining whether or not a person is unemployed during the survey week are thus quite precise, although there is some controversy about the appropriateness of the criteria used. Considerable criticism has been leveled against the government's unemployment concept, because its counting procedure simply identifies the number of unemployed persons without conveying the degree of social hardship associated with their joblessness. Job loss by a family breadwinner is entered into the head count in precisely the same way as that experienced by a teenaged part-time worker whose job provides pocket money.[3] Moreover, the official-unemployment measure does not reflect the hardship experienced by workers whose hours of work are reduced to part-time when they prefer to work full-time.[4]

Once the number of unemployed persons has been identified on the basis of the criteria noted above, the unemployment rate is computed as the ratio between the number of unemployed persons and the number in the labor force (i.e., number of civilian employees plus the number of unemployed persons).

$$U = \frac{\text{Number of unemployed persons}}{\text{labor force}}$$

Thus, in May of 1980, the Bureau of Labor Statistics reported an unemployment rate of 7.8 percent.* This was computed from the ratio

$$U = \frac{\text{Number of Unemployed}}{\text{Civilian Labor Force}} = \frac{8,154,000}{105,142,000} = 7.8$$

Unemployment and the Discouraged Worker

Apart from its lack of insight into the hardship implications of unemployment and enforced reductions in hours of work, the official unemployment figure does not reflect the experience of persons who are in the "think-they-cannot-get-a-job category" identified by the U.S.

---

[3]See pages 256–57 for alternative measures of unemployment, some of which are designed to reflect the social distress associated with job loss.

[4]While the reduction in employment as a result of enforced part-time work is not reflected in the measured unemployment rate, the Bureau of Labor Statistics keeps a record of part-time workers who want full-time work.

* Preliminary

Department of Labor. It will be recalled from Chapter 3 that the joblessness of discouraged workers is not reflected in the unemployment statistic, because this enumeration includes only persons who were actively seeking employment during the survey week. Persons who are not labor-force participants because they think they cannot get a job have left the labor force and are not counted as being unemployed. Thus, it is reasonable to infer that measured rates of unemployment understate the extent of the unemployment problem by excluding discouraged workers from the unemployment count. Table 13-1, therefore, recomputes the unemployment rate to reflect the joblessness of discouraged workers and compares it with the "official" unemployment rate for the period 1969–1978.

TABLE 13-1 *Civilian Unemployment Rates under Alternative Definitions, 1969–78*

| Year | *Unemployment Rates* | |
	All unemployed	Unemployed plus discouraged workers[1]
1969	2.1	2.4
1970	3.5	3.8
1971	4.4	4.7
1972	4.0	4.3
1973	3.2	3.5
1974	3.8	4.1
1975	6.7	7.2
1976	5.9	6.3
1977	7.0	8.1
1978	6.0	7.5

[2] "Discouraged workers" are defined as those who are not in the labor force because they believe they cannot find a job
SOURCE: U.S. Department of Labor.

Computing the unemployment rate to reflect the number of discouraged workers, as well as the number who are officially classified as unemployed, is useful because it provides a better perspective for interpreting the concept of "full employment." Even though full employment has never been regarded as a social goal to be reached at all costs, it has become increasingly difficult to achieve as other goals are given high priority. Control over inflation presents a particular problem.

Inflationary pressure is widely regarded as jeopardizing the economy's ability to maintain low levels of unemployment, for reasons that will be examined in later chapters. Nevertheless, given the policy obligation of achieving maximum or full employment, it is essential to establish a criterion for judging whether a particular excess supply of labor constitutes a problem that is sufficiently serious to warrant public intervention.

"Natural" Unemployment Rates and "NAIRU"

As has already been noted, there will always be some unemployment as certain workers find themselves "between jobs" or become new entrants into the labor market after leaving various nonmarket activities in order to seek out job openings. The unemployment they experience is typically temporary and is designated as "frictional" to reflect its association with normal job changes and the fact that it takes new workers some time to locate their first job. Thus, the unemployment rate associated with frictional unemployment is "normal" and exists even under conditions of full employment. This type of unemployment is quite different from involuntary unemployment. Involuntary unemployment exists if persons are willing to work at current wages but are unable to find work. Its presence suggests that there are pathological tendencies at work in the economy.

The unemployment rate associated with normal labor-market flows is sometimes called the "full employment rate of unemployment," the "natural rate of unemployment," or "NAIRU," the nonaccelerating inflation rate of unemployment, which is consistent with a balance between flows into and out of the labor market and a rate of inflation that remains constant (not necessarily zero) at its previous rate.[5]

How high a rate of unemployment is frictional and consistent with the natural rate of unemployment? This is a question that defies a precise answer not only because the concept is itself so amorphous but also because there are differences in judgment as to whether and when unemployment reflects a normal job-search process as opposed to a pathological tendency in the economy. Furthermore, the rate of unemployment that is likely to be associated with normal labor-market flows varies with factors that affect the duration and frequency of unemployment.

[5]Borrowing from the Austrian tradition, Milton Friedman reintroduced the adjective "natural" to convey the notion of a "tendency" under specified conditions. See his "The Role of Monetary Policy," *American Economic Review* 58 (March 1968). Thus, the natural rate of unemployment is not to be interpreted as being either optimal or unchangeable; it is a long-term rate that tends to prevail.

The duration of unemployment is the average length of time required to locate and accept a job after entry into the unemployment pool. This depends on such factors as the presence of employment services that facilitate contact between searchers and employers, the ability and willingness of unemployed workers to engage in search activities in order to locate jobs, and the availability of suitable jobs.

The frequency of unemployment is the number of episodes or "spells" of unemployment experienced per year. This magnitude reflects variations in the demand for labor among sectors as well the rate at which new workers enter the labor force. A large number of new labor-force entrants, such as would be associated with a large teenage population, raises the percentage of unemployment that can reasonably be interpreted as "frictional" or "natural."

The natural rate of unemployment is not, however, to be viewed as unchanging or immutable. On the contrary, it will change as the structure of the labor market and the composition of the labor force changes; the expectation is that as the average age of the population increases, the percent of unemployment that can reasonably be thought of as reflecting the natural unemployment rate will be reduced.

The conceptual and statistical difficulties of estimating the natural rate of unemployment notwithstanding, R. J. Gordon has made some estimates of the unemployment rates that were, in his judgment, consistent with balance between flows into and out of the labor market and expectations concerning wages and prices for the period 1960–1977. These estimates, which are included in Table 13-2, are usefully compared with the actual rates of unemployment, which are recorded in Column 2. Table 13-2 shows that from 1960 through 1964, the actual unemployment rate exceeded, sometimes substantially, the rate that would have been compatible with normal movements into and out of the labor force. The subsequent period, 1965–1970, was one of substantially "full employment." Since 1970, however, experience reflects a considerable lengthening in the average duration (in weeks) of unemployment as well as a substantial increase, particularly in 1975 and 1976, in the percentage of the labor force that was unemployed. In 1974 the annual average unemployment rate for all workers stood at 5.0 percent. In 1975 the unemployment rate was 8.5 percent, while in 1976 and 1977 the rates were 7.7 and 7.0 percent. At the close of 1978 the December unemployment rate for all workers was 5.9 percent.

Over the same period the natural rate of unemployment was estimated as being in the range of 5 to 6 percent.[6] The upward revision

---

[6] Table 13-2 records the estimated natural rate as 5.4 percent. However, it is generally agreed that it is more appropriate to conceive of the natural rate as reflecting a range rather than a specific percentage. Some economists consider Gordon's figures on the natural rate

TABLE 13-2 *May Unemployment Rates (Persons 16 Years and Over) and Percentage Distribution of Duration of Unemployment*

Years	Actual unemployment rate	Natural unemployment rate*	Total	Less than 5 weeks	11 to 14 weeks	15 to 26 weeks	27 weeks and over	Average means
1960	5.5%	4.4%	100%	44.6%	9.2%	13.0%	11.8%	12.8
1961	6.7	4.4	100	38.3	8.7	15.4	17.1	15.6
1962	5.5	4.4	100	42.4	8.3	13.6	15.0	14.7
1963	5.7	4.5	100	43.0	8.7	13.1	13.6	14.0
1964	5.2	4.6	100	44.8	8.4	12.9	12.7	13.3
1965	4.5	4.7	100	48.4	8.2	12.0	10.4	11.8
1966	3.8	4.8	100	54.9	7.3	19.3	18.4	10.4
1967	3.8	4.9	100	56.6	7.0	9.1	5.9	8.8
1968	3.6	4.9	100	56.6	7.0	9.1	5.5	8.4
1969	3.5	5.0	100	57.5	7.1	8.5	4.7	7.8
1970	4.9	5.1	100	52.3	8.1	10.4	5.7	8.7
1971	5.9	5.2	100	44.7	8.7	13.3	10.4	11.3
1972	5.6	5.3	100	45.9	7.6	12.3	11.6	12.0
1973	4.9	5.4	100	51.0	7.7	11.0	7.8	10.0
1974	5.6	5.4	100	50.6	8.2	11.1	7.3	9.7
1975	8.5	5.4	100	37.0	9.1	16.5	15.2	14.1
1976	7.7	5.4	100	38.3	13.1	13.7	18.3	15.8
1977	7.0	5.4	100	41.6	11.1	13.1	14.8	14.3
1978	6.0	5.4	100	46.1	15.1	12.3	10.5	11.9

[1] Not strictly comparable with earlier data due to population adjustments.

* Robert J. Gordon, *Macroeconomics* (Boston: Little, Brown and Co., 1978), Appendix B. Reprinted courtesy of the author.

SOURCE: Employment and Earnings Report, U.S. Department of Commerce.

since the 1960s in the estimated natural rate is believed to reflect the increased labor-force participation by women, teenagers, and persons from minority groups, all of whom are subject to more frequent spells of unemployment and generally higher rates of unemployment than that experienced by prime-age males. The proportion of women and young

---

of unemployment reflecting only demographic changes in the structure of the labor force as perhaps being too low for the 1970s, during which increases in the level of transfers may have reduced the hardship of unemployment and permitted longer and more frequent periods of job search.

persons in the labor force, as was noted in Chapter 2, has increased substantially since 1960. Employers, nevertheless, seek to fill their vacancies chiefly with prime-age males. Thus, the unemployment rate for women and young persons is disproportionately high, which raises the unemployment rate for the economy as a whole, even though there is continued upward pressure on wages and a strong market for prime-age males. Figure 13-3, which provides a graphic perspective about unemployment since 1960, represents the natural rate of unemployment (i.e., the rate that is regarded as being consistent with full employment) as ranging between 4 and 6 percent rather than as the specific percentages recorded in Table 13.2.

FIGURE 13-3 *Actual and Natural Unemployment since 1960*

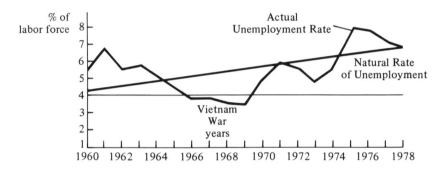

Turnover Rates

It is also enlightening to examine the problem of unemployment in terms of labor-force-turnover rates. Labor-force-turnover information is available for manufacturing establishments. Table 13-3 shows the rehire rate in manufacturing industries. Since 1960, manufacturing firms averaged 1.6 layoffs per 100 employees per month. During the same period they were rehiring 13 persons per 100 employees per month. The rehire rate—that is, the ratio of rehiring to layoffs—averaged 85 percent and did not drop below 70 percent in any year. Thus, the vast majority of those laid off in manufacturing industry between 1960 and 1975 were ultimately rehired by their original employees, although they may have taken interim jobs elsewhere.

It is relevant to note, however, as is shown in Table 13-4, that the labor-force-turnover picture changed between May 1973 and May 1975.[7]

[7] 1973 and 1975 were selected because both years reflect extremes in the economy's employment experience. The 1973 rate of 4.9 percent was the lowest of the decade, while the 8.5 percent rate of 1975 was the highest.

TABLE 13-3 *Labor-Turnover Rates in Manufacturing* (Per 100 employees)

	May 1973	May 1975
1. Total accessions	4.7	3.5
New hires	3.9	1.8
Recalls	0.8	1.7
2. Total separations	4.7	4.1
Quits	2.7	1.3
Layoffs	0.9	2.6
Other, including involuntary quits	1.1	0.2

SOURCE: *Employment and Earnings*, June 1973 and June 1975.

TABLE 13-4 *Unemployed Persons by Reason for Unemployment*

	May 1973 Percent	May 1975 Percent
Job losers	38.7	57.6
Job leavers	13.7	9.2
Re-entrants	32.5	23.5
New entrants	15.0	9.6
Total	100.0	100.0

When the average rate of unemployment is low, as it was in May 1973, the percentage of unemployment owing to job loss, as is recorded in Table 13-4, is relatively low. By contrast, when unemployment is high, as it was in May 1975, job loss is the chief reason for unemployment.

The Differential Incidence of Unemployment

The nature of the unemployment problem cannot be fully comprehended without noting that the impact of unemployment in terms of rates, duration, and frequency is very disparate among population groups. Table 13-5 records significant differences by sex, age, and race. Clearly, differentials between male and female unemployment are less significant than those associated with race and age. Nonwhite unemployment is substantially greater than white unemployment, and the disparate impact of unemployment on teenage youth has been particularly dramatic, as is reflected in Figure 13-4.

The teenage labor force typically increases between 30 and 40 percent with the closing of schools in June of each year. The average

TABLE 13-5 *Rates, Duration, and Frequency of Unemployment, by Age, Sex, and Race*

	Unemployment rate (percentage of labor force)		Average duration (weeks)		Average frequency (times per year unemployed)	
	May 1973	May 1975	May 1973	May 1975	May 1973	May 1975
Males						
16-10	12.1	18.1	8.8	11.0	0.72	0.86
25-34	7.1	14.9	9.8	14.9	0.38	0.52
35-44	2.4	5.8	16.1	18.0	0.08	0.17
Females						
16-19	13.3	19.3	7.1	9.3	0.98	1.08
25-34	7.9	13.3	8.0	10.4	0.50	0.67
35-44	3.5	7.3	11.1	16.2	0.16	0.23
White						
Males	3.4	7.2	12.9	15.5	0.14	0.24
Females	4.6	8.5	8.9	13.5	0.27	0.35
Nonwhite						
White	7.4	13.1	12.5	17.8	0.31	0.38
Females	8.9	13.5	10.7	13.4	0.43	0.53
Total	4.9	9.0	10.1	13.5	0.25	0.35

SOURCE: Employment and Earnings, June 1973 and June 1975.

annual rate of teenage unemployment is increased by the sharp rise in teenage unemployment that takes place each summer. The unemployment rate for all teenagers, as can be verified from Figure 13-4, experienced a sharp rise since the late 1950s relative to the rate for adult men.

While the unemployment problem of young persons is serious, particularly in terms of its magnitude, it is important to recognize that the kind of unemployment experienced by this group is quite different from that experienced by other persons. Referring again to Table 13-5, "Rates, Duration and Frequency of Unemployment by Age, Race and Sex," it is to be noted that while younger workers experience higher rates of unemployment than do other workers, the young tend to be

FIGURE 13-4 *Unemployment Rates since 1960: All Workers and Teenagers*

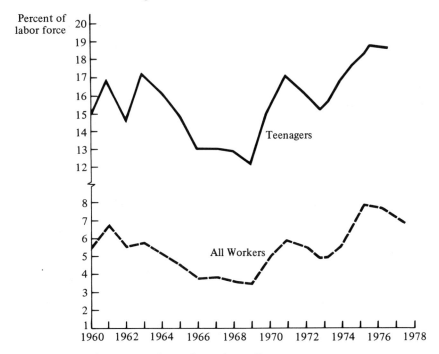

SOURCE: Employment and Earnings, Annually.

unemployed more often for shorter spells.[8] Older workers are unemployed less often but experience unemployment of longer duration. Viewed in this light, the unemployment problem of older workers is more serious than that confronting teenage workers. When the unemployment rate is high among experienced older workers, it suggests that the excess supply of labor is larger than that which is consistent with frictional unemployment. A critical question that arises when a high percentage of those who are unemployed are experienced workers in the prime-age groups who are job losers (as opposed to job leavers, reentrants, or new entrants) is whether a sufficient number of vacant jobs exist at current wages to reduce the excess supply of labor to a level that is consistent with frictional unemployment. Considerable analysis is required to answer this question. The section that follows examines the relationship between vacancies and employment.

[8] Martin Feldstein, "The Importance of Temporary Layoffs: An Empirical Analysis," *Brookings Papers on Economic Activity* 3 (1975): 735.

Relationship between Vacancies and Unemployment

A job vacancy is an unfilled job opening for which an employer is actually seeking a worker.[9] At the present time, comprehensive statistics of unfilled vacancies are not being compiled in the United States. However, there are data available in other economies, the United Kingdom among them, that show that vacancies and unemployment are negatively related along a curve such as that shown in Figure 13-5.[10] The essential characteristic of the curve is its convexity; it cannot touch either axis. Even a very tight labor market is characterized by some unemployment because a large number of vacancies encourages some workers to quit in search of a new job. Conversely, there are some unfilled vacancies even when the unemployment rate is high; typically, these openings are seeking workers with very special qualifications, or they are jobs with characteristics that make them unattractive even when unemployment rates are high.

FIGURE 13-5   *The Relationship between Vacancy and Unemployment Rates*

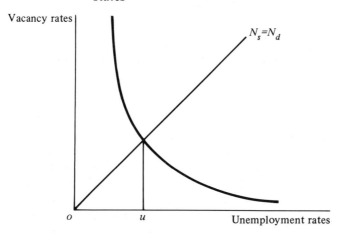

The relationship between job-vacancy rates and unemployment rates is useful for conceptualizing the state of excess labor supply or demand that characterizes the market if flows into and out of the labor

[9] Glenn Miller, "Job Vacancy Statistics," *Federal Reserve Bank of Kansas City Monthly Review* (June 1970): 12.

[10] This diagram was introduced by J. C. R. Dow and L. A. Dicks-Mireaux in "The Excess Demand for Labour: A Study of Conditions in Great Britain, 1946–56," *Oxford Economic Papers* 10 (February 1958): 1–33.

market are not equal. The supply of labor in the aggregate may be conceived of as the sum of the number employed, N_e, and the number, U, who are seeking work but are unemployed. Thus, the labor supply, N_s, is:

$$N_s = N_e + U \tag{1}$$

Similarly, the demand for labor in the aggregate is equal to N_e, the number of workers employed, plus V, the number of job vacancies. Thus the demand for labor is:

$$N_d = N_e + V \tag{2}$$

The excess demand (or supply) of labor (X) is thus:

$$X_d = N_d - N_s \tag{3}$$

$$X_s = N_s - N_d \tag{4}$$

Substituting equations (1) and (2) into (3) and (4) expresses the vacancies in comparison with the number of persons looking for work or, alternatively, the excess of persons looking for work in comparison with existing vacancies.

If the level of unemployment in the economy is *ou*, as in Figure 13-5, the relationship between job vacancies and unemployment coincides with the vector $N_s = N_d$, which represents equality between labor supply and labor demand. Unemployment *ou* represents "frictional unemployment." That is, it is the unemployment that corresponds to unfilled vacancies available in occupations and locations that make it possible to match workers and jobs through job search. As was suggested in Chapter 4, in which the notion of job search was introduced, the *duration* of unemployment depends on the relationship between the wage offers actually available and the aspiration level that workers have in mind when they seek employment. It is in this sense that unemployment of the sort represented by *ou* in Figure 13-5 is voluntary unemployment. If $N_s = N_d$, there is no excess supply of labor in the aggregate, and the expectation is that the duration of unemployment will be relatively brief, because there is a quantitative balance between the demand for the labor supply at a wage rate approximating that which people aspire to receive.

Under what conditions will such a balance between the demand for and the supply of labor be achieved? To gain insight into this question we require a theory of employment that is firmly rooted in the decision-making processes of households and business firms. Thus, the theory of household choice with respect to labor-force participation and hours of work and the theory of the employment decisions of business firms that were developed in Part I provide the foundation for the theory of employment that will be developed in the chapter that follows.

Concluding Remarks

It is useful to return once again to the problem of measuring unemployment. Because of the limitations of the "official" unemployment rate, the U.S. Bureau of Labor Statistics has developed a group of alternative unemployment measures, represented in Figure 13-6 as U-1 through U-7, that are representative of different opinions about the meaning and measurement of unemployment. The bureau regularly publishes U-1 through U-5 data; U-6 and U-7 can be calculated from their components.

1. The U-1 measure identifies the number of persons who have been unemployed forty-five weeks or longer as a percentage of the labor force.

2. The U-2 measure identifies as a percentage of the civilian labor force the number of persons unemployed because they were terminated at their last job.

3. The U-3 measure identifies as a percentage of the civilian labor force the number of household heads who are unemployed.

4. The U-4 measure identifies the number of unemployed persons seeking full-time jobs as a percentage of all those in the full-time labor force.

5. The U-5 measure is the percentage of persons in the civilian work force who are sixteen years or older who are not working but who are available for and are seeking work. This is the official unemployment rate. It can be viewed as the base series from which the other six measures can be constructed through addition or subtraction. The widespread acceptance of the U-5 measure derives from the fact that the only criterion of unemployment is whether job search took place. It involves no value judgments concerning a person's family or marital status, relative need for work, or personal characteristics.

6. The U-6 measure seeks to reflect involuntary part-time unemployment. It is constructed by adding one-half the number of persons seeking part-time work and one-half the number of persons employed involuntarily on part-time schedules who usually have or desire full-time work to the number of persons seeking full-time work.

7. The U-7 measure seeks to reflect the number of "discouraged" workers—the persons who are not looking for work because they believe there is no work available for them.

This recently developed array of seven unemployment rates illustrates a range of value judgments about unemployment in light of the psychological and economic hardship it imposes. In 1975 the series ranged from a low of 2.7 for U-1 to 10.7 for U-7.

FIGURE 13-6

Seven Ways to Measure Unemployment

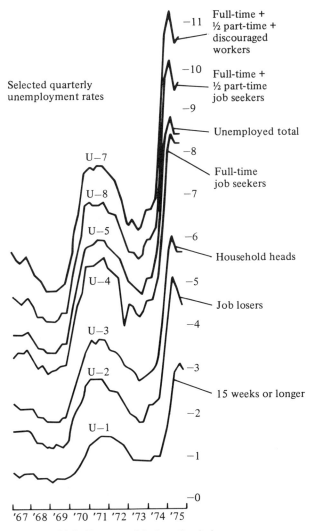

Selected quarterly
unemployment rates

SOURCE: U.S. Bureau of Labor Statistics

Suggestions for Further Reading

Charles Holt and M. H. David. *The Concept of Vacancies in a Dynamic Theory of the Labor Market: Measurement and Interpretation of Job Vacancies.* New York: National Bureau of Economic Research, 1966.

Martin Feldstein. "The Importance of Temporary Layoffs: An Empirical Analysis," *Brookings Papers on Economic Activity* 3 (1975).

14 Employment and Unemployment: Explaining the Evidence

Evidence about the nature and incidence of unemployment makes it quite clear that explanatory hypotheses must address the problem on two levels. What is required is first an hypothesis to explain unemployment levels in excess of the natural or frictional rate. Second, this hypothesis needs to be supplemented with additional analysis that explains the disparate incidence of unemployment among different population groups. At present, there is concern about both problems. Historically, however, the problem of the level of employment and unemployment in the economy as a whole was the only focus of analytical inquiry. The latter question was the particular concern of John Maynard Keynes, who addressed the issue in his important book *The General Theory of Employment Interest and Money*, which was published in 1936, during the Great Depression.

Writing from the vantage point of earlier experience, during which unemployment appeared to be "self-correcting" in the sense of bringing about wage adjustments that encouraged the reemployment of unemployed workers, Keynes observed that industrial economies were experiencing a type of unemployment that appeared not to be amenable to the market-clearing mechanism that was historically effective. During the 1930s the number of workers seeking employment at current wages appeared to be in excess of the number of job vacancies available to be filled; the type of unemployment that was being experienced was involuntary in the sense that it was not correctible by market forces. Expressed in terms of the relationships represented in Figure 14-1, the type of unemployment about which Keynes was so concerned corresponds to $o\bar{u}$ This level is greater than ou, the unemployment rate that corresponds conceptually to frictional unemployment, because it is

FIGURE 14-1 *Relationship between Vacancy and Unemployment Rates: Involuntary Unemployment*

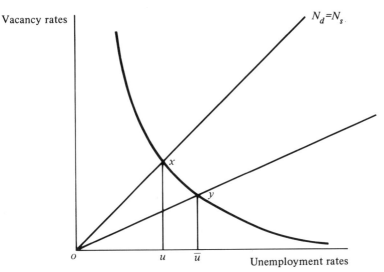

matched by vacancies. If N_d does not equal N_s the excess of unemployment is "involuntary" because it exceeds the unemployment associated with normal labor-market flows and the wage-rate changes that accompany them.

The critical question for an economy that is experiencing unemployment is whether the functioning of the price mechanism in the economy's labor and commodity markets can restore employment to a level at which the supply of labor is not in excess of the number of vacancies, so that policy intervention is not required. A theory of employment that is firmly rooted in the decision-making processes of households and business firms is required to provide insight into this question. Thus, the theory of household choice with respect to labor-force participation and hours of work, and the theory of the employment decisions of business firms, provide the foundation for the theory of employment on a macroeconomic level.

The Theory of Employment

The Microfoundations

Several aspects of the supply of and the demand for labor have already been noted. Specifically, workers were envisaged as allocating time to market and nonmarket activities in response to real wage offers. Decision making about employment at the level of the firm is also responsive to the level of real wages (i.e., the relationship between money wages and the price level) because this determines the profitability of providing more jobs. Increased employment requires that *real* wage levels be reduced.

The concern of employers with real wages is readily understood; from the standpoint of a prospective employer, it is profitable to hire an additional worker if his marginal-revenue product is expected to exceed the real-wage rate he must be paid. Employers are always ready to provide more employment if they can do so at a lower *real* wage; thus, the level of real wages is the "supply price" of employment.

Even though the wage bargain is struck in money terms, the employer's concern is with the ratio w/P, where w is the wage he pays and P, the average level of all prices. Thus, it will be profitable to offer additional employment at current wages only if the general price level rises. Alternatively, if the general price level remains constant, the required fall in real wages depends on a downward adjustment in money wages. The level of real wages will fall in either case, and the profitability of offering more employment will be enhanced.

The relationship between real and money wages may be illustrated in terms of the hypothetical data in Table 14-1, in which t_0, t_1, and t_2 represent separate calendar dates on which money wages, w, are \$6, \$5, and \$5, as recorded in Column 2. The assumed price level for each date is recorded in Column 3 and is expressed as a percentage of that which prevailed on date t_0, which is represented as 100. The last column is the real-wage level that reflects the relationship between the money wage and the price level. Thus, the real wage, or purchasing power, of a money wage of \$6, when the price level is at 100, is \$6. If, subsequently, the money wage falls (say, in consequence of unemployment) while the price level remains constant, the real-wage level will have fallen to \$5 (\$5/100 = \$5), making it profitable for employers to offer additional jobs.

This would not, however, be the case if in t_2 the price level *also* falls (say, to 80 percent of what it was in t_0), for the level of real wages would then have *risen* to \$6.25 (i.e. \$5/.80 = \$6.25), which would penalize employment. A cut in money wages promotes employment *only* if the

Table 14-1 *The Relationship between Money and Real Wages*

Date	Money wage	Price level $t_0 = 100$	$\dfrac{w}{P}$
t_0	\$6.00	100	\$6.00
t_1	5.00	100	5.00
t_2	5.00	80	6.25

price level is not also falling. Keynes thus rejected the traditional view that a reduction in the level of unemployment is contingent on reductions in money wages. He maintained, first, that workers are generally unwilling to accept cuts in their money wages, i.e., they are subject to "money illusion" and feel themselves to be better off when money wages are higher regardless of the price level. Second, he expected that the general price level would fall more rapidly than money wages during a depression, so that *real* wages would rise. If his conjecture is correct, the implication is that an across-the-board reduction in money wages, assuming it can be brought about, would be *adverse* rather than helpful in its effects during periods of unemployment.

Since Keynes's conjecture about the relationship between money and real wages over the cycle appeared to be important to his analysis, it quickly became a matter for empirical investigation. While the findings of these investigations are not conclusive,[1] studies by Tarshis and Dunlop concluded, on the basis of English and American data, that Keynes was wrong in his conjecture about their relationship.[2] More recently Ronald Bodkin has reexamined the relationship between real and money wages again using historical as well as postwar U.S. and Canadian data. His findings, which largely reconfirm those of Dunlop and Tarshis, are reported below as *Economics in Action 14:1*.

ECONOMICS IN ACTION 14:1

Real Wages and Cyclical Variations in Employment

Like Tarshis and Dunlop before him, Bodkin undertook to examine the evidence about the cyclical relationship between real wages and employment.[3] As an initial step to examining the statistical relationship between real wages and employment, real wages were computed by dividing money wages (measured in terms of payments to production workers) by a consumer price index and then "detrended" to correct for secular or long-term movements in the data. The presumption is that trend-corrected real wages will be negatively related to cyclical activity and, therefore, positively related to the rate of unemployment.

No significant association between detrended real wages and the rate of unemployment was established on the basis of Canadian

[1] James Tobin, "Money Wage Rates and Employment," in Seymour Harris, *The New Economics* (New York: Alfred A. Knopf, 1947).

[2] John T. Dunlop, "The Movement of Real and Money Wages," *Economic Journal* 48 (September 1938), and Loie Tarshis, "Changes in Real and Money Wages," *Economic Journal* 49 (September 1939).

[3] Ronald Bodkin, "Real Wages and Cyclical Variations in Employment: A Reexamination of The Evidence," *Canadian Journal of Economics* 2, 3 (August 1969).

historical data. However, analysis of U.S. data show trend adjusted real wages to be rising as the rate of unemployment falls. These results are consistent with the Dunlop-Tarshis finding that trend-adjusted real wages rise in periods of expanding employment.

The empirical finding that real wages do *not* behave as Keynes expected during depressed periods does not, however, undermine his argument that there "may exist no expedient by which labor as a whole can reduce its *real* wage to a given figure by making revised money bargains with entrepreneurs."[4] The critical point in Keynes's argument is that workers cannot reduce their real wages via so simple a measure as reducing their money wages. Real wage levels are not determined in the economy's labor markets. The money wage is set by institutional forces in the economy's labor markets, but the level of real wages is dependent on the level of employment, which is determined by the relationship between aggregate demand and supply. The behavior of these magnitudes is examined in the section that follows.

Aggregate Functions and Employment

Keynes's Aggregate-Supply Function

In *The General Theory*, Keynes identified the aggregate-supply price of a given amount of employment in terms of the "proceeds which will just make it worth the while of the entrepreneur to give that employment."[5] The implication is that the aggregate-supply schedule of the economy reflects the supply experiences of individual firms. For any individual producer, the supply price of a particular quantity of the commodity he will offer for sale is the price sufficient to provide the proceeds necessary to induce them to offer it to the market. In the short run, when the inputs of resources other than labor are fixed for the individual firm, the supply price of output is represented by the firm's marginal-cost curve. Since labor is the only variable input, the marginal cost of output is equal to the money-wage rate divided by the marginal product of labor or:

$$MC = \frac{w}{MP}$$

where w is the money-wage rate and MP is the marginal product of labor. Even if the wage rate is constant, a firm's marginal-cost curve rises beyond the point of diminishing returns; its supply curve is, therefore,

---

[4] *The General Theory of Employment, Interest and Money* (1936), p. 13.
[5] Keynes, *op. cit.*, p. 24.

upward-sloping.[6] Entrepreneurs are thus encouraged to increase output and employment only if they expect prices to rise.

A lateral summation of the marginal-cost curves of each of the firms in an industry yields an upward-sloping industry-supply curve like the curve SS' in Figure 14-2. This is a schedule that relates quantities of output supplied to expected market prices.

FIGURE 14-2 *Industry-Supply Curve*

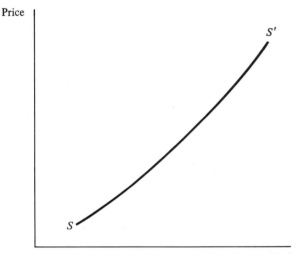

Quantity supplied

The aggregate-supply curve of the economy is readily derived from industry-supply curves, although the variables involved in the industry-supply curve are different from those that relate the supply price of output in the aggregate to its related volume of employment. Each industry-supply curve relates quantities of output to market prices and resembles Figure 14-2. Together they provide the information required to generate the economy's aggregate-supply curve or function.

Keynes did not illustrate the aggregate-supply schedule graphically. However, his verbal description, which identified employment as the most satisfactory measure of changes in current output, suggests that had he drawn an aggregate-supply curve he would have linked employment to required proceeds in current prices. The aggregate-supply curve is generated by multiplying each level of output (Y) by the average current price, p, required to make it profitable to employ the labor force

---

[6] See above, Chapter 6, p. 112.

necessary for its production. Thus, the aggregate-supply function represents money rather than real magnitudes; each of its points has a price level implicit in it.[7]

Table 14-2 illustrates the derivation of the aggregate-supply schedule or function in hypothetical terms. It is assumed that all output is produced in the private sector by "price taking" firms that employ varying labor inputs at an average money wage of $8,000 per year and use them in conjunction with a fixed stock of capital, K. The presumption is that diminishing returns are experienced as larger outputs are produced, which causes unit costs of production to rise at an increasing rate as output increases. Thus, if entrepreneurs in the aggregate are to provide employment for 30 million workers (Line 2), the wage bill (wN) would be $24 billion. The addition of a "markup" over wage costs to cover fixed cost and gross profit implies that entrepreneurs will require $50 billion in gross revenues to make it worthwhile to provide employment for 30 million workers. Thus, the supply price of employing 30 million workers, given the assumptions on which Table 14-2 is based, is $50 billion. This figure is recorded in the fourth column of Table 14-2. On the same assumptions, the aggregate level of proceeds necessary to employ 40 million workers is $70 billion. Employment levels of 50, 60, and 70 million workers require proceeds or levels of GNP of

TABLE 14-2 *Derivation of the Aggregate Supply Schedule*

N, Employment in millions	Wage bill wN	Fixed cost F	Z, (Aggregate supply price) or GNP in billions	Gross profit $\pi = Z-wN-F$
0	$ 0	$10	$ 0	$-10
30	24	10	50	16
40	32	10	70	28
50	40	10	95	45
60	48	10	125	67
70	54	10	160	96

[7] Sidney Weintraub represented the Z function on this basis. See his "A Macroeconomic Approach to the Theory of Wages," *American Economic review* (December 1956). This presentation links the aggregate-supply function of the macroeconomy to the employment and output decisions of individual firms. Weintraub's representation of the Z function, which this booadoptsts because of its appropriateness for examining employment differs from the standard presentation which shows aggregate supply as a 45° line representing the relationship between real expenditure and output when there is equilibrium in both commodity and money markets. A popular macroeconomic textbook, which is an exception in that it shows the Z function as the relationship between levels of proceeds (or GNP) and employment, is Wallace C. Peterson, *Income Employment and Economic Growth,* 3rd edition (New York: W. W. Norton & Co., 1974), pp. 111–115.

$95 billion, $125 billion, and $160 billion in order to make entrepreneurs willing to provide the related volume of employment.

Based on the data in Table 14-2, in which output does not increase proportionately with increases in employment, the aggregate-supply function is represented in Figure 14-3 as $Z = p \cdot q(N, \overline{K})$, where N represents variable labor inputs and $\overline{K}$ represents the short-run constant input of capital goods. Employment is plotted on the horizontal axis, and levels of Gross National Product in current dollars (i.e., $p \cdot q$) are on the vertical axis. The proceeds associated with each GNP level are computed by aggregating price-quantity magnitudes from industry-

FIGURE 14-3   *The Aggregate Supply Curve or "Z" Function*

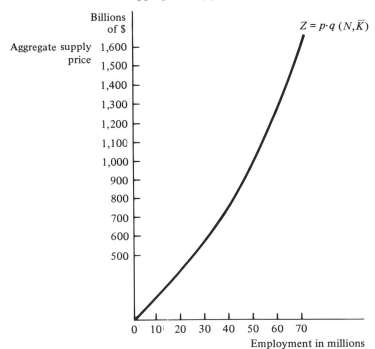

supply curves like that in Figure 14-2. By computing proceeds-employment relationships and aggregating them, it is possible to generate data like those hypothesized in Table 14-2, which shows the Z function in Column 4. The level of GNP required to support higher levels of employment rises, because marginal costs rise as output increases. Thus, the Z function represents the aggregate-supply price of employment and slopes upward at an increasing rate, as in Figure 14-3.

The Aggregate-Demand Schedule

While the Z function relates various possible levels of employment to the proceeds levels that are required to support them at current prices, the *actual* level of employment is determined by the interaction of the aggregate-supply schedule with the aggregate-demand schedule. The explanation that Keynes offered in his now classic work is that productive capacity is brought into use only if business expectations about profit opportunities are such that the demand for aggregate output will be high enough to insure its sale at prices that will cover its costs of production. The central theme of Keynes's *General Theory*, on which modern macrotheory is largely based, is that in the short run, during which productive capacity is relatively fixed, the level of aggregate effective demand is the critical force determining the level of income and employment.

The aggregate-demand function relates employment levels to the proceeds that businessmen expect to realize, in current dollars, from the sale of their output to households, other businesses, or government.[8] Thus the aggregate-demand function may be written as $D = \Phi(N)$. Expected sales proceeds depend on the level of consumption and investment expenditures. Representing household expenditures for consumption as C, business investment expenditures by I, and government expenditures as G, we see that the aggregate-demand schedule is: $DD = C + I + G$. It is represented graphically in Figure 14-4 as $D = \Phi N$.[9]

FIGURE 14-4 *Aggregate Functions and Employment*

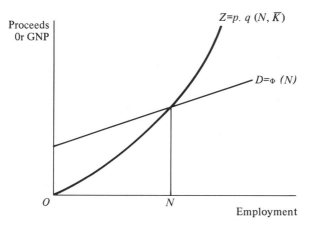

[8]The proceeds expected from foreign trade add to or reduce those coming from domestic trade by the amount of *net* foreign investment.

[9]This representation of the aggregate-demand schedule parallels that of the aggre-

The reason why aggregate demand is a function of employment (N) will be understood by examining its component parts: household expenditures, investment expenditures, and government expenditures. The latter are dependent on policy decisions, but consumption and investment expenditures are the result of endogenous forces operating in the economy.

The primary dependence of consumer expenditures on current and past income and borrowing is well established. Investment expenditures, on the other hand, are quite volatile, because they are undertaken in an environment of uncertainty. It is precisely because the stream of revenues that a new capital good can be expected to produce over a period of years is so unpredictable, that investment is the critical component of aggregate effective demand. Investment depends on expectations about the ability of new investment to yield income over an uncertain future period. If business pessimism reduces investment expenditures, expected proceeds from the sale of output may be less than is necessary for entrepreneurs to fully employ the labor force that is willing to work at the current level of real wages.

The level of employment is determined by the relationship between the aggregate-demand function and the aggregate-supply function. The two functions do *not* necessarily intersect at full employment levels of GNP. Every increase in output and employment that takes place as the economy expands along its aggregate-supply curve is not associated with a corresponding increase in demand.[10] When the aggregate-demand level is deficient, some of the labor seeking work will find itself confronted with unemployment that does not yield to job search. Alternatively expressed, the number of unemployed workers exceeds the number of vacant jobs employers are seeking to fill. The type of unemployment that results is involuntary in the sense that it cannot be eliminated through the price mechanism. Even where wages are not rigid for contractual reasons, workers resist wage cuts and legislation supports wage floors. However, even if it were possible to cut money wages, their influence is not transmitted to real wages. Real wages, as J. M. Keynes clearly showed, *are determined along with the level of employment by the level of aggregate demand.* If the level of aggregate demand forthcoming from consumption and investment demand is not sufficient to promote full

---

gate-supply schedule and differs from the conventional representation, which shows combinations of C + I expenditures and output. The advantage, from the point of view of this text, of conceiving the aggregate-demand schedule as relating employment levels to expected proceeds is that it focuses on the *employment* decision rather than the output decision.

[10] This is the essence of the generalization known as Say's Law, which is typically stated as holding that supply generates its own demand. Rejection of this generalization is an integral part of Keynes's disagreement with the classics.

employment, a state of demand deficiency will exist that will be associated with real wages that are too high for full employment. Given a money-wage level that labor resists reducing, the achievement of full employment requires a level of aggregate demand that is high enough to raise the general price level so that w/P, which is the level of real wages, is reduced. Unless this can be accomplished, the economy will experience involuntary unemployment.

Intergroup Differences in Employment and Unemployment

While the theory of demand explains the level of employment and unemployment, it does not explain the process of reentry into the labor market or why the impact of unemployment as well as the probability of reentry in the event of job loss is disparate among population groups. Much of the theoretical and empirical inquiry into employment problems since Keynes wrote has been addressed to these questions. The essential contribution of this ongoing research has been to develop the microeconomic foundations of macroeconomic analysis. It is now unlikely that macro- and microeconomics will ever again be "compartmentalized" as they were until the recent past.

The development of search theory has been a particularly fruitful avenue of recent research, and its marriage to the theory of employment, which is examined next, is an important step in the direction of greater realism.

The Process of Job Search

Contemporary research has shown that the majority of persons who are unemployed quit voluntarily or are new entrants or reentrants into the labor market. Entry into the labor market, as well as reentry after quitting or being laid off, imposes the need to search for a job opportunity. The search that is undertaken is not costless. Even the simplest model envisages the searcher as venturing out to locate job offers at a cost that includes all out-of-pocket expenditures, such as advertising and transportation and, if he is unemployed, the wages lost while searching.[11] A more complex model could incorporate the possibility of recalling offers previously rejected. The object of search models is to determine when the searcher will stop searching and accept an offer, at which point he exits to a state of employment. The decision-making process is thus analogous to that which governs other types of investment in human capital. That is, search is essentially an investment process, and unemployment can be interpreted as performing a socially valuable

[11]S. A. Lippman and John J. McCall, "Job Search," Part I, *Economic Inquiry* 14 (1976): 155–189.

function by promoting the allocation of workers into their best opportunities.

The premise is that the amount of search (i.e., the period of unemployment) depends on the probability distribution of wages that characterizes the offers made by employers. The searcher does not know precisely which wage offer will be located during a particular search day, but he is presumed to know from experience and search the distribution of wage offers that his services can command. Thus, on a given search day, the probability that a searcher will receive an offer of wage, W, is $F(W)$, where F is the (known) wage distribution from which the offers he receives are randomly generated. Since he knows the opportunity cost of his search efforts and the probability distribution of the wages his services can command, his reservation wage can be computed, i.e., it is possible to compute the wage at which the marginal cost of obtaining one additional job offer is equal to the expected marginal return of one more offer. The duration of job search thus varies inversely with the cost of obtaining additional offers. The availability of unemployment insurance and other forms of income maintenance during unemployment reduces the cost of job search. Thus, it has been suggested that it is financially worthwhile for workers receiving such payments to prolong the duration of their unemployment, because the combination of unemployment compensation (or other transfer income) coupled with the tax rate on earned income substantially reduces net earnings from employment.[12] Some workers who have been laid off appear to find it preferable to wait to be recalled to their old job rather than to engage in search.[13] The implication of this line of reasoning is that it is appropriate for government to adopt policies that will discourage workers from quitting their jobs and from prolonging their search if they do quit or are laid off. Arguments for reforming unemployment-compensation programs to accomplish these objectives are examined in Chapter 19.

Layoffs: Unemployment without Job Change

An important limitation of the traditional (depression) view of unemployment is that it does not relate to the kind of unemployment that arises in consequence of job layoffs. As was noted above, an individual can be laid off and thus be "unemployed" even though he reports to the household survey that he has a job. Layoffs are defined as "suspensions" without pay lasting or expected to last more than seven consecutive calendar days, and initiated by the employer without

[12] Martin J. Feldstein, "The Importance of Temporary Layoffs: An Empirical Analysis," *Brookings Papers on Economic Activity* 6 (1975): 725–744.

[13] Martin J. Feldstein, "The Economics of the New Unemployment," *Public Interest* 33 (Fall 1973): 3–42.

prejudice to the worker.[14] This definition includes permanent as well as temporary layoffs, but excludes discharges "for cause," retirement, and separations initiated by workers. The layoff phenomenon that is frequent in our economy ends in recall and involves no job search.[15]

The reasons why temporary layoffs are often the norm is not difficult to understand. Investment in firm specific capital coupled with employee preferences for stable employment are reflected in layoff (furlough) provisions in union contracts to forestall wage cuts. These provisions imply that a firm's response to a fall in demand is likely to take the form of temporary layoffs, scheduling changes, inventory accumulation, and perhaps even price reductions. A spell of unemployment that is initiated by a layoff is involuntary unemployment; however, the decision rule that leads to layoffs (in lieu of wage cuts) and that determines their duration is at least partly chosen by workers, as part of the contract package for which they bargain.

Inquiry into the magnitude and importance of layoffs also provides additional insight into the downward inflexibility of wages. Temporary layoffs and quasi-permanent employment provide two reasons for the downward wage rigidity that Keynes attributed to money illusion on the part of workers. The vast majority of unemployed workers are not part of the supply of labor to other firms. They thus have little effect on the supply conditions in the labor market generally. Workers who are on layoff typically do not force wage rates down by accepting other jobs at lower wages. Nor do firms reduce the offers they make to experienced workers. Since most of the experienced workers who are unemployed at any time are on layoff, new hiring must be done largely by attracting those who are employed elsewhere. Thus, wages tend to remain rigid.

Intergroup Differences in the Incidence of Unemployment

As was noted above, the impact of unemployment is quite different among different demographic groups. Since the number of employment separations do not rise greatly during a recession, because heavier layoffs are partially offset by reduced quits, the inference is that certain workers are "disadvantaged" because they experience particular difficulty in finding jobs. This phenomenon is not explained by the theory of aggregate demand. It suggests the relevance of investigating the flow of workers between jobs, unemployment, and nonparticipation in the labor force in order to identify differences among groups in the probability of finding a job in the event of unemployment. Such an investigation is reported as *Economics in Action 14:2.*

[14] *Employment and Earnings* 22 (November 1975): 135.
[15] Martin Feldstein, "The Importance of Temporary Layoffs: An Empirical Analysis," *op. cit.*, p. 739.

ECONOMICS IN ACTION 14:2

Intergroup Differences in Unemployment and in the Probability of Labor-Market Reentry

The Current Population Survey samples 55,000 households sub-divided into eight rotation groups, six of which are in the sample two consecutive months. This classification makes it possible to "track" respondents from one labor-market state to another. Labor-market states are identified as (1) the probability of transition from employment to unemployment; (2) the probability of transition from unemployment to not being in the labor force; (3) the probability of transition from unemployment to employment; (4) the probability of transition from employment to not being in the labor force; (5) the probability of transition from not being in the labor force to employment; and (6) the probability of transition from not being in the labor force to unemployment.

The analysis of labor-market flows in terms of this classification of labor-market states sheds light on the unemployment experiences of different demographic groups during periods of normal economic activity and during periods of recession.[16] In order to compare the impact of cyclical changes on different demographic groups, the flow rates in tight and loose labor markets were averaged each month for the period 1967–1973. Each month in the sample was identified as representing a tight or loose labor market, depending on whether the aggregate unemployment rate was above or below its mean.

The difference among groups between flows into jobs and flows into the pool of unemployed workers turns on the probability of successful labor-force entry. The probability of the flow from employment to unemployment includes not only the probability of being unemployed in the first instance but also the probability that some persons will become unemployed by first dropping out of the labor force and then reentering unsuccessfully.

For the labor force as a whole, a downswing is characterized by a low probability of making a transition from a state of unemployment to a state of employment. Between 1967 and 1973, 0.9 percentage points of the total increase of 1.7 percentage points in the unemployment rate are identified as being attributable to the decreased probability of making a transition to a state of employment from a state of unemployment.[17] An additional 0.5 percentage points of the unemployment rate is associated

[16] Stephen T. Marston, "Employment Instability and High Unemployment Rates," *Brookings Papers on Economic Activity* 1 (1976): 169–203.
[17] It is relevant that in discussing Marston's paper, Michael Wachter noted that the period 1967–1973 includes only a mild recession without massive layoffs.

with labor-force entrants who have a lower chance of finding a job. Thus, 1.4 percentage points of the cyclical differential in unemployment was found to be attributable to the difficulties unemployed workers and new entrants have in finding a job, and only 0.3 of a percentage point was found to be due to employment separations.

While the deteriorating probability that unemployed workers will find a job is the main factor in raising unemployment rates during a period of cyclical decline, there are important differences across demographic groups in the relative probability of achieving successful entry into the labor force. There is a high risk of separation from employment among primary workers. But, even though job loss takes a high toll, the probability of labor-force entry changes little for this group. Secondary workers are, however, characterized by higher rates of nonparticipation in the labor force than is the case with prime-age white males. A deterioration in the probability of successful labor-force entry therefore increases the measured unemployment rate of this group. Among secondary workers the total flow from employment into unemployment is increased in consequence of persons reentering the labor force unsuccessfully and becoming unemployed. Among these groups failure to achieve successful labor-force entry rather than employment instability was found to be the major factor increasing their unemployment in a declining economy.

Alternative Hypotheses about Unemployment among Secondary Workers

The reasons why secondary workers experience greater difficulty than white prime-age males in achieving successful labor-force entry is not discernible from the analysis of labor-market states and is a matter of considerable controversy. The limits to the upward mobility that they experience is reflected in their earnings-age-income profiles. Data from the Survey of Economic Opportunity are the basis of the age profile of hourly wages for white and black males and females that are reproduced in Figure 14-5. One investigation which used these data concluded that the notion of a career with steady opportunity for advancement is relevant only for white males. This group experiences wage increases from age twenty through age fifty-four.[18] By contrast, black males and women of both races make progress only from ages twenty through twenty-four; from ages twenty-five to thirty-four and beyond their wage profiles are practically flat.

The uneven distribution of wages among the four sex-race groups

---

[18] Robert E. Hall, "Why Is the Unemployment Rate So High at Full Employment?" *Brookings Papers on Economic Activity* 3 (1970): 369–410.

FIGURE 14-5 *Age Profile of Wages, by Sex and Race, 1966*

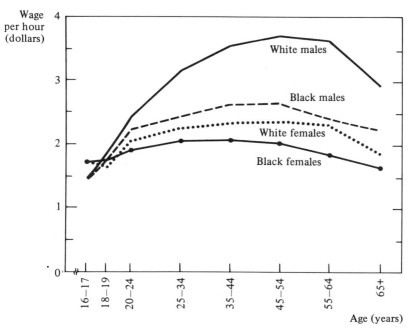

SOURCE: Survey of Economic Opportunity, conducted by U.S. Bureau of Census, Spring 1967.

shown in Figure 14-5 is paralled by a similar uneven distribution in the impact of unemployment, as shown in Table 14-3. Unemployment in the United States remains relatively high at full employment because large fractions of some groups in the labor force experience abnormally frequent changes in jobs with frequent periods of unemployment between jobs. Their experience, according to a leading hypothesis, reflects differences in opportunity. Thus, Hall observes that whites are willing to work steadily at low-paying jobs because they know they can advance up a ladder by establishing a stable employment record. Blacks, on the other hand, do not have the same opportunity, and are therefore likely to leave low-paying jobs in a few months or a year.[19] Racial differences among women are not as pronounced, presumably because women of both races tend to be excluded from the job ladder. However, women as well as nonwhites exhibit a lesser commitment to the labor

[19] Hall, *op. cit.*, p. 395.

TABLE 14-3   *Estimates of Weeks of Unemployment, by Race, Sex, and Wage Groups, 1966*

Hourly wage in dollars	Men		Women	
	White	Black	White	Black
0-1.50	4.3	9.4	1.3	1.0
1.50-1.75	2.8	8.3	1.1	1.3
1.75-2.00	2.8	4.9	1.0	1.6
2.00—2.50	3.0	2.7	0.8	1.2
2.50-3.00	2.0	0.0	0.9	0.3
3.00 or more	1.4	−1.0	0.0	0.6

SOURCE: Robert E. Hall, "Wages, Income and Hours of Work in the U.S. Labor Force." Working Paper 62, (Massachusetts Institute of Technology, Department of Economics, August 1970).

market. Often there are jobs available, but there is a "mismatch" between vacancies and the skills unemployed workers have to offer.

In particular, the high unemployment rates of the early and later 1960s and during the 1970s reflect the presence in the economy of large numbers of unskilled and poorly educated workers, who are frequently available only in the wrong locations.[20] Their skills often do not match the requirements of job vacancies. Many jobs are available, but because these do not offer training or advancement opportunities, workers have low attendance and high quit rates. The rewards from stable employment are not great enough to encourage long-term employment. Among young people, the unemployment effects of weak job commitment are reinforced by the seasonal character of the labor-force activity of students. Since school attendance is the major activity of about 40 percent of persons in the labor force ages sixteen through twenty-one, this is reflected in the statistical picture of youth unemployment. If those who are looking for part-time work are not counted, the unemployment rate falls by as much as 5 percentage points. The high unemployment rates among youthful workers is to a considerable extent a reflection of the commitment, in America, of providing more years of schooling than is typical in other countries.[21]

There is considerable controversy about the reasons that underlie the poor-jobs, poor-work-habits syndrome. One view is that firms cannot afford to offer useful on-the-job training to a worker whose net product during the period of training must be at least equal to his wage. The

[20] The increase in the natural rate of unemployment noted above reflects the presence of these groups in the labor market.

[21] Martin Feldstein, "The Economics of the New Unemployment," *op. cit.*, pp. 9–12.

current minimum-wage law, it is held, prevents many young people from accepting jobs that provide valuable experience even though the pay is low. Only those who come to the market with some skill and sufficient education are productive enough to permit employers to pay at least the minimum wage and also provide opportunities for training and advancement. The worker who is disadvantaged, whether by youth or other characteristics, brings little to the labor market. In the short run, the minimum-wage law deters their unemployment; in the long run it contributes toward making those who start off with low skills part of the permanent poor, because it often precludes the kind of training that would qualify them for jobs other than the dead-end jobs that they tend to quit. Some of the ways of removing the barrier that the minimum-wage law imposes to better on-the-job training and experience are examined in Chapter 17.

It is important to recognize, however, that not everyone agrees that minimum-wage legislation has an adverse impact on the employment experiences and work behavior of disadvantaged groups. The proponents of the dual-labor-market hypothesis, as was already examined above, offers an alternative explanation. They maintain that discriminatory practices deprive nonwhites and women of the opportunity to try for attractive jobs. Thus, there are two queues rather than one. The nonwhite and female queue is in a constant state of flux, as these workers take unskilled jobs at a low wage rate. They quit after a relatively short time before reentering to take a similar low-paying, dead-end job, which they quit or from which they are laid off because the firms they work for have little need for a skilled or stable work force. More important, in the view of proponents of the dual-labor-markets hypothesis, secondary workers find employment in industries that function on the periphery of the economy. These industries are comprised of firms that lack market power and produce goods or services that have low skill and low capital requirements. Not only do they have little need for a skilled work force and, therefore, little incentive to offer training and promotion opportunities; they would also find it unprofitable to encourage stable work behavior on the part of their employees, because they are confronted with variable demands. Unlike the firms of the concentrated sector, which retain highly skilled technical and professional workers and respond to declines in demand by reducing output rather than price, firms on the periphery respond by contracting output and laying off workers.

Even in the concentrated sector, however, job stability is characteristic only of certain job clusters, which entail assignments having specific skill requirements. Workers in the lower tier of the primary sector thus experience layoffs when aggregate demand declines and are recalled when demand improves. However, the chief impact of unemployment is concentrated on workers in the secondary sector who are precluded from access to job ladders in the primary market. The policy implication of this interpretation is twofold. First, it is necessary to maintain a level of aggregate demand, through monetary and fiscal policy, that will insure the growth of the GNP and rising living standards. Insufficient aggregate demand is associated with an insufficient volume of job vacancies to prevent involuntary unemployment. Second, it is desirable to adopt the kind of public policy that will eliminate the most menial jobs (e.g., through health and safety regulations and minimum-wage legislation) and to create more "good" jobs in order to facilitate the upward mobility of women and minority workers.[22]

Concluding Remarks

There is an important further dimension to the unemployment problem that developed during the 1970s. Unlike the unemployment of the 1930s and 1940s, the unemployment which is being experienced now is associated with inflationary forces. Theoretical inquiry into the causes of inflationary pressure and its relationship to unemployment reflects areas of fundamental disagreement among the participants, not only on a technical level, but, as is already evident in the preceding discussion, on a philosophical level as well. The coupling of these high unemployment rates with inflation has emerged as the great economic dilemma challenging us today.

Chapter 15 focuses on the mainstream view that is associated with writers who, like Milton Friedman, lay the blame for inflation chiefly on monetary and fiscal excesses. Chapter 16 examines the challenge to their interpretation of inflationary forces, which is emanating chiefly, though not exclusively, from modern interpreters of J. M. Keynes. There are several strands to the controversy that has developed among them, for Friedman and his associates also claim a Keynesian heritage. The disagreement between the Keynesians and those who are leading what they perceive to be a return to the Keynes of the *General Theory* has important implications for understanding the functioning of labor markets and alternative-policy prescriptions.

[22] Eli Ginzberg, "The Job Problem," *Scientific American* 237 (July–December, 1977): 43–51.

Suggestions for Further Reading

Paul Davidson and Eugene Smolensky. *Aggregate Supply and Demand.* New York: Harper and Row, 1964, Chapter 9.

Martin Feldstein. "The Economics of the New Unemployment." *Public Interest* 33 (Fall 1973).

Eli Ginzberg. "The Job Problem." *Scientific American* 237 (July–December 1977): 43–51.

Robert E. Hall. "Turnover in the Labor Force." *Brookings Papers on Economic Activity* 3 (1972).

Stephen T. Marston. "Employment Instability and High Unemployment Rates." *Brookings Papers on Economic Activity* 1 (1976).

George L. Perry. "Unemployment Flows in the U.S. Labor Markets." *Brookings Papers in Economic Activity* 2 (1972).

Wallace C. Peterson. "Income Employment and Economic Growth," 3rd edition. New York: W. W. Norton & Co., 1974, Chapters 5–7.

Sidney Weintraub. "A Macroeconomic Approach to the Theory of Wages." *American Economic Review* 46, 5 (December 1956).

15 Inflation and Unemployment: Rational Expectations and Search Models

While the unemployment that accompanies economic stagnation was the focus of academic and government economists during the two decades following the Great Depression of the 1930s, a very different problem is now confronting the economy. When the decade of the 1970s began the unemployment rate was 5.9 percent and the economy was *simultaneously* experiencing inflationary price increases.

Historically, rising prices and low levels of unemployment characterized the prosperity phase of the business cycle, while falling prices, accompanied by high unemployment levels, were associated with periods of depression. Thus, the 1970s experience of rising prices and rising rates of unemployment, as exhibited in Table 15-1, confronted economists and policymakers with a totally new problem.[1] "Stagflation" and "slumpflation," as the phenomena of simultaneous price inflation and unchanged or decreasing levels of employment and output came to be called, was completely contrary to previous experience, in which higher unemployment levels were accompanied by falling prices. The necessity for explaining inflationary pressure in economies that have unemployed resources and for formulating appropriate policies to achieve the twin goals of containing inflation while maintaining satisfactory employment levels presents an intellectual puzzle, about which disagreement continues and which, thus far, has defied effective policy action.

---

[1] Inflationary pressures were a source of concern throughout the 1960s as well; however, unemployment rates were falling from 1964 through 1969.

278/

TABLE 15-1 *U.S. Unemployment Rate (%) and Cost-of-Living Index (Usually Called Consumer Price Index = CPI) 1958–1978*

	UNEMPLOYMENT (%)	CPI (1967 = 100)
1958	6.8	86.6
1959	5.5	87.3
1960	5.6	88.7
1961	6.7	89.6
1962	5.6	90.6
1963	5.7	91.7
1964	5.2	92.9
1965	4.6	94.5
1966	3.9	97.2
1967	3.8	100.0
1968	3.6	104.2
1969	3.5	109.8
1970	4.9	116.3
1971	5.9	121.3
1972	5.6	125.3
1973	4.9	133.1
1974	5.6	147.7
1975	8.5	161.2
1976	7.7	170.5
1977	7.0	181.5
1978	6.0	194.7
1979	5.8	231.8
1980	7.8**	233.2*

**Preliminary May 1980.
*Preliminary January 1980.
SOURCE: *Economic Report of the President* (January 1979).

The analytical and policy differences among modern economists is particularly evident in their differing explanations of the persistence of the dual problem of unemployment and inflation. With respect to economic analysis (whose policy implications are left chiefly to discussion in Part III), the focal point of their theoretical investigation has been similar: to identify the forces that "trigger" inflation in the economy and to explicate the microeconomic processes that underlie aggregate price and wage changes. The latter represent a whole new area of research that reflects the increasing awareness that macro- and microeconomics are not neatly compartmentalized: there are microfoundations that underlie the employment and inflation phenomena observed on a macroeconomic level.[2]

[2] The early recognition of this relationship by Sidney Weintraub was noted in Chapter 14. He has refined his early effort to extend the analysis of J. M. Keynes to explain

A major difference among modern economists with respect to explaining macroeconomic magnitudes is their conception of the way in which labor markets function. All agree that inflationary pressures are inherent in a strong economy. But the position of the majority (whom we generally refer to as "neoclassical" economists because of their views about the functioning of the price mechanism) is that the wage-price spiral of recent decades can be explained in terms of a mechanism that functions *endogenously* within the price system. Their theory of the determination of the *level* of wages is, therefore, consistent with their hypothesis concerning the *structure* of wages that developed in Chapters 8–11 in Part I. Their critics, who include a group generally referred to as "post-Keynesians," maintain that wage rates are established exogenously. They thus interpret the relationship between wage and price levels quite differently from the way their neoclassical counterparts do.[3] As was the case in Part I, our inquiry again begins with the neoclassical or mainstream view and introduces the alternative interpretation (in this case, that of the post-Keynesians) at a later point in the discussion.

Phillips Curves

An apparatus that has become known as the "Phillips curve" is a useful starting point for examining the two leading hypotheses that are being offered to explain the wage-price spiral.[4] Phillips curves stem from a 1958 British study that showed that the rate of change of wage rates was related to the level of unemployment over a hundred years of British history. Because the change in wage rates is related to inflation, this

---

inflation and income distribution in numerous books and articles. His most recent formulation is *Capitalism's Inflation and Unemployment Crisis* (Reading, Mass.: Addison-Wesley Publishing Company, 1978). A later but also pioneering effort in the direction of examining the microeconomic foundations of inflation and unemployment is Edmund Phelps, *et al., Microeconomic Foundations of Employment and Inflation Theory* (New York: W. W. Norton & Co., 1970). The differences between the hypotheses they offer concerning inflation reflect the differences between the two leading schools of thought on this problem.

[3] In emphasizing wages as being exogenously established (i.e., wages are determined by social and political forces rather than through the price mechanism), the post-Keynesians maintain their greater fidelity to the premises of *The General Theory*. See, for example, Alfred Eichner and J. A. Kregel, "An Essay on Post-Keynesian Theory: A New Paradigm in Economics," *Journal of Economic Literature* 13 (December 1975).

[4] The study of inflation has recently shifted from an analysis of the relative strength of "demand pull" and "cost push" elements to the relationship of prices implied in the Phillips curve. Among those who maintain that demand-pull and cost-push forces cannot be isolated is, in particular, F. D. Holzman, "Inflation: Cost-Push and Demand-Pull," *American Economic Review* 50 (March 1970): 24–42. More recently, the article by Helmut Frisch "Inflation Theory 1963–1975: A Second Generation Survey," *Journal of Economic Literature* 15 (December 1977): 1289–1314, reviews the large literature on inflation theory that has been published since 1960.

research appears to be relevant in relation to the difficulties experienced by the United States and other Western economies in achieving the dual goal of price-level stability and full employment.[5]

ECONOMICS IN ACTION 15:1

Money-Wage-Rate Changes and Unemployment

A. W. Phillips's study of the relationship between percentage changes in wage rates and the percentage unemployed of the civilian labor force for the periods 1861–1913, 1913–1948, and 1948–1957 implied that, leaving aside the war years, during which rising import prices generated a wage-price spiral, a stable money-wage level was compatible with a 5.5 percent unemployment rate. Alternatively expressed, the evidence suggested that for the period studied, the rate of increase of money wages could have been held to the 2 to 3 percent increase in labor productivity, with about a 2.5 percent rate of unemployment. A plot of the relationship between money-wage-rate changes and unemployment for the period 1861–1913 yielded a convex downward-sloping curve, which is reproduced in Figure 15-1 from the original study.[6]

Shortly after the publication of Phillips's study, Paul Samuelson and Robert Solow undertook to establish empirical evidence for a Phillips curve in the United States.[7] They concluded that the price index would have to rise substantially if unemployment were to be reduced to no more than the 3 percent level historically associated with "full employment." Later studies by Bhatia and France provided a further basis for the view that there might be a "trade-off" between rates of unemployment and rates of inflation in the U.S. economy.[8]

---

[5]A statistical relationship between unemployment and inflation was identified by Irving Fisher prior to Phillips's study. See Irving Fisher, "A Statistical Relation between Unemployment and Price Changes," *International Labour Review* (June 1926): 785–92, reprinted in *Journal of Political Economy* (March/April 1973): 596–602.

[6]A. W. Phillips, "The Relation Between Unemployment and the Rate of Change of Money Wage Rates in the United Kingdom 1862–1957," *Economica* (1958). The original Phillips curve as fitted to British data for the period 1861–1957 during which money wages were, in fact, flexible downward; part of the original curve, therefore, lies below the vertical axis. Because of the downward rigidity of wages in the postwar period, it has become conventional to represent a curve without negative wage changes and which "flattens out" as it approaches the employment axis.

[7]Paul Samuelson and Robert Solow, "Analytical Aspects of Anti-Inflation Policy," *American Economic Review Papers and Proceedings* 1 (1960).

[8]R. J. Bhatia, "Unemployment and Rate of Change in Money Earnings in the United States, 1900–1958," *Economica* (August 1961): 284–90, and R. R. France, "Wages, Unemployment and Prices in the United States, 1890–1932, 1947–57," *Industrial Labor Relations Review* (January 1962): 171–190.

FIGURE 15-1 *The Statistical Phillips Curve*

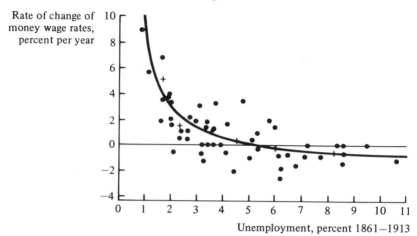

SOURCE: A. W. Phillips, "The Relation between Unemployment and the Rate of Change in Money-Wage Rates in the United Kingdom, 1862–1957," *Economica* (1958).

Subsequent evidence concerning the Phillips curve in the United States is considerably less clear-cut. Roger Spencer's study identified three different relationships between rates of inflation and the rate of unemployment over the course of the business cycle he examined.[9] Both the rate of inflation and the unemployment rate fell during the recovery year of 1964. An accelerating rate of inflation did not take place until employment reached approximately 4.5 percent in 1965. It was not until the recession phase of 1969–1970 that the unemployment rate and the rate of change in consumer prices increased simultaneously. Here the evidence suggested that the "tighter" the labor market, the greater the upward pressure on wage rates and price. This evidence was widely interpreted as implying that an economy can hold down its rate of inflation only if it is willing to "tolerate" more unemployment. Alternatively, if lower employment levels are pursued as a matter of policy, then inflationary price increases will follow as a matter of course. These findings are statistical, but the "puzzle" of simultaneous increases in unemployment and rates of inflation gave impetus to efforts to "explain" Phillips curves in theoretical terms.

[9] Roger Spencer, "The National Plans to Curb Unemployment and Inflation," *Federal Reserve Bank of St. Louis Review* 55 (April 1973).

Neoclassical Interpretations of Inflation and Unemployment

Excess Demand in the Labor Market

It deserves to be emphasized that the relationships of the Phillips curve do not constitute a theory of inflation nor do they support any particular theory concerning the cause of inflation. The first step in the direction of erecting a theoretical scaffolding to fit the empirical evidence was provided in an early (1960) inquiry by R. G. Lipsey.[10] In his effort to provide a theoretical foundation for the empirically established relation of the Phillips curve, Lipsey inferred that an increase in money wages reflects a state of excess demand in the labor markets. The wage rates that are hammered out at the bargaining table are, in his view, essentially a ratification or rubber stamp of labor-market pressures generated by excess demand.

The relationship between excess demand in the labor market and wages and between wages and unemployment is shown in Figure 15-2 and 15-3, A and B. In Figure 15-2, excess demand for labor is represented on the horizontal axis as $(N_d - N_s)/N_s$ where N_d represents the planned demand for labor and N_s represents planned supply. An increase in the planned demand for labor generates an increase in the money-wage rate along the reaction function R. Because the magnitudes involved are *planned* rather than actual magnitudes, they are not empirically observable. But it may be inferred that a *negative* relationship exists

FIGURE   15-2   *Excess Labor Demand and Wage Rates*

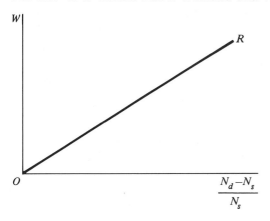

[10] R. G. Lipsey, "The Relation Between Unemployment and the Rate of Change in Money Wage Rates in the United Kingdom, 1862–1957: A Further Analysis," *Economica* (1960).

FIGURE 15-3   *Excess Labor Demand and Wage-Rate Increases*

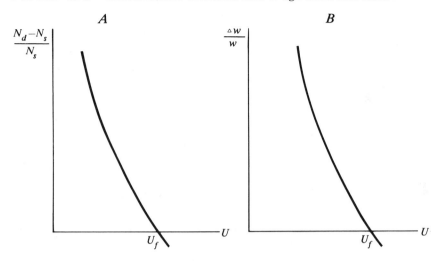

between excess demand for labor and the unemployment rate. Thus in Figure 15-3A excess demand for labor is represented on the vertical axis and unemployment is on the horizontal. If $N_d - N_s = 0$, so that the number of job seekers equals the number of vacancies (i.e., $V = U$), the amount of unemployment is U_f, which represents the frictional or natural employment associated with incomplete information.

Figure 15-3B relates the rate of change in money wages to excess demand for labor. On the basis of the relationship between excess labor demand and wage increases represented in Figure 15-2 $\Delta w/w$, which is the rate of change in money wages, is substituted for $(N_d - N_s)/N_s$ and related to the unemployment rate, U. Thus, if the number of job seekers equals the number of vacancies (i.e., $V = U$), there is no upward pressure on wages such as would be experienced if there were an excess demand for labor, i.e. $\frac{\Delta w}{w} = 0$. An excess demand for labor, such as accompanies lower unemployment rates, increases wage rates; i.e., $\Delta w/w$ increases as U decreases to less than U_f. These relationships generate a Phillips curve for a representative labor market, as in Figure 15-3B. Subsequent aggregation of individual functions would generate a Phillips curve for the entire labor market, which represents the trade-off that is believed to exist between wage-rate changes and the unemployment rate.

Some writers believe that the kind of inflation that now confronts the economy is of a sort which can be stopped only by acquiescing to a higher unemployment rate. If this is indeed the case, it raises a "cruel dilemma" for fiscal and monetary policy.[11] It was in the hope of minimizing this dilemma that manpower policy was formulated during the 1960s to encourage a *leftward shift* of the Phillips curve by retraining unemployed workers to fill existing vacancies. These policy considerations are examined further in Part III, Chapter 18.

The Persistence of a "Natural" Level of Unemployment

The Phillips-Lipsey concept of excess demand sparked a large number of econometric studies, including one by the OECD that undertook to explain inflation in six countries.[12] All of the labor-market-demand-pressure variables used to study wage inflation, among them l/u, $V - U$, and $l/u - v$, proved to be significant for the six countries studied. However, by the end of the 1960s, when efforts to improve the Phillips relationship by policy measures to shift the curve to the left proved to be unsuccessful, it was inferred that the trade-off between the rate of inflation and the rate of unemployment is a short-run relationship. Policymakers cannot keep unemployment permanently below the "natural" level of unemployment without setting off an accelerated inflationary spiral. Two alternative theories have been offered to rationalize this possibility. Milton Friedman's explanatory hypothesis proceeds in terms of worker responses to "unexpected inflation." Subsequently, this hypothesis was combined with some essentials derived from the theory of worker-search behavior. This analysis was used to develop a theory about the mechanism through which wages and prices are raised while unemployment returns to its "natural" level, in spite of policy measures to reduce it.

Adaptive-Expectations Theory

The hypothesis that there is a "natural" level of unemployment, which tends to reassert itself in spite of policy measures to lower the rate, implies that the downward-sloping Phillips' curve is a short-run phenomenon. The "trade-off" between increasing unemployment rates and rising prices is not experienced in the long run because the natural unemployment rate is reestablished. The long-run relationship between price levels and unemployment rates (i.e., the long-run Phillips curve) is

[11] Edmund S. Phelps, "Money Wage Dynamics and Labor Market Equilibrium," Discussion Paper No. 70 (University of Pennsylvania: 1967). See also Paul A. Samuelson and Robert M. Solow, "Analytical Aspects of Anti-Inflation Policy," *American Economic Review* 50 (May 1960): 177–194.

[12] *Inflation, the Present Problem*, Report by the Secretary General, Organization for Economic Cooperation and Development (Paris: 1970).

therefore constant and may be represented by a vertical line, such as U_n in Figure 15-4.

On what basis can a long-run vertical Phillips curve be rationalized? A leading hypothesis is predicated on the premise that people adapt their expectations when actual events show them to be inappropriate.[13] Thus, people formulate their economic plans on the basis of their expectations regarding wage and price levels. Expectations mirror the aggregate-demand conditions of the past. If, subsequently, *actual* levels of wages and prices differ from their expected levels, people reformulate their expectations for the future. The internal mechanism of the economy subsequently crystallizes expectations into aggregate-demand curve and price-and-wage changes.

The role of adaptive expectations in generating continued inflationary pressure and persistent unemployment may be visualized in terms of Figure 15-4, in which the rate of increase in wage rates, $\Delta w/w$, is a proxy for the rate of increase in prices, and QQ and $\hat{Q}\hat{Q}$ are short-run Phillips curves. The vertical curve U_n is the "natural" unemployment rate (which is consistent with "frictional" unemployment) for the economy; it represents the long-run normal relationship in which there is

FIGURE 15-4 *The Long-Run Phillips Curve*

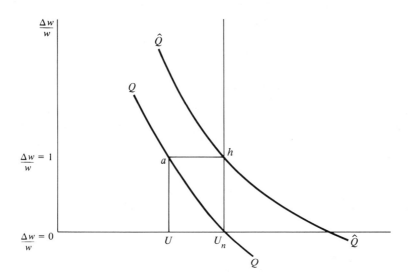

[13] The notion of adaptive expectations was first introduced by Phillip Cagan in "The Monetary Dynamics of Hyper-inflation," in Milton Friedman, ed., *Studies in the Quantity Theory of Money* (Chicago: University of Chicago Press, 1956), pp. 15–117.

no trade-off between unemployment and inflation. If, therefore, the expected rate of inflation is zero (i.e., $\Delta w/w = 0$), the relevant short-run Phillips curve QQ passes through the vertical Phillips curve at $\Delta w/w = 0$. This is the "natural" level of unemployment, which will tend to prevail in spite of efforts to achieve lower rates of unemployment.

If, for example, there is no expectation of further inflation and monetary or fiscal policy is used in an effort to reduce unemployment (say, from U_n to U, as in Figure 15-4), inflationary expectations are likely to be generated. According to the adaptive-expectations hypothesis, the behavioral changes that follow stimulative monetary and/or fiscal policy will generate increases in the price level and also *negate* policy efforts to reduce the unemployment level. The scenario is as follows: First, stimulative efforts raise the aggregate demand for goods and services. Businessmen are likely to respond initially to increased demands for output by driving down inventories. But if they perceive increased demand as being more than transitory, they will employ additional labor. The smaller the excess supply of labor in the market (i.e., the greater the excess demand for labor), the higher the actual level of wages will become in relation to the expected wage rates. Rising money wages affect employer pricing decisions as well as workers' decisions about labor-market behavior.

The second part of the scenario is worker responses to rising money wages, which they interpret as representing higher *real* wages: i.e., workers respond to money illusion and do not expect inflation. Consequently, they reevaluate their time allocation between market and nonmarket activity. In terms of Figure 15-4, they move from x to a point such as a on a short-run Phillips curve like QQ. This reflects the collective decision to allocate more time to market activity, so that the unemployment rate declines in the short run from U_n to U, as the objectives of stimulative monetary and fiscal policy are achieved.

There are, however, likely to be further effects. The hypothesis envisions supply-side influences as output and employment levels increase. The marginal cost of output will increase even without a rise in wage levels and necessitate an increase in commodity prices. The rise in wage levels that accompanies excess labor demand will exacerbate the rise in commodity prices.

The experience of rising commodity prices eventually makes workers aware that they have been "fooled" into interpreting higher money wages as representing higher real wages, because they did not expect inflation. When the actual rate of inflation is positive rather than zero (say, $\Delta w/w = 1$), as in Figure 15-4, real wages prove to be lower than expected, which causes workers to reevaluate their work-leisure choices. The lower real wages associated with higher commodity prices makes employment less attractive. This may be described as a movement from point *a* on *QQ* to *b* on $\hat{Q}\hat{Q}$. The necessity for adapting to a wage-price level that differs from the expected one is associated with different work-leisure choices (and, thus, a different employment level for the economy as a whole). The concluding part of the adaptive-expectations hypothesis is thus that market activity is less attractive at a lower real-wage level, and unemployment is increased, say, back to U_n the "natural" rate. This level of unemployment reflects revised work-leisure choices that accompany current expectations with respect to wage and price levels. When unemployment is at the "natural" rate, according to the adaptive-expectations hypothesis, there is no excess supply in the labor market, and the actual rate of wage inflation will be equal to the expected rate.

Market-Search Theories of the Phillips Relationship

The conclusion that the trade-off between increasing wages and prices and lower rates of unemployment is a short-run phenomenon is shared by a number of writers who have utilized the theory of market search in order to support the view that workers respond to *real* wage rates and that there is a "natural" or equilibrium rate of unemployment for the economy. Their models have been received with particular enthusiasm, because they focus attention on the microeconomic foundations of the employment-inflation phenomenon. The addition of search theory to the adaptive-expectations model is an important step in the direction of greater realism. It serves to remove the assumption of perfect information and conceives of employers and employees as making decisions in labor markets in which the market-clearing wage is not "given" and known to all participants and in which the cost of obtaining information is not zero. The analysis rests on the premise that there is an interaction between the two key stocks of the labor market. These are the number of unemployed workers and the number of unfilled jobs; their relationship is governed by the search behavior of job seekers and employers.[14]

The relationship between the number of searchers and the number of job vacancies is conceived to determine the parameters of the probability distribution of wage offers. If there is neither an excess demand nor supply of labor, the probability distribution remains unchanged. Analogously, an excess demand for labor, i.e., a situation in which the number of unfilled vacancies exceeds the number of unemployed workers, raises the probability distribution and thus the expectations that govern worker search. This becomes the critical factor

---

[14]Charles C. Holt, "Job Search, Phillips Wage Relations and Union Influence: Theory and Evidence," in Edmund Phelps, et al., *Microeconomic Foundations of Employment and Inflation Theory* (New York: W. W. Norton & Co., 1970), p. 59.

in generating inflationary wage increases, according to the market-search theories of the Phillips relationship.

It will be recalled from Chapter 4 that at the microeconomic level, the rate of wage change an individual worker expects as a result of job search depends on the rate of change in wages generally and the duration of the workers' unemployment.[15] Thus, the job-search hypothesis of wage change maintains that the average rate of change of wages between jobs for all unemployed workers passing through the market to fill job vacancies reflects the interaction of the search behavior of employed and unemployed workers and the hiring decisions of employers, given the level of vacancies.[16]

The rate of money wages currently prevailing is influential on the rate of wage change in the economy because searchers adjust their aspirations to the wages they see others receiving. If wage offers are high enough to cause job search by employed workers, while those who are unemployed quickly find new jobs or are rehired, it implies that employers are responding to a tight labor market by raising wages. Because workers tend to quit more readily when employment opportunities are available, the number of unfilled vacancies can rise quite markedly in a tight labor market without this having a significant effect in reducing the rate of unemployment. Thus, it is the *change* in the unemployment rate that is critical in determining the wage increases that firms must offer in order to fill their vacancies when the labor market becomes tighter.[17]

The rate of change of money wages also is believed to depend on the difficulties employers experience in their efforts to maintain the work force at desired levels while coping with quits and recruiting problems. The vacancy level is thus a major determining influence. The higher the number of vacancies and the lower the level of unemployment, the higher the probability of quits and therefore the greater the stock of workers who are unemployed because they are searching. In combination, these circumstances are seen as facilitating continued inflationary pressure, which is accompanied by *persistent positive levels of unemployed resources.*[18] In short, the market-search theory of the Phillips relationship comes to the same conclusion as the adaptive-expectations

---

[15] See above, Chapter 4.

[16] Charles C. Holt, *op. cit.*, p. 65.

[17] Edmund Phelps, "Money Wage Dynamics," in Edmund Phelps, *et al., Microeconomic Foundation of Employment and Inflation Theory* (New York: W. W. Norton & Co., 1970), p. 135.

[18] Conversely, at high levels of unemployment, workers tend to be laid off when they are no longer needed. It takes them longer to find jobs, and new jobs are likely to be at lower wages or require higher performance standards. Holt believes the process could make wages generally fall, although unemployment would have to be high in order for this to happen. See C. C. Holt, *Job Search, op. cit.*, p. 72.

theory, i.e., a higher rate of inflation cannot achieve a lasting reduction in the rate of unemployment below the natural level. The equilibrium rate of unemployment corresponds to a point on the short-run Phillips curve, i.e., the equilibrium locus is vertical. Thus, the job-search models conclude that no trade-off exists, in the long run, between inflation and unemployment. A policy of inflationary expansion to reduce unemployment can be accomplished only at the cost of increasing inflation and continued disequilibrium. The policy is temporarily effective, because it causes suboptimal decisions that are rooted in imperfect information. In the long run, the economy will settle down to a natural rate of unemployment, which is primarily a function of information cost.

Institutional Inconsistencies Relating to Search Models

While the marriage of the job-search model to the adaptive-expectations hypothesis of inflation is widely accepted, it is not without its limitations. It neglects important aspects of the functioning of labor markets that were examined in earlier chapters. The notion that employers respond readily to labor shortages by raising wage rates underestimates the cost of changing wages and the institutional alternatives that have developed to limit the frequency with which they are made.[19] It has been observed that when faced with labor shortages, firms "frequently lower hiring standards, raise expenditures on recruitment, and contract out work before raising wages. ...." In part, this represents the expectation that labor shortages will be temporary while, with money wages rigid downward, a wage increase would be permanent.

The implication of the search hypothesis that excess demand for labor systematically raises wages above worker expectations also overlooks the influence of the structure of labor markets. As has already been noted, there is considerable internal mobility, e.g., semiskilled workers within a plant are promoted from the unskilled grades. Thus, excess demand may have the effect of shortening the queue, which enables less preferred workers who are willing to work at current wage rates to become employed. The net effect of the internal structure of the labor market is to reduce the number of ports of entry. The fewer the ports of entry, the lesser the opportunity for workers outside a firm to be offered more high-paid jobs. This is an effect that has been observed to be operative in several countries.[20] Institutional forces thus contribute to a

---

[19] Albert Rees, "The Phillips Curve as a Menu for Policy Choice," *Economica* 37 (August 1970).

[20] Derek Robinson, "Wage Drift, Fringe Benefits and Manpower Distribution: A Study of Employer Practices in a Full Employment Labor Market" (Paris: O.E.C.D., 1968).

"stickiness" of wages that is compatible with "correct" wage expectations on the part of workers. The logic in terms of which search theory explains the inflationary prices thus appears to be at least partly negated by institutional influences on wage rates.

The Role of the Money Supply

Milton Friedman once remarked, "Inflation is always and everywhere a monetary phenomenon."[21] Yet the preceding discussion said nothing about the role of the money supply in generating price-level increases. Since adaptive expectations and search models envision inflationary pressure as being generated by inflationary expectations that reflect the state of aggregate demand, the inference, in light of Friedman's observation, is that the process is related to changes in the money supply.

The money supply consists of currency and checking accounts (demand deposits) in banks, which belong to households, businesses, and government. Currency now consists chiefly of Federal Reserve notes, which the Federal Reserve banks circulate as the public's need for cash changes. The volume of demand deposits, which represent about 85 percent of the money supply, is controlled by various Federal Reserve monetary tools. These are used in conducting monetary policy, which is concerned with controlling the level of interest rates in order to achieve the price level and employment objectives that the Federal Reserve Board considers appropriate, given the state of the economy.

While there are various ways in which the Federal Reserve system may stimulate the economy, the technique that is most frequently used is to offer to purchase bonds in the open market at attractive prices.[22] The proceeds that banks and private individuals (who deposit in banks) receive from these sales increase the level of bank reserves, which lowers interest rates. This, in turn, stimulates business borrowing and thus investment, which is a major component of aggregate-effective demand. Monetary growth thus has the effect of increasing employment and output. Its subsequent effect on the price level, as envisioned by the adaptive-expectations and search models, lends itself to illustration in terms of the aggregate-demand-and-supply apparatus introduced in Chapter 14.

In Figure 15-5, the level of employment is at N, output is at Q_n, which is consistent with the natural output level, and the price level is at

[21] Milton Friedman, *Inflation: Causes and Consequences* (Asia Publishing House, 1963), reprinted in *Dollars and Deficits* (Englewood Cliffs, N.J.: Prentice Hall, 1968), p. 39.

[22] The money stock is similarly increased if the expansion proceeds via fiscal policy that is financed by bond sales to the Federal Reserve banks.

FIGURE 15-5 *The Price-Level Effects of an Increased Money Supply*

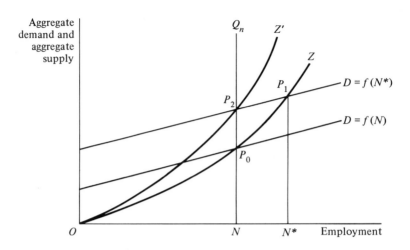

P_0, where it is expected to remain.[23] If the unemployment level associated with N is considered unacceptably high, so that intervention is required, then stimulative monetary policy might be used to raise the level of aggregate-effective demand. In terms of Figure 15-5, this would mean that the aggregate-demand function $D = f(N)$ shifts upward so that the new function is $D' = f(N^*)$. Employment thus increases to N^*, and the price level rises to P_1, even though the expectation is that the price level would remain a P_0.[24] Price expectations are not fulfilled because, as noted in Chapter 6, the supply price of output increases as employment expands because of diminishing returns in the short run. Even if money wages remain the same, as employment expands, commodity prices will rise. A movement along Z as aggregate demand increases from $D = f(N)$ to $D' = f(N^*)$ is thus associated with a higher price level P_1.

How much will the price level rise when the increase in employment is achieved by means of stimulative monetary policy, i.e., an increase in the size of the money supply? In terms of Figure 15-5, the inflation rate is $\Delta P = (P_1 - P_0)/P_0$. This rate of increase will not be as large as the increase in the growth rate of money, for the increase in employment

---

[23] It will be recalled that both the aggregate-demand and aggregate-supply functions are drawn in terms of current dollars. Thus, there is a price level implicit in each point of the curves.

[24] If the labor force is constant, so that the increase in employment reflects movement of workers from the unemployed pool into jobs, the change form N to N^* in Figure 15-5 is precisely equivalent to the move from U_n to U in Figure 15-4.

also raises real output, which reduces the gap between actual output and potential output. Arthur Okun has produced statistical evidence that in the short run a 1 percent reduction in the unemployment rate is accompanied by a 3 percent increase in real output (income). This relationship between short-run changes in employment and changes in real output is popularly designated as "Okun's Law".[25] It provides some insight into the effect of an increase in the money supply on the price level. An increase in output also increases the *real* demand for money, i.e., it raises B/P, where B represents the money balances (currency and demand deposits) that the public wishes to hold, and P is the price level. Because of the increase in B/P in the short run, ΔP, the rate of inflation, will be less than the increase in the money supply. Thus, in the short run

$$\Delta P = \Delta m - \left(\frac{\Delta B}{\Delta P}\right)$$

Therefore, if the money stock increases by 10 percent, and the increase in real output raises the demand for real-money balances by 7 percent, the rate of inflation would be only 3 percent, i.e., $\Delta P = .10 - .07 = .03$ percent.

This short-run impact of the increase in the money supply is, however, based on the expectation that the price level will remain at its original level. This expectation is disappointed when the price level increases to P_1 and workers discover that real wages are less than they expected. In order to protect real-wage levels in the face of expected inflation, workers will bargain for higher money wages. In order to fill their vacancies in a tightening labor market, firms will have to pay higher wages, which they expect to pass on in the form of higher prices. The aggregate-supply curve in Figure 15-5 will, therefore, be shifted leftward from Z to Z'. The extent of the shift reflects the higher wage costs that are based on inflationary expectations. The tighter the labor market, the greater the likelihood that wages will rise more rapidly than the actual rate of inflation. Thus, in the view of those who explain the inflationary process in terms of the adaptive-expectations hypothesis, the expected rate of inflation operates in conjunction with the increase in the money supply to determine the rate of inflation. Inflation is higher the higher the expected rate of inflation. Inflationary expectations are critical because when inflation is expected, wages are bid up and firms pass on the increases in the form of higher prices.

The size of the GNP gap, which reflects the state of the labor market, is also critical. The smaller the gap between actual output and

[25] Arthur Okun, "Upward Mobility in a High Pressure Economy," *Brookings Papers on Economic Activity* 2 (1973).

potential output, the tighter the labor market, and, thus, the wage increases that labor will seek in order to keep up with the expected rate of inflation. Thus, it is quite possible, within the framework of models premised on the assumption that market participants adapt their behavior to the state of their expectations, to have both inflation and unemployment so that the economy experiences *stagflation*, as it has during the decade of the 1970s.

The phenomenon of stagflation can also be explained in terms of Figure 15-5. Stagflation occurs when the shift of the aggregate-supply function reduces employment back to N, at which unemployment and output are once again at their natural levels, but the price level is at P_2. The expectation that the price level will continue at P_2 keeps wages from being pressured downward in spite of unemployment. If, subsequently, the actual rate of inflation coincides with the expected rate, then, according to inflation hypotheses that are predicated on expectations-adaptive behavior, the price level will remain constant at P_2. This level is permanently higher than P_0, the level at which it was before the money stock was increased to stimulate aggregate demand. The policy implication is clear; in terms of the adaptive-expectations model, monetary or fiscal policy aimed at reducing the unemployment level below its natural rate cannot succeed in the long run. The increase in output and employment is only temporary, but the increase in the price level is permanent. Once the price level has risen, so that inflationary expectations are formed, a downward correction can be accomplished only by a degree of monetary and fiscal "tightness" that will lead people to expect the price level to fall. This implies that in the short run unemployment will increase to levels that are in excess of the natural level. The problem would then be one of expanding the economy once again while inhibiting inflationary expectations.

Concluding Remarks

A large segment of the economics profession, as well as of the nation's policymakers, is persuaded by expectations hypotheses of inflation. The common feature of these hypotheses is that they interpret continued inflationary pressure as being generated by inflationary expectations, which reflect the state of aggregate demand. The expectation of higher prices is associated with real-wage reductions; this causes workers to bargain for higher money wages in order to protect real wages and/or to reevaluate their allocation of time between market and nonmarket activity in order to search for wage offers consistent with their real-wage desires.

The implications of this view of worker behavior and the functioning of the labor market is twofold. The first is that the process of bargaining for money wages also establishes the level of *real* wages. The second implication is that unemployment in excess of the natural level is voluntary, in the sense that it reflects a reallocation of time between market and nonmarket activity.

This view of the functioning of labor markets is quite different from Keynes's view that while workers bargain for money wages, the bargaining process does not also establish real-wage levels; the latter are determined by the level of aggregate demand. To the extent that a reduction in employment is the result of *layoffs* rather than quits (and, as has been seen, layoffs accounted for about two-thirds of total separations), the inference is that unemployment is *involuntary* rather than voluntary in nature. Thus the wage-cost-markup hypothesis offers an alternative explanation of inflation, which professes to be more faithful to the tradition of Keynes. It begins with the premise that money-wage bargains do not establish real wages, and rejects the notion that there is a natural rate of unemployment that tends to reassert itself. This hypothesis is examined in Chapter 16.

Suggestions for Further Reading

Charles C. Holt. "Job Search, Phillips Wage Relations and Union Influence: Theory and Evidence," in Edmund Phelps, *et al., Microeconomic Foundations of Employment and Inflation Theory*. (New York: W. W. Norton & Co., 1970), pp. 59ff.

Helmut Frisch. "Inflation Theory, 1963–1975: A Second Generation Survey." *Journal of Economic Literature* 15 (December 1977): 1289–1314.

A. W. Phillips. "The Relation Between Unemployment and the Rate of Change of Money Wage Rates in the United Kingdom, 1862–1957." *Economica* (1958).

Arthur Okun. "Upward Mobility in a High Pressure Economy." *Brookings Papers on Economic Activity* 2 (1973).

16 *Inflation and Unemployment: The Wage-Markup Hypothesis*

The adaptive-expectations and search hypotheses of inflation identify forces that operate on the demand side of commodity and labor markets to generate inflationary expectations. The expectation of higher prices is associated with real-wage reductions, which cause workers to reevaluate their allocation of time between employment and nonmarket activity. Thus, the presence of unemployment during periods of rising prices has been interpreted as evidence that the economy is characterized by some "natural level" of unemployment that monetary and fiscal policy can reduce only temporarily and only at the expense of generating continuous inflationary pressure.

Unlike writers who view adaptive behavior to unexpected inflation or search for higher-wage bids in a tight labor market as the key link in generating a short-run Phillips relationship and inflationary pressure, post-Keynesian writers have a different explanation for the observed phenomenon of stagflation. They view their explanation as being essentially more consistent with Keynes's own view of the inflationary process, which interprets the price level as being determined by the relationship between the aggregate-wage bill and laborers' average productivity. Their analysis of the critical magnitudes underlying the dual problem of inflation and unemployment is less widely accepted than the analysis presented in the preceding chapter, which is the mainstream view. However, the post-Keynesian analysis of inflation provides the theoretical foundation for most of the incomes-policy formulae that have been offered to deal with the problem of inflation when unemployment is at unacceptably high levels.

Inflation and the Wage-Cost-Labor Productivity Relationship

Whereas modern monetarists conceive of changes in the money supply as generating unexpected inflation and decreases in the real wage, which restore the actual rate of unemployment to the natural level, Keynes's view is that changes in the money supply act chiefly on aggregate output, Q, rather than on the price level, P. The relationship between changes in wage rates and labor productivity is identified as the critical determinant of the price level.

One way of examining Keynes's perception of the relationship between wage-rate and price-level changes is to proceed from the truism that at any level of output total proceeds, Z, are equal to the quantities of the goods sold multiplied by their prices. Thus:

$$Z = \Sigma pq = PQ \tag{1}$$

where Σpq is the summation of total revenues, P is the level of all prices, and Q is aggregate output. If now the average wage per employee is represented by w while the markup over wages is k, and N is the volume of employment, then for the economy as a whole

$$PQ = kwN^1 \tag{2}$$

The magnitudes affecting the price level can then be exposed by rearranging. Thus:

$$P = \frac{kwN}{Q} \tag{3}$$

The average product of labor, Q/N, can be denoted more simply as A. Thus:

$$P = \frac{kw}{A} \tag{4}$$

The critical relationship with respect to the behavior of the price level is, therefore, between wage and salary payments and labor productivity. Keynes's theory of the price level is predicated on the relationship expressed in the price-level equation $P = kw/A$, which is derived from the identity $PQ = Z$.[2]

---

[1] This is consistent with profit maximization at the level of the firm, i.e., Q for each firm is associated with $P = MRP = w + k$. See Chapter 7.

[2] This formulation was introduced by Sidney Weintraub. See his *Classical Keynesianism, Monetary Theory and the Price Level* (Philadelphia: Chilton Company, 1961),

Needless to say, equation (4) is not a theory. But if the markup k, of prices over unit-labor costs is constant, as is maintained on the basis of empirical study, the implication is that an increase in the price level is related to a rising w/A ratio. It follows that achievement of a steady price level requires that increases in wage rates must correspond to increases in the average productivity of labor.[3]

The Structural Model of Inflation

Several writers have identified the "productivity gap" as the cause of inflation. Their views have become crystallized in their emphasis on "structural" factors as underlying the tendency toward inflation in industrial westernized countries.[4] In particular, they observe that (1) there is a difference in the rate of growth of productivity in the manufacturing and service sectors of the economy, productivity growth in the latter being much slower than in the former; (2) money wages in both sectors are increasing at a uniform rate; the rate of growth being determined by productivity increases in the manufacturing sector; and (3) prices and money wages are characterized by downward inflexibility.

The different productivity characteristics of the manufacturing and service sectors, coupled with a uniform growth of money wages, generates a permanent cost pressure in the service sector while cost plus pricing engenders cost-push inflation. The process is accentuated by the high-income and low-price elasticity that characterize the demand for services.[5] Thus, cost-push inflation is generated in the service sector in a closed economy.[6] The structural model is a *cost-push* model in that it emphasizes an increase in unit costs rather than excess demand in explaining increases in the general price level.

The Wage-Cost-Markup Hypothesis

In common with the structural hypothesis, the wage-cost-markup hypothesis of inflation, which builds on the price equation $P = kw/A$,

---

Chapter 3; also *A General Theory of the Price Level, Output, Income Distribution and Economic Growth* (Philadelphia: Chilton Company, 1959), Chapter 2.

[3]Typically, k is in the neighborhood of 2, though it has been closer to 1.9 in recent years. At 2, half of every dollar received as sales proceeds goes to labor costs, while the other half goes for tax payments, interest, rent, depreciation, and profits. See Sidney Weintraub, *Some Aspects of Wage Theory and Policy* (Philadelphia: 1963), pp. 176–178.

[4]See in particular William J. Baumol, "Macroeconomics of Unbalanced Growth; The Anatomy of Urban Crisis," *American Economic Review* 57 (June 1967): 415–426; and Paul Streeton, "Wages, Prices and Productivity," *Kyklos* 15 (1962): 723–733.

[5]That is, increases in income increase the demands for services more than proportionally, while increases in price reduce demands less than proportionally.

[6]In an economy that is "open," the transmission mechanism must take into account the world market. See Odd Aukrust, "A Model of the Price and Income Distribution Mechanism of An Open Economy," *Review of Income and Wealth* 16 (March 1970): 51–78.

emphasizes wage increases in excess of labor productivity as the source of inflationary pressure. But unlike the structural hypothesis, it also integrates the role of demand-side as well as supply-side influences. It argues that increases in unit labor costs (w/A) have been the critical factor in recent inflationary experience. However, this hypothesis is neither a "cost-push" nor a "wage push" theory of the price level. Increases in wages and salaries are seen as shifting the aggregate-demand schedule upward, because they generate consumption demands while also shifting the aggregate-supply (i.e., Z) function because of their effect on costs.

Table 16-1 displays movements in w, A, and k from 1950 to 1974 for the U.S. and Canada. According to Weintraub's analysis, any increase in P must, in one way or another, have worked through w, k, and A relationships. In a closed economy, it is the relationship between w and A that is critical. This relationship is reflected, in the first instance, in the slope of the Z function.[7] Each point on the aggregate-supply function OZ, which is reproduced in Figure 16-1, shows the functional relationship between employment and the money outlays that would be associated with providing the related number of jobs. Since this function is expressed in money terms, each point on the Z function also contains a price level. It rises with employment, because diminishing returns increase marginal costs and, therefore, the revenues that are necessary to make an increase in employment profitable from the standpoint of entrepreneurs.

TABLE 16-1 *Five-Year Averages of Indexes of WCM Components, United States and Canada, 1950–1974*

	United States, 1958 = 100				Canada, 1961 = 100			
Period	k	w	A	P	k	w	A	P
1950—1954	104	77	89	87	106	65	81	85
1955—1959	101	97	99	97	104	86	95	94
1960—1964	101	118	113	105	101	105	104	102
1965—1969	98	148	126	115	99	11	118	118
1970—1974	96	206	137	144	95	203	130	150

Note: Figures for Canada are from GNP data; an exclusion of public-administration and defense salaries led to no significant differences in the series. The *P*-term denotes the GNP deflator. For the United States the data refer to GBP components, including the GBP deflator.

SOURCE: Sidney Weintraub, *Capitalism's Inflation and Employment Crisis*, p. 55. Reprinted with permission.

[7] In an open economy, it is necessary also to take into account the proportion of imports relative to exports. See Sidney Weintraub, *Capitalism's Inflation and Unemployment Crisis* (Reading, Pa.: Addison-Wesley Publishing Co., 1978), p. 55.

FIGURE 16-1   *The Case of "Slumpflation"*

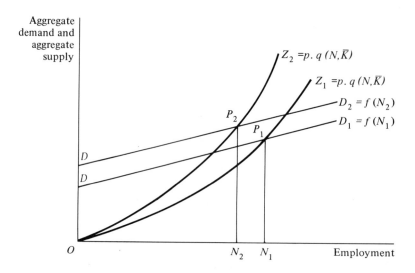

Each point on the aggregate-demand function, DD_1, which is also shown in Figure 16-1, has a price level in it that corresponds to that in the Z function. For example, the price level implicit in Z_1 corresponds to that implicit in D_1, while the higher price level implicit in Z_2 corresponds to that in D_2.

Post-Keynesians have utilized aggregate-demand and -supply functions expressed in money terms as a useful apparatus for explaining the behavior of the price level on the basis of the relationship between changes in money-wage rates and labor productivity. A change in the money wage, such as might result from a new wage agreement, shifts the aggregate-supply curve, via its effect on the cost curves of individual firms and, through them, on industry-supply curves. It also affects the aggregate-demand curve via its influence on consumer spending. Thus, if wages are increased (say, as a result of a new contract) and there is a constant markup, k, there will be an upward shift in both the aggregate-demand and -supply schedules from D_1 and Z_1 to D_2 and Z_2. The shift in the aggregate-demand function reflects the impact of the wage increase on increased consumer spending. The upward shift of the aggregate-supply function to Z_2 reflects the impact of the wage increase on industry-supply curves based on the relationship between wage rates and labor productivity. The relationship between the wage increase and labor productivity is therefore critical.

According to post-Keynesian thinkers, the wage-cost-markup formula $w + k = p = MRP$ is the microeconomic basis for understanding the relationship between money-wage rates, labor productivity, and the price level. Employers hire the amount of labor at which labor's marginal-revenue product is equal to the money-wage-rate plus a markup to cover fiscal costs. From an employer's point of view, the relationship between wages and labor productivity must be consistent with profit goals. Thus, if the productivity of labor rises at the rate of 3 percent in a year (which is approximately the rate at which labor productivity grew until the recent past), wages can also rise by 3 percent. This means that the ratio between wages and labor's marginal-revenue product (w/MRP) and therefore marginal cost is unchanged. For the economy as a whole, proportionate change in wages-and-labor productivity is consistent with profit maximization at an unchanged price level.

If, on the other hand, the percentage increase in wage rates exceeds the percentage increase in the marginal productivity of labor, the ratio of w to MRP will have increased. Thus, prices will have to rise to cover the difference between percentage changes in the MRP of labor and percentage changes in w. Post-Keynesians interpret American experience during the last twenty-five years as implying that this has been the relationship between labor productivity, hourly compensation, and the price level. A price-level increase of 7.3 percent was accompanied, in 1951, by an increase in compensation per man hour of 9.8 percent and a productivity increase of 2.9 percent. In 1961, productivity increased by 3.3 percent, compensation increased by 3.5 percent, and the price level increased by only 0.6 percent. More recently, in 1976, productivity increased 4.0 percent, compensation per man hour increased 7.7 percent, while the price level advanced by 5.2 percent.[8] These experiences are interpreted as evidence that price-level stability will elude us if the rate of increase in compensation per man hour increases at a higher rate than increases in productivity per man hour. Inflationary pressures have recently been reinforced by bad crops and the energy crisis generated by the price increases demanded by the OPEC countries. In the post-Keynesian view, however, these forces chiefly exacerbate inflationary tendencies that have their root in the imbalance between labor productivity and labor compensation.

If labor productivity remains constant or increases less than money wages rise, per-unit cost-of-production increases cause the leftward shift of the Z function from Z_1 to Z_2, to exceed the upward shift of D_1 to D_2. Thus, in Figure 16-1, an increase in money wages is associated with a *smaller* volume of employment, N_2, and a *higher* general price level.[9] The

[8]1976 figures are from *Monthly Labor Review* (July 1977) and *Survey of Current Business* (April 1977). Other data are from *Annual Report of the Council of Economic Advisors* (January 1977): 229.

[9]If the usual assumption of a constant markup is replaced by a variable one, then the decline in productivity due to diminishing returns will raise costs but squeeze profits and, conceivably, have the effect of dampening the increase of the wage-price process. The assumption of a constant markup over wages is one of several alternative theories about the process of income distribution in the economy.

wage-cost-markup hypothesis is thus analytically capable of explaining why inflation can occur simultaneously with unemployment. A general wage increase that is not accompanied by a corresponding increase in labor productivity not only increases the price level but results in a lower level of employment. This occurs because the leftward shift of the Z function is greater than the upward shift (via increased consumer expenditures) of the aggregate-demand function. This is "slumpflation"; i.e., an increase in the price level accompanied by a reduction in output and employment. This problem, according to the wage-cost-markup hypothesis, will not yield to a tight-money policy. Rather, it calls for a policy to curb wage increases that are in excess of labor productivity. Such policy measures are particularly essential in light of recent evidence on labor productivity. While output per worker grew at an average rate of 3.3 percent per year during the two decades after World War II, there is recent evidence that the rise in productivity has slackened to a rate of 1.8 percent.[10] A study by William Freund suggested that the slowing of productivity growth may have more to do with the buildup of inflation than has generally been recognized. The rationale for this argument is examined next.

The "Multiplier Effect" of Productivity Changes on Inflation

Productivity changes have generally been regarded as having only a relatively small effect in aggravating or mitigating inflation. However, a new study by William Freund suggests that a small productivity change may have a large "multiplier" effect on inflation. This effect derives partly from the convention of negotiating wage increases based on past inflation and productivity increases that are *assumed* to be equivalent to the historical 3 percent rate. If this productivity increase were *actually realized*, unit labor costs would remain unchanged, so that there would be no additional inflationary pressure. However, if, as the evidence suggests, productivity growth has slowed down, while workers get wage increases based on the 3 percent historical rate of increase, unit labor costs will rise. Since the rate of inflation has *roughly reflected* changes in unit-labor costs, an increase in labor costs in excess of productivity increases will be inflationary. If for example, productivity increases by 1.5 percent, while wages increases 3 percent, inflation will increase by 1.5 percent.

Inflation will be exacerbated in the following year if workers get wage increases that reflect past inflation and the expected 3 percent productivity increase. If workers get wage increases of 4.5 percent (1.5 percent for past inflation and 3 percent for expected productivity

---

[10]William C. Freund, "Reaching a Higher Standard of Living," Office of Economic Research, The New York Stock Exchange (January 1979).

increases) while the actual productivity increase is only 1.5 percent, unit-labor costs and therefore the rate of inflation will increase by 3 percent.

In succeeding years, the inflationary impact of wage increases based on past inflation plus the historical productivity factor will increase in a multiplier process. Based on an assumed actual-productivity increase of 1.5 percent, the rate of inflation will be 9 percent in the eighth year.[11] Thus, the productivity lag of recent years has been underestimated with respect to both its magnitude and its inflationary potential. In combination with the institutionalization of the practice of negotiating for wage increases that offset past price increases, the productivity lag has been significant in the buildup of inflation. Apart from the obvious importance of fostering productivity improvements by encouraging research and development, capital spending, saving, risk taking, better matches between job seekers and vacancies, and improved education and training, the productivity lag calls for a policy to curb excessive wage increases.

The alternative prescription of tight money and fiscal restraint to control inflation has been administered on the premise that the "trade-off" between inflation and unemployment is unavoidable. This premise neglects the possibility that the unemployment problem can be attacked by using monetary and fiscal policy to provide the leverage to aggregate demand that is required in order to help the economy achieve its employment goals while the inflation problem is combated with other weapons. There are various techniques, known by the general term "incomes policy," or "income gearing," that can be used to hold wage and price increases in check. We have already had some experience in this country, albeit very half-hearted, with incomes policy. Future policy cannot, of course, be predicted with much certainty, but it seems entirely reasonable to surmise, given the apparent inability of monetary and fiscal restraint to curb rising prices without simultaneously increasing unemployment, that a serious incomes policy may be undertaken.[12]

U.S. Experience with Incomes Policy

The critical importance of the relationship between money-wage increases and labor productivity was given official recognition in the

---

[11] Freund, *op. cit.*, p. 26.

[12] It deserves to be noted that Arthur Burns, until January 1978 Chairman of the Federal Reserve System, and Governor Henry Wallach of the Federal Reserve Board, concur on the need for policies to restrain wage and salary increases. A joint letter signed by Walter Heller, Arthur Okun, Robert Solow, James Tobin, Henry Wallach, and Sidney Weintraub endorsing some form of incomes policy to accomplish this objective appeared in the *New York Times*, March 12, 1978, p. 18.

1962 annual report of the Council of Economic Advisors. This report expressed a rationale for imposing general wage-and-price guideposts in order to achieve price stability.[13] The 1964 Annual Report of the Council of Economic Advisors noted that the trend of productivity advances was approximately 3.2 percent, and the report of 1966 recommended the adoption of 3.2 percent as the guidepost for wage-rate increases. The recommendation for price guideposts to be imposed along with wage guideposts was offered to keep prices stable and the distribution of income unchanged.

Since gains in labor productivity vary widely among firms and industries, the guidepost principle implies that firms and industries that experience productivity trends in excess of the national average should reduce their prices to reflect this differential while granting wage increases equal to the average productivity gain in the economy. Analogously, firms having smaller productivity gains while granting wage increases in excess of productivity increases would increase their prices. Thus, some prices would rise while others would fall, but on average, the guidepost principle is compatible with price stability.

Both labor and industry observed the guideposts reasonably well until mid-1966. Conceivably, labor's cooperation was related to the fact that unemployment was not much in excess of 5 percent since 1962 while the Consumer Price Index rose by less than 2 percent for the same period. But by 1966 the economy experienced an upsurge, during which unemployment was reduced to a level of 3.8 percent. The wage guidepost of 3.2 percent subsequently yielded to the pressure of unions to "catch up," and the labor settlements of the period typically exceeded the 3.2 percent wage guidepost. Price guideposts were similarly violated by firms with price-making powers, and by the end of 1966 consumer prices had risen by 3.3 percent. As a consequence, recommendation of a 3.2 percent wage guidepost for 1967 seemed pointless, and the council refrained from announcing one. The first U.S. experience with guideposts thus came to an abrupt halt.

The Nixon administration, which came into office in January 1969, made known its opposition to incomes policy and for more than two years attacked inflation through monetary and fiscal policy. These policies met with little success, and on August 15, 1971, the president abruptly shifted to a policy of market intervention, which took the form of a ninety-day freeze on virtually all wages and prices. This "Phase I" was followed by "Phase II," which provided a new system of wage-and-price guideposts with compliance required by law. Appraisal of Phase II-controls indicate that the effects of six quarters of control

---

[13] The rationale for guideposts was again expressed in the *Annual Reports* of January 1977, pp. 120–134; February 1968, pp. 120–128; and January 1969, pp. 118–121.

produced an average reduction in the annual rate of inflation of about 2.0 percentage points and some alteration in the rate of change of wages. There was also an average reduction in the rate of unemployment of 0.2 percentage points and an increase in the average rate of productivity of about 1.0 percentage points.[14] These results reflect both the general support for and compliance with regulations established to achieve stabilization goals.

The administrative machinery set up for Phase II included a Pay Board, which had the responsibility of setting wage guideposts, and a Price Commission to administer prices. The basic standard established for new labor contracts, as specified in November 1971, was 5.5 percent. The rationale was that if the average rate of increase in labor compensation could be held to that level, given a labor-productivity trend of about 3 percent per year, and nonlabor costs that rose at a rate of about 2.5 percent, prices would increase no more than 2.5 percent per year. These rates were expected to maintain existing profit margins and the division of income between wages and profit.

The Phase II price-control program was terminated in January 1973 with virtually the same abruptness as its introduction. Phase III was a largely voluntary program of price control, during which inflation reached its highest rate since the Korean War.

There is considerable controversy about the interpretation of this experience. Some analysts maintain that the premature ending of Phase II was itself the major cause of intensified inflation. Others maintain that the 1973 inflation reflected a change in the nature of the inflationary forces at work.[15] Specifically, it has been argued that inflation was precipitated by the sharp increase in food prices, the change in the international economic situation, and capacity changes in several basic-materials industries. Supply shortages had developed in the agricultural sector, while, at the same time, the devaluation of the dollar in the international money market raised the prices of U.S. imports. Other analysts, however, argue that the rise in farm and oil prices constitute *relative* price surges but do not generate price-level inflation. This is not to say that increases in food and energy prices do not have serious implications, but these sectoral increases as well as increases in import outlay will be offset by reductions in other sectors unless wages

---

[14] Econometric studies that approximate these results include those of R. F. Lanzillotti and B. Roberts, "An Assessment of the U.S. Experiment With an Income Policy," Tulane Conference on Income Policy (April 1973); and B. Askin and J. Kraft, *Econometric Wage and Price Models: Assessing the Impact of the Economic Stabilization Program* (Boston: 1974).

[15] Barry Bosworth, "The Inflation Problem during Phase III," *Papers and Proceedings of the American Economic Association* (May 1974).

have risen in excess of labor productivity or profits have become inflated.[16]

Both Congress and the public were sharply critical of Phase III, and by mid-June of 1973, President Nixon once again sharply reversed direction and imposed a second price freeze. Phase IV was ushered in on August 12, 1973, and mandated a combination of controls and decontrols in industries that did not exhibit major cost pressures. Phase IV came to an end with the expiration of the Economic Stabilization Act on April 30, 1974. This brought to an end a thirty-two-month episode of controls whose objective it was to restrain both wage-push and profit-push forces.

Early in 1979, President Carter suggested the use of the present federal-income-tax system as a mechanism for inducing workers to accept wage increases that do not exceed 7 percent. Several alternative policies, which will be examined in Chapter 17, have been offered over the last several years. These are likely to receive serious consideration as doubts increase about the adequacy of traditional measures of fiscal and monetary policy to achieve the president's targets of 4.8 percent unemployment and 4 percent inflation growth. Preliminary estimates put unemployment at 7.8 percent of the labor force in May 1980 and this is expected to increase. Yet the concern is that even this high rate of unemployment will fail to bring about the desired disinflation effect; the average rate of wage inflation during 1979 approximated 8 percent and the rate of price inflation was in excess of 13 percent. Although somewhat abated by mid-1980 the pattern of wage and price inflation is stubborn. However, experience with incomes policy suggests that it is alterable. It is worth recalling that during the early 1960s, a pattern of about 3.5 percent wage inflation and a 1.5 percent price inflation was maintained during a recovery that reduced unemployment from 7 percent in 1961 to about 4 percent by the end of 1965. One would probably be overoptimistic to think that this low rate of price inflation can again be achieved in the foreseeable future. But there are several proposals, including one suggested by President Carter in January 1979, to induce business and labor to comply with disinflationary guideposts.

Concluding Remarks

Inquiry into the problems of "stagflation" and "slumpflation" reveals essentially the same dichotomy among economists with respect to explaining the *level* of wages as was encountered in Part I with respect to explaining the *structure* of wages. Macroeconomists who are of neo-

---

[16] Sidney Weintraub, *Capitalism's Inflation and Unemployment Crisis* (Reading, Pa.: Addison-Wesley Publishing Co., 1978), Chapter 3.

classical persuasion maintain that the level of money wages can be explained in terms of the operation of the price mechanism. In their view, wages are simply one set of prices in the economy; they interpret the growth of money wages and the rate of unemployment as reflecting the degree of excess demand and supply (of labor). Higher rates of unemployment imply an excess supply of labor and a real-wage level that is too high to be compatible with lower rates of unemployment; conversely, if the rate of increase in money wages and prices is accelerated, the inference is that the labor market is tight; i.e., $V > U$. A tight labor market, in turn, is interpreted as reflecting an excess demand for goods, because the demand for factors is a derived demand. In a tight labor market, it is argued, employers must raise their money-wage offers to fill their vacancies. Unemployment, therefore, declines as money wages increase.

According to the mainstream view, the unemployment that accompanies high and rising wage rates is voluntary; workers choose to search for wage bids that they believe will improve their positions in real terms. In spite of policy to reduce unemployment, its rate will return to a level that Friedman, Phelps, and Holt conceive to represent the "natural unemployment rate." The long-run Phillips curve is, therefore, believed to be vertical and to coincide with the volume of unemployment that is consistent with the natural unemployment rate. The implication is that monetary and fiscal efforts to reduce the level of unemployment below the natural rate are not only doomed to failure but will, in addition, exacerbate the problem of inflation. Thus, the natural-unemployment-rate hypothesis has implicit in it the presumption that an increase in the quantity of money, M, that enters the economy via monetary or fiscal policy makes its impact felt on P, the general price level, which is comprised of commodity and factor prices (including wage rates).

The assumption that the demand for labor is derived from the demand for commodities and that wage-rate increases are not generated without a prior excess demand for commodities is central to the preceding argument, which assumes that the behavior of the labor market is symmetrical to that of commodity markets. Post-Keynesians are among those who are not persuaded by this mainstream view of wage rates and labor-market behavior. They view the establishment of wage rates as being *exogenous* to the system rather than occurring *endogenously* within the framework of the price system. Unlike the proponents of expectations and search models they interpret the problem of inflation as reflecting a more rapid increase in wage rates than can be supported by the productivity of labor; in short, the ratio of w/A is held to be critical in determining the general level of prices.

Their rejection of the determining role of the quantity of money should, in no way, be interpreted as implying that "money doesn't matter" or that monetary policy is unimportant. The quantity of money assuredly matters, and monetary policy has an important role. However, the effect of changes in M is thought to be on Q and N (the volume of output and the level of employment) and not on P (the price level). A change in the quantity of money alters *the rate of interest*, which affects the level of aggregate demand through its impact on investment decisions.[17]

Modern followers of Keynes maintain that "once price inflation is underway . . . extra money is imperative for maintaining Q and Y. Without a ΔM flow the inflation and unemployment script of stagflation and slumpflation woes will materialize."[18] Thus, modern followers of Keynes would not agree that the economy is confronted with a kind of inflation that can be stopped only by increasing the unemployment rate through lower aggregate demand, which poses "a cruel dilemma" for fiscal and monetary policy.[19] Their alternative is to use wage/price controls (i.e., incomes policy) as a weapon for containing prices without the need for sacrificing employment levels. These policy recommendations will be examined in detail in Part III, Chapter 18.

Suggestions for Further Reading

William Baumol. "Macroeconomics of Unbalanced Growth: The Anatomy of Urban Crisis." *American Economic Review* 57 (June 1967): 415–426.

William Freund. "Reaching a Higher Standard of Living." Office of Economic Research, The New York Stock Exchange (January 1979).

Barry Bosworth. "The Inflation Problem During Phase III." *Papers and Proceedings of the American Economic Association* (May 1974).

Paul Streeton. "Wages, Prices and Productivity." *Kyklos* 15 (1962): 723–733.

Sidney Weintraub. *Capitalism's Inflation and Unemployment Crisis* Reading, Pa.: Addison-Wesley Publishing Co., 1978.

---

[17] It is relevant to note in this connection that unlike the quantity theorists, who view changes in the money supply as being exogenously determined, Keynes' followers identify money as being an *endogenous* magnitude that varies in response to the investment and finance decisions made in the economy. Concerning the controversy about the role of money see, in particular, Hyman Minsky, *John Maynard Keynes*, and Sidney Weintraub, *Capitalism's Inflation and Employment Crisis,* Chapter 4, "Money-Wage Economy."

[18] Weintraub, *op. cit.,* p. 69.

[19] This policy view is expressed on behalf of modern neoclassical economists by Edmund Phelps in "Money Wage Dynamics and Labor Market Equilibrium," *University of Pennsylvania Discussion Paper No. 70* (1967).

17 *The Wage Share and Its Distribution*

The economy's level of employment and output together with the wage rates established in the labor markets of the economy, determine the size of the wage share, W, in national income. Thus, $W = PQ/wN$ where wN is the wage bill and PQ is the total revenue generated by the nation's employment. Alternatively expressed, the wage share is the fraction of total revenue paid to wage-earners.

Identification (and explanation) of the *wage share* has historically been associated with the hypothesis that earnings are properly thought of as factor shares that reward the performance of particular functions in the production process. Classical economists identified capitalists, land-owners, and laborers as the "great trinity" of factors of production whose shares in the nation's product are received in the form of profit, rent, and wages. Their studies sparked a lively interest in the problem of "income distribution," as the problem of explaining the relative shares of the factors came to be known.

During the 1930s, interest in the problem of income distribution slackened as J. M. Keynes' influence shifted the attention of economists to the problem of the level of employment and income. However, since World War II, there has been a revival of concern with the problem of income shares, largely as a result of renewed interest in the related problem of economic growth. Unfortunately, as will be seen, there is no consensus concerning the behavior of income shares during the present century. Nor is there a generally accepted body of theoretical principles that either neoclassical theorists or their critics accept. In the midst of their controversies, the labor economist is more concerned with the distribution of personal income than he is with the relative size of the share represented by wages and profits.

The distribution of personal income reflects factor payments and additions to or subtractions from national (or earned) income resulting from business and government transfers. Transfers augment factor payments, thereby raising personal income above earnings for some persons, while others receive personal incomes that are less than earnings. Social security and other taxes, wages accrued but not dispersed, and undistributed profits are typical among the several items that cause personal income to differ from national (or earned) income.

The special concern that is now being accorded to the distribution of personal income (as distinct from the functional or factoral distribution of income) reflects the finding that in modern economies variances in *labor* income are the chief sources of income inequality. Property ownership is a less important source of disparity among income recipients than is the differential command over labor income. As a result, it is the distribution of labor income that is of particular interest.[1] Similarly, it is the distribution of labor income to which policymakers have addressed their attention. The rationale for policies of income insurance and assurance, which will be examined in Part III, derives largely from the inference that income distribution cannot be left entirely to the marketplace. These inferences are closely related to the structure of wages and the effect that this structure has on the distribution of labor income and the wage share.

The Functional Distribution of Income

The Size of the Wage Share

Data compiled by the U.S. Department of Commerce on wage salaries, and wage supplements displayed in Table 17-1 show that labor's share in the national income was 76 percent in 1978. There is no firm consensus concerning the comparison of this percentage relationship with earlier proportional relationships. On the one hand, Department of Commerce data for 1929, which are also shown in Table 17-1, indicate that during that year employee compensation comprised only 60.2 percent of national income. For the period 1948–1957, it averaged 66.78 percent, which represents an increase of 6.27 percent over the 60.51 percent it averaged for the period 1920–1929.

On the surface these calculations suggest that there has been a small shift to labor from other income receivers. It has, however been argued that the wage share remained constant between 1929 and 1950 in spite of the evidence given above. Its constancy is maintained on the basis of accounting conventions that omit returns on the capital component used in the government sector so that its output is wholly represented by the

---

[1] Thus, Jan Tinbergen's *Income Distribution: Analysis and Policies* (Amsterdam, North Holland: 1975) is concerned only with labor income.

TABLE   17-1   *The Distribution of National Income, 1929, 1950, and 1978 (Billions of $)*

	1929 Billions of Dollars	%*	1950 Billions of Dollars	%*	1978 Billions of Dollars	%*
Compensation of employees	$51.1	60.2	$154.8	65.3	$1301.2	75.9
Proprietors income from business and professional	14.9	17.5	13.5	5.7	$112.9	6.4
Net interest	4.7	5.5	7.1	3.0	106.1	6.4
Corporate profits (before taxes)	9.2	10.8	33.7	14.7	202.4	10.9
Rental income	4.9	5.7	27.1	11.3	47.6	.4
Total	$84.8		$236.2		$1703.6	

*Does not total 100% because of rounding

compensation of its employees.[2] The seeming increase in labor's share is partly accounted for by the expansion of the government sector. Furthermore, part of the increase in employee compensation reflects the decline in the earnings of those who are self-employed. The increasing importance of the corporate form of organization and the decline in self-employment have both contributed to increasing the statistical wage share, thereby obscuring its historical constancy.

The historical constancy of the wage share is consistent with findings about production functions in a study conducted by the late Paul Douglas (together with Charles W. Cobb) for the period 1899–1922. These investigators concluded that a 1 percent increase in labor inputs with a constant input of capital will increase output by three-fourths of 1 percent, while a 1 percent increase in capital inputs, with labor constant, will increase output by one-fourth of 1 percent.[3] Thus the elasticity of substitution between labor and capital is approximately one. This finding is consistent with a 3 to 1 constant ratio in the shares of the national product which labor and capital have historically received.

Figure 17-1 illustrates the basis for an historically constant relationship between factor shares, given Douglas' findings about their elasticity of substitution in production. The curve E_{lk} represents the elasticity of substitution between labor and capital which is equal to one

[2] Edward Denison, "Income Types and the Size Distribution," *American Economic Review* (May 1954): 254–269.

[3] Paul Douglas, *The Theory of Wages* (New York: The Macmillan Co., 1934); also Paul Douglas and Crace Gunn, "Further Measurements of Marginal Productivity," *Quarterly Journal of Economics* (May 1940): 339–428.

FIGURE   17-1   *The Case of Constant Factor Shares*

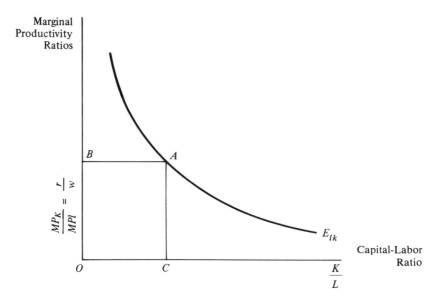

at any point along the curve.[4] The capital-labor ratio is measured along the horizontal axis while the ratio of the marginal productivities of labor and capital is measured along the vertical axis. Thus, if we pick a point, A, on the elasticity of substitution curve E_{lk} and identify the rectangle $OBAC$, then the distance

$$OB = r/w \text{ and}$$
$$OC = K/L$$
Multiplying OB and OC
$$OB \cdot OC = \frac{r}{w} \cdot \frac{K}{L} = \frac{w \cdot l}{r \cdot k} = \frac{\text{Labor Income}}{\text{Property Income}}$$

A movement along the elasticity curve reflects a change in input mix in response to a change in relative factor prices, as was examined in Chapter 6. If, for example, capital has become cheap relative to labor, producers will substitute capital for labor. This will increase the demand for capital relative to labor, thereby limiting the fall in interest rates relative to wage rates. A small increase in the capital/labor input ratio K/L is therefore offset by a decrease in r/w, where r is the price of capital and w is the price of labor. Thus, if the elasticity of substitution is one and the prices of labor and capital approximate their respective

---

[4]Technically, E_{lk} is a rectangular hyperbola, for the area under such a curve is constant for all points.

marginal products, the expression $(r/w)(K/L)$ remains constant, which implies that labor and property shares also remain constant.[5]

The informed observations of J. M. Keynes and the empirical studies of Klein and Kosabud concur that the ratio of the wage share and the capital share has been constant. Just prior to the outbreak of World War II, J. M. Keynes observed that "the stability of the proportion of the national dividend accruing to labor is one of the most surprising yet best-established facts in the whole range of economic statistics."[6] More than two decades later, the constancy of the wage share relative to the profit share was identified as one of the "great ratios of econometrics."[7] Additional credence is given the argument that the wage share has been stable by the finding that unions have not been successful in raising the wage share.[8] Kerr finds no evidence that collective bargaining has had a "permanent effect" except perhaps in highly unionized metropolitan areas. While there may have been a slow secular shift to labor since 1900, most of it came about before 1929 (thus antedating the modern trade-union movement), and it occurred chiefly in the non-manufacturing sectors.

Evidence of a Rising Wage Share

There is, however, contradictory evidence that supports the view that the wage share has been rising. Irving Kravis used three methods to identify the behavior of the wage share. The first estimated the amount of labor supplied by proprietors and their families and inputed a wage to it. This method identified the return to capital in the unincorporated sector as a residual. He also estimated the amount of capital used in the unincorporated sector and inputed its return so that the labor share emerges as a residual. Finally, he combined the two previous methods. The results of all three methods are summarized in Table 17-2. Kravis's computations show a substantial rise since 1900 in the labor share.[9]

---

[5] If the elasticity of substitution between labor and capital were less than one, the factor whose supply is growing more rapidly would experience a greater fall in price so that its share in national income would fall. Conversely, if the elasticity were greater than one, the share of the more rapidly growing factor would rise.

[6] J. M. Keynes, "Relative Movements of Real Wages and Output," *Economic Journal* 49 (March 1939): 48.

[7] Laurence Klein and Richard Kosabud, "Some Econometrics of Growth: Great Ratios of Econometrics," *Quarterly Journal of Economics* 75 (May 1961): 173–198.

[8] Clark Kerr, "Labor's Income Share and the Labor Movement," in G. W. Taylor and F. C. Pieron, eds., *New Concepts in Wage Determination* (New York: McGraw-Hill, 1957); and N. J. Simler, *The Impact of Unionism on Wage-Income Ratios in the Manufacturing Sector of the Economy* (Minneapolis: University of Minnesota Press, 1961).

[9] Irving B. Kravis, "Relative Income Shares in Fact and Theory," *American Economic Review* (December 1959).

TABLE 17-2 *Estimates of Labor's Share in National Income, Selected Periods 1900–1958*

	1st Method	2nd Method	3rd Method
1900—1909	69.4	67.8	67.9
1920—1929	70.8	71.5	71.2
1948—1958	77.0	77.3	76.8

SOURCE: Irving B. Kravis, "Relative Income Shares in Fact and Theory," *American Economic Reveiw* (December 1959). Reprinted with permission.

How can these findings be reconciled with the fact that the amount of physical capital per unit of output has increased? The latter development suggests that, other things being equal, one would expect that the *property* share of income would have risen unless there are other influences that offset the effect of increasing amounts of physical capital. One such factor is, no doubt, the decline in the relative price of new capital goods as a result of improvements in the technology of their production. This would tend to reduce the relative price of capital services. Furthermore, it is not just the quantity of physical capital per unit of output that has increased. The quantity of *human* capital, as has been seen, has also increased. The inference is that inputs of human capital per man hour have increased at a more rapid rate than the increase in physical capital and that the wage share has increased in consequence. One reason for the inference that inputs of human capital have increased is that the technological changes that accompany the growth of physical capital typically also require higher skill levels on the part of the work force that is to use the new capital.

A rising wage share can also be rationalized in terms of institutional changes. Specifically, minimum-wage legislation in conjunction with public employment is increasingly serving as a redistribution device. Collective bargaining may tend to reduce the relative price of bargaining. Further, unions increasingly bargain the volume of employment along with the wage rate, so that bargained wage increases are less likely to be offset by reduced employment. The effect of these influences has not yet been evaluted statistically, but it would not be surprising if when it is, the historical constancy of the wage share turns out to be a thing of the past.

Family Differences in Income Distribution

The Stability of Family Shares

While there is no consensus concerning the trend of the relative shares being received by wage earners and the recipients of property incomes, there is fairly clear evidence that the distribution of income among families, ranked by fifths, has remained remarkably constant since World War II. Family income typically represents the pooled resources of family members. It thus reflects the number, sex, and age of family members, their labor-force participation, their earnings from the jobs at which they work, their property income, and any transfers received from government.

Most families are husband-wife families with a male working head. Earnings, as was noted in Chapter 4, typically increase with age. Thus, the earnings of males aged twenty-five to sixty-four are more unequal than those of males aged thirty-five to forty-four. There has, however, been no change in the relative inequality of income among adult males. Some writers suggest that this stability appears to be the result of forces that have operated to offset one another.[10] On the one hand, there has been a narrowing of schooling differentials, which has served to reduce the inequality of lifetime income. On the other hand, improved financial aid for schooling and training has, conceivably, resulted in greater investments in those persons who have greater ability, which would tend to increase inequality.

In spite of an increase in the proportion of wives who have earnings, this has not resulted in greater equality in family income, because there has not been a positive correlation between the annual earnings of husbands and wives.[11] This is reflected in Table 17-3, which records the percentage share of aggregate money income before taxes received by

TABLE 17-3 *Share of Aggregate Income before Taxes Received by Each Fifth of Families, Ranked by Income, Selected Years 1947–1977*

(Percent)

Income Rank	1947	1957	1967	1972	1976
Total families	100.0	100.0	100.0	100.0	100.0
Lowest fifth	5.1	5.0	5.5	5.4	6.0
Second fifth	11.8	12.6	12.4	11.9	12.0
Third fifth	16.7	18.1	17.9	17.5	17.0
Fourth fifth	23.2	23.7	23.9	23.9	24.0
Highest fifth	43.3	40.5	40.4	41.4	41.0

[1] The income (before taxes) boundaries of each fifth in 1975 were: lowest fifth, under $6,914; second fifth, $6,914 to $11,465; third fifth, $11,465 to $16,000; fourth fifth, $16,000 to $22,037; highest fifth, over $22,037; top 5 percent, over $34,144.
SOURCE: Department of Commerce, Bureau of the Census.

[10] See Barry Chiswick and June O'Neill, eds., *Human Resources and Income Distribution* (New York: W. W. Norton & Co., 1977), p. 8.
[11] As Chiswick and O'Neill note, men and women with high earning potentials are more likely to marry; but a woman is more likely to work, the lower her husband's income. *Op. cit.*, p. 7.

each fifth of families ranked by income. The share being received by the top 5 percent of families declined by a mere 1.3 percent between 1947 and 1957 and has varied almost imperceptibly since that time. Since aggregate income has been rising over the period, the average being received by each quintile has increased at about the same rate. The rich have not become richer, but neither have the poor been able to achieve significant improvement in their relative positions. Some redistribution occurred during World War II, but in spite of more than forty years of progressive-income taxation, minimum-wage laws, and transfer-payment programs, the distribution of cash incomes in the United States has remained remarkably constant. Some of the policy measures that aim at a more equalitarian distribution will be examined in Chapter 20.

The cyclical behavior of the income-distribution pattern is also a matter of concern. It was noted in Chapter 13 that an increasing rate and duration of employment has a different impact on different groups of workers. Workers with more schooling and more extensive labor-market experience have a lower rate of unemployment than workers with lesser skills and schooling. Since wage rates are relatively sticky during periods of declining employment, the increase in the inequality of earned income that is observed during a recession reflects more frequent layoffs and layoffs of longer duration among some members of the working population. There is, furthermore, a distinct inverse relationship between the likelihood of poverty and the number of weeks one works. Economic security depends less upon whether one works than on how much and at what kind of job one works. Thus we turn our attention to identifying, specifically, the incomes of the "working poor" and the nature of their work experience as a basis for examining, in Part III, the kinds of policies that have been adopted to ameliorate their condition.

The Working Poor

The Size of the Poverty Population

Some background information is essential before the problems of the working poor can be addressed. A criterion of poverty and an appreciation of the size of the poverty population are a useful beginning.

In the United States social-policy developments have led to the identification of poverty in terms of a family's ability to obtain the goods and services required to meet certain specified minimum needs. The President's Council of Economic Advisors established a poverty line of $3,000 per annum in 1963 as being required for a typical family of four persons. This estimate was predicated on the assumption of minimum nutritional requirements as estimated by the Department of Agriculture for the Social Security Administration and extended to arrive at a total budget of $3,000 for food and nonfood items for a poor family. The council's poverty standard was subsequently refined by Mollie Orshansky, of the Social Security Administration, to take into account the size of the family, whether it was headed by a man or a woman, and whether it was farm or nonfarm. She estimated that a nonfarm family of two adults and two children required a minimum of $3,130 in 1963.[12] According to current standards, a 1970 income of less than $3,968 is a basis for counting a family of four as being among the poor. Table 17-4 summarizes the 1970 poverty standard for farm and nonfarm families of various sizes. It indicates that in 1970 the number of poor Americans was about 25.5 million persons. Compared with the 1963 estimate of 34 million, this figure represents a rather considerable reduction in the incidence of poverty to approximately one in eight as compared to one in five.

TABLE 17-4   *The Poverty Population and Its Labor-Force Status*

The Poverty Population, 1970

	U.S. Population	Persons in Poverty	Poverty Rate
All persons	202,556,000	25,522,000	12.6%
white	176,566,000	17,480,000	9.9
black	22,768,000	7,650,000	33.6
Aged persons	20,050,000	4,709,000	24.6
Children (under 18)	69,995,000	10,493,000	15.0

SOURCE: U.S. Bureau of the Census

The labor-force status of those who are poor as compared with the nonpoor is a matter of particular importance, because it reflects the potential of this group to participate in the employment- and income-

[12] Mollie Orshansky, "Counting the Poor: Another Look at the Poverty Profile," *Social Security Bulletin* (January 1965).

generating programs that will be examined in Part III. It will be recalled from Chapter 2 that a person is in the labor force if he is either employed or actively seeking employment. Those who are temporarily out of work because of illness, bad weather, a labor dispute, or vacation are also classified as "in the labor force."

Table 17-5 provides perspective about the labor-force status of the poor as compared with the nonpoor. It is particularly revealing because it shows that the poor participate in the labor force less than the nonpoor do. Of the population classified as poor, 43 percent were not in the labor force in 1969 (the year used in the last census estimate).

TABLE 17-5 *Labor-Force Status of the Poor and Nonpoor, 1969*

Population	*In the labor force*	*Out of the labor force*
All Persons		
Nonpoor	91%	9%
Poor	57	43
Aged persons		
Nonpoor	23	77
Poor	16	84
Persons in male-headed		
families with children		
Nonpoor	98	2
Poor	84	16
Persons in female-headed		
families with children		
Nonpoor	80	20
Poor	50	50

Note: Family members are classified by the labor-force status of the family head.
SOURCE: U.S. Bureau of the Census and U.S. Department of Labor.

This differential rate of labor-force participation between the poor and the nonpoor is not a basis for inferring that the poor are fundamentally less work oriented than the nonpoor. A relevant fact, which is apparent in Table 17-5, is that the poverty population includes a relatively large number of persons who are older than sixty-five years. Normally this age group participates in the labor force to a lesser extent than younger persons do. Poor families are also disproportionately headed by females. Women, as has already been noted, typically have a smaller labor-force attachment than do males because of their greater responsibility for household management.

These observations suggest that the poverty problem is susceptible to labor-market solution only to a minimal extent. Of those who did not work in 1976, over one-third were keeping house, one-fourth were ill or disabled, and only 3 percent reported their inability to find a job. These facts are consistent with the finding that almost the entire gain in the reduction of poverty since the mid-1960s can be accounted for by income transfers. The relative importance of transfer payments as a source of personal income is displayed in Table 17-6.[13]

TABLE 17-6   *Percentage Sources of Personal Income Selected Years*

Type	1946	1960	1969	1978
Wages and salaries	63.2%	68.0%	69.0%	64.3%
Proprietors income	20.6	11.8	8.9	7.6
Rental income	3.1	3.5	2.4	1.7
Dividends and personal interest	6.8	9.0	10.5	12.3
Transfer payments	6.4	7.2	8.9	14.1

SOURCE: Economic Report of the President, 1979.

The survey of empirical findings about income distribution in the United States that has been examined in this chapter underscores that the matter of income redistribution is not one of high priority in this country, except as it relates to the very poor. The relative shares that are being earned from labor effort and property ownership have exhibited a pattern of relative constancy over more than three decades. The distribution of personal income among families has also remained remarkably stable. There has been a substantial increase of cash-transfer payments since 1946, but their burden appears to have been distributed quite equally among the recipients of other incomes, because the taxes that support them include payroll as well as income taxes. There is no evidence that the differentials that are present in the pattern of personal-income distribution are viewed as requiring any kind of corrective policy, except on behalf of the poverty population.

Even though the poverty problem appears to be amenable to labor-market solution only to a minimal extent, there are nevertheless some persons whose positions would improve if access to full-time work at better wages could be accomplished.[14] In 1970 there were more than 1

[13] The distribution figures include only cash income. In-kind benefits such as food stamps, rent subsidies, medicare, and medicaid are not included.

[14] Barry Schiller maintains that unemployment contributed to the low economic status of as many as 25 percent of all non-aged poor families. See Barry Schiller, *The Economics of Poverty and Discrimination* (New York: Prentice-Hall, 1973), p. 38.

million household heads of poor families who worked full-time. Indeed, the number of poor year-round workers is in excess of the number of poor part-time workers. The poverty of their families, in spite of regular employment, is partly the result of their very low wages and, second, of their having above-average needs, either as a result of family size or special circumstances, such as illness. As shown Table 17-7, the incomes of 36 percent of the families whose head worked full-time, year round, in 1970 was under $2,000, when the wages of other family members is included. Their experience poses the question of whether their problem might be amenable to improvement through legislated wage minima.

Theoretical inquiry into the likely impact of minimum-wage legislation has recently been enriched by the development of models that incorporate both a "covered" sector, in which the legislated minimum prevails, and an "uncovered" sector, in which it does not. The analytical objectives are to examine and provide empirical estimates of (1) the disemployment and unemployment effects of minimum-wage legislation, (2) the effect on the wage structure, and (3) the effect on the distribution of income. While present concern is only with the distributional aspects of minimum-wage legislation, analysis is necessarily predicated on a basic understanding of its employment and unemployment effects. The section that follows develops a theoretical model for this purpose.[15]

TABLE 17-7   *Incomes of the Working Poor, 1970*

	Percent of families
Under $2,000	36%
$2,000—$2,999	19
$3,000—$3,999	20
$4,000—$4,999	15
$5,000—$5,999	9
$6,000 +	1
	100%

Number of families 1,068,000
SOURCE: U.S. Bureau of the Census.

The Effects of Minimum-Wage Legislation

The Theoretical Model

In principle, the introduction of a minimum wage can generate several possible effects that lend themselves to diagrammatic analysis, as

[15] This is the model developed by Jacob Mincer in "Unemployment Effects of Minimum Wages," *Journal of Political Economy* 84 (August 1976, Pt. 2): s87–s104.

in Figures 17-2 A and B. One possible effect is that work in the covered sector (Diagram A) becomes relatively more attractive than nonmarket activity or work in the uncovered sector as the wage is raised from w_o, to w_c. This may increase labor-force participation in the covered sector causing labor to flow out of the uncovered sector. This tends to raise wages in the uncovered sector (Diagram B) from w_o to w_u, as the labor-supply curve moves leftward in the uncovered sector from S_u to S'_u.

FIGURE 17-2   *The Effects of Minimum-Wage Legislation*

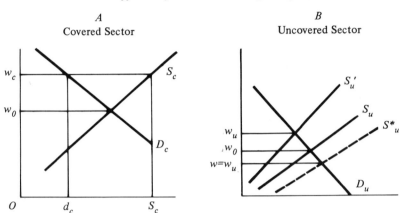

<table>
<tr><td align="center">A
Covered Sector</td><td align="center">B
Uncovered Sector</td></tr>
</table>

An alternative possibility is that the introduction of a minimum wage of W_c in the covered sector creates an excess supply of labor $OS_c - Od_c$ which is *added* to the supply in the uncovered sector.[16] As supply shifts to S_u^* the wage in the uncovered sector is bid down, establishing the uncovered equilibrium wage of $w = w_u$. Workers in the covered industry are better off as a result of the legislated minimum, W_c. How workers in the uncovered sector fare depends on whether they continue to participate in the labor force.

Investigation of the impact of a minimum wage requires recognition that persons who do not become employed in the covered sector at the legislated minimum may prefer to remain unemployed until a job in the covered sector becomes available. Workers who become disemployed in the covered sector may leave the labor force in preference to accepting a wage in the uncovered sector that is below their "shadow price" in the covered sector. This serves to weaken the demand pressure on wages in the uncovered sector. The wage in the uncovered sector may not fall all

---

[16] This is the assumption made by Finis Welch in "Minimum Wage Legislation in the United States," *Economics Inquiry* 12 (September 1974): 285–318.

the way to $w = w_u$ but may remain above that level for workers who have uncovered jobs. It is thus theoretically possible that workers in the uncovered sector could become better off as a result of minimum-wage legislation, along with those in the covered sector, although wages in the uncovered sector cannot rise as much as wages in the covered sector.[17]

The division of the outflow of workers from the covered sector into reemployment in the uncovered sector and withdrawals from the labor force depends on the demand-and-supply elasticities of labor in the uncovered sector. Some of the workers leaving the covered sector will be reabsorbed in the uncovered sector, but others may leave the labor force. Thus, the unemployment that arises in consequence of an increase in the minimum wage understates the disemployment of which it is only one part.[18] The other two parts are reemployment in the uncovered sector at lower wages than before, and labor-force withdrawals. The relationship between labor-force withdrawals and minimum-wage hikes implies that there may be a relationship between the rise in the minimum-wage level and the growth in the number of welfare recipients. The extent to which this is the case is, of course, an empirical question, as is the question of magnitude of the labor force and unemployment effects. Some empirical findings on the latter effects are examined as *Economics in Action*: 17:1.

ECONOMICS IN ACTION 17:1

Do Increases in Wage Minima Decrease Employment among Low-Wage Groups?

An empirical study by Jacob Mincer of the unemployment and labor-force effects of an increase in the minimum wage established that the requirement of paying the minimum-wage has a significant effect on labor-force participation and employment except for males aged twenty-five to sixty-four, nonwhite males sixty-five plus, and nonwhite females twenty plus.[19] Using Bureau of Labor Statistics data to identify

[17]While reduced labor-force participation is a theoretical possibility, the empirical evidence is that its effect on teenage workers is weak. See James F. Ragan, Jr., "Minimum Wages and The Youth Labor Market," *Review of Economics and Statistics* LIX (May 1977): 129–136.

[18]Mincer, "Unemployment Effects of Minimum Wages," *op. cit.*

[19]Other studies that reached essentially the same conclusion are Marvin Kosters and Finis Welch, "The Effects of Minimum Wages on the Distribution of Changes in Aggregate Employment," *American Economic Review* (June 1972): 323–332; and Douglas K. Adie, "Teenage Unemployment and Real Federal Minimum Wages," *Journal of Political Economy* (March/April 1973): 435–441. Daniel Hamermesh has recently surveyed fifteen studies that estimate how overall employment demand depends on the relative price of labor and capital and finds elasticities of substitution ranging from a low value of 0.15 to a high value of 1.0, with a long-run median estimate of close to 0.75. See Daniel

ten age-sex-color population groups, he established that the unemployment effects were substantially smaller than disemployment for most groups for the period 1954–1969. Labor-force participation diminishes in consequence of increases in the minimum wage. The largest negative effects were observed in relation to nonwhite males ages twenty through twenty-four, white males ages twenty through twenty-four, white teenagers, and nonwhite males ages twenty-five through sixty-four.

The largest disemployment effects were observed among teenagers, nonwhite males (twenty through twenty-four), white teenagers, and white males (twenty through twenty-four). The labor-force and employment effects of the minimum wage are greater for nonwhite than for white groups. The employment effects are larger than the labor-force effects, except among nonwhite teenagers and white males ages sixty-five plus and older. This evidence implies that minimum-wage legislation causes flows from the covered sector into the uncovered sector and, subsequently, out of the labor force. The largest increase in the unemployment rate is observed for nonwhite males (twenty to twenty-four), followed by nonwhite teenagers and white teenagers. Thus, Mincer's findings with respect to the effect of increases in the minimum wage confirm the earlier finding of other studies.

Other Aspects of Minimum-Wage Research

A major difficulty in unemployment studies is their inability to deal with supply-side phenomena such as population growth.[20] Studies that focus on *employment* rather than unemployment may therefore produce more definitive results. Such studies indicate that a 25 percent increase in minimum-wage rates decreases teenage employment by roughly 3.5 to 5.5 percent.[21] Unexpectedly, these studies find that white teenagers suffer employment losses from minimum wages but black teenagers do not.[22]

Very little evidence exists about the employment effects of mini-

---

Hamermesh, "Econometric Studies of Labor Demand and Their Application to Policy Analysis," *Journal of Human Resources* XI (1977); and "Policy Content of Quantitative Minimum Wage Research," *Industrial Relations Research Association Series, Proceedings* (27th Annual Winter Meeting, 1974).

[20] Robert S. Goldfarb, "Policy Content of Quantitative Minimum Wage Research," *Industrial Relations Research Association Series, Proceedings* (27th Annual Winter Meeting, 1974).

[21] Masanori Hashimoto and Jacob Mincer, "Employment and Unemployment Effects of Minimum Wages" (unpublished manuscript, August 1971); Finis Welch, "Minimum Wage Legislation in the United States." The paper by Hashimoto and Mincer appears in Mincer, *op. cit.* These two studies also have some estimates of effects on groups other than teenagers.

[22] Welch, *op. cit.*, argues that this finding is related to problems of sample size in the employment data.

mum-wage legislation on groups other than teenagers. One writer has suggested that when employment involves hiring costs, the requirement to pay a minimum wage affects the *kind* rather than the quantity of labor that is hired. Labor that is viewed as "more stable" (adults) might be substituted for labor viewed as being less stable (teenagers).[23] The analysis in Chapter 7, which examined the employment decisions of price-making firms suggests that the cost increases inherent in minimum-wage requirements do not necessarily result in reduced commodity demands, because they do not invariably necessitate higher commodity prices. Most commodities are not sold in competitive markets, in which price-taking sellers maximize profits (minimize losses) by varying their outputs in order to equate costs at the margin to the marginal revenue the market dictates for them. Except for the primary-foodstuffs and certain raw-materials and services markets, the industries in the private-enterprise sector of the economy are largely oligopolistic in structure. In these oligopolistic markets, small numbers of relatively large firms maintain a "fix price" market by varying their volume of output. Their demand for labor reflects the level of output they wish to produce.

While most of the empirical work relating to the impact of minimum-wage legislation has focused on its disemployment impact, relatively little work has been done in connection with its effect on the distribution of income. Minimum-wage legislation, as already noted, is advocated chiefly as a tool for redistributing income, but its effectiveness in accomplishing this objective has not been the subject of investigation until recently, because of lack of data. This omission has recently been remedied. The U.S. Department of Labor now interviews the same households for its survey of family incomes as it uses for surveys of wage rates. The merger of the two data sources has yielded the insights reported as *Economics in Action* 17:2: The Impact of Minimum Wages on Family Incomes.

ECONOMICS IN ACTION 17:2

The Impact of Minimum Wages of Family Incomes

The recently available data on the correlation between low wages and low family income pose the matter of the impact of minimum-wage legislation in a different light from that of the employment perspective in which it is typically considered.[24] When minimum-wage legislation is viewed as a means of altering the pattern of personal-income distribu-

---

[23] Goldfarb, *op. cit.*, p. 268.

[24] Edward M. Gramlich, "Impact of Minimum Wages on other Wages, Employment and Family Incomes," *Brookings Papers on Economic Activity* 2 (1976): 409–461.

tion, the critical question is whether the benefits, in terms of income redistribution, outweigh the penalty imposed on employment.

The correlations that were identified between low wages and low incomes are markedly different for adults and teenagers. For adults the correlation between low wages and low family incomes is not perfect but is fairly close. The median family income for adult workers earning below $2 per hour in 1973 was $7,576, or 1.77 times the poverty line for a family of four in 1972. By contrast, the median family income for workers making more than $4 an hour was $15,100, which is twice as high. However, even with the fairly strong correlation between low wages and low family incomes, 12 percent of the low-wage adult workers were part of families that had incomes in excess of $15,000, and 15 percent were part of families with incomes above the median for the economy as a whole. This finding suggests that minimum-wage legislation has a "spillover" benefit for high-income families. The spillover effect is particularly marked for teenage workers. Approximately 40 percent of low-wage teenagers are in families with incomes above $15,000, and fewer than 7 percent of low-wage teenagers were in poverty-level families. The implication of these findings is that minimum-wage legislation is unlikely to have strong redistributive effects. The spillover of benefits to the teenagers of high-income families, who are not likely to head up the low-income families of the next generation, suggests that the effectiveness of minimum-wage legislation as a means for redistributing income is limited.

Concluding Remarks

The patterns of personal-income distribution that have been examined in this chapter are the outcome of the differential structure of wages that was examined in Part I and the differential impact of the economy's employment experience on different groups. No attempt has been made to examine alternative theories of income distribution. While some scholars are optimistic that there will be an eventual convergence of alternative theories,[25] the underlying political ideologies and social philosophies inherent in competing theories are so diverse that the question of their possible synthesis will not be pursued further. Instead, attention is shifted in Part III to the policy sphere.

Economic policy is concerned with the use of tools to influence or achieve goals that, in a free-enterprise economy, reflect a social consensus.

---

[25] See in particular Gain Singh Sabota, "Theories of Personal Income Distribution: A Survey," *Journal of Economic Literature* XVI (March 1978): 1–41; and Mark Blaug, "Human Capital Theory: A Slightly Jaundiced Survey," *Journal of Economic Literature* XIV (September 1976): 839.

Its formulation and successful administration depend quite as much on the prevailing social philosophy and attitudes as they do on the issues it is intended to address. There appears to be a consensus that the labor market is among the sectors of the economy that require some degree of policy intervention. The prevailing point of view is that while society is willing to alleviate the most severe hardships of the poverty population, it is not willing to undertake policies that will drastically alter the distribution of income. Attention has been directed, instead, to those critical variables that underlie personal earnings—namely, employment levels and individual access to opportunities. The consensus is that these magnitudes are appropriate for policy manipulation. These policies can be further supplemented, if all else fails and satisfactory employment levels are not achieved, by policies of income insurance and assurance. Three main policy areas will, therefore, be addressed in Part III. These are first, to examine the policy implications of the Employment Act of 1946 and the Full Employment and Balanced Growth Act of 1978. Both commit the federal government to the pursuit of policies to reduce and maintain employment rates at acceptably low levels. The achievement of this objective has, thus far, been impeded by a conspicious lack of success in formulating policies that will also contain inflationary pressure. The policy aspects of this "cruel dilemma" are the subject of Chapter 18.

Chapter 19 is concerned with policy that seeks to enhance the labor-force participation and employability of persons of working age. Commitment to a policy of achieving and maintaining high levels of employment implies that government will also assume responsibility for promoting the employability and productivity of all who seek employment opportunities in the labor market. The disparate incidence of unemployment among various population subgroups is as much a focus for policy-making as is the general level of unemployment. A labor-market policy that fails to achieve high levels of employment either falls heavily on those groups who are least employable or it redistributes job opportunities and incomes so that the misery of unemployment is shared rather than reduced.

The concluding chapter of this book is concerned with policies to insure and assure income. Such measures are intended to cope with the fact of labor-market failure. Income insurance is provided under the unemployment-compensation system for workers who lose their jobs. Income assurance, i.e., income that is unrelated to previous labor-market activity, is made available under specified circumstances to persons and families who are unable to earn labor income.

Labor-Market Policy

18 Labor-Policy Issues: Employment, Inflation, Employability, and Income

The most critical aspect of policy intervention in the labor market concerns the problem of the level and impact of unemployment. The Employment Act of 1946, to which reference has been made several times as a landmark piece of legislation in our economy, states that "...it is the continuing policy and responsibility of the federal government to use all practicable means...for creating and maintaining...conditions under which there will be afforded useful employment opportunities...for those able, willing, and seeking to work, and to promote maximum employment, production, and purchasing power."

The preamble to the Full Employment and Balanced Growth Act of 1978 reiterated this policy goal and expressed the further objective "to translate into practical reality the right of all Americans who are able, willing, and seeking work to full opportunity for useful paid employment at fair rates of compensation...." It further asserts "the responsibility of the federal government to use all practicable programs and policies to promote full employment, production, ... real income, balanced growth, adequate productivity growth...."

To this end the president is required to establish annual numerical goals for employment and unemployment as well as medium-term goals for three successive calendar years. The requirement for employment objectives for specific subgroups of the labor force, including youth, women, minorities, handicapped persons, veterans, and older persons is specifically recognized. The medium-term numerical goal is to reduce the rate of unemployment to not more than 3 percent among individuals aged twenty and over and 4 percent among individuals aged sixteen and over within a period not extending beyond the fifth calender year after the first economic report which the president is required to submit to the Congress. Our most recent legislation thus reflects a firm commitment to achieve specific employment and unemployment goals for the economy as a whole, with special attention to the labor-market problems of particular groups.

The Full Employment and Balanced Growth Act also recognizes that the formulation of employment policy is unavoidably intertwined with anti-inflationary policy. The ideal, of course, is to achieve reasonably full employment while restraining the inflationary pressure that appears to be inevitable in a tightening labor market. The specific objective that has been incorporated into the act is to reduce the rate of inflation to not more than 3 percent within a period not extending beyond the fifth calendar year after the first required Presidential Economic Report. It is further mandated that the policies adopted for reducing the rate of inflation "shall not impede achievement of the goals and timetable specified for the reduction of unemployment."

Achievement of the policy objectives set forth in the Full Employment and Balanced Growth Act of 1978 impose a requirement, first, for identifying the root causes of the unemployment problem as it is currently being experienced. This kind of analysis necessarily underlies effective policy formation. Appropriate policy in an economy that is experiencing unemployment in consequence of inadequate demand is quite different from that which is appropriate in an economy that is experiencing frictional or structural unemployment. The first concern of this chapter, therefore, is to reexamine how employment policy was formulated over the last several decades in order to address alternative types of unemployment problems. The kinds of policy alternatives that are presently being offered reflect the lessons that have been learned from this experience.

The formulation of employment policy in the present setting is complicated by the directive that Congress has given that the goal of reducing the rate of inflation must not be allowed to infringe on the goals that have been adopted for the achievement of full employment. The act specifically states that "sole dependence upon fiscal or monetary policies or both to combat inflation can exacerbate both inflation and unemployment." Congress urges that fiscal and monetary policies be coordinated with specific policies in order to combat inflation. The policies that are recommended include (1) an effective information system to monitor and analyze inflationary trends in individual economic sectors; (2) programs and policies for alleviating shortages of goods, services, labor, and capital, with particular emphasis on food, energy, and critical industrial materials; (3) the establishment of stockpiles of agricultural commodities and other critical materials; (4) encouragement to labor and management to increase productivity; (5) the encouragement of competition in the private sector and improvement of the economic climate for the growth of small business; (6) removal and/or modification of such government restrictions and regulations as add unnecessarily to inflationary costs; (7) increasing exports and improving the international competitive position of agriculture, business, and industry; and (8) such other administrative actions and recommendations as the President deems desirable in order to promote reasonable price stability.[1]

President Carter's recommendation of a policy to establish "real-wage insurance" proposes that workers agreeing to comply with the voluntary 7 percent pay standard will be given a tax-credit cushion if inflation subsequently exceeds 7 percent. The administration estimates that the plan could cut a half a percentage point off the rate of inflation if enough workers agree to cooperate. In offering his proposal for real wage insurance for which several groups of workers, among them the Communications Workers, the United Autoworkers, the American Federation of State, County and Municipal Employees and the Teamsters, expressed their qualified support, the administration has focused new attention on *incomes policy* as an anti-inflation weapon.[2] The reemergence of incomes policy as a serious policy alternative has stimulated new interest in a variety of tax-oriented proposals that academic and government economists have been urging for a number of years. The common feature of these proposals, which are examined in the second part of this chapter, is their recommendation that excessive advances in the price level be restrained by adopting a policy of basing wage increases on productivity improvements.

Formulating Policies to Combat Unemployment

Inadequate Demand or Structural Unemployment?

A fundamental contribution of the Keynesian revolution was that it redirected attention away from the notion that the economy is always characterized by powerful tendencies toward full-employment equilibrium. Two lessons for practical policy emerged as economists examined the nature of economies characterized by less than full employment. The first is that long and severe depressions, characterized by falling wages and prices, are not a prerequisite for restoring increases in aggregate demand and real spending. The second is that increased spending can be achieved directly through expansionary fiscal policy, i.e., through reduced taxes or deficit-financed government expenditures.

[1] Public Law 95-523, October 27, 1978, Section 8.

[2] Robert Flanagan examines the conceptual and administrative issues raised by real-wage insurance in his article "Real Wage Insurance as a Compliance Incentive," *Eastern Economics Journal* V, 3 (1979).

These lessons were never more relevant than during the widespread unemployment miseries of the 1930s and the early years of World War II, which the United States entered in 1941. The reduction in unemployment that was achieved during the war was substantial, and virtually full employment was maintained into the mid-1950s. But the late 1950s and early 1960s, as was noted in Chapter 13, were, once again, years during which the economy experienced unemployment. The economy remained generally prosperous, but unemployment reached a recession high of 6.8 percent in 1958. Thus, the unemployment problem appeared to differ from that experienced during the 1930s. The persistence of unemployment in a prosperous economy precipitated a controversy between those who asserted Keynes's diagnosis of inadequate aggregate demand and those who offered the alternate view that the economy was experiencing *structural* unemployment. The distinction between these two hypotheses of unemployment became crucial from the standpoint of policy.

The proponents of the inadequate-demand theory, whose most prominent advocate was Walter Heller, then chairman of the Council of Economic Advisors, argued that persistent unemployment was the aftermath of the incomplete recovery from the 1957–1958 recession. The solution he recommended was expansionary fiscal policy.

The structuralists, on the other hand, maintained that changes in industry skill requirements relative to the skill availabilities of the labor force were at the root of the problem. In their view, a structural mismatch had developed in the economy so that there was unemployment in spite of an adequate level of aggregate demand. The problem, as they saw matters, was that the labor force had not adapted itself, either geographically or in terms of its skills, to the changes in labor requirements that had taken place. Because they believed the problem to be structural, they recommended policies that aimed at adapting the unemployed to available job openings by retraining and relocation. Thus, the structuralists are closely aligned to the human-capital theorists in their policy recommendations. Workers are unemployed because they lack the skills they need to make it worthwhile to employ them at present wage levels. Such measures would, they believed, produce a leftward shift of the Phillips curve and reduce the unemployment rate at the current level of income. They opposed policy to increase aggregate demand on the grounds that it would generate inflation, as bottlenecks appeared in particular sectors in consequence of supply shortages.

In 1961, the Joint Economic Committee held hearings with a view to identifying whether inadequate demand or structural factors were responsible for the excessive unemployment that had persisted since late 1957.[3] The debate was prolonged and extensive. The inadequate-demand

[3] Charles Schilling, "Recent Inflation in the United States," Study Paper No. 1, Joint Economic Committee Study of Employment Growth and Price Levels (Washington, D.C.: U.S. Government Printing Office, 1957).

view finally prevailed and was given policy implementation in the income-tax cut of 1964. By 1965 the unemployment rate was reduced below 5 percent and subsequently fell to below 4 percent, where it remained from 1966 to 1969. This success suggests that inadequate demand was chiefly responsible for the prolonged period of unemployment between 1958 and 1965.[4] The unemployment rate increased as the demand for goods and services declined during the recession. The reemployment of those who were laid off was impeded not only by the uncertainty of recovery but also by rehiring delays that were associated with the relatively large pool of unemployed workers and the increased productivity of workers who retained their jobs.

In the light of these difficulties, government assumed responsibility for promoting the employability and productivity of workers who were disadvantaged in the labor market. Recognizing that the burden of unemployment falls most heavily on those groups that are least employable, federal manpower programs were introduced in 1962 to reduce high unemployment and high labor turnover among specific groups of disadvantaged workers, by providing training to qualify them for higher-paying jobs that they would be less likely to quit. The basic premise was that those who are chronically unemployed are disadvantaged chiefly because of limited investments in education and training, i.e., they are deficient in human capital. The programs that were initiated to upgrade them in terms of education and skill training, and to provide better access to jobs, placement services, and relocation, will be examined in Chapter 19.

The Origin of Public-Service Employment

The experiences of the period between 1969 and 1974 appeared to convince the Nixon administration that a trade-off between unemployment and inflation is unavoidable. Unemployment in 1969 was at the lowest level achieved without controls, but inflation was accelerating. Furthermore, the effort to check inflation via fiscal and monetary restraint without serious unemployment proved unsuccessful. Unemployment rates reached 6.6 percent by January of 1971.[5] The subsequent easing of monetary and fiscal restraints (a policy reversal that was undoubtedly influenced by the imminent election) reduced unemployment to 5.2 by November of 1972. The downward trend of unemployment continued and reached a low of 4.6 percent in October of 1973. But inflation surged upward from the 3.5 percent rate of 1971 to 7 percent in 1973 and reached 11 percent in 1974. The advent of "double digit" inflation provoked a reluctant (and half-hearted) policy of

---

[4] It is also relevant to note that, in addition to the tax cut, the economy was greatly stimulated by spending for the Vietnam War.

[5] See Chapter 13, Table 13-1.

wage-and-price control.[6] Inflation was tagged "Public Enemy Number One." The administration pursued an anti-inflationary fiscal policy, while the Federal Reserve Board, also engaging in an anti-inflationary effort, allowed the money supply to decline. Simultaneously, however, unemployment rose to 8.9 percent in March of 1975, which was the highest rate posted since 1941.

Unwilling to allow unemployment to remain above 5 percent, Congress gave consideration to tax cuts, public works, and public-service employment. The administration, however, continued to regard hyper-inflation as a bigger threat than unemployment. Ultimately, administration reluctance to use fiscal and monetary policy to create jobs provoked congressional efforts to introduce public-service employment. A presidential veto spurred Congress to try again in 1971, this time via the Emergency Employment Act. It was signed into law to initiate a job-creation program by making available a $2.25 billion budget to state and local governments to employ approximately 150,000 unemployed persons. In 1974, continued recession led Congress to pass the Emergency Jobs and Unemployment Assistance Act, which added Title VI to the Comprehensive Employment and Training Act (CETA) of 1973. CETA, which became operative in 1974, provided additional public-service slots.

In the Comprehensive Employment and Training Act of 1973 (CETA), responsibility for formulating and managing manpower programs was shifted to state and local governments ("S and L's"), and an increase in the funding of PSE was provided under Titles II and VI of CETA. In excess of 300,000 PSE slots were funded under all CETA titles between 1975 and 1977.[7]

Numerous proposals have been brought before Congress to expand PSE programs. The Humphrey-Hawkins bill was among the proposals that envisioned a considerable expansion in funding, but its passage as the Full Employment and Balanced Growth Act of 1978 included no specific provision for further funding. However, the act makes it clear that there is strong sentiment in Congress against tolerating high rates of unemployment in order to limit inflation. This stance suggests that Congress would undertake aggressive action to reduce the unemployment rate if it substantially exceeds the mandated maximum. In this light it is relevant to examine the likely effectiveness of a public-service-employment policy, should Congress determine that it is necessary to provide jobs on the public payroll for those persons who cannot get employment in the private sector.

---

[6] See Chapter 16 above for details.

[7] The same act also extended unemployment insurance up to sixty-five weeks.

PSE and the Unemployment-Inflation Trade off

Direct job creation has been advocated as a policy tool that has the potential for mitigating the conflict between the goal of reducing unemployment and controlling inflation. It is conceived to offer the short-run possibility of diminishing the inflationary pressure that accompanies higher rates of employment in an economy that is experiencing a cyclical upswing. In the long run, PSE is conceived to offer the prospect of reducing NAIRU, the nonaccelerating inflation rate of unemployment.[8] The mechanism for accomplishing these objectives is to adopt policies that will shift the demand for labor to secondary workers. Such a shift may be desirable because unemployment among them does not contribute to holding down the advancing wage costs that accompany inflation. Thus a policy that provides public-service employment for secondary workers (and *only* for them) may reduce aggregate unemployment without generating additional inflationary pressure and may even moderate inflation. The potential effectiveness of such a policy is dependent on its being limited to persons whose search behavior would be responsive to wages that are high relative to what could be earned in the private sector and in jobs that are more "attractive" than those typically offered to disadvantaged workers, whose employment normally would not generate inflationary wage increases.

The employment gains that might be achieved via job creation in the public sector result from the substitution of low-wage workers for high-wage workers in a proportion that would maintain (or increase) total output while reducing the total number of persons who are unemployed. Achievement of this objective is dependent first on the nature of the production functions governing the input-output behavior in production activities employing both types of labor. It also depends on the effect that their unemployment has on their respective wage rates. If, for example, three secondary workers can be substituted in a particular activity for one primary worker without any change in output, then one hundred unemployed secondary workers could be employed in place of thirty-three primary workers. The number of unemployed persons is thus reduced by sixty-seven.[9] The aggregate number of unemployed persons is reduced by changing the "mix" of the unemployed; that is, the amount of secondary unemployment is reduced while the unemployment of primary workers is increased. Since unemployment among primary workers has a moderating influence on wage inflation, the short-run trade-off between unemployment and

---

[8] Martin N. Bailey and James Tobin, *Brookings Papers on Economic Activity* 2 (1977).
[9] This hypothetical illustration is offered by Bailey and Tobin, *op. cit.*, pp. 517–518.

inflation may be improved as a result of a public-service employment program.

The long-run effects, however, result from the adjustments that follow in the relative wage levels of primary and secondary workers. Provision of public employment for secondary workers would increase the relative wage they would command in the *private* sector as their unemployment rates fall. Primary workers may, therefore, be substituted for secondary workers in the private sector. If this is the case, it will *diminish* the effectiveness of public-sector employment. The worst possible case is that in the long run, the number of secondary workers employed in public jobs will be equal to the number displaced from private employment.[10] There is thus a theoretical basis for skepticism about the prospect for the long-run success of direct job creation. The case for direct job creation, therefore, rests chiefly on its short-run effectiveness in diminishing inflationary pressure and in distributing the burden of unemployment more equitably. The extent to which either of these effects occurs is, of course, an empirical problem. Some empirical evidence about the short-run employment effects of direct job creation are examined in *Economics in Action* 18:1.

ECONOMICS IN ACTION 18:1

The Effects of Public-Service-Employment Policy

Two alternative public-service programs were simulated to assess the difference that such a policy would have made to unemployment rates, the rate of price change, the GNP, and the fiscal responsibility of federal and nonfederal governments during the period 1973–1975.[11] The program format chosen for simulation included (1) eligibility standards for admission to and continuance in public-service employment (PSE), (2) a wage schedule for participants' wages based on occupational history and skill in private employment, (3) the assumption that persons who want public-service jobs and meet the eligibility requirement are accepted at the prescribed wage, (4) an automatic and relatively quick response to worsening employment conditions, and (5) the stipulation that the monetary authority maintains interest rates within a range compatible with government's financing the program.

The simulation also required certain assumptions about the behavior of institutions and persons who are eligible to participate in the

---

[10] Bailey and Tobin, *op. cit.*, p. 525.

[11] Barbara Bergman and Robert L. Bennett, "Macroeconomic Effects of a Humphrey-Hawkins Type Program," *Papers and Proceedings of the American Economic Association* (February 1977): 265–270.

program. Specifically, it was assumed that persons who are eligible for unemployment insurance will want to get on public-service employment less often than those who are not eligible. It is assumed that the probability is .1 that a person will want to shift from unemployment-insurance entitlement to PSE if additional weeks of unemployment-insurance coverage remain. Alternatively, the probability of a shift to public-service employment is assumed to be 1.0 if no weeks of coverage remain. It is also assumed that persons on unemployment insurance and on public-service employment will continue to search for regular jobs and will accept 75 percent as many jobs offers as persons who are ineligible for these opportunities.

The simulation also assumed that the federal government will purchase fourteen-cents' worth of materials and training services from the private sector for each dollar of public-service-employment wages and will hire five additional federal workers for each 100 public-service-employment workers to administer the program. Finally, it is

TABLE 18-A   *Simulated Effects of Two Variants of a* PSE *Program (All dollar figures in billions at annual rates)*

	Civilian Unemployment Rate (%)				% of Civilian Labor force on PSE		GNP deflator			
	Actual	Simulated			Simulated		Actual	Simulated		
Date	No PSE	No PSE	Lo PSE	Hi PSE	Lo PSE	Hi PSE	No PSE	No PSE	Lo PSE	Hi PSE
1973 I	5.0	5.0	4.8	4.6	0.3	0.7	150	152	152	153
1973 II	4.9	4.6	4.6	4.5	0.3	0.7	153	154	154	155
1973 III	4.8	4.7	4.5	4.7	0.4	0.7	156	158	158	158
1973 IV	4.7	4.6	4.7	4.7	0.2	0.6	159	160	161	161
1974 I	5.1	4.9	4.7	4.6	0.4	1.0	164	164	165	164
1974 II	5.1	5.5	5.0	4.8	0.5	0.9	167	166	166	165
1974 III	5.5	6.1	5.6	5.4	0.6	0.8	172	170	170	169
1974 IV	6.6	7.0	6.5	5.8	0.4	1.2	178	174	174	173
1975 I	8.3	7.8	6.7	5.5	0.8	1.6	182	177	177	175
1975 II	8.9	8.0	6.4	5.0	0.9	1.6	184	181	181	179
1975 III	8.4	8.2	6.8	5.2	0.8	1.3	186	183	183	181
1975 IV	8.3	8.4	6.5	5.0	1.5	1.5	189	188	188	186
MEAN	6.3	6.2	5.6	5.0	0.6	1.1	170	169	169	168

SOURCE: Barbara Bergman and Robert Bennett, "Macroeconomic Effects of a Humphrey-Hawkins Type Program," *Papers and Proceedings of American Economics Association* (February 1977).

assumed that welfare payments will be decreased by ten cents for every dollar of public-service employment wages paid.

The model was run for the years 1973–75 on alternative assumptions of no public-service employment and high public-service employment. Table 18-A summarizes the effect of the programs in moderating the force of recession on unemployment rates using both assumptions. Significant improvement in the aggregate rate of unemployment becomes apparent in the second quarter of 1974. It continues through 1975, even if the amount of public-service employment is assumed to be low. Meanwhile, the net costs to the treasury were relatively low, and neither program causes the business firms whose behavior is simulated to raise prices faster than they rose in fact. The simulated rate of inflation, as is represented by the GNP deflator under various assumptions about the size of public-service employment, approximates the actual rate recorded in Table 18-A.

Additional Aspects of PSE

While an expanded public-service-employment program seems a promising technique for coping with unacceptably high levels of unemployment, it is not without drawbacks. These are associated with the multiple purposes of PSE. The program is conceived as being (1) a countercyclical program, (2) an antipoverty program, and (3) a revenue-sharing program. One of the chief limitations of the PSE approach is that it is quite possible that the S and L's will use their PSE subsidies to pay employees who have already been hired, or for workers who would have been hired in the absence of the program. This kind of "fiscal substitution" is a problem that appears to be inherent in a PSE approach, which functions as a disguised form of revenue sharing.

The actual size of the fiscal-substitution effect is, of course, an empirical question. A study prepared under the auspices of the National Planning Association estimated a fiscal substitution effect of .46 after one year.[12] Subsequent studies produced conflicting results; however, they verify that the fiscal-substitution effect is substantial.[13] The greater the substitution of federal funds for state and local funds, the less effective PSE becomes as an employment program.[14]

[12] *An Evaluation of the Economic Impact Project of the Public Employment Program,* Manpower Administration, U.S. Department of Labor Control No. 42-2-001-11 Final Report (May 1974).

[13] *Brookings Papers in Economic Activity* (1978) and George E. Johnson and James D. Tomola, "An Impact of the Public Employment Program," Technical Analysis Paper No. 17 (Washington, D.C.: Office of Evaluation, ASPER, U.S. Department of Labor).

[14] George E. Johnson and James D. Tomala, "The Fiscal Substitution Effect of Alternative Approaches to Public Service Employment Policy," *Journal of Human Resources* XII, 1 (Winter 1977).

While the fiscal-substitution effect limits the impact of the PSE program on total employment, it may nevertheless be effective as an antipoverty program if it alters the composition of employment toward groups that are relatively disadvantaged with respect to the labor market. The law provides that special attention be given to disadvantaged workers, but it is apparently difficult to translate this policy into effective action. Specifically, there is evidence that the persons who are hired into public-service unemployment are predominantly whites with nine or more years of education.[15]

The qualifications and characteristics of these persons suggest that they are likely to have a better-than-average chance of finding jobs in the private sector. However, once placed in public service, these persons presumably have less time and less incentive to search for private-sector employment, so their employment in the public sector may result in lesser incentive to search for private-sector emloyment, and their employment in the public sector may represent a less productive use of their capabilities than would result from private employment, could it be made available. The fact that a high proportion of the persons who are placed into public-service employment are not truly disadvantaged appears to be associated with the tendency for public-service-employment legislation to create jobs of a type that are more typically associated with permanent careers.

The more career oriented public-service jobs become, the more difficult it becomes for the jobs created to be temporary. In principle, a public employment program should be phased out in countercyclical fashion. This type of timing requires that the jobs created be of the kind that can both be quickly provided and terminated as opportunities improve in the private sector. This implies that the jobs created be of such a nature that they require only very short and nonspecific training and that they lend themselves to being filled by persons of various ages with a wide range of previous training and experience. It is clearly difficult to plan a program that incorporates all these features.

ECONOMICS IN ACTION 18:2

The Impact of a Tax Cut as an Alternative Employment Policy

A tax cut can, in principle, be used as an alternative to public-service employment. The critical question at issue is the relative efficiency of the two mechanisms for creating increments of employment.

---

[15] B. Chiswick and J. O'Neill, *Human Resources and Income Distribution*, p. 117.

The Council of Economic Advisors addressed itself to this question by estimating the number of jobs created and paid for under a $1 billion public-service-employment program as compared with an equivalent federal tax cut.[16] It was estimated that a $1 million PSE program could pay for approximately 110,000 job opportunities at $9,000 per job. However, it was also estimated that part of these jobs would merely displace jobs that state and local governments would normally have generated without federal aid. On the basis of past experience, it was estimated that a PSE program only initially creates more jobs than can be achieved by means of a tax reduction. These estimates are summarized in Table 18-B. The PSE program is more effective *initially* while the performance effect of a tax cut continues to increase. If the objective of a program is to increase aggregate employment as much and as rapidly as possible, a PSE program can be more effective in the short run (per unit of budget deficit) than any other type of fiscal policy if the fiscal-substitution effect is small.[17]

TABLE 18-B *Estimated Employment-Creating Effect of Alternative Programs*

Additional employment due to:	By end of quarter							
	1	2	3	4	5	6	7	8
Reduction in federal taxes[1]	1.1	4.5	10.2	17.8	26.2	34.6	43.0	51.4
Public service employment	41.3	74.3	60.5	47.5	25.7	19.2	11.0	11.0
Total jobs created	42.4	78.8	70.7	65.3	51.9	53.8	54.0	62.4

[1] Assumptions—Time pattern of a reduction of federal personal-income taxes assumed to be same as under the PSE programs (Table 18-1).

End of quarter	Multiplier
1	.4
2	.8
3	1.2
4 and thereafter	1.5

Magnitude of tax reduction assumed to be $125 million in first quarter and $250 million in each of the following quarters.

SOURCE: Barry Chiswick and June O'Neill, eds., *Human Resources and Income Distribution* (New York: W. W. Norton & Co., 1977), p. 122.

[16] Supplement to the 1976 Report of the Council of Economic Advisors.
[17] George E. Johnson, "Evaluating the Macroeconomic Effects of Public Service Programs," in *Evaluating the Labor Market Effects of Social Programs*, Orley Ashenfelter and James Blum, eds. (Princeton, N.J.: Princeton University Press, 1976).

While the number of jobs created by a one-million-dollar public-service employment program are considerably diminished, whereas those generated by a tax reduction are enhanced, it is relevant to recognize that time is of the essence when an economy is confronted with a serious unemployment problem. The longer the time that elapses before jobs are restored, the more precipitous the decline may become. Delay is likely to increase the magnitude of the problem, thereby expanding the magnitude of the effort that is required to halt the contraction of employment. Thus, the *speed* of the impact of the policy must be considered as much as the size of the impact in guiding the choice between PSE and tax cuts as employment-policy tools.

Wage Subsidies to Increase Employment

The payment of wage subsidies to employers to encourage them to hire disadvantaged workers has also been advocated as a means of altering the mix of employment in their favor while also improving the inflation-unemployment trade-off. One proposal, which relates specifically to teenage workers, suggests giving all teenagers vouchers that could be used either for schooling or to subsidize employers who hire them.[18] This proposal has not been translated into policy. However, under the Concentrated Employment Program (CEP), employers are reimbursed for the costs of job training to encourage them to hire workers they would otherwise not consider. Reimbursement of training costs incurred by firms that locate plants in or near slum areas is provided for under the Jobs Opportunities in the Business Sector (JOBS) program. The Revenue Act of 1978 also provides for tax credits up to 50 percent of the wages paid to individuals who are members of "targeted groups." These groups include persons receiving vocational rehabilitation, economically disadvantaged youths, economically disadvantaged Vietnam veterans, SSI recipients, general-assistance recipients, youths participating in cooperative-education programs, and economically disadvantaged ex-convicts. Tax credits are not available to employers receiving federally funded payments to provide on-the-job training for such persons.

From the standpoint of the employee, a wage-subsidy scheme is intended to have essentially the same effect as direct-job creation. That is, the intent of the subsidy would be to change the relative wage paid by firms for secondary as compared with primary labor. Primary workers become relatively more expensive to employ if, in effect, a subsidy reduces the relative cost of employing secondary workers. Thus, the

---

[18] Martin S. Feldstein, "Lowering the Permanent Rate of Unemployment," A Study for the Joint Economic Committee 93:1 (GPO, 1973).

unemployment rate of secondary workers would tend to decline as this group is substituted for primary workers in the private sector. However, it has been argued that wage subsidies do not promise the same reduction in frictional unemployment as does direct-job creation.[19] The basis for this conclusion is that while there is an additional incentive to employers to hire disadvantaged workers, their job-search behavior may not be modified, because their relative wage is the same as it would be without the wage subsidy. The actual impact of wage subsidies on employment, as is the case with public-service employment, is an empirical question that requires further investigation in order to test the theoretical conclusions that have been reached about the effectiveness of alternative ways of changing the employment mix in favor of disadvantaged workers.

Anti-Inflation Policies

An Overview of Macroeconomic Anti-inflation Policies

Fiscal and monetary policy are the policy "work horses" on which reliance has been placed in order to control the economy's level of output and employment. Fiscal policy utilizes the mechanism of treasury expenditures and revenues and the management of the public debt in order to alter the level of aggregate effective demand. Monetary policy is similarly aimed at controlling the level of aggregate demand but does so via control over bank reserves and thus interest rates and business investment. Both monetary and fiscal policy affect wage rates and prices through the operation of market forces. Their inadequacies when the economy is experiencing the dual problem of inflation and unemployment have led many economists to propose that they be supplemented by some form of tax-based incomes policy (TIP). Such a program would utilize a tax penalty or reward, or a combination of both, to provide an incentive to employers and/or employees to reduce the wage increases that are agreed upon when wage agreements are negotiated.

Alternative Proposals: The "Carrot" of an Employee TIP

A proposal put forward by Arthur Okun of the Brookings Institution in 1977 would require setting a threshold rate of wage increase that is consistent with productivity advances.[20] Workers would be offered an incentive in the form of a tax rebate to restrain the rise in hourly compensation below the threshold. The Okun TIP proposal would give a

---

[19] Martin N. Bailey and James Tobin, *op. cit.*, p. 513.

[20] Arthur M. Okun, "The Great Stagflation: Anti-Inflation not Anti-Growth," *Vital Speeches of the Day* (December 1, 1977): 120–125.

tax rebate, equal to one point of the normal payroll tax for each point by which the rate of wage increase is below the threshold rate, to each employee of firms holding the increase in average compensation per hour below the threshold rate of wage increase. The proposal calls for tax compensations (up to the social-security wage ceiling) to restrain take-home pay. The reward (or penalty) for each employee would be related to the average wage increase granted by the firm rather than to the individual employee's own wage increase. The rationale for this feature is that the objective of an employee TIP is not to discourage merit upgrading of individual employees, but to discourage increases in the wage structure of the firm.[21]

An employee TIP could, in principle, be readily implemented by using the present tax-withholding system. The program would be entirely administered by the employer and place no compliance burden on the individual employee, who would simply be informed of his TIP tax credit or surcharge on his paycheck and on his W2 forms.

The impact of a TIP program on union behavior can be examined in terms of a collective-bargaining model. The interaction between a union and management may be envisioned with the aid of a diagram like that in Figure 18-1, in which the P curve represents the union "push" for wage increases while the R curve represents management's resistance. A union's push for additional increases is positive at every tentative wage increase (W_1). Thus, showing wage increases on the horizontal axis, and bargaining pressure on the vertical, the "push" curve slopes downward because the higher the tentative wage increase, the smaller the union push is likely to be. On the basis of the observations made in Chapter 9, we know that the level of unemployment and the wage increases won by other unions affect the bargaining stance adopted by a particular union. Thus, it may be inferred that the union-push curve at each W_i will be higher (1) the higher the rate of wage increase that has recently been achieved by other workers, and (2) the lower the current rate of unemployment. Two other factors affect the degree of "push" at a tentative W_i. It is expected that (3) the push will be greater, the higher the expected rate of price increase, and (4) the higher the net profit rate that firms are expected to realize from a given wage increase. Factors (3) and (4) are uniquely related to the market power of price-taking firms.

Management resistance to wage increases is represented by the R curve in Figure 18-1. Its position reflects the effect that a proposed wage increase is expected to have on the firm's level of net profit. The larger

---

[21] Okun has argued that the political process virtually requires that wage penalties be imposed on firms, while wage rewards must be given and made universally available to workers. See "Comments and Discussion," *Brookings Papers on Economic Activity* 2 (1978): 349–361.

FIGURE 18-1   *Wage-Bargaining under an Employee TIP Program*

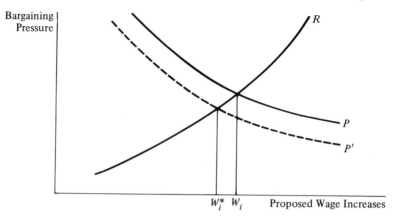

the wage increase that is being sought, the lower the level of net profit will be. In particular, a decline in net profit implies that a firm will be more likely to have to finance investment by external borrowing rather than from retained earnings, which will raise the cost of capital. Thus, management will be more resistant to a proposed W_i (1) the lower its level of net profit at the current wage and (2) the greater the reduction in net profit that is expected to result if the proposed W_i is achieved. Thus, the expected level of profit affects both the union-push curve and the management-resistance curve, and, consequently, the rate of wage increase that actually results.

An employee of TIP would exert its impact by influencing the position of the union-push curve. Two factors in addition to those noted above are important. Specifically, the union-push curve will be higher if the proposed W_i (1) represents a larger increment in after-tax income. The union will bargain harder, the larger the number of after-tax dollars that are involved in a proposed wage increase. The union will also bargain harder if (2) a proposed wage increase is expected to represent a smaller increment in *real* (i.e., inflation-adjusted) after-tax income.[22] Factor (1) is the incentive or substitution effect; factor (2) is the income effect. The overall effectiveness of an employee TIP program reflects their joint influence on the position of the union-push curve in a bargaining situation.

Some possibilities are illustrated in Figure 18-1. Because an employee TIP reduces the after-tax gain from a given increase in wages, the expected effect of factor (1) is that the union-push curve will be depressed from P to P^1 so the proposed wage increase is reduced from W_i

[22] Laurence S. Seidman, "Tax Based Incomes Policy," *Brookings Papers on Economic Activity* 2 (1978): 329.

to W_i^* The extent to which this will be the case, however, also depends on the influence of factor (2), the income effect. If employees believe TIP will lower the rate of inflation, then the income effect will reenforce the substitution (incentive) effect in pressuring the union-push curve down to the left. Conversely, if employees are pessimistic about the inflation-lowering possibilities of TIP, they are likely to push for a higher wage increase, even though it will impose a tax penalty for exceeding the threshold rate. In this case, the income effect will work against the substitution effect, and the net effect on the position of the union-push curve is not predictable in terms of economic principle.

It is possible to add an additional feature to the employee TIP in which the federal government could "insure" cooperating workers by granting additional tax rebates if they are penalized by price inflation.[23] The "carrots" of the Okun proposal are thus intended as incentives that will make it unneccessary for government to intervene directly in setting wages or prices. The proposal has been offered on the premise that competitive forces would continue to govern the choices of unions and business as they incorporate tax savings and tax costs into their decision making.

The "Stick" of an Employer TIP

An alternative Tax-Based Incomes Policy (TIP) proposal is offered by Henry Wallich (governor of the Federal Reserve System) and Sidney Weintraub of the University of Pennsylvania. This proposal, which was initially offered in 1971, is premised on using the tax system in a *punitive* way to limit the wage increases firms grant their workers.[24] They propose that the (approximately) thousand largest corporations, in terms of numbers of employees in the economy, be required to compute the net value added per full-time employee. They would also compute their average wage and salary bill. If this computation reflects an average pay increase of 5 percent or less, the presumption is that the firm has adhered to a noninflationary pay norm. The firm's liability for corporate taxes would be based on the relationship between the pay increases the firm grants and the average product gain achieved by its workers. If, for example, the wage guidepost were 5.5 percent and the firm granted a wage increase of 6.5 percent, the corporate-profits-tax liability of the firm would increase by some multiple of the present base corporate-profit-tax-rate of 48 percent. Thus the rate, t, for a particular firm is

$$t = b + m(w - n), m > 0$$

---

[23] This feature of the Okun proposal has been incorporated into President Carter's real-wage proposal.

[24] Henry Wallich and Sidney Weintraub, "A Tax-Based Incomes Policy," *Journal of Economic Issues* (June 1971).

where b = the base corporate-profit-tax rate, w = the average rate of increase in the wages of a particular firm, n = the TIP target rate of increase for wages, and m = the TIP multiplier.

Firms would be relieved of a supplemental tax liability if the value added, in constant dollars per employee, increased while the firm's pay boost did not exceed the target rate. The target rate could be exceeded by some limited amount (say, 1 percent for every 3 percent superior showing in corrected average productivity) by industries that exhibit exceptional productivity. Thus, the intent of an employer-penalty TIP is to "stiffen the backbone of businessmen" so that they will be less likely to yield to wage settlements that are in excess of the gain in average labor productivity.

The expected impact of an employer TIP can also be illustrated in terms of a collective-bargaining model. The employer-resistance curve is expected to shift leftward to R' as in Figure 18-2. If for example, the likely wage increase without TIP is $W_i = 8\%$, the imposition of TIP will strengthen employer resistance and reduce the wage increase to (say) $W_i^* = 6\%$.[25]

FIGURE 18-2 *Wage-Bargaining under an Employer TIP*

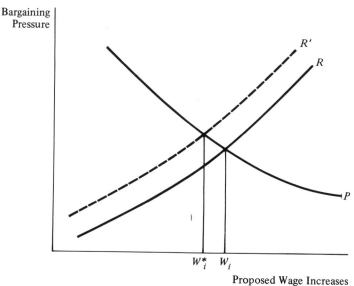

[25] Laurence Seidman, *op. cit.*, pp. 316–319, has argued that a penalty TIP would provide a stronger incentive to control wage increases than a reward TIP with the same TIP

The CAIP Proposal

More recently, Weintraub has offered a Contract-Award Incomes Policy (CAIP) as an alternative anti-inflationary proposal. This proposal is conceived as being less of a departure from tradition than other TIP plans, because it builds on a now prevailing provision in the Davis-Bacon Act. This act requires that workers on federal or federally assisted construction projects be paid "prevailing wages," a term usually interpreted to mean that they will be paid the maximum rates prevailing within a fifty-mile radius of the site. By analogy, Weintraub asks, why not a ceiling on annual rates of pay change?[26] Such a ceiling would require little more than the insertion of a clause into government contracts that successful bidders be required to adhere to an annual limit of 5 percent in the average wage-and-salary increase that can be granted over the life of the contract. Among the penalties that might be meted out to violators he suggests that future bids might be rejected for a specified number of years (say, three) and that cost excesses could be precluded as cost deductions for tax purposes in computing company profits.

Since such a proposal would affect a large segment of the construction industry, it would help mitigate inflationary pressure in a leading sector of the wage-push process. As a natural extension of a provision of the Davis-Bacon Act, Weintraub envisions this proposal as providing a mechanism for relating wage incomes to productivity trends in a manner that is compatible with a market economy, while avoiding the adverse affect which stringent monetary and fiscal policy has on employment. It also has an historical precedent that other proposals do not have.

Reservations concerning TIP Proposals

The Possibility of Tax Shifting

The most difficult test confronting TIP may be its capability to restrain wage-price increases in oligopolistic industries that confront strong unions in their labor market. The size of the wage increase that results in this type of bargaining situation reflects the interaction of union "push" and management resistance in "key" industries; their wage increases are typically matched by others in the industry and sometimes

---

multiplier. However, Gordon has examined this issue empirically and concluded that there is no evidence for this assertion. See "Comments and Discussion," *Brookings Papers on Economic Activity* 2 (1978): 352–353.

[26] Sidney Weintraub, "TIP to STOP Inflation," Frank M. Engle Lecture, April 13, 1978, The American College, Bryn Mawr, Pennsylvania.

spill over into other industries. Since this pattern of wage increases assumes that they are passed on to consumers in the form of higher prices, it has been argued that the price-setting powers of oligopolistic firms pose a threat to the effectiveness of TIP.[27]

There are, however, reasons for discounting tax shifting as a serious threat.[28] In the first place, it is not certain that firms will be able to raise gross profit significantly, even if they have reserve market power. In some industries, import competition is an impediment that limits the extent to which prices can be increased. The ultimate weapon, however, is the sequence in which a firm's profit is taxed. The Internal Revenue Service "goes last." Thus, even if a firm can raise its price sufficiently high to raise gross profit, the tax on larger gross profits makes it virtually impossible to circumvent TIP. The possibility of a shift of the TIP penalty in the form of higher prices could arise only if the Internal Revenue Service "goes first" with respect to levying taxes, while the firm goes last.[29]

TIP and the Frequency of Strikes

A second concern that arises in connection with the Wallich-Weintraub proposal is that by encouraging employees to resist excessive union demands, it will also increase the frequency and duration of strikes.[30] The implicit presumption of the Wallach-Weintraub proposal is that union demands will decline over time. This is not necessarily the case. A union may have some minimum demand for which it is prepared to strike.

Wallich and Weintraub recognize this possibility but maintain that a union that does not take TIP into account in its demands is not maximizing the benefits that it achieves for its members. Nevertheless, unions do not always maximize, which suggests not only that there may be more strikes if a TIP program is adopted but also that there may be government intervention to settle strikes. This may be a factor that itself contributes to more generous wage settlements in order to settle strikes, and that thereby undermines the effectiveness of TIP.[31]

Administrative Problems

One of the principal claims in favor of TIP proposals is that substantial new administrative costs would not be involved. The

[27] Albert Rees, "New Policies to Fight Inflation: Sources of Skepticism," *Brookings Papers on Economic Activity* 2 (1978).

[28] Lawrence Seidman, *op. cit.*

[29] The firm would "go last" if the tax penalty were levied on the firm's wage bill rather than on net profit.

[30] Albert Rees, "New Policies to Fight Inflation: Sources of Skepticism," *op. cit.*

[31] Rees, *op. cit.*, pp. 467–473.

Wallich-Weintraub proposal and the Okun proposal would both be administered through the Internal Revenue Service. This does not, however, mean that there would not be a whole range of administrative problems. If, for example, the "carrot approach" is used, the provision of tax reductions for workers who have not exceeded the threshold raises a number of vexing administrative problems. Firms would have to inform workers on their W-2 forms that they qualify for a tax break. This implies a need to audit workers' tax returns and a method for recovering inappropriate tax reductions.[32] Collecting excess subsidies from firms is administratively superior to having IRS collect from every worker directly, but, in effect, it imposes upon employers the costs of failure to restrain wages and prices. This difficulty suggests that the "stick approach," which imposes penalties on firms, is preferable on administrative grounds to a "carrot approach," which offers tax breaks to workers.[33]

An administrative problem also arises in connection with measuring elements of labor compensation and distinguishing these items from nonwage compensation. Firms, as well as unions, have an incentive for expanding nonwage benefits (i.e., pensions, stock options, group-insurance plans, etc.) if TIP limits wage increases. Administration of TIP requires identification of all forms of compensation that are not included in a firm's wage payments, because they are, nevertheless, passed through into price increases. General rules for the evaluation of nonwage benefits are easy to formulate but difficult to administer.[34]

A different sort of problem is likely to arise from the fact that TIP proposals are aimed only at wage control and expect to control prices indirectly. Labor is likely to react very negatively to any anti-inflation program that does not include some form of direct price control. Yet administrative problems increase several-fold when control is extended from wages to prices, particularly when new products are involved, when quality changes take place, or if mergers or other developments associated with a dynamic economy occur. Administration of price controls is also complicated by the necessity of identifying separately such mandated cost increases as are imposed by occupational-safety standards (OSHA) and pollution controls for the purpose of permitting them to be passed through to higher prices.

The administrative problems of TIP are minimized if the policy is limited to business taxpayers, if it does not apply to small companies, and if it is limited to controlling excessive wage increases and not extended to controlling price increases directly. Administrative problems

---

[32] Larry L. Dildine and Emil M. Sunley, "Administrative Problems of Tax-Based Incomes Policies," *Brookings Papers on Economic Activity* 2 (1978).

[33] Dildine and Sunley, *op. cit.*, p. 365.

[34] Dildine and Sunley, *op. cit.*, p. 373.

are further minimized if the penalties (rewards) of TIP are enforced only when firms exceed (fall below) the wage threshold instead of applying over the whole range of possible wage changes.[35]

Concluding Remarks

The most attractive feature that is claimed for the various TIP proposals for controlling inflation is that they provide a mechanism for relating wage incomes to productivity trends in a manner compatible with a market economy, while also making it possible to avoid the adverse effects that traditional monetary and fiscal demand-restraining measures have on employment. However, they are administratively more complex than their proponents generally recognize. Moreover, TIP proposals are generally viewed as "just another form of control." Yet the qualified endorsement that some unions have given to President Carter's proposal for real-wage insurance indicates that labor's resistance to a reward TIP would be less than its resistance to a penalty TIP.

While tax-based-incomes-policy proposals are highly promising as measures to control inflation without adversely affecting the level or incidence of unemployment, an ongoing requirement exists to improve the functioning of labor markets. The human-resources or manpower policies of the 1960s were in part crisis-oriented responses to the economic and social aftermath of World War II, but they were also responses to the long-term demographic changes examined in Chapter 2. In order to be effective, the economy's policies to encourage employment and employability must be responsive to those trends. Except for immigration, the population base from which the labor force will be derived is already in existence. Everyone who will enter the labor market through 1990 is already alive, and labor-force-participation rates do not change rapidly from already established patterns. Thus, the characteristics of the people available for employment are a critical variable.

Human-resources policy is addressed specifically to maintaining and improving the employability of persons in the labor force. The assumption of these policies is that the level of aggregate effective demand will be adequate to generate a demand for workers. Somewhere "out there" there must be jobs for suitable workers if policies to promote employability are to be effective. Chapter 19, which follows, examines human-resources policy as it has evolved from the 1960s to the present, as an adjunct to the policies for maintaining employment that were examined in this chapter.

---

[35] Seidman has proposed that penalties (rewards) apply over the full range of wage changes. See "Tax-Based Incomes Policies," *Brookings Papers on Economic Activity* 2 (1978).

Suggestions for Further Reading

Barbara Bergman and Robert L. Bennett. "Macroeconomic Effects of a Humphrey-Hawkins Type Program." *Papers and Proceedings of the American Economic Association* (February 1977): 265–270.

Albert Rees. "New Policies to Fight Inflation: Source of Skepticism." *Brookings Papers on Economic Activity* 2 (1978).

Lawrence Seidman. "Tax Based Incomes Policy." *Brookings Papers on Economic Activity* 2 (1978).

Sidney Weintraub. "TIP to Stop Inflation." Frank M. Engle Lecture, April 13, 1978, The American College, Bryn Mawr, Pennsylvania.

19 Employability and Human-Resources Policy

The policies to achieve long-run improvement in the level of employment in the private sector are necessarily predicated on the assumption that individuals will have characteristics and capabilities that make them attractive employees, and that they will have access to the opportunities that employment policy generates. Thus, "manpower policy" or "human-resources policy," as it is now being called, which came into existence in 1962 with the passage of the Manpower Development and Training Act (MDTA), directed policy attention to the supply side of the labor problem by addressing the problems of labor-force participation and employability. Human-resources policy is an essential complement to employment policy. Long-term reductions in the full employment rate of unemployment require improvements in the marketable skills of disadvantaged workers and a speedier matching of jobs and workers.

The Analytical Basis in Current Policy

Contemporary human-resources policy is an outgrowth of the response to the unemployment problems that emerged at the end of the 1950s. From the standpoint of economic analysis, it is firmly rooted in both micro- and macroeconomic theory. Since the economy was generally prosperous, the unemployment problem was widely diagnosed as being one of frictional unemployment. The presumption was that jobs existed but that workers and jobs were mismatched. Retraining and relocation would facilitate a better mesh between vacancies and unemployed workers.

The federal manpower programs that were initiated in 1962 emphasized the training of unemployed workers in high-unemployment regions. The premise of these programs was that with proper training, those who are chronically unemployed will be able to find employment.

Thus, starting in the late 1960s, continued high unemployment and frequent spells of unemployment by specific groups of disadvantaged workers became identified by most economists as a supply-side problem of the labor market. The inability of these workers to find and hold stable employment was interpreted as reflecting their inadequate investment in their own human capital. Counseling, training, and skill upgrading to aid them in their search for attractive employment opportunities was the policy recommended to reduce their unemployment and their high turnover rate.

The discussion in Chapter 4 of the impediments that confront individuals in responding to the potential for economic gains from human-capital investment suggests that exclusive reliance cannot be placed on the market system to supply the kind and number of professional, skilled, and trained individuals the economy has come to require. The strong commitment to a long-run policy of full employment, as espoused in the Full Employment and Balanced Growth Act, is essential, but a policy that is aimed at shifting workers (and jobs) out of the secondary sector is an essential adjunct to it. The premise is that some individuals are unable to respond to the incentives of the marketplace and that government must assume responsibility for promoting the employability and productivity of all who seek employment opportunities in the labor market.

Phase I: Area Redevelopment and Retraining

The first piece of legislation to be passed was the Area Redevelopment Act of 1961, which, as its title implies, was intended to attack the problem of the economically depressed areas of the economy and assist unemployed persons in finding employment near their homes by attracting new industries. There was, however, no significant economic improvement in the depressed regions where funds were spent,[1] nor did the policy help reduce unemployment rates in the economy as a whole.[2] The ARA was thus terminated after only four years.

The Manpower Development and Training Act of 1962 had a far greater scope than the legislation that preceded it, and reflected a basic philosophical change concerning the appropriate role of government in relation to the development of human resources. Title I of the act required the Secretary of Labor to "improve the adequacy of the nation's manpower development efforts to meet foreseeable manpower needs and

[1] G. L. Mangum, *The Emergence of Manpower Policy* (New York: Holt, Rinehart and Winston, 1967).

[2] The unemployment rate by the year's end was 5.5 percent. This reflects a loss of consensus to the commitment to maintain full employment as required by the Full Employment Act of 1946.

recommend needed adjustments . . . ." It also required the president of the United States to submit an annual *Manpower Report of the President*. The authors of this bill envisioned Title I as a major step in the direction of comprehensive manpower planning in the United States.

Title II, the training title, was to be the *modus operandi* for effecting it. It authorized a federally financed, state-operated training program to retrain mature, experienced adult workers who had become unemployed as a result of technological change. This was to be accomplished by means of a broad package of manpower services, including testing, counseling, job placement, and identification of individuals suitable for occupational training in classrooms and by "on the job" training. These responsibilities were to be shared by the U.S. Department of Labor, the Department of Health, Education, and Welfare, and various state agencies.

Title III of the act, unlike ARA, which funded depressed areas only, provided for the allocation of funds to all the states in the union. The formula for distributing these monies reflected a) the proportion of the labor force in the state in relation to the labor force in the economy as a whole, b) the proportion of unemployed persons in the state relative to the economy as a whole, c) the proportion of insured unemployed persons in the state relative to the total number of insured employed in the state, d) the average unemployment-compensation benefits paid weekly by the state, and e) the availability of full-time employment in the state. Provision was made under this section of the act for the payment of training allowances equivalent to the average unemployment compensation paid by the state, to provide for some minimum income during the training period.

Phase Two: Concern with the Economically Disadvantaged

Further development of human-resources policy in the following year reflected still another dimension of concern—concern with unemployment rates among the youth of the economy. The unemployment rate among teenagers was close to 15 percent between 1961 and 1962 as compared with only 3.6 percent among married men. A proposal was made to deal with the problem of unemployed youth by establishing a Youth Conservation Corps, modeled after the Civilian Conservation Corps of the New Deal era, but the bill failed to win the legislative support of the House.

The Manpower Development and Training Act was amended in 1963 to respond to the need for training youthful workers. The Vocational Educational Act, also passed in 1963, responded to the same need through an appropriation of funds by Congress to increase federal matching grants from $55 billion in 1963 to $255 billion in 1968. The purpose of this act was to reach those who had either completed their formal educations and were preparing to enter the labor market or who, if already in it, needed to upgrade their skills or learn new ones. These individuals were to be assured access to high-quality vocational education, geared to existing or anticipated opportunities for gainful employment and to the prospective trainees' abilities to benefit from a training program. Its intent was to focus on the employment problems of four main groups: (1) those in high school, (2) those who had completed their formal education (or discontinued it) and were preparing to enter the labor market, (3) those already in the labor market who required new skills or needed to upgrade existing ones, and (4) individuals with special educational and employment handicaps. Their needs were to be provided for by means of direct grants to the states.

Vocational programs that the states planned were reviewed by the U.S. Commissioner of Education, although this is now a formality. Many of the states have utilized the funds received through the grants program for constructing vocational schools with facilities and equipment for providing a wide range of training opportunities.

Phase Three: Subsidizing Employment in the Private Sector

The Economic Opportunity Act of 1964 went even further in the direction of attempting to meet the specific needs of the poor and the disadvantaged. It specifically provided for three manpower programs: the Job Corps, the Neighborhood Youth Corps, and Work Experience and Training. The intent of the Job Corps was to improve the employment opportunities of disadvantaged young people aged sixteen through twenty-one by means of basic education and residential training. This "away from home" education and training program undertook the very ambitious objective of altering the attitudes, motivations, and life-styles of its enrollees by removing them from their normal home environment.

The program was short-lived in its original form. Program evaluation indicated results that were too inconclusive to justify the expense of its continuance without modification. The program was eventually transferred to the U.S. Labor Department, which reorganized it to utilize training centers in the home communities of enrollees.

The "war on poverty" through manpower policy advanced even further in the direction of a positive role for government in relation to providing employment opportunities for the economically disadvantaged, as the 1960s drew to a close. The decision that government would subsidize private employment was a major step undertaken in 1967, when the Secretary of Labor announced that the Labor Department would undertake a Concentrated Employment Program (CEP). Its aim was to focus the MDTA effort chiefly on training the disadvantaged and subsequently channel them into jobs after completion of their training.

Under the Jobs Opportunities in the Business Sector program employers were reimbursed for the costs of on-the-job training in order to encourage them to hire workers whom they would not otherwise consider employing. One feature of the reimbursement program was the payment of subsidies, in the guise of reimbursement for training costs, to firms to encourage them to locate plants in or near the slums.

The Neighborhood Youth Corps combined an in-school, out-of-school program to assist disadvantaged young people. The chief purpose of the in-school program is to aid school retention. This feature of the program appears to be successful. New York City enrollees have had higher retention rates than fellow students with similar demographic characteristics. The out-of-school program, which provides employment and income for enrollees, has had more dubious results. There is little evidence that the program has enhanced the employability of enrollees by more than would have been accomplished by the normal passage of time.[3]

Phase Four: Decentralizing Manpower Programs

Still another change in human-resources policy was introduced in late 1967 with the amendment of the Economic Opportunity Act to decentralize decision making about governmentally assisted programs. The rationale for transferring programs to the community level was that local problems seemed to require action at the local level. The transition was not, however, completed until December 1973, with the passage of the Comprehensive Employment and Training Act, which replaced both the Economic Opportunity Act and the Manpower Development and Training Act. Its Title I provided for a human-resources-planning capability in each city, county, or state having a population of over a hundred thousand. These jurisdictions receive federal funds to mount programs for their own labor-market situations and disadvantaged workers. It also provides for a fund-allocation formula based on unemployment rather than on poverty. Title I funds can also be used to provide public-service employment on the decision of state or local planning bodies.

Title II, as already noted, provides a permanent program of public-job creation for the disadvantaged in areas that experience above-average levels of unemployment.

Title III of the act provides for continued efforts at a national level for migrant workers and Indians living on reservations. The Job Corps was also continued under Title IV, while Title V established a National

[3] Garth Mangum, "MDTA: A Decade of Achievement," in S. L. Wolfbein, ed., *Manpower Policy Perspectives* (Philadelphia: Temple University School of Business, 1974), p. 114.

Commission on Manpower Policy in order to evaluate the effectiveness of policy and to recommend changes.

Equal Economic Opportunity

Since a large proportion of the beneficiaries of human-resources policy are members of minority populations, it is almost axiomatic that efforts to improve their skills must proceed in tandem with efforts to improve their access to jobs. This is to some degree a matter of information and counseling, but it is also a matter of policy to promote equal economic opportunities. The first Fair Employment Practices Committee (FEPC) was created on executive order by President Roosevelt in 1941. But it was not until President Kennedy's executive order in 1961 that the federal government undertook responsibility to "promote the full realization of equal-employment opportunity." Specifically, the federal government pledged to end discrimination in its own departments and to enforce equal opportunity in private firms working under federal contracts if they did not undertake affirmative-action programs. Subsequently, the Civil Rights Act of 1964 forbade, under its title VII, discrimination by corporations, unions, and any other groups participating in labor markets. The Equal Employment Opportunity Commission (EEOC) was delegated the responsibility of enforcement.

Together with the office of Federal Contract Compliance, the EEOC has worked toward eliminating discrimination. The blue-collar unions have the potential for facilitating employment for large numbers of minority workers, particularly in the construction industry. However, the "Philadelphia Plan," which proposed to increase the proportion of new black recruits into the building trades, has not been well received. A major reason appears to be the job fears stirred up by increasing unemployment. The reluctance of government to actually carry out the threat of contract termination has also been a negative factor.

This is not to say, of course, that federal efforts to promote the employment rights that are an essential adjunct to its human-resources policy have been without impact. Executive orders to promote equal opportunity and the enactment of legislation to achieve it are important in establishing the principle that discrimination is not acceptable, even though enforcement apparently lags behind principle.

Evaluating the Earnings Impact of Human-Resources Policy

Cost-Benefit Analysis: The Establishment of PPBS

During the last two decades cost-benefit and cost-effectiveness analysis has become an accepted technique for appraising the appropriateness of investments made by the public sector in unplanned economies. This technique was initially developed to evaluate a variety of projects, such as the generation of hydroelectric power and the development of water-recreational facilities. Its present status as a budget tool dates from the sixties, when it came to be used to guide decision making with respect to alternative military hardwares. As Secretary of the Department of Defense, Robert McNamara required that the "cost effectiveness" of each program undertaken be evaluated. This technique for taking account of the vast number of factors that needed to be considered in connection with the allocation of defense dollars and resources was regarded so favorably that the "Planning, Programming-Budgeting System" (PPBS) was extended by executive order to all executive agencies and branches.[4]

More recently, cost-benefit and cost-effectiveness analysis has been utilized to determine patterns of land use, develop traffic networks, and plan educational programs. The common element in all these investment projects is that they yield services that are not sold (and that in some cases do not even have a counterpart in the private sector). The inputs that are used in their production are usually purchased from the private sector, so that the object of the analysis is to compare the costs of using these resources in alternative projects with the benefits they make possible.

It is useful to distinguish between cost-benefit analysis and cost-effectiveness analysis. Both methods are in use for guiding decision making but lend themselves to the solution of problems that differ chiefly in respect to the possibility of attaching monetary values to the "gains" associated with expenditures. These gains generally represent a variety of objectives that a program might be engineered to achieve, depending on the desirability of achieving one objective rather than another.

Clearly, many investments in the public sector have both economic and noneconomic objectives. For example, the educational service provided by a school system can be evaluated in part by the earnings of its graduates. But it also encourages the development of "good citizens" and the pleasure they derive from being educated. These gains cannot be given expression in monetary terms. Thus, cost-benefit analysis is useful only for allocating resources to achieve purposes whose results can be evaluated in monetary terms, whereas cost-effectiveness analysis is useful for guiding the allocation of resources to achieve objectives whose purposes do not lend themselves to being evaluated in monetary terms.

Cost-Benefit Analysis and Social Choices

The application of cost-benefit and cost-effectiveness techniques for accomplishing particular objectives can, obviously, be undertaken only

---

[4] Executive Office of the President Bureau of the Budget. Bulletin No. 66-3 to heads of department and establishments (Washington: October 12, 1965).

after society has made a decision with respect to its "preferences" about public goals. Conflict about which public use of resources will have the highest priority is, of course, minimized in a dictatorship. In a democracy, the ideal is to arrive at a consensus that reflects individual preferences. To examine at this juncture the theoretical problems of achieving consensus would take us too far from our immediate concern.[5] The fact is that specification of what the goals of our educational system should be remains as one of the major unsettled issues of our society. There is a conflict between those who advocate that we maximize the rate of return on public investment in education and training and those who question the propriety of government expenditures as a way of facilitating investment in human capital by disadvantaged groups who are beyond "self-help" measures. Reconciliation of these positions is clearly a matter of ongoing controversy, which is manifesting itself in a variety of ways. The most relevant aspect of this controversy, from the standpoint of the labor economist, is our present commitment in the United States to the human-resources policy initiated by the passage of the Manpower Development and Training Act of 1962.

There is so much controversy concerning the results of our experience with the human-resources development programs introduced as a result of MDTA and its amendments that it seems especially useful to remind ourselves of the criteria for program evaluation to which we committed ourselves under the Planning Program and Budgeting System. PPBS requires that before any expenditure can be incorporated into the federal budget, the goals of the program be clearly specified. Goal specification is a fundamental preliminary to the identification of alternative ways of achieving an objective and to estimating the costs and benefits that are expected to be associated with each alternative. The selection of the alternative that is to become incorporated as a budget item is predicated on the determination of the most favorable cost/benefit ratio. Given the requirements of the PPBS system, it is unavoidable that the evaluation of the human-resource programs of the past decade proceed in the light of PPBS requirements.

ECONOMICS IN ACTION 18:1

MDTA: Some Evidence of Positive Results

Observers who view the program's accomplishments as having been positive do so chiefly on the basis of the evidence they perceive that enrollees have experienced improvements in employment and earnings. One generally favorable assessment of the effect of training focused on trainees who started under the Manpower Development and Training

---

[5] Arrow's study of this problem is a modern classic. See Kenneth Arrow, *Social Choice and Individual Values* (New York: John Wiley and Sons, Inc., 1963).

Act (MDTA) during the first three months of 1964 and completed training that year.[6]

Several disadvantages are associated with choosing to analyze the experience of trainees from so early a cohort. One disadvantage is that the program of the early 1960s focused on those who were most trainable, whereas in the later 1960s the program became geared to disadvantaged workers. This difference is reflected in the sharp increase in the number of dropouts from the training program for the later period, and in the decline in the average age and educational level of trainees. However, study of the 1964 cohort has the advantage of making it possible to follow the cohort's progress in the labor market after training by matching the progress record on each trainee with his social-security earnings history. The Social Security Administration has a year-by-year earnings history for each social-security account since 1950, which can be used subject to confidentiality restrictions. A further possible advantage is that if tax estimates of trainee effects can be generated in the early years of the program, these may serve as benchmarks against which to assess whether it is desirable to make further changes in the nature of government efforts in the training area.

Table 19-A provides sample statistics on longitudinal-earnings records of individuals aged sixteen to sixty-four in four trainee and comparison groups classified by race and sex. All of the trainee group experienced considerable declines in earnings in 1964, the year of training, and experienced increases in earnings after training. Part of the observed earnings increase following training may simply be a return to an earnings path that was temporarily interrupted. It is, however, statistically possible to construct an unbiased estimate of the true training effects.[7] When this is done the findings are that costs were about $1,800 per trainee, which includes sums for trainee stipends. Making the assumption that stipend transfer costs are only slightly different from foregone-earnings costs implies that a permanent increase in earnings of about $180 per year are necessary for discounted benefits to equal costs at a discount rate of 10 percent. This requirement appeared to be roughly satisfied for the male cohorts and was considerably exceeded by the female cohorts.

Other Considerations

Who Shall Be Served?

While the income increases experienced by MDTA enrollees give evidence of the positive results of the program, other considerations have

[6] Orley Ashenfelter, "Estimating the Effect of Training Programs on Earnings," *Review of Economics and Statistics* (February 1978): 47–57.

[7] Orley Ashenfelter, *op. cit.*, pp. 51–53.

TABLE 19-A *Mean Earnings prior, during, and subsequent to Training for 1964 MDTA Classroom Trainees and a Comparison Group*

	White Males		Black Males		White Females		Black Females	
	Trainees	Comparison Group	Trainees	Comparison Group	Trainees	Comparison Group	Trainees	Comparison Group
1959	$1,443	$2,588	$ 904	$1,438	$ 635	$ 987	$ 384	$ 616
1960	1,533	2,699	976	1,521	687	1,076	440	693
1961	1,572	2,782	1,017	1,573	719	1,163	471	737
1962	1,843	2,963	1,211	1,742	813	1,308	566	843
1963	1,810	3,108	1,182	1,896	748	1,433	531	937
1964	1,551	3,275	1,273	2,121	838	1,580	688	1,060
1965	2,923	3,458	2,327	2,338	1,747	1,698	1,441	1,198
1966	3,750	4,351	2,983	2,919	2,024	1,990	1,794	1,461
1967	3,964	4,430	3,048	3,097	2,244	2,144	1,977	1,678
1968	4.401	4,955	3,409	3,487	2,398	2,339	2,160	1,920
1969	$4,717	$5,033	$3,714	$3,681	$2,646	$2,444	$2,457	$2,133
Number of Observations	7,326	40,921	2,133	6,472	2,730	28,142	1,356	5,192

SOURCE: Orley Ashenfelter, "Estimating the Effect of Treasury Programs on Earnings," *Review of Economics and Statistics* (February 1978): 51. Reprinted with permission.

contributed to the controversy that continues to surround our human-resources programs. A consideration of particular importance is the question of who shall be served. The present policy intent is to expend public funds to achieve a redistribution of income in favor of those who are identifiable as disadvantaged. Persons are considered to be disadvantaged if they are poor and without satisfactory employment because of their age (under twenty-two or over forty-four), minority status, physical or emotional handicaps, and/or lack of a high-school education. The requirement is that the disadvantaged be given priority in enrollment so that not less than 65 percent of total enrollment opportunities will be filled by individuals who satisfy the foregoing criteria. Federal human-resources programs have been criticized, on the one hand, because the avowed objective of favoring the disadvantaged has not been fulfilled and, on the other hand, for having adopted this objective in the first place.

Limited budgets have resulted in a tendency to serve those requiring only limited remediation and to focus on training for those occupations that require only limited amounts of training. It has been charged that service to the disadvantaged is penalized because training is provided under conditions and with facilities that cater to serving the secondary-labor market. Most MDTA projects have not been integrated into community colleges and other mainstream institutions.

Other observers question the wisdom and desirability of concentrating MDTA programs on the disadvantaged. These programs do succeed in upgrading semiunemployables so that they are able to take paid employment in jobs at the bottom of the skill ladder. But this implies that those who already have the requisite skills remain to compete with them. The result is that already crowded fields become even more crowded. Thus it may be urged that adult-training programs be geared to all steps in the skill ladder. This would, conceivably, limit rather than accentuate the "crowding" that feeds the secondary-labor market, while it would at at the same time avoid the tendency to displace one group of poor workers by another, through the use of public expenditures to acomplish this end.

The expansion of training opportunities at more advanced levels of the skill ladder may also have a salutary impact as an anti-inflation measure that does not involve an unemployment trade-off. Training workers to fill job vacancies requiring considerable skill (especially if accompanied by programs that encouraged worker migration to regions in which job vacancies exist) is greatly preferred as a measure for checking inflation to those that restrain the level of demand and generate unemployment.

The Implications of Demographic Changes

Some aspects of our present demographic trends are encouraging in regard to resources training. As noted in Chapter 2, the persons who will be in the labor force in 1990 have already been born. The key variable will thus be their rates of labor-force participation. The total labor force in 1978 averaged 98.5 million persons; approximately 63.2 percent of the population aged sixteen years or older were either working or looking for work. Given the continuation of the present trend of labor-force participation, which has been moving slowly upward over the past twenty years, and assuming that unemployment declines to 4 percent by 1985, the Bureau of Labor Statistics projects 103.3 million persons in the labor force by 1980, 109.7 million by 1985, and 114.7 million by 1990.[8] During 1978, growth in the civilian labor force was concentrated among women 16 and over, who accounted for two-thirds of the gain. Women's labor-force-participation rates had already reached 50 percent at the end

---

[8] C. T. Bowman and T. H. Morlan, "Revised Projects of the U.S. Economy to 1980 and 1985," *Monthly Labor Review* (March 1976); U.S. Department of Labor, "The Structure of the U.S. Economy in 1980 and 1985," Bulletin 1831 (Washington, D.C.: 1975).

of 1978 and are expected to continue their upward trend. The male labor-force-participation rate was 77.9 percent in 1978 and is expected to increase to 79.6 percent by 1990.

The most remarkable labor-force development between 1960 and 1977 was the increase in the number of younger workers. Teenagers either working or looking for work increased from 5.2 million in 1960 to 11.7 by 1977. The twenty to twenty-four-year age group also experienced a rapid growth through 1960. A definite slowdown in growth will occur for both these groups in the next fifteen years. The largest absolute increase during the closing years of the 1970s will be in the group twenty-five to thirty-four years of age, and in the thirty-five to forty-four-year age group in the 1980s. Thus, declining numbers of inexperienced teenagers and young adults will need to be absorbed by the labor market after 1980. This change will be accounted for primarily by the decline in the number of white males. Female teenagers in the labor force will continue to increase steadily in the 1980s, and the number of nonwhites will increase substantially. The number of blacks aged sixteen and older is projected to increase 12.1 percent by 1980 and 32.2 percent by 1990. The still relatively young twenty-five to forty-four-year black age group will be rising and will account for a larger proportion of the labor force after 1980. The median age of the labor force is expected to be thirty-five years by 1980 and thirty-seven years by 1990.

The labor force is expected to have more education by 1980 than it did twenty years ago and be more homogenous in its educational attainment. This will remove one of the important factors contributing to the higher unemployment rates experienced by the nonwhite population generally and by nonwhite teenagers in particular.

The problem of employability is expected to be particularly critical for women, because the traditional opportunities for educated women in teaching and the health-care professions will not provide an adequate source of demand. The potential for an overeducated female-labor supply is present unless women make more substantial inroads into the more traditionally male occupations.

The concern already evinced during the 1970s about a relative oversupply of college graduates seems to be emerging as a problem of smaller dimensions than was anticipated. The prospective surplus through 1985 is not large. The projected gap appears to be on the order of 700,000 for the period 1980–1985, considering replacement and growth needs in occupations now requiring college graduates and the educational upgrading that is expected to take place for jobs not previously requiring a college education. If the growth rate of the economy is more rapid than expected, this projected surplus could be eliminated. The expectation is not so much for a rising rate of unemployment among those who are college educated but that jobs not previously requiring a post-high-school education will expand their requirements. This suggests that at least some of those who pursued education in order to achieve upward mobility in the labor market face the prospect of lack of opportunity to profit from their investment. Workers who have capacities but lack credentials may well continue to be disadvantaged, because employers have an available supply of workers with college training. This suggests the need for synchronizing education to the labor requirements of employers, a matter to which virtually no interest has been paid as yet in this country. There are many occupations for which college education is a prerequisite but that have a skill content that could be taught in a one- or two-year vocational technical program.

About a third of the occupations in our economy require formal preentry training at the secondary- or post-secondary-school level. Funds are often wasted by providing training in the schools for skills best learned on the job. Ideally, skill training should be more separable from academic education, so that a prospective worker could have more flexibility. A worker could then choose to focus on job content and move quickly into employment. Alternatively, one could combine skill training with an academic education to enhance his chances of advancement and/or satisfy personal and cultural preferences.

The second third of U.S. jobs require skills that are acquired most effectively on the job. These are best left to employers' training capabilities. The chief concern of public policy here is to promote free access and preentry assistance to those who are competitively disadvantaged.

The remaining third of U.S. jobs require only minimum levels of competency in reading, writing, oral communication, and operating a motor vehicle. The lack of these skills is less often a barrier to labor-market success than moral values, self-confidence, and attitudes about the work place. Improving the employability of the disadvantaged by means of a remedial program must be aimed at identifying these personal deficiencies, which require elimination on an individual basis. Development of the diagnostic tools and methods is a research task that may well require federal sponsorship; their implementation is, however, a task that must necessarily be undertaken on a local level.

There is also a requirement for a program to meet mid-career needs—particularly for programs leading to career changes. Such programs are to provide skills and information that contribute to upward mobility and/or mid-career changes. Some employers are developing such programs, but neither the colleges nor the state legislatures, who conceive their responsibility to be teaching youth, have shown much interest. The requirement that 5 percent of CETA funds be spent for vocational education has encouraged some training innovations and has resulted in the provision of a limited number of stipends for training.

Other areas in which human-resources policy has an important task are in (*a*) providing information about the existence of jobs, (*b*) providing services that acquaint workers with labor-market practices, and (*c*) reducing discrimination in employment. This continues to be important. All these efforts, however, are predicated on assuring that the level of employment will provide opportunities for employable workers. Job creation is a matter of critical importance. The expenditures associated with human-resources policy is a waste of resources in a slack economy. It can also be a waste in an economy that is experiencing sectoral imbalances.

Urban Decay and Minority Prospects

The cross-migratory pattern of whites to suburban areas and blacks to central cities has been the greatest single factor in bringing about a general improvement in economic opportunities for black workers. The large exodus of white males from inner-city jobs, as they changed their residences, resulted in significantly greater employment opportunities for black workers.

But inner cities are no longer growth centers. The number of jobs in inner cities have increased only about 5 percent in the past decade, which compares very unfavorably with increases of about 45 percent in suburban areas and about 20 percent in rural areas. These differential rates of growth do not augur well for the black population, which is predominantly urban, while more than 90 percent of the growth of jobs between 1959 and 1969 took place in suburban and rural areas. The job opportunities that are likely to open up for blacks as a result of white out-migration will necessarily be modest (particularly in cities such as Atlanta, Gary, Washington, and Philadelphia, which are approaching or have exceeded a 50 percent black population). New jobs for minority workers will thus be largely dependent on the expansion of inner-city economies. The unemployment problem is particularly acute in inner cities, where unemployment rates among blacks have run as much as 40 percent in recent years, although there have been gains by black workers in inner cities generally. However, as migratory patterns become stabilized so that white turnover provides fewer employment opportunities for blacks while, at the same time, urban areas fail to participate in the growth of the rest of the economy, continued improvement in the labor-market prospects of black workers seems destined to be limited. Even vigilant enforcement of equal-opportunity legislation can do little to enhance employment opportunities if urban decay continues. The problems of black and minority workers generally present far broader problems than those relating to aggregate demand and the functioning of labor markets.

Concluding Remarks

The premise of the federal manpower programs that were initiated in 1962 was that with proper training those who are chronically underprivileged will be able to find employment. This is consistent with the prevailing view that the continued high unemployment and frequent spells of unemployment by specific groups of disadvantaged workers is a supply-side problem in the labor market.

However, when viewed from the perspective of those whose analysis of the labor market proceeds in terms of the dual-market hypothesis, this explanation of the disparate unemployment and high-turnover problems of disadvantaged workers is, as was examined in Chapter 12, quite untenable. According to their view, the secondary labor market has no need for a highly productive or motivated labor supply. They maintain that in the periphery outside of the economy's core industries, firms are characterized by low skill requirements, low wages, low capital requirements, and a lack of market power. Typically, these firms cannot afford to encourage stable work behavior by their employees or develop the career ladders that characterize the primary sector. While unemployment in the primary sector is often a transition to a better, higher-paying job, in the secondary sector it is essentially a process of shuttling from one poorly paid job to another.[9] None of these jobs provide specific on-the-job training or an opportunity for advancement; thus, workers have little incentive to perform well.

In the view of those who view the labor market as dual, the potential effectiveness of skill-training programs is questionable. They argue that much of the training that workers require to perform satisfactorily in the primary sector can be learned only on the job. Primary-sector skills are the result of "learning by doing" in association with social acceptability in a group that also performs a teaching function. Thus, the dualists emphasize policies to reduce discrimination and remove restrictive practices (e.g., occupational licensing and restrictive apprenticeship programs). They stress the importance of supplementing these policies by legislative changes that will shift jobs, and thus the demand for labor, out of the secondary sector and into the primary sector. The establishment of higher minimum wages, which reduce the wage differential between primary and secondary jobs, and the extension of social legislation (e.g., social-security and unemployment-insurance coverage)

---

[9] Peter B. Doeringer and Michael J. Piore, "Unemployment and the Dual Labor Market," *Public Interest* 38 (Winter 1975): 71.

have already accomplished this shift, to some degree, for unskilled construction labor, office cleaning, and longshoring. Hotel and hospital jobs seem likely candidates for similar shifts.

Even if one does not share the views of those who espouse the dual-labor-markets hypothesis, it is clear that a strong commitment to a long-run full-employment policy, which will contribute to the expansion of jobs in the primary sector, is an essential adjunct to any policy aimed at shifting jobs and workers out of the secondary sector. The requirement is for a larger number of primary-sector jobs in the aggregate; this can be accomplished only if there is a commitment to a level of aggregate demand that is high enough to keep the unemployment rate within the range that is consistent with frictional unemployment.

Looking ahead to the 1980s and beyond, when the projected size of the U.S. labor force is in excess of 103 million persons with some 55 million in the prime-age group (between twenty-five and forty-four years), it would appear that the availability of employment opportunities, particularly good employment opportunities, will become critical.[10] The very size of this projected labor force, which reflects the impact of the baby boom of the 1940s and 1950s on the labor market, may portend continued economic growth and a high-enough level of aggregate demand to generate adequate employment opportunities. But if these employment opportunities fail to materialize in sufficient volume, it may well be that whatever reservations presently remain toward government as the employer of last resort will evaporate. The notion of government as an employer of last resort has gained some degree of public acceptance in this country. Large numbers of public-service jobs have been created under CETA. The view that job creation is an essential complement to monetary and fiscal policy for keeping economies on the path of full employment has gained in acceptance even though, at the present time, the public appears considerably disenchanted with government, particularly federal government.

Much of what happens in the future will reflect the attitudes of the population aged twenty-five to forty-four, which will represent the largest population group of 1980. It is a certainty that the viewpoints and attitudes of this group, the veterans of Vietnam, the campus rebels of the 1960s, and the political and social activists of the 1970s, are fundamentally different from those of the present prime-age group in the labor market. The recent extensions of the retirement age to seventy is likely to further complicate the employment problems of this age group, in spite of the fact that their average educational level will probably exceed that of older workers. It is impossible to predict the outcome of the additional

[10]Garth L. Mangum *Employability, Employment and Income* (Salt Lake City, Olympus Publishing Company, 1967) Chapter 6.

frustrations that are certain to materialize in the work place. But it is not impossible that the present-day reservations about direct job creation against unemployment will evaporate, if this becomes necessary, in order to meet the needs of the next generation of workers.

Suggestions for Further Reading

Peter B. Doeringer and Micheal J. Piore "Unemployment and the Dual Labor Market" *Public Interest* 38, (Winter 1975).

Garth L. Mangum, *Employability, Employment and Income* (Salt Lake City, Olympus Publishing Co., 1976) Chapter 6.

20 *Income Insurance and Assurance*

The magnitude of transfer payments (i.e., payments unrelated to current participation in the economic process) to insure or assure income has already been noted.[1] Some payments, such as unemployment compensation and old-age, survivors', and disability insurance (OASDI), insure income and are related to previous work. Other transfers, such as aid for families with dependent children (AFDC) and supplementary security income, assure income by distributing cash to individuals and families on the basis of need. The latter are frequently supplemented by distributions in kind in the form of food stamps, medicaid, school-lunch programs, and the like. Their primary purpose is to redistribute income or assure an adequate consumption of goods or services that are considered essential, although they are sometimes also intended to increase future earnings.

Transfers that involve cash payments have provoked considerable controversy because of their possible adverse effect on the supply of labor. Economic principle suggests that labor-force-participation rates and the number of hours worked will be adversely affected if income is provided without work. Even unemployment insurance, which has become an institution since it was introduced during the 1930s, is not universally applauded. Its partial replacement of income for workers whose employment has been terminated without fault on their part and its cushioning of the adverse effects of unemployment is viewed as a positive feature. So is the encouragement it gives to job choice, which is seen as improving the distribution of labor. However, it is also regarded as delaying the reabsorption of workers into employment. There is valuable empirical evidence about these critical issues that will be examined after some of the details of these programs are considered.

[1] See Chapter 17.

Unemployment-Compensation Programs

The unemployment-compensation system was brought into being by the Social Security Act of 1935. This nationwide program is administered by the states according to federal guidelines. It is supplemented by federal unemployment-insurance programs covering railroad workers, federal civilian employees, recent veterans, and persons unemployed because of foreign imports. In addition, special unemployment assistance (SUA) was added in January 1975 to provide temporary assistance to wage and salary workers not included in a regular federal or state program. The details of these programs are examined next.

Eligibility and Benefits

The rules and practices of the unemployment-compensation system vary from state to state. However, in general, eligibility is contingent on a one-year period of employment in a covered industry. Eligibility is also dependent on the cause of unemployment. Job layoff assures eligibility in all states. Conversely, voluntary separation without "good cause" is a basis for disqualification, although the criterion of "good cause" is highly variable from state to state. Some thirty states permit the payment of benefits after a disqualification period, even if unemployment is not associated with "good cause." Persons receiving social-security benefits are denied unemployment benefits, or receive only reduced benefits, in thirteen states.

Unemployment benefits are paid only to persons who are available for and are actively seeking employment. A "suitable" job offer cannot be rejected, although criteria of "suitability," like those of "good cause," are subject to variable interpretation. Some states require that the claimant visit the local office on a weekly or bi-weekly basis and present evidence of job search, in order to collect benefits. Other states, however, allow benefit checks to be mailed and require little or no proof that the claimant is engaged in job search.

The duration of benefits generally increases up to twenty-six weeks with the amount of "coverage" or work experience the individual has accumulated. This is the case in forty-three states. The other seven provide all eligible persons with benefits for the same number of weeks. The amount of the benefit varies from about one-half of the worker's wage before taxes, up to a maximum of ninety dollars per week. For more than 70 percent of all covered workers, several states provide an additional allowance for dependent children or wives who are not employed.

Unemployment benefits are not taxable in the U.S. (which is not the case in the United Kingdom or Canada). Thus, the rate at which lost income is replaced is quite high, e.g., for workers earning $150 per week, about 60 percent of wages and fringe benefits are replaced by unemployment insurance. It is this feature that is widely believed to be the source of a "substitution effect" that is thought to reduce the supply of labor.

Funding and Coverage

Approximately 80 percent of all workers are potentially eligible for coverage by the unemployment-insurance system. This represents approximately a 20 percent increase since 1950. The increase is partly due to the historical decline in the proportion of the labor force in agriculture, self-employment, and unpaid employment in family business. Special unemployment assistance (SUA) extended coverage to some 12 million workers not covered by the regular program. These are chiefly state and local government employees and farm and domestic workers. Under legislation passed in 1976, approximately 9 million of the wage and salary workers currently covered by SUA will eventually be included in state coverage so that their employers will contribute to the unemployment-insurance fund. Domestics working part-time, employees on small farms, unpaid workers in family businesses, and self-employed workers currently remain uncovered by unemployment insurance.

State unemployment-insurance systems are funded by taxes levied on employers in proportion to the base wages and salaries (usually up to $4,200 annually) they pay their workers. Increases in the taxable-earnings base have been proposed because unemployment-insurance funds have been reduced to very low levels by the recent high claims levels that resulted from recession. Depletion has been accelerated by temporary programs extending the duration of the benefits. As a result of 1970 legislation, benefits were permanently increased to thirty-nine weeks during periods of high unemployment. Federal supplemental benefits (FSB), which were legislated in 1975, added twenty-six weeks of additional benefits, thereby temporarily extending benefits to sixty-five weeks. These benefits were reduced in 1976 in states with low unemployment rates and were phased out in March 1977. In some cases, state unemployment benefits are supplemented by funds accumulated under union contracts. These additions, unlike those received from state and federal sources, are taxable income. The 1975 recession also depleted many of the private unemployment-benefit funds.

While unemployment-insurance coverage has been substantially broadened over the last twenty years, there has been a decline in the proportion of unemployed workers who are eligible to receive benefits under regular state programs. This is, no doubt, related to the change in the composition of the labor force. As was noted in Chapter 2, many women and young workers have only sporadic attachment to the labor force. In consequence of their unstable labor-force status, they often do not meet the eligibility requirements for coverage. But for men over twenty-five years of age, there has been a marked increase in the proportion eligible for benefits. It is this increase, together with the extended duration of coverage and the size of the benefits, that is being implicated in connection with the extended duration of unemployment. The presumption is that duration and level of unemployment-insurance benefits have an effect on the work-leisure choice. Economics in Action 20:1 summarizes an empirical study that examined the effect of partial-benefit schedules on the incentive to work.

ECONOMICS IN ACTION 20:1

The Effect of Partial Benefits

Most beneficiaries of unemployment insurance are totally unemployed, but large numbers have some concurrent earnings. Six states offset all earnings with a comparable reduction in benefits, i.e., there is a 100 percent marginal rate starting with the first dollar of earnings. The majority disregard an amount of earnings equal to one-fifth of the weekly benefit rate, although there are also other formulas. In principle, it would seem that such partial-benefit schedules, which abruptly cancel benefits rather than allowing them to diminish gradually with earnings, create a point at which a work disincentive appears.

Evidence for examining the effect on work behavior of adjusting benefits to changes in concurrent earnings was provided by an analysis of a 5 percent sample of more than 5,000 checks paid for weeks of partial employment in Wisconsin in 1967.[2] The distribution was bimodal, i.e., it exhibited two peaks. Lower-paid workers group mainly at the first peak, as is reflected in Figure 20-1, while those who are more highly paid group at both peaks.

This behavior suggests that the unemployed identify the combination of earnings and benefits that will maximize their incomes with a minimum work effort and that they have the freedom to make appropriate work arrangements. Partial-benefit schedules, which pay either the full benefit (i.e., where the marginal tax rate is zero) or no benefit (i.e., when the marginal tax rate is infinite), are most likely to result in calculated limits to work effort. The latter are contrary to the policy objectives of the program. A partial-benefits program, which shifts abruptly from a marginal tax rate of zero to one that is infinite, is simple to administer but has a built-in work disincentive that a more complex schedule would tend to avoid.

[2] Raymond Munts, "Partial Benefit Schedules in Unemployment Insurance: Their Effect on Work Incentive," *Journal of Human Resources* V (Winter 1970): 160–176.

FIGURE 20-1 *Number of Weekly Benefit Payments by the Ratio of the Beneficiary's Weekly Earnings to His Weekly-Benefit Rate*

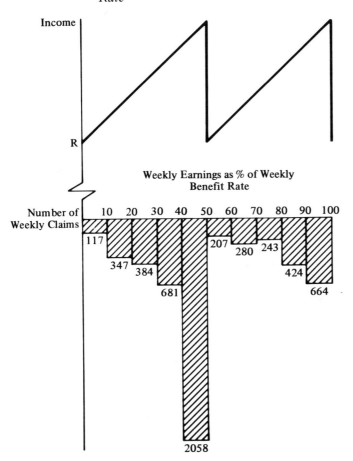

SOURCE: Raymond Munts, "Partial Benefit Schedules in Unemployment Insurance: Their Effect on Work Incentive," *Journal of Human Resources* 5 (Spring 1970): 170. Reprinted with permission.

Income-Assurance Programs

Table 20-1, Federal Income-Assurance Programs, summarizes the key program characteristics and the dollar amounts of the federal programs currently in effect. These programs, which distribute income in cash or kind, have added substantially to the growth of the federal budget. Excluding pensions paid to military and civilian government employees and railroad workers, federal transfer payments amounted to $178.4 billion in 1978, which equals 44.5 percent of the federal budget of $400.4 billion. OASDI (typically referred to as "social security") is the largest program, both in terms of the number of beneficiaries and size of expenditures. This program, which has been in existence since 1935, is a federally funded and administered system for providing retirement income to wage and salary workers. It imposes no restriction on the amount of property or other pension income a beneficiary may receive. The original intent of the program was dual: to maintain the purchasing power of retired and disabled family heads and the families of deceased workers, and to open employment opportunities for younger workers. The high unemployment levels prevailing during the 1930s led to a program that encouraged retirement at age sixty-five (or age sixty-two with reduced benefits) while also discouraging further labor-market participation by reducing the benefits paid if earnings exceeded the stipulated maximum per month for persons younger than seventy-two years. Thus, sixty-five became the traditional and frequently mandatory retirement age. The Age Discrimination in Employment Act, passed in 1977, now enables older persons to postpone retirement to age seventy if

Table 20-1   *Federal Income Assurance Programs*

Variable.	1975	1976	1977 Estimate
Outlays providing income maintenance	139,997	164,354	177,075
A. Outlays for social insurance programs:	93,528	110,858	120,820
1. Social security (HEW)	76,589	87,942	100,104
A. OASDI	54,839	62,245	70,572
B. Disability insurance	7,630	9,141	10,768
C. Hospital insurance	10,355	11,869	12,960
D. Supplementary medical insurance	3,765	4,687	5,804
2. Railroad retirement (Railroad Retirement Board)	3,034	3,322	3,624
3. Unemployment insurance (Labor)	12,761	18,315	15,748
A. State programs	11,958	16,878	14,832
B. Special unemployment assistance	183	800	300
C. Railroad unemployment	67	164	176
D. Unemployment compensation for federal employees and ex-servicemen	553	473	440
4. Other:	1,144	1,289	1,344
A. Special benefits for disabled coal miners (Labor and HEW)	945	980	933
B. Trade-adjustment activities (Labor)	13	60	120
C. Federal employees workers' compensation	186	249	291

B. Outlays for public assistance:	24,172	28,377	28,639
1. Supplemental Security Income	4,081	4,545	5,245
2. Public assistance maintenance payments (HEW)	4,592	5,200	5,625
3. Medicaid (HEW)	6,840	8,184	8,703
4. Assistance to refugees (HEW)	70	135	128
5. Food stamps (USDA)	4,357	5,283	4,307
6. Child nutrition (USDA)	1,832	2,333	2,000
7. Special mild (USDA)	124	103	—
8. Public housing (HUD)	1,312	1,429	1,489
9. Rent and mortgage interest supplements (HUD)	761	866	1,062
10. General assistance to Indians (Interior)	48	50	53
11. Removal of surplus commodities (USDA)	155	249	27
C. Outlays for retirement of ex-government employees and for disability, dependency, and indemnity compensation of veterans:	21,940	25,119	27,616
1. Public health service officers' retirement (HEW)	21	24	28
2. Medical care for retired commissioned officers (HEW)	5	6	7
3. Veterans Administration:	8,139	8,782	8,679
A. Disability and dependency, and indemnity compensation	4,680	5,114	5,220
B. Veterans and survivors pensions	2,739	2,914	2,771
C. Life insurance (net subsidy)	527	544	568
D. Other veterans benefits	193	210	120
4. Department of Defense (military):	6,790	7,920	8,935
A. Military retirement	6,242	7,325	8,247
B. Medical care for retirees	548	595	688
5. Civil Service Commission retirement	6,825	8,198	9,753
6. Department of Transportation, Coast Guard retirement	105	122	133
7. Department of State, Foreign Service retirement	53	65	79
8. Department of Commerce, NOAA officers' retirement	2	2	2

SOURCE: U.S. Budget, 1977.

they choose.[3] Retired workers can earn up to $4,000 annually if they are between sixty-five and seventy years of age without a reduction in benefits; benefits are reduced by one dollar for each two dollars of earnings on earnings above that amount.

[3] Persons in executive positions whose retirement income will be at least $27,000 annually or who are tenured professors in institutions of higher learning are excluded from this option until 1982. They may be retired at age sixty-five.

The intent of the legislation that created the social-security program was that the program be self-financed from a payroll tax levied jointly on workers and their employers. The anticipated relationship between contributions and benefits began to change in 1939, when it was provided that persons who retired early would receive benefits in excess of the actuarial value of the taxes paid and that their dependents would receive benefits without a requirement for additional taxes. Thus, a couple receives 150 percent of the benefit to which a retiring male worker is entitled if the wife is also of retirement age and has not acquired insurance on her own behalf. By 1950 the program had become essentially a currently funded one, in which employed persons, in effect, pay the benefits of those who are retired.

The current-funding provision requires the payment of 12.25 percent tax equally shared by workers and their employers, on wages up to $29,000. Approximately 90 percent of all wage and salary earners are covered by the program and are required to make contributions amounting to 4.95 percent of their earnings. Workers who are self-employed pay a tax of 7 percent on the first $15,300 of their earnings. Federal civilian employees are under a separate retirement program and are excluded from the social-security system, as are some state and local employees.[4]

Congress has periodically legislated increases in taxes and benefits. Starting in 1975, the level of benefits has been "indexed" to relate it to price increases. The taxable-earnings base has also been indexed approximately to changes in the average covered wage. It thus will increase automatically over time. However, projections of the social-security system show that program costs, relative to payroll receipts, are likely to rise so markedly that receipts will fall short of benefits. The magnitude of the tax shortfall depends on the birth rate, the rate of inflation, and the rate of growth of real wages. Even the most optimistic assumptions imply that payroll taxes will have to be increased to 15 percent of the total payroll by the year 2030. This will represent a 50 percent increase over the present tax rate.[5]

The high rate of these social-security projections is partly attributable to what is termed the "double indexing" provision of the 1972 legislation. The formula for computing benefits calls for averaging the twenty highest years of earnings. The number of years included in the average increases by one year each year until thirty-five years of earnings are included as a basis for computing benefits. These benefits are

---

[4] Virtually all persons who are sixty-five or older receive medicare or medicaid benefits in addition to cash benefits.

[5] Barry Chiswick and June O'Neill, eds., *Human Resources and Income Distribution, op. cit.*, pp. 132–133.

automatically adjusted to keep pace with changes in the Consumer Price Index (CPI). Each increase of 3 percent or more in the CPI increases the percentages in the benefit formula by an equivalent percentage. However, an additional inflationary influence derives from the provision of a 1972 amendment to the law that automatically raises the maximum wage to be included under social-security coverage in accordance with the rate of increase in average money wages. Benefits are thus doubly affected by inflation. Inflation increases wages, which causes workers to move up on the benefit schedule, and it also adjusts the schedule automatically so that each upward step yields a higher dollar benefit.[6] Thus, if high rates of inflation continue, it is possible that a retiree will eventually receive monthly benefits that are higher than his monthly earnings.

Aid to Families with Dependent Children

Figure 20-2 reflects the relationship between AFDC expenditures and unemployment from 1940 to 1975. The magnitude of the program has increased significantly over the years; the number of AFDC recipients almost tripled in the decade between 1965 and 1975. This increase reflects several influences. One is the intensive publicity put forth about the benefits available by the various agencies concerned with the poverty population and their efforts to identify eligible families. It also reflects a liberalization of eligibility requirements, particularly with respect to residence, and the rising level of benefits that have helped to make participation attractive. The introduction of the food-stamp program in 1965 and medicaid in 1966, with essentially the same eligibility standards, probably contributed further to the expansion of the program, because it implied that eligibility for one provided access to the other.

More recently, the rate of increase in the number of AFDC families has slowed down. This reflects a more careful screening of program participants for eligibility and the efforts of some states (notably California and Michigan) to locate fathers responsible for child support. The Child Support Program of 1975 extended this program to the country as a whole, effective as of 1976.

---

[6] The progressive nature of the benefit formula (whose computation formula adds 120 percent of the first $110 of average monthly earnings and 44 percent of the next $290, with further reductions down to 20 percent of average monthly earnings) implies that the greatest impact on benefits derives from the adjustment of the formula rather than from a move up the schedule. The resulting tendency toward accelerated inflation has led to a number of proposals for "decoupling." A prominent proposal was presented by William C. L. Hsiao, who headed the U.S. Senate Committee on Finance in 1974. The Hsiao proposal calls for computing both earnings and benefits in constant dollars of a particular year so that workers having comparable earnings histories in real terms would receive the same benefits even though they retire in different years.

FIGURE 20-2   *Aid to Families with Dependent Children and Unemployment in the United States, 1940–1975*

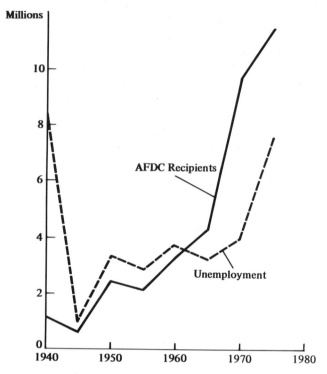

SOURCE: *Employment and Training Report of the President*, 1976.

The rapid growth of the AFDC program has led to measures intended to encourage AFDC mothers to become employed. Training is provided and a monetary incentive is offered by reducing the loss of benefits from the 100 percent marginal tax rate that has prevailed in most states. The Work Incentive Program (WIN), introduced in 1967 as a result of an amendment to the Social Security Act, provided that the first thirty dollars of net monthly income (i.e., net after work-related expenses) will be disregarded before reducing benefits by sixty-seven cents for each dollar of earnings. Some states allow amounts in excess of thirty dollars to be disregarded as a basis for computing benefits and are more generous in regard to work-related expenses. Thus, the marginal tax rate varies substantially among the states.

Additional work incentives were provided by legislation passed in 1972. WIN II, as the program is known, requires all employable AFDC recipients to register for training or placement as a condition for receiving welfare payments. Generally, persons who are sixteen or older who are not students or disabled, and women whose children are older than six years, are considered employable. The program also provides for child-care services, subsidies to employers to hire AFDC recipients, and for subsidies for public-service employment.

The employment effects of this legislation have not yet been evaluated, but the response to work incentives appears to have been weak. Employment rates are higher in states where the effective-benefit tax rate is lower. However, it is estimated that even with a zero effective tax rate on benefits, the percentage of the current population of AFDC mothers who would work is unlikely to exceed 25 percent.[7] The reduction in the marginal tax rate appears to have been offset by rising cash and in-kind benefits.

A major factor in explaining the limited effectiveness of work-incentive measures is to be found in the characteristics of AFDC mothers themselves. Their low level of education appears to be particularly relevant. They are also characterized by a higher incidence of physical and mental disabilities than is the case for the female population generally. Given these factors, together with taxes and other work-related expenses, an AFDC mother may find that her AFDC benefits approximate the earnings that can be derived from paid employment.

AFDC-UF

Twenty-six states participate in the AFDC program for unemployed fathers (AFDC-UF), which provides aid to families in which a non-disabled father is present but currently unemployed. For the family to be eligible for benefits, the father must have been unemployed for at least thirty days or, if employed, must be working 100 hours per month or less. Previous employment must either have been in an uncovered industry, or, if it was in one covered by unemployment insurance, benefits must have expired.[8] Typically, the average cash benefits under the AFDC-UF program approximate the average monthly benefits of a worker eligible for unemployment compensation, except for low-wage workers with several children. It is possible, under these circumstances, that AFDC-UF benefits could exceed those that can be received from unemployment compensation.

The effect of the 1975 Supreme Court decision is to shift some

---

[7] B. Chiswick and J. O'Neill, eds., *op. cit.*, p. 46.

[8] In June 1975 the Supreme Court ruled that a family cannot be excluded from AFDC-UF benefits solely because of eligibility for state or federal unemployment-insurance benefits.

portion of the cost of unemployment from employer-financed trust funds to the general revenues of state and federal governments. It may also increase AFDC-UF participation, which raises, once again, the question of the potential effect of transfer payments on the incentive to work. The popular expectation is that the potential adverse effect of such transfer payments on the incentive to work will be negative. The Graduated Work Incentive Experiment, which was examined in Chapter 2 above, does not, however, lend much support to this widely held view. Its findings, as were reported above, was that poor and near-poor male household heads who participated in the income-maintenance experiment did not significantly reduce their labor-force participation. Their overall response to tax rates that on the average cut net wages in half, and to income guarantees that were equal to a substantial fraction of preexperimental income, are hardly detectable.

Further analysis of the responses of the population that participated in the experiment captured some additional evidence about their labor-market behavior. The impact of the negative income tax on job search is of particular interest. Any payment that a worker receives when he is not working lowers the cost of job search and raises the expected wage of the job offer eventually accepted.[9] The effect of the subsidy on the rate of job change or turnover is reported as *Economics in Action* 20:2.

ECONOMICS IN ACTION 20:2

The Effect of Work-Incentive Payments on Job Change

Personal characteristics such as age, education, and the ethnic group of husbands participating in the Graduated Work-Incentive Experiment, as well as the nature of the job individuals hold, are expected to be important in determining their labor-turnover behavior. The general finding was that the rate of job change is depressed among husbands in participating families.[10] This effect was more pronounced for whites in the low-education, low-wage part of the sample. Families with low normal or potential earnings who were covered by generous plans (among the eight different plans included in the experiment) also exhibited a shorter duration of unemployment.

There is also evidence that work-incentive payments have quite different effects across groups on the nature of the new job, if a job

[9] See pp. 136–138 above.

[10] Harold W. Watts, et al., "The Labor Supply Response of Husbands," Symposium on the Graduated Work Incentive Experiment, *Journal of Human Resources* IX, 2 (1974): 181–200.

change occurs. Using average-earnings or occupational-status scores to characterize new jobs and initial jobs, the finding is that the subsidy has quite different effects, depending on the person's capacity for improvement. Younger, better-educated, and initially better-situated workers exhibit a tendency to benefit from a job change that is related to the presence of the incentive-payment plan. By contrast, husbands who are older, less well educated, and whose initial employment is a low-paying, low-status job do not show relative improvement when they change jobs. While husbands in participating families evidence reduced turnover as a whole, the group with unused potential appears more able to realize it in the presence of the income subsidy. These findings, however, represent only weak tendencies, which require further study and replication in the independent data.

The Relevance of Health to Labor-Supply Response

The labor-supply responses reported above and in Chapter 2 relate to the behavior of "healthy" husbands. Since it is now well established that health status affects labor supply, the expectation was that the health status of participants in the work-incentive experiment would interact with the income subsidy.

Good health was equated with having one chronic illness at most and missing fewer than seven days of work in the year preceding the experiment. Within the framework of this definition, only 68 percent of the sample was healthy. On the average, husbands in control families worked about four hours less if they were "unhealthy." For husbands in the experimental group, the differential is closer to six hours. This finding suggests that the income subsidy allows a more pronounced response to poor health. There is also evidence that hourly earnings are lower for husbands having impaired health. The effect of poor health on the earnings of husbands in control families was approximately nine dollars and fifty cents per week, as compared with a differential of twenty dollars and fifty cents for husbands participating in a payment plan. These results imply that the larger response to illness is particularly concentrated among those with low earnings.[11] It is important to note, however, that the tendency for health status to introduce patterned interaction is weak and attains significance only during the first year.

Concluding Remarks

The income-maintenance experiment is of particular interest in the light of current reappraisals of the welfare system. These programs have

---

[11] Watts, *op. cit.*, p. 198.

provided income guarantees that exceed the earnings of the poorest among the working poor in several states. The disincentives to work that the system has generated, together with the growth of female-headed households and the adverse effects of denying cash benefits to intact families with fathers present, have led to widespread public concern and resentment.

The understandable fear of the public is that any system of transfer payments encourages large numbers of persons—able-bodied prime-age males among them—to "live on the dole." The income-maintenance experiment seems to suggest that the fear is not as well founded as is popularly believed. It is also interesting to note that, as one aspect of the Graduated Work Incentive Experiment, an effort was made to introduce such social-psychological characteristics as are typically associated with "the culture of poverty." The moral values, attitudes, and character traits that are typically associated with the poverty population are generally believed to be the root of the differential response to economic stimuli that are thought to separate the poor from the nonpoor. The variables used for this analysis related to work involvement, anomie, occupational flexibility, self-esteem, perception of financial need, and time orientation (i.e., present versus future focus). All of these variables figure importantly in the poverty-population studies that sociologists have conducted. The results gleaned from the Graduated Work-Incentive Study do not support the notion that the attitudes and psychological characteristics of poor husbands have a substantial effect on their labor supply or their response to an income subsidy.[12] On the contrary, the evidence is that the poor are generally highly motivated to work and to earn income. External forces may frustrate them and lead to a variety of "bad" characteristics, but these, in the judgment of the analysts, are a consequence rather than a cause of labor-supply outcomes.

It would, however, be premature to conclude that the Graduated Work-Incentive Experiment provides a definitive guide to policy. The fact that the experiment lasted only three years provides a basis for possible underestimation as well as overestimation of its impact on labor supply.[13] On the one hand, the short-term nature of the program, which temporarily reduces the price of leisure, may underestimate the probable extent to which a permanent-income program will reduce the supply of labor. Workers may be reluctant to give up permanent attachments to the labor market for temporaty benefits. On the other hand, it may be that the experimental program overestimates the labor-supply reduction that would result from a permanent program, because those who are eligible are under pressure to take advantage of the program while it lasts. Either way, the impact of a temporary program may be misleading.

[12] Watts, *et al., op. cit.,* p. 198.

[13] Irwin Garfinkel, "Income Transfer Programs and Work Effort: A Review," Introduction to *How Income Supplements Can Affect Work Behavior,* Paper 13, Joint Economic Committee, Congress of the United States (February 18, 1974).

TABLE 20-2 *Percentage Changes in the Labor Supply of Prime-Age Married Male Beneficiaries in Response to Negative-Income-Tax Programs*

Study	Data source-year[1]	Per $1,000 increase in maximum benefit payment (the "guarantee")	Per 10 percentage points increase in the tax rate (benefit-less rate)[1]
Ashenfelter-Heckman	SMSA aggregates, 1960 Census.	−1.0	0
Ashenfelter-Heckman	SEO—1967	−3.5	+1.5
Bowen-Finegan	SMSA aggregates, 1960 Census.	−3.0	−.3
Garfinkel-Masters	SEO—1967	−.6	−0.2
Greenberg-Kosters	SEO—1967	−5.2	+5.0
Hall	SEO—1967	−6.0	+3.0
Hill	SEO—1967	−14	+2.0
Kalachek-Raines	CPS—1967	−5.3	−5.0

[1] The SMSA aggregate studies are based on averages for the 100 largest standard metropolitan statistical areas taken from the 1960 Census. The current population survey (CPS) is an annual survey taken of a random sample of the U.S. population. The survey of economic opportunity (SEO) was specially designed to get better measures of the economic status of the poor, and in addition some groups of poor people were oversampled.

The guarantee effects for the first 5 studies are calculated directly from the author's reported nonemployment income or other income coefficients. For the last 3 studies the guarantee effect is calculated by converting the total income elasticity, reported in table 9.1 in (8), to a linear slope coefficient. The labor supply figure used to convert the elasticity to the slope coefficient was 2,000 hours per year for all 3 studies while the income figures used were 6,000 for Kalachek-Raines, 5,000 for Hall, and 4,000 for Hill. The income figures are crude approximations of the means of the sample used by the authors. Where the authors ran separate labor supply equations for blacks and whites, a weighted average (.33 for blacks, .66 for whites) of their results was used.

With the exception of those reported for the Bowen-Finegan and Garfinkel-Masters studies, all tax rate effects are calculated from a wage rate elasticity derived by adding the income and substitution elasticities reported in table 9.1 in (8). The tax rate effect for the Bowen-Finegan study is derived directly from their earnings coefficient evaluated at initial earnings of $4,000. The tax rate effect for the Garfinkel-Masters study is derived from preliminary unpublished results. Where the authors ran separate labor supply equations for blacks and whites, a weighted average (.33 for blacks, .66 for whites) of their results was used.

NOTE—In all of the studies except Ashenfelter-Heckman (3) and Bowen-Finegan, labor supply is defined either as annual hours worked or annual hours in the labor force. In the Ashenfelter-Heckman and Bowen-Finegan study, labor supply is defined as the labor force participation rate in the SMSA in the week prior to the survey. The Garfinkel-Masters measure of labor supply does not include overtime or moonlighting. For a discussion of the implications of using different measures of labor supply see (13) and (15).

To calculate the effect of an NIT with a $3,000 guarantee and a 50-percent tax rate, multiply the figure in the guarantee column by 3 and the figure in the tax rate column by 5. Thus, the Garfinkel-Masters results indicate that such an NIT would lead to a 2.81 percent $[3(-.6) + (-.2)]$ reduction in the labor supply of male heads.

SOURCE: Irving Garfinkel, "Income Transfer Programs and Work Effort: A Review," *op. cit.,* p. 15.

An equally serious problem is that several studies that used the 1967 Survey of Economic Opportunity as their data base arrived at different percentage changes in the labor-supply effect of a $1,000 increase in the guarantee and a 10 percent increase in the tax rate. These differences, which are summarized in Table 20-2, are so wide that they do not really provide definitive guidance for policy formulation. The differences among the studies listed in Table 20-2 are the result of alternative methodologies with respect to measuring nonemployment income and wage rates as well as to differences in the sample used. These limitations suggest that much more empirical evidence is required before sufficiently valid conclusions can be reached about the vital matter of income maintenance to serve as a guide to effective policy. This is particularly the case when these studies are examined in light of others undertaken by sociologists. The latter view any attempt to examine the behavior of the poverty population in terms of their response to what is regarded as "rational economic incentives" as being very limited in perspective. It may be that the differential responses to negative-income programs reflected by Table 20-2 can be reconciled by reexamining them in the light of various sociological studies.[14]

Suggestions for Further Reading

Glen C. Cain, ed. "Symposium on the Graduated Work Incentive Experiment." *Journal of Human Resources* 9, 2 (1974).

Barry Chiswick and June O'Neill. *Human Resources and Income Distribution.* New York: W. W. Norton & Co., 1977.

Raymond Munts. "Partial Benefit Schedules in Unemployment Insurance: Their Effect on Work Incentive." *Journal of Human Resources* V (Winter 1970), pp. 160–176.

[14] See, for example, Samuel Z. Klausner, "Six Years in the Lives of the Impoverished: An Examination of the WIN Thesis," Center for Research on the Acts of Man (1978).

Index